Dangerous Intercourse

A VOLUME IN THE SERIES

THE UNITED STATES IN THE WORLD

Edited by Benjamin A. Coates, Emily Conroy-Krutz, Paul A. Kramer, and Judy Tzu-Chun Wu

Founding Series Editors: Mark Philip Bradley and Paul A. Kramer

A list of titles in this series is available at cornellpress.cornell.edu.

Dangerous Intercourse

Gender and Interracial Relations in the
American Colonial Philippines, 1898-1946

Tessa Winkelmann

Cornell University Press
Ithaca and London

First published 2022 by Cornell University Press

Library of Congress Cataloging-in-Publication Data

Names: Winkelmann, Tessa, 1981– author.
Title: Dangerous intercourse: gender and interracial relations in the American colonial Philippines, 1898–1946 / Tessa Winkelmann.
Description: Ithaca: Cornell University Press, 2022. | Series: The United States in the world | Includes bibliographical references and index.
Identifiers: LCCN 2022012905 (print) | LCCN 2022012906 (ebook) | ISBN 9781501767074 (hardcover) | ISBN 9781501767081 (pdf) | ISBN 9781501767098 (epub)
Subjects: LCSH: Miscegenation—Social aspects—Philippines. | Miscegenation—Political aspects—Philippines. | Interracial couples—Philippines. | Interracial marriage—Philippines. | Racially mixed families—Philippines. | Racially mixed children—Philippines. | Philippines—Colonization—Social aspects. | Philippines—History—1898–1946.
Classification: LCC GN254 .W56 2022 (print) | LCC GN254 (ebook) | DDC 306.84/509599—dc23/eng/20220422
LC record available at https://lccn.loc.gov/2022012905
LC ebook record available at https://lccn.loc.gov/2022012906

Contents

Acknowledgments

I wish that I did not have to start these acknowledgments with loss, especially at a time when so many are experiencing their own grief. For me, that loss has coincided with the conclusion of this project. Much of this book is about how Filipinas made things happen, even under the pressure of extreme duress. Life for many of my friends in the Philippines is still like this. Susan Quimpo, Gayia Beyer, and Ged Hidalgo all hoped and worked to make big changes in the face of ongoing national crises—environmental racism, poverty, a fractured political system, the debris of imperialism, and so on. When I first started thinking about and researching this book, I wasn't sure that I would be able to do all the work I felt was necessary to complete the project. These three helped assure me that it could be done and forged my initial contacts with the people who would ultimately appear in the book. I signed up for Susan's brainchild, Tagalog On Site, when I was a master's student in ethnic studies at San Francisco State University. I wanted to build my conversational, reading, and writing skills in a language I grew up with but was never expected to really know. While learning Filipino with other Filipino Americans in Manila, we met Gayia, who introduced us to her family and ancestral homelands in Banaue, and Ged, who literally navigated us all around Manila so that we could buy *load* for our phones and attempt to use our language skills in public. Whenever I expressed to them my hesitance about doing this project, they were always reassuring with a quick, "Of course you can do it, why not?" *Maraming salamat sa inyong tulong, mga kapatid.* We lost Susan, a never smoker but a lifelong resident of one of the traffic capitals of the world, in the summer of 2020 to severe emphysema. We lost Gayia and Ged to COVID-19 in the first half of 2021, when much of the first world had already vaccinated those with preexisting conditions. These preventable deaths gut-wrenchingly highlight the continued precarity of those in postcolonial nations, especially women. I dedicate this book to you, *mga tatlong diwata.* Thank you for being the lifeline of this book.

Trying to finish a research-based book while navigating the teaching and service demands of a tenure-track job and raising two toddlers as a first-generation woman of color was (and is) no small task. I needed so much help, and in so many different ways—financially, academically, emotionally, and physically. This is my road map.

The research for this book would have been impossible without the generous support of the Fulbright Institute of International Education fellowship and the amazing support of the Manila-based Philippine-American Educational Foundation (PAEF) staff, Marj Tolentino, Esmeralda "EC" Cunanan, Yolly Casas, and Eileen "Con" Valdecañas. I could not have navigated (literally!) the embassies and archives without them. Research grants at the Bentley Historical Library at the University of Michigan and the Newberry Library in Chicago allowed me to spend months rather than days immersed in the archives. A Ford Foundation postdoctoral fellowship was awarded to me at a crucial time. Baby two was on the way, and time away from teaching responsibilities for writing and childcare was very much needed.

At the University of Illinois, I was fortunate to find support both financially and in the form of mentorship and community. My mentor and adviser, Augusto Espiritu, was instrumental in guiding me to this project when I, as a new graduate student in history with no prior experience in the field, felt like a fish out of water. His help along the way, as well as the guidance of my dissertation committee—Kristin Hoganson, Leslie Reagan, and Dave Roediger—gave this project its shape and substance. Kristin was, in many ways, the co-adviser of my graduate project, and I have benefited from, and continue to benefit from, her expertise in the field of the United States and the world, as well as her belief in and generous support of my work. A community of scholars and friends sustained me in Illinois, whether it was reading drafts of my work or helping me navigate how to present at my first academic conference. Thank you to Moon Kie Jung, Caroline Yang, Junaid Rana, Martin Manalansan, Kathy Oberdeck, J. B. Capino, Genevieve Clutario, Christine Peralta, Long Bui, Constancio Arnaldo, Norma Marrun, Mary Ellerbe, Christine Lyke, Clarence Lang, Yaejoon Kwon, Vince Pham,

Shantel Martinez, Merin Thomas, Glenn Lopez, Mark Sanchez, Utathya Chattopadhyaya, Sonia Mariscal, Cynthia Marasigan, and Joyce Mariano.

At the University of Nevada, Las Vegas, I have been lucky to be able to share academic space with one of the most diverse undergraduate populations in the United States. Thank you to all the students who have helped me become a stronger teacher. Isi Miranda, Marimar Rivera, Annie Delgado, and Sana Azim all provided tremendous support for this project, helping me with translations, securing photo permissions, and doing research, and I was so fortunate to work with you all. Learning from and working with my colleagues here has made the book better and made me a better scholar. Thank you to Raquel Casas, William Bauer, Mark Padoongpatt, Miriam Melton-Villanueva, Jeff Schauer, A. B. Wilkinson, Carlos Dimas, Austin Dean, David Tanenhaus, Andy Kirk, Claytee White, Stefani Evans, Priscilla Finley, Yuko Shinozaki, Sheila Bock, Michael Alarid, Heather Nepa, Annette Amdal, and Shontai Zuniga. Susan Johnson, newly arrived to our department, organized a manuscript workshop for me, as well as workshops for several other junior faculty members. I am grateful to have had the opportunity to share the draft in such a supportive forum and thankful that colleagues and readers still attended virtually amid an unfolding global pandemic. Thank you to Mary Renda and William Bauer for your thoughtful, insightful, and detailed comments, which pushed this work over the finish line.

Other friends and mentors have also taken time out of their busy schedules and lives to read, comment on, and support this work. Thank you to Judy Wu, Vernadette Gonzalez, and JoAnna Poblete for providing early feedback and encouragement on the manuscript when it was still a dissertation. I don't know how you all take on as much as you do and still find time to make such important contributions to the lives of young scholars and junior faculty. I have learned so much from you and am always in awe. Chris Capozzola, Simeon Man, Margaret Rhee, Adrian De Leon, and Joy Sales have always been encouraging and supportive, and I am so glad we share many of the same conference circuits. Susan Crame and her extended family took a chance answering an Instagram message from me regarding their colonial-era descendants. Thank you for believing I was not a catfish and for sharing your history with me. Anna Gonzalez was the first Filipina woman I saw in a position of power when I started as an undergrad at the University of California, Irvine. She got me started on this path early on, and I am so thankful that she saw something in me to nurture.

In the Philippines, so many people opened their homes to me and offered their assistance, and this project would not have come together without them.

Thank you to the Santos-Chee family for always opening your home to this wayward cousin whenever I visit. Tanya and Auntie Bridgette Hamada similarly housed me so that I could be close to the archives at Ateneo and the University of the Philippines (UP). Waldette Cueto's help at the American Historical Collection and beyond was invaluable. Thank you to Mario Feir and Stephen Feldman for welcoming me into your home to browse your collection of rare Filipiniana and for your care in preserving this heritage. A special thanks to Marc Chavez, whom I first met at the UP archives when I was looking at the H. Otley Beyer papers. Marc still offers to help me when I can't physically be in the Philippines to request documents. Thank you so much for your friendship over the years and for the huge stacks of old colonial documents that you somehow always manage to get for me. I value both the documents and your friendship immensely, but mostly your friendship. I am so fortunate to have met other students and Filipino Americans—Jennifer Buison, V Fixmer-Oraiz, Natalie Fixmer-Oraiz, Tarhata Brazal, Espie Santiago, Patty Tumang, Meds Medina, Laurel Fantauzzo—who have become friends, community, and support systems both in the United States and in the Philippines. Thank you, *mga kapatid*.

The time freed up to revise and complete this book was possible only because of the many women who helped me raise my children. I don't know what I can say that can convey how grateful I am that you came into our lives during a global pandemic and agreed to feed, clothe, and care for Ada and Simon. Chasity Saunders, Ashley Smith, Sara Kalaoram, Iana Relampagos—you made my children's lives better. You made my life better. I hope that one day I can give you back some of what you gave us.

Support and childcare from both blood and chosen family members have also been invaluable for the completion of this book. Thank you, Overgaards—especially Tita Joy, who loves Ada and Simon so much that she is always willing to come to Las Vegas for weeks at a time to help out. My mom helped show me early on the resilience of immigrant women of color, even when faced with crushing odds in this society. You may not have been actively teaching, but I was actively learning. My dad gave me the resources to fund my language-learning trip to the Philippines, even though I think it made him sad I wasn't also actively trying to learn German, and even though he, like much of my family, still doesn't completely understand what I do. "That paper" I'm writing is finally done, everyone! Christina Winkelmann and Morgan Swift always opened their home to us and, along with Joelle Gazmen and Felicia Tsang, made frequent trips to Las Vegas that helped maintain my sanity. They also listened to my job talks and kept me abreast of the latest pop cultural items that, for some reason, had stopped filtering down to me. May you reap all the rewards there are. The Poppel family—Deborah, David, Becca, and Ben—took on the lion's share of childcare duty when in town, allowing me free weekends to visit local archives or hole up in my office to write. Deborah and David committed to frequent cross-country trips to help us out, and even though the pandemic made visits rarer, all that freed-up time added up. I offer my humble thanks. Our fur fam Peter and Daisy were steadfast and constant writing companions and usually low maintenance. We miss you every day, Peter. Finally, Zack, Ada, and Simon have had to put up with my absence due to this book more than anyone. I am so lucky to have a partner who takes that word seriously and who parents, cleans, cooks, and supports in ways that silently acknowledge and refuse the patriarchy of our society, which marks all those tasks as mine alone. Ada and Simon, the COVID-19 pandemic took away playgrounds, preschool, friends, visits from family, trips to the grocery store, and more. I am sorry that I was also gone for so much of it working on this book. I hope when you're older you don't remember having missed out on so much. Mommy will remember and feel bad enough for all of us. You three are the best things in my life. This book is for you.

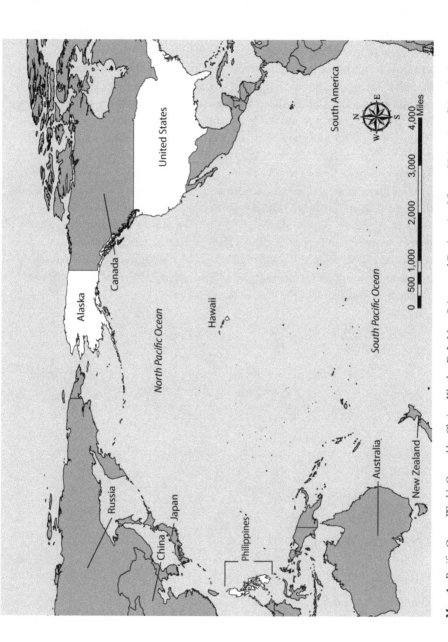

Map 1. Pacific Ocean World. Created by Chrissy Klenke, DeLaMare Science and Engineering Library, University of Nevada, Reno.

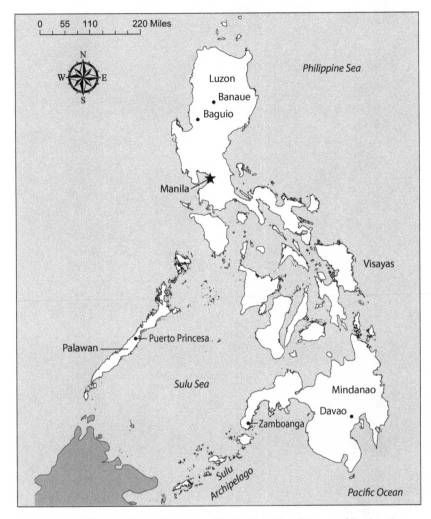

Map 2. The Philippines. Created by Chrissy Klenke, DeLaMare Science and Engineering Library, University of Nevada, Reno.

Introduction

Dangerous Intercourse: Romantic Pretense
and Colonial Violence

"You have an island as beautiful as your women," said William Howard Taft, the leader of the Second Philippine Commission and the soon-to-be president of the United States. He was speaking to a delegation of Filipino representatives on the Philippine island of Marinduque in 1901 as part of a larger effort to demonstrate the United States' "benevolent" intentions and to secure the cooperation and loyalty of Filipinos around the archipelago in the cause of the US imperial mission.[1] Dr. Trinidad H. Pardo de Tavera, a prominent Filipino intellectual traveling with Taft's party, likewise stated in 1901 at a commission dinner: "We found that Americans were not slow in making the acquaintance of our women; what was more, they did not smile only on the pretty ones, as was the wont of that class which formerly set up first claim to women's smiles in this country."[2] At the same time that Taft's party toured the islands and made overtures of interracial attraction, Filipinos and approximately 100,000 American troops were engaged in a bloody war that would last well into the next decade.[3] At the onset of the American occupation in 1898, US troops, civilians, and entrepreneurs alike quickly took part in and spurred the growth of the sexual economies they encountered in the islands. So began the colonial romance between the United States and the Philippines, a relationship wherein interracial intercourse and suggestions of social and sexual attraction veiled and sanitized various types of violence occurring across the archipelago.

Where US history has spilled—and often violently combusted—across various geographies, boundaries, and borders, social and sexual relationships between American citizens and non-American citizens have been a consistent form of colonial engagement. American colonial liaisons literally courted those communities and individuals whose land and resources were coveted by the settler colonial state. In North America, many of these lands were eventually incorporated in some manner into the US body politic, typically by deception or force. As Americans closed in toward the Pacific Coast, they propelled the dissolution and rebuilding of local governments, changes in ownership and use of the land, and the transformation of societies and cultures. The various forms of social and sexual relations that arose in contact zones and Indigenous borderlands greased the wheels of many of these reformations of US empire. The formation of the US empire across the Pacific was no different; that is to say, social and sexual contact continued to be just as important to the building and maintaining of US imperial goals outside the settler colonial metropole. As reflected in the comments of Commissioner Taft, marshaling ideas of interracial romance, desire, or attraction could obscure and salve the violence of imperial occupation and convey the purported benevolence of the American colonial state in the Philippines.

Dangerous Intercourse marks the first comprehensive study of crossing sexual color lines in a US overseas colonial geography. During the period of formal US colonial rule of the Philippines, most Americans and Filipinos came to know one another through the violence of the Philippine-American War, but others became acquainted through interracial intercourse—social and sexual relations that were often just as violent and just as dangerous as the relations forged through warfare. Filipinos and Americans mingled and danced together in social spaces and at formal parties known as bailes; worked together in clubs, schools, and charitable organizations; and even lived alongside one another as Filipinos came to be employed as cooks, drivers, and maids in American homes. Filipinos and Americans traveling together for the Taft Commission, for example, attended luncheons, bailes, and meetings together and often shared close living quarters during their trips. Sexual relations, too, were varied and expressed in different ways, from the short term and informal, as in the sexual economy, to the more enduring and formal, as with cohabitation and marriage. Much to the chagrin of many colonial officials, transgressions of the sexual color line were not infrequent or isolated incidents. Government reports lamented the "presence in a large majority of the towns of the archipelago of dissolute, drunken and lawless Americans, who are willing to associate with low Filipino women."[4] As one American bemoaned, "Every civilian I had thus far met were married or living with native women."[5]

Race and "Romance" on the Frontier: The Farthest West

When American troops first arrived in the Philippines on the eve of the Spanish-American War, they entered a society shaped by over three hundred years of interracial intercourse. The Spanish Empire first gained a foothold in the archipelago in the late 1500s, after conquistadors wrested power and territory away from the local Muslim rulers who controlled the largest port settlements in northern Luzon, the central Visayan Islands, and southern Mindanao, the three main geographies that make up the Philippine archipelago. With the Philippines, the Spanish crown acquired its only colony in the Asia-Pacific region and the base of their commercial exchange with China. Spanish friars quickly went to work proselytizing among the Muslims descended mostly from the Malay Peninsula and the Indigenous populations throughout the islands, although their conversion work found success mostly among the populous lowlands of Luzon and the Visayas, and less so in the northern and southernmost regions of the Philippines. The Manila galleon trade, a circuitous mercantile system that connected the Philippines with the rest of the Spanish Empire, lasted for over two centuries and ensured the profitability of the colony. Manila-built galleon ships laden with goods from Asia sailed for Acapulco in Spanish Mexico, where cargo then continued on to Havana and Seville. This lucrative shipboard trade lasted until revolution in Mexico ousted the Spanish from one of their largest possessions in North America in the early 1800s. By then Manila had become a bustling and racially diverse cosmopolitan port city that welcomed various European travelers and was inhabited by Chinese merchants, Indigenous vendors and laborers, Spanish soldiers, friars and landed gentry, and many mixed-race individuals who began to identify as Filipinos.[6] Like the Americans who would come after them, Spanish, Chinese, and European settlers in the islands often married or cohabited with native women, establishing connections to local communities and resources. These intermarriages and mixed liaisons served them well, as by the time the Americans arrived en masse in 1898, many of the most successful and wealthy residents of the islands were descended from mestizo (mixed-race) families. So normalized was the presence of people of mixed ancestry that many of the first informants of the new American regime were Chinese mestizos, Spanish mestizos (who often self-identified and were known simply as Filipinos), and other Europeans who were married to native women.

Around the turn of the century, American imperialists were looking to join the ranks of the older European powers they still largely emulated and thus had a mind to develop military strength and accumulate territorial possessions abroad, a desire that coincided with the so-called closing of the American frontier reported in the 1890 US census. According to the report, the western part of the continent had been fully settled. No more land to tame meant fewer outlets for the strenuous development of American civilization, and US politicians and civilians alike worried about flagging masculinity and vitality as a result. When Spain's hold over its colonial possessions faltered as anticolonial revolutions took root, the United States watched intently, already eyeing the "pearl of the orient" in the Pacific as well as Cuba and Puerto Rico in the Caribbean. Fighting "a splendid little war" against Spain, imperialists reasoned, could advance the multiple goals of revitalizing American manliness, accumulating strategic territories for military buildup, and developing access to new markets.[7] While the US declaration of war against Spain was avowedly due to Spanish abuses against Cubans and the sinking of the USS *Maine*, the first battle of the war took place not in the Caribbean but halfway around the world in Manila Bay. Americans had long coveted the Philippines as a stepping-stone to the fabled markets of China, much as their Spanish predecessors had centuries earlier. In December 1898, the United States signed a peace treaty with Spain that brought Cuba, Puerto Rico, Guam, and the Philippines under various forms of US control and occupation. President McKinley established the First Philippine Commission (also known as the Schurman Commission, named after commission leader Jacob Gould Schurman) in January 1899, tasking its members with assessing the state of the "new possession" and prescribing a plan of action for the governance of the islands. The commission also served as the initial governing body of the colony. When Filipino revolutionaries realized that the US military had no intention of leaving the islands after the defeat of Spain, they trained their weapons on the Americans and declared war in February 1899. The United States thus fulfilled its myriad expansionist aims through both the Spanish-American War and the subsequent Philippine-American War.

American officials deployed to the Philippines began their colonial state-building plans even as the violence of the war raged around them. The United States declared the war against the Filipinos over in 1902, though fighting would continue throughout the islands for well into the next decade. Colonial officials established a local insular government and responded to continued Filipino calls for independence in a slow and piecemeal manner. In the first of these moves, the American government allowed the formation of a Philippine assembly to join the American commission as a bicameral legislature in 1907.[8] In 1912, with the upcoming presidency of Woodrow

Wilson, the first Democrat elected since annexation, Filipino nationalists saw a chance to push the issue of independence and began drafting legislation to advance their goals. Filipinization efforts under the governor-generalship of Francis Burton Harrison (an appointee of Wilson) opened more political opportunities to Filipinos, as the insular government actively sought to replace most low-level Americans in the civil service with Filipinos. The Jones Act of 1916 formally expressed a commitment from the United States to eventual Philippine independence and stipulated that an elected Philippine senate would replace the US commission in the legislature. However, the executive office of the governor-general—the highest office—was still held by an American appointed by the US president. By the 1930s, Filipino desires for independence coalesced with American desires to stem the tide of migrants from the colony to the metropole, and legislation was passed in 1934 that would somewhat satisfy both parties. The Tydings-McDuffie Act, also known as the Philippine Independence Act, laid out a ten-year path to independence, the end of the governor-generalship in favor of an elected Philippine president, and changed the status of the islands from colony to commonwealth. It also changed the status of Filipinos from US nationals to aliens, limiting the previously unrestricted travel of the colonial "wards" to the United States to a total of fifty immigrants per year. The United States finally granted independence on July 4, 1946, but by then the deep sociopolitical imperial ties that connected the two nations all but guaranteed the longevity of uneven relations. One of the places where this unevenness is still most visible is in the shape of interracial intercourse between Americans and Filipinos. From the notorious rest and recreation port cities that cater to foreign navies and sex tourists to the prevalence of the pen-pal bride system that has normalized the outmarriage and migration of Filipina women, the modern iterations of interracial relations continue to signify ongoing imperial dominance and are part of a long genealogy of dangerous intercourse in the islands. Indeed, the dangerous ideas about Filipina sexuality fashioned by imperialists at the turn of the century continue to be at the center of contemporary American notions of the Philippines and its people. These durable ideas shape the realities of Filipina women today, and indeed, of Asian and Asian American women more broadly.

Americans and Filipinos began fraternizing and engaging romantically and sexually almost immediately upon the 1898 arrival of troops in Manila, and the American military government took its cues from the recently defeated Spanish regime in terms of how to approach such encounters. American officials, for example, often maintained rather than eradicated red-light districts previously established and maintained by Spanish colonial authorities and quickly became acquainted with the social mores and practices regarding sexual relationships. Army medical personnel took note of the prevalence of interracial sexual intercourse early on in the occupation, with one surgeon reporting that American soldiers became "habituated to the repulsiveness of the native women." The surgeon continues: "Sexual immorality is more common, with a notable increase in venereal disease."[9] But unruly transgressions of the sexual color line were not new terrain for Americans. Indeed, the settler colonial possibilities that unfolded in North America were indelibly shaped by interracial intercourse, from French fur traders who gained access to pelts via intermarriage with Indigenous women in New France, to the Anglo settlers who married landowning Mexican women in the wake of the US war against Mexico.[10] The extent to which European and American settlers penetrated Indigenous nations in North America via intermarriage has been well documented.[11] Interracial relations on the so-called frontiers of what would eventually be incorporated into the United States created opportunities for white settlers to access myriad resources and land through the kinship networks they married into. The consolidation of the settler colonial United States was aided and supported along the way by such relations. Even prior to the formation of the United States, ideas about racial mixing informed how early colonists imagined the burgeoning nation. The racialist thinking of newly minted Americans was imbued with their knowledge of the Spanish classificatory *casta* system as well as the revolts of African and mixed-race people in the Caribbean colonies.[12] Interracial intercourse helped to secure land and capital, as sexual violence against enslaved Black women guaranteed white owners a continuous supply of slaves born into bondage. By 1913, thirty of the forty-eight states had anti-miscegenation laws prohibiting interracial marriage and sexual intercourse between whites and nonwhites. These laws protected white supremacy by drawing tighter restrictions around who could and who could not access the material wealth accumulated through whiteness.[13]

As a proven tool of settler colonialism, interracial intercourse continued to aid in the dispossession of Indigenous people as the western "frontier" expanded into the Pacific Ocean. More than two thousand miles away, missionaries, plantation owners, and other businesspeople achieved their aim of seizing power away from native Hawaiians and eventually annexing the island nation as a wayward piece of the growing United States.[14] American colonists and tourists described Hawaiian women as "squaws," a derogatory label that originated from Anglo men's observations of Indigenous women in North America. This slur continued to find new life beyond the American West and, indeed, well beyond our ostensible fiftieth state.[15] As Americans made their way deeper into the Asia-Pacific world, or to what I refer to here as "the farthest west," they again harnessed interracial intercourse to disperse American influence in a nation more than seven thousand islands strong. The sexual economy in the Philippines remained the largest site of interracial liaison in the first several decades of American occupation, but as American settler communities became more established, mixed-race families became a more conspicuous presence. With the aid of interracial sexual relations, colonists firmly entrenched themselves and US empire in the islands; inroads were made into local Indigenous communities, lands were secured and turned into sharecropping ventures or speculated as plantations and homesteads, and American mestizos were incorporated into the already mixed population of the Philippines.

Dangerous Intercourse proceeds from the understanding that it is impossible to understand these interracial relations, marriages, families, sexual transactions, and so on, outside a framework that considers this longer history of settler colonialism in the United States. The continuities are too many and the stakes are too great to proceed otherwise. The various projects of settler colonialism around the globe are projects built on a foundation of land dispossession and exploitation. The structures that emerge in settler colonial societies often involve state-sponsored genocide and other violent schemes of Indigenous removal to make way for Anglo-European settlement and the establishment of a new ruling foreign polity.[16] Settler colonialism does not operate under a stable set of strictures but often adjusts to local conditions, being historically specific but also durable. As Indigenous scholars point out, the contemporary settler state reproduces itself through the more contemporary logics of multiculturalism and inclusion.[17] In the United States, settlers came to include nonwhite individuals as well, although the bicoastal incorporation of Indigenous land was a process that relied on the ideology of manifest destiny—the idea that an anointed white population was meant to take the land, make it profitable, and serve as an example for other nations. While I do not define the US-occupied Philippines as a settler colonial project necessarily, I do recognize that much of the story presented here revolves around American settlers who bought and sold local land and who married or cohabited with Filipinas, and that settler colonial logics imbued every step of the US process of colonization in the islands. As an unincorporated territory, however, the Philippines and its colonial governance was not beholden to the Constitution or federal laws, nor was it decidedly on a path to statehood, as Indigenous lands (incorporated territory) in the United States were understood to be.[18] As the colonial method of imperialism relies on some degree of settlement, it might be more accurate to think of the Philippines during this period as an American colony with settlers rather than an American settler colony.[19] So while American settlers played a vital role in advancing US imperial possibilities in the archipelago, the Philippines was eventually granted independence, even though independence did not ultimately free the nation from American influence and subjugation.

Transgressions of the sexual color line were not the only settler-tested strategies that US empire brought to the Philippines. Many of the high- and low-ranking military personnel sent to the islands, for example, had participated in the genocidal wars against Native nations in North America in the late 1800s, and they employed the tactics and lessons learned there to their punitive expeditions in the Philippines.[20] Indeed, ideas of "Indianness" that Americans cultivated in the settler colonial state imbued and created "conditions of possibility for U.S. empire to manifest its intent."[21] Many Americans at the turn of the century made it clear that they understood the Philippines as part of the mythic settler narrative of the US West. American colonial officials, for example, constantly described the inhabitants of the Philippines as "Indians," and the islands as a frontier zone.[22] President Theodore Roosevelt expressed this sentiment in his 1902 Memorial Day speech, in which he stressed the importance of maintaining the islands: "As we grow in power and prosperity, so will our interests grow in that furthest west which is the immemorial east."[23] Later in 1912, President-Elect Woodrow Wilson, who sought to cut ties with the colony, stated of the US-Philippines relationship: "The Philippine Islands are at present our frontier, but I hope we presently are to deprive ourselves of that frontier."[24] This study asks us to reorient our geographical framework to understand this vast ocean world— specifically current and former possessions of the United States, such as Hawaii and the Philippines—as also belonging to a western historical trajectory, and to consider how the domestic settler colonial history informed the shape of imperialism in the Philippines.

Crossing the sexual color line in the domestic settler state, as in the Philippines, built and made durable the US empire. Key to the story of the US colonial state in the Philippines were the sociosexual relationships that made imperial desires into realities. Indeed, dangerous intercourse was not a peripheral outcome of the occupation of the islands; rather, it was a cornerstone. Because of this, my understanding of both settler colonialism in the United States and the colonization of the Philippines is one that must include an analysis of gendered dimensions of power. It would be an incomplete analysis of such relations in the new far-flung colony if we did not recall how white intermarried settlers chipped away at Indigenous landholdings by various legal and illegal methods; how Indigenous wives helped Anglo-European expeditions to chart cartographies; or how mestizo or mixed-race descendants could or could not inherit property, vote, or be considered a full citizen under US federal or state laws.[25] Studying the importance of interracial American-Filipino couples who hosted and toured colonial officials around the Philippines demands this hindsight, because Americans in the Philippines were also looking back transpacifically. The supposed unfitness of Filipina women to offer proper home influences to young white American men mirrored the logic of Indigenous child removal and facilitated justifications of colonial occupation.[26] Anthropologists intent on documenting Philippine racial types took their cues from their understanding of Indianness as well. The colonization of the Philippines was an imperial adventure that many Americans were already well acquainted with and readily prepared for.

Imperial policy in the colony, however, necessitated a tempered approach to handling racial intermingling, as Americans were ostensibly present in the archipelago on a benevolent mission of goodwill and kindness. The enforcement of anti-miscegenation laws in the Philippines could undermine such a position. Thus, what was admissible racial policy for the domestic homeland would not necessarily follow the flag to the Philippines.[27] As such, interracial intercourse at the colonial site could and often did support imperial claims of amity. Indeed, the colonial policy of benevolence and instances of interracial intercourse between Americans and Filipinos could be mutually supportive of each other. As in the continental United States, where miscegenation laws trod lightly in cases of cohabitation and marriages with Indigenous women due to considerations of land and property acquisition, a similar practical averseness to upholding racist strictures in the name of advancing colonial goals persisted in the Philippines.[28] While imperialism in the Pacific was unable to rely on the wholesale export of American segregation and anti-miscegenation laws that would belie its commitment to some semblance of social equality, it could rely instead on the everyday racism of Americans to police sexual encounters, define and limit citizenship, and structure innovations in imperial rule.[29]

In addition to redirecting and complicating our geographical gaze, this story shifts how we might understand the significance of places considered peripheral, or less a part of US history. This is not a narrative that simply considers a few mixed-race families and scandalous interracial incidents that occurred in a small island nation, the hinterlands of an imperial power. While most of the events highlighted in *Dangerous Intercourse* unfold primarily in the Philippines, this story relies on global movement: Americans looking to seek their fortunes on the so-called frontier in the farthest west, letters and post-cards sent back and forth between friends, and passenger-laden transport ships plying the transpacific. Progressive reformers, prohibitionists, suffragists, and others in the metropole learned of the boozy and salacious reputations that the troops garnered in Manila and pushed through legislation prohibiting liquor and beer on US bases at home and abroad, a major victory for the Anti-Saloon League and their allies, which predated Prohibition by more than ten years. Many Filipinos used the debauchery of the troops to point out the hypocrisy of US rule, saying that moral conditions in the city of Manila had declined upon the departure of the Spanish. American and British travelers defended the imperial pursuits of their respective countries by comparing the prevalence of red-light districts and other vice economies in various colonial port cities, such as Yokohama, Hong Kong, and Manila. Women from all over Southeast Asia who worked in the sexual economy traveled to the Philippines, drawn in by the influx of US troops. Some found their first American clients on board the ships bound for Manila Bay.[30] Black and white Americans alike who had relations with Filipina women were dubbed "squaw men," a pejorative term originally applied to white men in the American West who married Indigenous women.[31] The transnational and transimperial mobility of people, things, and ideas are at the heart of this narrative.

Encounters and liaisons such as those described in *Dangerous Intercourse* have been theorized as various types of "intimacy" by scholars of postcolonial studies, gender and women's studies, and other fields. Though I often use intimacy and intercourse interchangeably here, I favor the term "intercourse" as an analytic through which to understand these interracial encounters for several reasons. First, and on a very basic level of word choice and definition, "intercourse" connotes both sex and social contact and does not necessarily intuit closeness, affinity, or trust. The former, in my observance, more accurately reflect the realities of what interracial relations looked like. Though many white settlers imagined their relations with Filipinos to be characterized by intimate knowledge and closeness, these things were often lacking in the relationships considered here. Much of the sexual contact between Americans and Filipinos was transactional labor for the many women engaged in this type of work.[32] Though I, like postcolonial theorists, highlight that intimacies reproduced categories of difference and were rooted in the violence of imperialism, my use and understanding of intercourse stresses the logical, rational, and intellectual nature of the decision making processes of the mostly Filipina women who entered into relations with Americans. Additionally, I have lifted the period specific "intercourse" from the historical archive. In 1899, the US military distributed sanitation circulars to troops bound for the Philippines emblazoned with this warning about Filipinos: "Intercourse with them will be dangerous." It was a warning against both casual social encounters and sexual ones, meant to protect troops from moral degeneration as well as venereal diseases.[33] At the turn of the century, intercourse would have just as likely signified social interaction as much as (if not more so than) sexual engagement. Finally, as I contemplated a US-based historiography of colonial intimacies, I first concluded that this was not a well-developed field, at least not in the same way that the field of European colonial intimacies is developed.[34] I soon realized this conclusion was wrong, as it was based on a narrow understanding of what counted as colonial intimacies. The field is very vibrant, but it is not just found within the cross section of the fields of US imperialism and gender studies but also largely found within Native American studies and histories of the US West. My failure to link the two areas was due to a continued hesitance (both in and out of the academy) to connect the so-called imperial turn in US history to the larger global histories of empire, as well as a hesitance to connect the US island empire that began to take shape in 1898 to a longer history of US settler colonialism. My works seeks to address this by putting the rich scholarship on kinship networks and middle grounds within the settler colonial nation in conversation with works on overseas colonial intimacies to trace the continuities and also the disconnects as Americans crossed the Pacific in search of new lands to conquer. My choice to favor "intercourse," then, is also a part of the work of drawing these fields more closely together.

Similarly, the overarching idea of "dangerous intercourse" allows for a broad reading of interracial sexual relations and the different stakes and consequences for those that chose to cross the sexual color line. As postcolonial studies and Native American studies scholars have shown, relationships between colonized and colonizer were inherently violent, inflicting not only physical and bodily harm but also mental and emotional harm.[35] In the Philippines, certain dangers existed for both white and Black American men in the Philippines who engaged sexually with the local population, such as the ostracism of their countrymen, being derided as degenerates, or being passed over for prestigious jobs servicing the empire. Black Americans in the archipelago faced the additional realities of having their relations with the local population—which were often just as exploitative and uneven as those between whites and Filipinas—policed in more institutionalized ways than those of their white counterparts, via more frequent troop rotations or propaganda conveying that their presence would be a bad influence on local communities. For the most part, consequences for white men were relatively few, as the more isolated colonial geography allowed greater access to sexual experimentation with and exploitation of the native Filipino population, often with less legal and social consequences.[36] Filipina women, on the other hand, often entered into such relationships less willingly, or as a result of more constrained life choices in a rapidly shifting colonial regime. So while many Americans could dodge the legal and even the social dangers of interracial intercourse in the colony, Filipinas who became entangled with Americans often found themselves negotiating precarious positions.

In addition to the commonly understood dangers that many Filipina women risked when they formed relations with Americans, such as rape, injury, death, defamation of character, financial ruin, and abandonment, they also faced everyday violence and racism from their American husbands, which reverberated far beyond the home. For example, while American men who married Filipinas were often ostracized from the larger American community in the colony because they had "gone native," they too expressed and shared the racist views of their countrymen. White husbands and liaisons expressed their racist ideas and understandings of the Philippines and Filipinos through the ubiquitous slights and violence directed at their spouses and sexual partners, even as they simultaneously expressed companionate attachment. Indeed, expressions of interracial love, sexual attraction, or friendship demonstrated no more anti-imperial or antiracist ideology than the expressions of overt racism that helped justify colonial occupation.

The physical and social dangers that embroiled those engaged in mixed relations extended beyond the so-called private, as moralists incited criticism of the imperial occupation and the US government by pointing to the flourishing sexual economies in the islands. Interracial marriages and cohabitation caused a stir among Americans at home and in the colony despite the usefulness of more formal relations (like marriage) in legitimizing the benevolent mission of the United States. However, instances of domestic and sexual violence, the expansive sexual economy, and non-heteronormative or queer sexual encounters possessed the incendiary potential to loosen the seams of the American reputation in the colony. Instances of rape or other "unmentionable liberties" not only put into question the idea of American moral superiority but provided fuel for Filipino nationalists in their campaign for immediate independence.[37] Thus, the control of certain types of interracial intercourse—or at least the control of the public narrative about them—could be more urgent and important than the control of other less explosive types of relations.

Ultimately, while both Filipinos and Americans could potentially secure political, socioeconomic, and cultural power in the new colonial order through intercourse, this work stresses the unevenness of such gains within a deeply exploitative colonial society. Any disruption of colonial bedrock ideas of racial superiority due to dangerous intercourse were fleeting, and those Americans who entered into interracial relationships were easily discounted by other colonialists as degenerates, lacking proper home influences in the dangerous and lurid islands. Filipino families could potentially gain more stability, standing, or wealth through certain associations or kin connections to Americans, although their relationships often also helped to fulfill the goals of the colonial state. Mixed families, for instance, might be pointed to by colonial officials and supporters—with or without their consent—as embodiments of successful Americanization in the tropics. So while individuals could fare well enough through their transgressive relations, the aims of the colonial government were ultimately also served. In this way, crossing social and sexual color lines facilitated imperial consolidation and empire building in very long-lasting and consequential ways.[38] Mixed-race couples participated as settler colonists and literally guided colonial officials on their incursions into native communities. Interracial attractions and families were pointed to as legitimating examples of American goodwill and commitment to the welfare of the local population. Even red-light districts, which generated so much negative media attention from Americans and Filipinos alike, ultimately attracted profitable colonial tourism and, according to colonial doctors and officials, alleviated soldier dissatisfaction at being stationed for so long in a place so far away from home. While interracial intercourse posed a set of dangerous possibilities to colonial officials, it was also of vital importance to the consolidation of imperial rule and legitimacy in the Philippines.

Dangerous Intercourse is organized along chronological and thematic lines. The first two chapters deal with securing and creating the colonial state. Chapter 1 begins by looking at the day-to-day lives of women in the Philippines and how their lives shifted with the arrival of the largest group of Americans to have resided at any one time in the Philippines: the US military. Enlisted men became acquainted with Filipinas immediately upon their arrival in the Philippines. Their ubiquitous presence in the islands, and how local populations responded to this presence, shaped initial relations between colonizer and colonized. The revolutionary Filipino government and the US military government both marshaled tropes of dangerous intercourse to direct the outcome of the Philippine-American War. Chapter 2 describes how different regional norms, cultures, and geographies shaped interracial relations. A comparison of the northern and southern Philippine "frontiers" demonstrates how regional imperial control was solidified through the presence and management of interracial intercourse. The US colonial borderlands of the northern Cordillera mountains attracted sporadic settlement from colonial officials and academics who often married into the local communities, while Mindanao—the southernmost region with a predominantly Muslim population—became a region of US-sponsored settler colonialism that facilitated Christian immigration (of both Americans and Filipinos) and land appropriation. Colonial agents at both sites drew from the settler colonial strategies of the domestic homeland, while the Indigenous and Muslim inhabitants attempted to advance their own goals as liminal societies within the archipelago.

Chapters three and four deal more with those who stayed, or settled, in the islands, and how they, together with Filipinos, lived with dangerous intercourse. Chapter 3 explores the blurred line between social and sexual intercourse in the US colony, as both American and Filipino reformers attempted to police the relations that haunted and informed all aspects of colonial society. Many spaces of colonial sociality—the bustling streets of Manila, cabaret dance halls, or bailes—were viewed as dangerous gateway locales that could potentially facilitate the more dangerous problem of sexual intercourse. Every dangerous gateway, however, had empire-building potential or utility, whether it was advancing the facade of diplomatic relations via social conviviality or helping to attract business capital to America's new possession in the Pacific. Filipinos participated in reform efforts to eradicate interracial intercourse, often with their own agendas for shaping the direction of colonial rule, rather than for the protection and sanctity of white American bodies. While chapter 3 explores how Americans and Filipinos socially policed intercourse in the absence of legal barriers, chapter 4 examines the colonial courts and their treatment of interracial relations, focusing on cases involving criminal and family law. Men who committed murder or other grave crimes involving their Filipina wives or lovers often skirted the harshest punishments unless they were not white. Filipinas and mixed-race children became embroiled in court cases during which judges and claimants constantly questioned their legitimacy as wives, mothers, and children, reflecting the precarious legal nature of interracial unions. While some women found success in the colonial courts, winning custody of their children or getting spousal support for abandonment, others were stripped of their inheritance or told that the courts did not recognize them as the natural children of American colonists. What all these cases highlighted was the fact that despite US overtures of familial relations with the Philippines, even formal spouses (Filipina women) and mixed-race offspring were consistently understood as illegible members of American families even if the law said otherwise.

The last two chapters look at how Americans, Filipinos, and mixed-race offspring reflected on or (re)imagined US empire, particularly in the later years of US rule. Chapter 5 shifts gears to look at imperial cultural productions I dub "imperial fiction" (namely poetry, memoir, and novels) produced by American expatriates and Filipino writers. Here I explore imperial fiction from every decade of the colonial occupation. American expats embraced a time-honored settler society tradition by producing literature that literally rewrote the history of US empire in the Philippines, imagining it as a union of two peoples rather than a violent occupation. Filipino writers also used interracial intercourse as a literary trope but did so most often as a point from which to critique US presence in the islands, not romanticize it.

Finally, chapter 6 focuses on the descendants of interracial couples. While American philanthropic organizations denigrated American mestizos as the potentially dangerous collateral damage of empire—that is, as quasi-Americans who might incite rebellion against the benevolent American presence—well-to-do American mestizos distanced themselves from such characterizations. Instead, elite mixed offspring formed their own societies, modeled after US settler societies, and fashioned themselves as the dutiful children of heroic Americans. Because this small population of non-abandoned mestizos had the recognition of their fathers and some access to American resources and citizenship, they, unlike their less fortunate and more numerous counterparts, often achieved a semi-elevated status, not necessarily as respectable Americans (like the image they attempted to project) but as assured Americanized Filipinos. Both of these narratives, one created by colonialist philanthropic organizations and the other by elite American mestizo society, shifted the discourse of child abandonment in the Philippines away from American immorality and hypocrisy and turned it into a story of American benevolence, responsibility, and settler respectability.

Interracial intimacy was and continues to be used to imagine the US-Philippine relationship, even though most of the acts of transgressive intercourse outlined here were not characterized by tender closeness or attachment. While Americans at the turn of the century often described the Philippines alternately as friend, child, and damsel in distress, perhaps the most prolific popular imagery and discourse about the archipelago and its imperial occupation by Americans in the first half of the twentieth century focused on ideas of romantic interracial love and interest (figs. 0.1 and 0.2).[39]

Figure 0.1. "He Can't Let Go," *Puck*, November 23, 1898. The Philippines is represented as a woman in need of rescue. Uncle Sam pulls her from a cliff, saving her from "Spanish misrule" and "Aguinaldoism."

Figure 0.2. "Columbia Is by No Means Enthusiastic by This Transaction." *Life*, December 8, 1898. Uncle Sam pays Spain for possession of the captive Philippines. The chained woman flirtatiously gestures to Uncle Sam while Columbia, a feminized personification of America, looks on.

Such a pervasive and durable imagining obscures and denies the brutality of imperial conquest and how actual interracial intercourse in the islands was largely characterized by and made possible through colonial violence. The postwar militarization of the Pacific theater perpetuates this dangerous intercourse today. The idea that social and sexual interracial intercourse is a sign or symptom of positive racial relations—an idea that is contemporarily espoused by the ideologies of multiculturalism and neoliberalism, especially in discourses of mixed-race identity—is not a new one. As this project illustrates, the logic that interracial intercourse equals tolerance and equality was used at the turn of the century to ensure the legitimacy and longevity of overseas American imperialism.

Perhaps one of the most conspicuous signifiers of the disconnect between interracial intercourse and racial liberalism (and perhaps the longest-lived embodiment of the imperial US–Philippine romance) is the historic and continued presence of American mestizos in the islands. The mixed-race descendants and children of Filipinas and primarily American servicemen but also tourists and civilians have occupied a liminal space in Philippine society and an almost nonexistent one in the United States since the early 1900s. Then described by Americans and Filipinos as American mestizos and now as Amerasians (a postwar political classification of the mixed-race children originating from occupied Southeast Asian nations), this population has largely gone unnoticed by the American public at large for over a century. Most mestizos and Amerasians living in the Philippines—both historically and contemporarily—were abandoned by their American fathers and raised by their mothers and other extended family members. The large and conspicuous Amerasian population today, especially in the various militarized port cities of the Philippines, inspires various forms of anti-American resistance and sentiment, as local communities are unable to escape the striking unevenness of international relations literally staring them in the face. The Philippine Amerasian population has grown significantly since the turn of the twentieth century, especially during and after World War II. Even while the US government has acknowledged other Amerasian populations across Asia (via federal immigration laws like the Amerasian Homecoming Act), those in the Philippines remain largely ignored. As a US wartime ally and "friend," the Philippines existed outside the humanitarian impulse, as if Amerasians there were not the by-product of warfare and violence but the result of romance and commitment; as if only Spain and Japan were imperial occupiers, while the United States was something else; as if the United States' history with the Philippines was somehow exceptional.

Ultimately, this project traces a genealogy of the US-Philippine "romance" that has persisted since the turn of the twentieth century, a romance that has buttressed ideas of US exceptionalism while denying and obscuring the colonial violence and inequality that is the foundation of imperial occupations. By centering relations typically understood as positive and even loving, relations that often intuitively suggest positive interactions and obscure violence, it is my hope that the romanticism surrounding historic and contemporary US-Philippine relations can be broken down and interrogated more effectively, and in so doing, shift the dangerous ideas about Asian and Asian American women's sexuality and availability that continue to shape their lives. As this project will demonstrate, it is not just the disembodied notion of a figurative interracial romance that continues to sustain exceptionalist ideas about the nature of US imperialism in the Philippines but actual romances, family formations, and sexual relationships.

Chapter 1

Marshaling Interracial Intercourse during the Philippine-American War, 1898–1902

Juliana Lopez had heard of the atrocities committed by the American soldiers against women in the islands. How could she not have? For the many Filipino, Indigenous, Spanish, Chinese, and other residents of Manila, it was a daily occurrence born out of the ongoing war and splashed across the pages of American- and Filipino-run presses alike.[1] There was always some drunk soldier getting into a fight in the nearby red-light district, hurling barbs and fists at passersby on the streets. Sometimes a night of debauchery would end more gruesomely, like when a Black soldier from the Twenty-Fourth Infantry shot two brothel "inmates." Some said he did it because the women insulted him with a racial slur, while others said he pulled the trigger after the women attempted to rob him.[2] Stories about the US military demanding people's homes, taking liberties with women, and destroying crops and livestock reached Manila from outlying towns, which was why Juliana was so worried when her sister Andrea wrote to her in late December 1901 with the news that American soldiers had overtaken their family home in Batangas, just a few hours south of Manila Bay. Andrea was worried too. In a letter to Juliana, she recounted that the military was forcing her to leave and that she would likely do so out of fear that they might "commit some outrage upon her person."[3] Ultimately, however, Andrea did not comply. It was bad enough that three of her brothers had been arrested days before the commandeering of her home, taken away by the US military to be thrown in jail with little explanation. This latest injustice was too much and she refused to go, allowing the Americans to occupy all parts of the house except her own living quarters and room. Juliana pressed her sister to leave before some violation of her honor occurred, but after a few weeks Andrea had fallen into a routine living among the soldiers and assured Juliana that she was all right for now. Despite this reassurance, Juliana feared for her sister and prayed that she would not be "insulted" by the troops.[4]

The story of the Lopez family and their experiences during the Philippine-American War would become known to imperialists and anti-imperialists on both sides of the Pacific. The letters written back and forth to one another were first part of a transnational effort to release the three Lopez Brothers—Cipriano, Manuel, and Lorenzo—from jail. Clemencia Lopez, one of the eldest of the four Lopez sisters, traveled to Boston on a mission to petition US president Theodore Roosevelt for their release. But the family letters also became part of a larger anti-imperialist agenda, and Clemencia was soon speaking before American crowds on the state of the war in the Philippines, Filipina women's social status in society, and the Filipino desire for national independence. At one such speaking engagement before the New England Woman Suffrage Association in May 1902, she brought up the precarity of women's bodily integrity in the Philippines in light of the Philippine-American War, saying that because many wives were so devoted to their husbands' war efforts, they too were exposed to the "attacks of the enemy."[5] The American Anti-Imperialist League (AAIL) used Clemencia's tour around the United States, as well as her family's letters, to promote its goal of non-annexation of the Philippines. Fiske Warren—a well-known anti-imperialist and an acquaintance of the Lopez family—edited and published (using a pseudonym) the family's letters, which detailed the injustices they endured at the hands of Americans during the war. While many Americans supported the AAIL and came to sympathize with the people and social world that Clemencia Lopez described at her speaking engagements, it was not enough to turn the tide of the US occupation after the war. That is not to say that the impact of Clemencia's visit to the United States and the publication of *The Story of the Lopez Family* were not enduring. The Lopez brothers told Juliana and Andrea about the better treatment they received at the hands of their American captors after their sister began to garner attention stateside, and they were finally released in May 1902, two months after Clemencia's petition was presented before the US Senate. The Lopez family story stayed with people, and in 1915, American Walter Jaeger reminded *New York Times* readers of the wartime "outrages upon married women and girls" committed by US soldiers in the Philippines, which he had likely learned

of from either attending one of Clemencia Lopez's talks or reading the published letters. His opinion piece was a response to the widespread condemnation of Germans and Germany after the sinking of the RMS *Lusitania* by
U-boats earlier that month. The United States, Jaeger pressed, was not without its own shameful history in times of war.[6]

Dangerous intercourse, as a reality, most often materialized in the ubiquitous physical sexual violence that occurred around the archipelago during
the Philippine-American War. While it was an everyday reality that informed
the lives of women like Juliana and Andrea Lopez, as well as the more vulnerable women who worked within the sexual economy, dangerous intercourse was also an idea, one that was commonly marshaled as a tool to
advance various goals and desired outcomes of the occupation. For Filipina
women with a platform like Clemencia Lopez, the reality of sexual violence
in the Philippines could be mustered as a way to draw attention to the hypocrisy of purported American benevolence and gain support for immediate independence. Unfortunately for Lopez and women across the archipelago,
US military officials in the Philippines who were not interested in giving
up their new possession in the Pacific also harnessed ideas of dangerous intercourse as part of the processes of colonial state-building. Army surgeons,
chaplains, officers, and soldiers were all drawn in to discussions about interracial intercourse, especially as soldiers became targets of anti-imperialists
and Filipinos alike for their debauchery and as high rates of syphilis took
more and more men away from their wartime duties. For the military officials responsible for wresting the Philippines out of Filipino hands, it was
expedient to direct the discourse around dangerous intercourse in ways that
tempered the criticism and culpability of the troops. At the same time, Filipinos engaged with US troops in ways that sought to wrest some of that
power back, with ideas of dangerous intercourse playing a leading role.

Dangerous intercourse had always been a contested site of empire, which
Filipinos and Americans both understood and used in different ways to direct
the outcome of US occupation of the Philippines. During the Philippine-
American War, interracial sexual relations were a particularly important site of
imperial negotiations. Discursively, dangerous intercourse was an exception-
ally powerful tool to wield in order to convey the egregious and unforgivable.
Walter Jaeger's 1915 condemnation of rape at the turn of the century, for example, was deemed a more powerfully persuasive device to make his point
about historical US wartime atrocities than the more recent 1913 Bud Bagsak
massacre of over five hundred Muslims from the southern Philippines by

American and native troops. The take-no-prisoners massacre was the latest in a series of ongoing campaigns to pacify the peoples of the Philippine islands. At the same time, Americans had little sympathy for the "fanatical" Moros, as they were called.[7] These "semi-civilized" non-Christians did not garner the same sympathy as did Juliana Lopez, a well-read, wealthy Christian Filipina who approximated Anglo-European ideals of feminine virtue. Lopez's position and status made her an apt messenger to deliver condemnations of rape, and she was but one voice that would marshal dangerous intercourse in the name of independence. Many Filipinos—from the revolutionary government to nationalist playwrights to poorer women concerned for their safety—used real and imagined sexual violence and dangerous intercourse not just to seek justice for violated women but as a symbol of the broader usurpation of the gendered homeland to rally criticism of the United States.

So much of how Filipinos formed ideas about the US occupation stemmed from interactions with the troops. As the largest American presence in the Philippines during the first decade of the occupation, prior to the large influx of entrepreneurs, teachers, families, and others, the figure of the American soldier was the ubiquitous representation of America in the archipelago. As recorded in 1900 by Daniel Williams, secretary of the Second Philippine Commission, army life in Manila was "an ever-present reality, the city being a huge military camp swarming with khaki-clad soldiers. . . . Among Americans the military element predominates."[8] For those Americans in the military, interracial intercourse was also understood as dangerous, though not because of concern for the bodily integrity of Filipina women or the injustice done to the burgeoning nation. Rather, American military discourse about interracial sexual contact largely emphasized the danger to the American male body and, by extension, the American colonial state in the Philippines.[9] As moralists on both sides of the Pacific received news of troop debauchery and regulated prostitution and used these reports to criticize the colonial occupation, military officials found that depicting Filipinas as lewd and diseased was the best way to deflect attention away from soldier immorality and maintain the moral high ground. The discourse about Filipina women that flowed from the US military in the Philippines was one that primarily depicted them as prostitutes anchored within the vice economies throughout the islands.[10] This constructed "knowledge" of Filipina sexuality allowed the US military, and the broader imperial mission, to justify its presence and claim a morally imperative place in the islands. While the bodies of women became contested sites from which transnational debates were forged and fought, the voices of Filipina women could have particular amplitude, especially when criticisms came from elites that embodied idealized womanhood, like Clemencia Lopez.[11]

American and Filipino experiences with interracial intercourse did not begin with the outbreak of hostilities in 1899 but rather had longer foundations. For Americans, centuries of hemispheric expansion and settler colonialism had informed ideas about interracial mixing. This long experience shaped ideas about who did and did not have a place in the US nation and culminated in the state-by-state adoption of anti-miscegenation laws, effectively barring whites and nonwhites from marrying. Filipinos built their understanding of interracial intercourse through centuries of Spanish colonialism and regional travel and trade. Intermarriage in the Philippines between local inhabitants and the newer Chinese and Spanish populations in particular informed Filipino perspectives on such relations, and while they had for the most part come to be an accepted part of Philippine society and culture, the lechery of Spanish friars in their sexual exploitation of Filipinas fueled revolutionary sentiment. While many Filipinos claimed with ambivalence or pride some European ancestry through friar lineages, they were also critical of the immorality of the religious men who had long held disproportionate power in the islands. For Filipinos and Americans attempting to sway the outcome of the Philippine-American War and public sentiment about annexation versus independence, marshaling real and imagined interracial intercourse was in many ways business as usual. As this chapter highlights, both Filipinos and Americans tried—in vastly uneven ways—to shape narratives about sexuality and to control interracial intercourse in order to see their vision of the Philippines emerge.

Marshaling Dangerous Intercourse for Inang-Bayan (Motherland)

The Lopez family's descriptions of sexual violence were not the first indictments of American rule, nor would they be the last. Just days after the outbreak of the Philippine-American War in early February 1899, *El Heraldo Filipino*—the Tagalog-language newspaper and major press organ of the Filipino revolutionary government—published "Hibik namin" (Our plea), an incendiary call to arms against the new American occupying forces. Written in lyric form, "Hibik namin" followed the Filipino literary tradition of previous "*hibiks*," or poetic protestations against colonial rule and the subjugation that arose from it.[12]

Pagkatanto naming ng kuhilang asal	We have known the wicked conduct
Nang americanong labis nang kasamaan	these scoundrels, blasted Americans
Sa sakit nang loob ang kulang na lamang	The hurt we have been inflicted
Ay maubos kaming sa mapo'y lumual . . .	Could wipe us off this earth . . .
Di pa sukat yaong madling kahayupang,	Why, when at every house they enter,
Ginagawa nila sa pakikipaglaban,	Should they violate every woman they capture?
Pano't ang babayeng abutan sa bahay	There are the acts of brutality in war
Na mapasok nila'y linalapastangan.	This is the height of cruelty in battle.[13]

The nine authors condemned the US occupation of the Philippines, decrying the rape of Filipina women by American soldiers and warning Filipino collaborators not to trust the promises of the Americans, for once they got what they were after, "Kayo'y ilulubog sa inyo ring dugo" (They will drown you in your own blood).[14] Unlike allusions to interracial intercourse that would be made a few years later by US commission leader William Taft and Filipino intellectual Trinidad Pardo de Tavera—allusions meant to signify positive American-Filipino relations, the poem's use of intercourse was meant as a rallying cry for Filipinos to align with the suppressed revolutionary government. The message was clear—dangerous intercourse was just that: dangerous.

Scholars have long maintained that empire was (and continues to be) an important site of knowledge production.[15] Domestic and overseas colonialism relied on certain knowledge to justify conquest, and also created knowledge about the people and places that were taken as colonies. Ideas about race, gender, class, sexuality, and so on shaped and were shaped by the expansionist efforts of the United States, both at home and abroad. But this was not a one-sided project. Colonized populations created their own knowledge of imperial processes and foreign occupiers as well. In the case of Filipinos during the Philippine-American War, dangerous intercourse was largely synonymous with sexual violence against Filipina women. Propagandists and nationalists mobilized ideas of dangerous intercourse—and the corresponding depiction of American troops as sexually depraved—as a politically savvy way to advance the nationalist goal of immediate independence. They often did not have to look far for their damning accounts of soldier abuses toward women, as the realities of sexual harassment and violence informed day-to-day life, even prior to the formal declaration of war against the Americans.[16] Much of the knowledge that Filipinos formulated about US martial masculinity was anchored in previous experiences with the Spanish Empire and the wartime atrocities that unfolded all around them. Filipino men and women simply had to point to the myriad incidences of sexual violence and debauchery to lay claim to their own abilities to rule the nation effectively and in the better interests of the native population. This was what made interracial intercourse so immediately dangerous for the stability of the US occupation in the islands and why deploying it as a discursive wartime tool was so imperative for Filipinos.

"Hibik namin" was one of the first wartime denunciations of the American occupation to highlight that annexation was dangerous to the bodily integrity and lives of Filipina women. In this poem, the nine authors' depiction of rape easily stands in for the violation of Philippine sovereignty by the United States. The poem describes the signs of a patriarchal society organized around women's domestic and reproductive labor, a vision commonly shared among the Europeanized and other Filipino elites that led and supported the revolutionary government. Idealized Filipina womanhood is clear in the verses in which the imperiled woman is described as "Asawang angel" (a wife who is an angel) and "dalaga kayang uliran nang linis" (a maiden who is pure and clean). The transgressions of the occupying force brought shame and shattered honor, "Kapag inabuta't kanilang nagipit, Ang puri'y siya nang mulang pagkalait." The feminine virtues embodied by the hispanized Maria Clara figure—one popularized by Filipino revolutionary martyr José Rizal in his novel on the evils of Spanish colonization—were largely constructed throughout the Spanish period but remained an embedded archetype embraced by many Filipino men and women throughout the American period.[17] In many subversive Philippine plays and literature from the time of the Philippine-American War, the virtuous woman is often the intended symbol of the nation, at risk of being defiled or otherwise suffering at the hands of another, typically the character that stands in for the colonial occupier.[18]

Like much of the Filipino discourse around dangerous intercourse, "Hibik namin" was a battle cry for the defense of transgressed Filipinas against Americans, in which the violation of the Filipina body stood in for the violation of the *inang-bayan*, or motherland. Contemporary Filipino scholars have pointed to the metaphorical nature of "Hibik namin" by drawing attention to the ambiguity of the authorship. In particular, they highlight that the names of the nine women signatories who authored the poem—Victoria Lactaw, Felipa Kapuloan, Feliza Kahatol, Victoria Mausig, Patricia Himagsik, Salvadora Dimagiba, Dolores Katindig, Honorata Dimauga, and Deodata Liwanag—are likely pseudonyms. That all of the chosen surnames have patriotic imagery or undertones (*kapuluan*/archipelago, *kahatol*/judgment, *himagsik*/rebellion, *dimagiba*/indestructible, *katindig*/defending one's beliefs, *liwanag*/beacon of light) has even led some scholars to speculate that the authors might have just as likely been men using the trope of idealized womanhood to incite rebellion and support for the cause of independence. At the same time, it was quite common for women of the time, especially of the elite classes, to ascribe to notions of "proper" and idealized womanhood themselves. Women took active roles in the successive revolutionary uprisings that occurred in the Philippines, acting as spies, provisioners, and even combatants.[19] Filipinas often wrote for and to newspapers, and many went into publishing themselves, starting newspapers and magazines of their own.[20]

While no consensus exists as to the authorship of "Hibik namin," its being ostensibly written by nine educated and virtuous women, who by their own account subscribed to gendered notions of woman as virginal wife and mother, gave the poem additional weightiness. The gravitas of "Hibik namin" was only possible because of the faithfulness to the rigid Maria Clara trope. In other words, only a particular type of womanhood in peril would be useful in Filipino campaigns against the occupying forces. Women that did not fit the particularly judicious mold—poor women, women in the sexual economy, Indigenous women—were less effective (if at all) in conveying the patriotic message of admonition. That the US project of empire relied on ideas of Filipinos as uncivilized, immoral, and sexual available only served to reinforce the valorization of some women over other more marginalized women, as Filipino elites sought to distance themselves from the narratives that Americans projected onto them. Herein lay the irony of revolutionary efforts to harness the idea of dangerous intercourse as a tool against empire. Filipino elites who highlighted depraved American sexuality as a way to advocate their own ability to lead and represent the people of the islands thoughtfully excluded from their idealized vision of the motherland those most vulnerable to sexual abuse from the invading forces.

The leader and president of the revolutionary government, Emilio Aguinaldo, favored the symbolism of dangerous intercourse in his public proclamations before and during the war. In August 1898, just a few months after American troops defeated the Spanish forces in Manila Bay and began pouring into the major cities, Aguinaldo administered an oath to Filipinos newly elected to serve as municipal council members. He praised their dedication to the "long cherished aspirations of our Fatherland" that "Filipinos should be the ones to govern the sons of this land."[21] Though he used masculine imagery to describe the prospects for self-rule and political participation, he shifted to femininizing the Philippines when he called on the newly sworn in officials to protect the nation from the threats to liberty that still emanated from the United States and other foreign elements: "The Philippine Islands, our beloved Native Land, on account of their riches and fertility, like a maiden of enchanting beauty, are coveted and sought by the foreign squadrons which from the bay gaze with admiration upon her, and stare, enamored by her marvelous and peculiar attraction. . . . Let us not bring upon her any sorrow through our lack of union."[22] Kristin Hoganson, Victor Mendoza, and others have pointed to the metaphor of marriage used by imperialists and anti-imperialists in describing the US-Philippines relationship, but less attention has been focused on how Filipino revolutionaries used this same language to advance their goals for the *inang-bayan*.[23] According to Aguinaldo, if Filipino men, united in the cause of liberty, claimed the marriage bed, it would make it more difficult for American imperialists to find excuses to intervene in the islands. A civil war among Filipinos, he warned, would give the foreign powers the opportunity they needed to ravish and exploit the islands, forcing the Philippines into an undesired marriage. However, it was not just any men he envisioned as suitable marriage partners for the maiden Philippines but specifically the hispanized or elite men from central and southern Luzon, whose provinces he took care to mention by name.[24]

The marriage metaphor was particularly apt, as Americans were quick to point out and attack the preponderance of cohabitation across the archipelago (rather than formalized marriage) as symptomatic of widespread Filipino immorality. As missionaries and civilians reported regarding local marital practices, formalized marriage was rare through the islands amongst the poorer classes because of the high fees charged by the previous Spanish religious orders. According to Homer Stuntz, reverend of the Methodist Episcopal Church and an early missionary in the Philippines, "The length to which friars went in getting money from the people almost pass belief. Marriage could only be had of the friar. Civil marriage was not possible, of course, where Rome had absolute sway. . . . Poor people practically abandoned all idea of marriage." The greed of the friars and the lack of access to marital contracts, he concluded, caused demoralization among the people, and "the idea of chastity, for which the Tagalog, Pampangan, and Ilocano people especially are noted, was seriously impaired." His own religious order, he claimed, had performed more than two thousand marriages in the past three years, righting the wrong of cohabitation and sex without marriage.[25] These descriptions of the pervasiveness of common-law marriage without religious or civil sanctity took root among Americans and further bolstered US claims of moral superiority over both the Spanish empire and Filipinos. The promotion of marriage was one of the earliest endeavors of both the revolutionary government and the American colonial state. Civil marriage was on the docket when Aguinaldo's administration began its organization of the newly freed Philippines. Just days before the revolutionary leader declared the Philippines an independent nation, his administration had released a set of rules indicating the new direction forward in all areas of governance. According to his decree dated June 20, 1898, marriage would be conducted primarily through chief commissioners of towns. If contracts were obtained through these civil servants, a priest could then provide a religious marriage.[26]

The revolutionary government faced dilemmas with this new rule, as native clergy complained about the lack of religious authority, and many Filipinos in the highly catholicized archipelago favored marriage through the church and saw the new proclamation as a violation of their religious freedoms. Gregorio Araneta, the secretary of justice under the revolutionary government, received complaints about the new marriage rules and gave his estimation that civil marriage should be primarily encouraged but that people should not be prevented from seeking marriage within the church.[27] The American occupiers also sought to address the issue of marriage. Under the military leadership of Elwell Otis—the military governor of the Philippines during the war against the Filipinos—and aided by local elite and prominent lawyer Cayetano Arellano, the establishment of civil marriages was prioritized and seen as a way to sway local sentiment away from the revolutionary camp. Arellano understood that marriage laws were a hot-button issue for the local population in light of the previous Spanish strictures. During the previous year, Arellano had served as the secretary of foreign affairs under the revolutionary government when it had begun pronouncing the new laws and decrees of the nation, including the marriage law. He would have been familiar with the troubles that the revolutionary government faced in its promotion of civil marriage rather than marriage through the church. Specifically, how could the revolutionaries decisively break from the policies of the unpopular Spanish friars while not alienating the Filipino clergy and followers of the Catholic Church, who made up the bulk of the population?[28] Arellano likely hoped that his advice to enact civil marriage with the option for religious marriage would both satisfy local

Catholics and signal to the Americans that he (and of course other Filipinos) were capable of embracing "modern" civil codes. In December 1899, not long after the war broke out, Otis put forth a general order that outlined the creation and recognition of civil marriage in addition to marriage solemnized by priests and religious orders.[29] This became the basis of the marriage law under the American civil government. Arellano's aid to the military government served him well, and he was later appointed by the US government to the position of chief justice of the Philippine Supreme Court, a position he remained in until 1920.

Almost a year after the outbreak of the war, Aguinaldo again used the imagery of dangerous intercourse as the revolutionary government urged Filipinos not to cooperate with the American military government. Many people across the archipelago had grown weary of the past year of warfare and were beginning to surrender their arms to the Americans. To engender more patriotism and call on Filipinos to join the war rather than "fold [their] arms" while the enemy invaded, he turned again to the useful gendered symbolism of dangerous intercourse. If Filipinos sat back or, worse, became collaborators, he proclaimed, there would be no country to "offer our beautiful maidens." "Can our dignity consent, and will it perhaps consent that the Filipino women bow their heads and bend their delicate necks before the haughty foreigners? No, never, never!!!! Rather death!!!!!"[30] The continued allusion to the US military as usurpers of not only land but also women was as militarily expedient for Filipinos as it was for Americans, especially as Filipino civilians complained to Aguinaldo's government that members of the revolutionary army were committing the same types of atrocities—theft, burning homes, raping women—as the US troops. Aguinaldo understood that wartime atrocities committed by Filipinos against one another would only favor the "plans of our enemies, the Americans," and decreed in the first days of the war that such crimes would be treated as military crimes, although this commandment was only heeded by some.[31] Indeed, Filipino collaborators who urged surrender turned the metaphor of dangerous intercourse on their erstwhile compatriots, feeding information about Filipino crimes such as rape to Americans and others critical of Aguinaldo's rule and advised, "Do not believe the reports that the Americans have injured women—no, rather the contrary, because such a thing is forbidden by them."[32]

The revolutionary government was well aware of the fact that most Americans thought them racially inferior and prone to all the vices and immorality that imperial nations associated with those they conquered. Filipino attempts to shape the discursive sphere about dangerous intercourse and sexuality in general was often in response to and in refusal of these American perceptions. It is true that Filipino ideas of gender and sexuality had been shaped by centuries of contact with Spanish expectations and norms as well as regional flows of trade and travel, but American ideas about racial hierarchies played a very immediate role in local attempts to demonstrate the capacity for self-rule. Aguinaldo himself was alerted to the fact that the American "foreign element" was making complaints about US troops contracting syphilis and other venereal diseases after visiting local brothels. Just a few months after the occupation by the US military and six months before Filipinos would declare war on the new arrivals, Emiliano Riego de Dios—the governor-general of Cavite, just south of Manila—wrote to Aguinaldo alerting him to the new sanitation regulations he hoped to enact in light of these complaints. Riego de Dios and the city officials had come up with a regulatory plan to examine women in the various houses of prostitution, and they hoped the revolutionary government would approve. As if to make a stronger case for approval, the Cavite officials stated that they would enact the regulations with "the most decorous publicity for the compliance therewith, in order that the diseases previously mentioned shall not continue to develop in the form observed by the foreign element." Riego de Dios also hoped to "prevent all kinds of scandals in the houses of prostitution."[33] Both Riego de Dios and Aguinaldo understood the stakes of an ostentatious display of sanitation regulations, as local and national prospects for independence were on the line, with the eyes of the Americans appraisingly fixed on the Philippines. They understood prostitution as dangerous not only or even primarily for being a vector of disease but for potentially impeding prospects for independence. Being able to adequately sanitize prostitution (or at least project the appearance of sanitation) was imperative for appearing modern and not in need of benevolent assistance or intervention. Both men hoped that shifting the discourse around Filipino inferiority would aid independence goals and eventually allow them to take a leading role in the running of a new nation. Apparently some non-idealized women, such as those who worked within the sexual vice economy, could constitute some part of the new nation as long as their bodies and livelihoods were obtrusively controlled by Filipino men.

Marshaling Dangerous Intercourse for Empire

Prostitution was also understood by Americans as a hub of dangerous intercourse, although for them the danger was not wrapped up with protecting

Figure 1.1. "Hobson Reaches the Philippines, and the Girls Are Ready." *Life*, January 26, 1899. Depictions of Filipinos at the time typically relied on the more well-known racist caricatures of Black and Indigenous people.

prospects for Philippine independence. Rather, for the mostly military American population in the islands during the war, prostitution threatened the bodily health of troops essential for combat and hence imperiled military rule over the colonial state. When the US Army arrived in the Philippines, first to fight the Spanish and then, after overstaying their welcome, to fight the Filipinos, many of the troops were already familiar with the narrative of the lascivious Filipina. Some would have seen the depictions of seminude Filipina women (mostly modeled after popular racist depictions of Indigenous and Black Americans) that featured prominently in the press coverage of annexation debates in the United States (fig. 1.1).[34]

Others, like those enlisted in the Eighth Army Corps, read about the dangers of overfamiliarity with local women in the shipboard literature distributed to them on their way to the Pacific. In 1899, Lieutenant Colonel Henry Lippincott, the chief surgeon of the United States Army, created a sanitation circular to be distributed freely to troops bound for the islands, in which he warned that "intercourse with them will be dangerous." "The natives are notoriously careless of all sanitary laws, and are infected with numerous diseases. . . . Under no circumstances have any communications with suspected people, and thus avoid carrying infection to the camp. All kinds of venereal diseases are very prevalent among the natives in the towns."[35] Lippincott had gotten much of his experience in the field alongside famed Indian fighter George Custer during the Great Plains Wars as a first lieutenant of the Seventh US Cavalry.[36] Tapped in 1898 to return to military service just days after the Battle of Manila Bay against the Spanish but prior to the formal outbreak of the Philippine-American War, Lippincott was one of several surgeons whose frontier experience, in the estimation of the War Department, made him ideal for the tropical service.[37] His circular was likely influenced by his time spent tending to the sick and wounded in the central plains and the Southwest and reflected a wariness of the treachery of the native population in the Philippines. Lippincott's warning, however, failed to take root among the enlisted men, as American soldiers sought out "immoral pursuits" and entertainment off base almost immediately upon arrival in the Philippines in 1898.

The American characterization of Filipinas as lurid disease carriers was one that easily gained a foothold, especially as transnational debates around prohibition and prostitution came to center squarely on the US military, much of which was, at the turn of the century, stationed in the Philippines. At the onset of the Philippine-American War, the United States sent more than 100,000 troops abroad to fight for continued possession of the islands.[38] American civilians never numbered over nine thousand in the islands during the American colonial and commonwealth periods, their numbers totaling around 8,135 in the 1903 census, 5,774 in the 1918 census, and 8,709 in the 1939 census.[39] The war marked a period of immense growth for the US military, which increased more than fivefold in just a few short years, from about 43,000 enrolled troops in 1897 to about 235,000 in 1898.[40] Of these 235,000 troops, 200,000 served in the Philippines between 1900 and 1902 alone. Unlike in the aftermath of the US Civil War, when active-duty troops dropped to near prewar levels and rounded out at around 25,000–35,000 members, troop strength in the aftermath of the Spanish and Philippine wars never dropped below 100,000 again. As the initial tether between the United States and the Philippines, the military began the process of colonial state-building in the islands, from pacifying the revolutionary army to building up local infrastructure in ways that suited Anglo-European tastes to producing and disseminating knowledge about the locale that bolstered the moral and civilizational imperative of the empire. The colonial process of knowledge production was one that was largely second nature to Americans at this point, as depicting foreign and nonwhite women as sexually promiscuous and dangerous was a well-used tool of not just US empire but Anglo-European empire more generally.

From the barbaric African woman who supposedly experienced pain-free childbirth to the lascivious native "squaw" who was incompatible with Anglo notions of femininity to the white-approximating and sexually available Mexican woman of the US-Mexico borderlands, ideas of gender and sexuality had long played a role in the formation of a US national identity that reified white heteronormative sexuality.[41] The material consequences of such knowledge production were significant, as ideas about nonwhite women sustained the logics of chattel slavery, Indigenous land dispossession, and the imperial conquest of neighboring nations. The gendered knowledge production about the Philippines took shape in much the same way that it did in the domestic homeland, pitting martial/frontier masculinity against the dangers of the diseased nonwhite woman. In the first four years of military rule (prior to civil rule in late 1902), the Philippines saw a proliferation of a "porno-tropics" discourse, or the sexual fetishization of the land and the people as a way to imagine and justify violent masculine conquest.[42] Depicting Filipinas as such was militarily advantageous because it helped justify imperial violence and also legitimated the civilizing mission of the United States, which purported the uplift of "uncivilized" Filipinos as a primary aim of annexation.

Because US soldiers were so visible, their actions often came to reflect on the military and nonmilitary American populations alike. Much to the chagrin of colonial officials who attempted to build a favorable reputation for US rule in the islands, troops in Manila and across the archipelago soon gained notoriety for their drunken and bawdy behavior. Local American newspapers in Manila often reported the latest incidents of soldiers "disturbing the peace," engaging in drunk and disorderly conduct, "visiting the dens of immorality" in "known vice districts," fighting in the streets over Filipina women, or being charged with the battery or murder of Filipinos.[43] One American, reflecting on the early state of colonial policy in the Philippines, described the "lack of control over the drink evil which was so notable during the early occupation of Manila by Americans. It is an undoubted fact that the excesses of our soldiers in this regard were extreme, and had a disastrous influence upon our prestige with the natives." The soldier-driven liquor trade, he continued, was so excessive that "the city seemed surrendered to a saturnalia of drunkenness."[44] Holding soldiers accountable for their behavior was a delicate matter, as their labor was integral to the processes of empire building in the islands. Military officials often did what they could to smooth over soldier abuses toward Filipinos, and for the most part, impunity was the norm. That, however, did not stop critics from demanding change. When reports of the troops' debauchery began traversing the Pacific, American officials were faced with a public relations nightmare.

Like Filipinos who harnessed ideas of dangerous intercourse as a way to negotiate empire, the US military marshaled ideas about interracial relations and sexuality as a way to garner and maintain control over the direction of empire. Threats to military governance of the islands came from two main arenas: anti-imperialists and American reformers, and Filipinos. The preponderance of military-produced discourse from the Philippine-American War period that characterized Filipinas as libidinous was in many ways a response to the vigorous attempts made by the reform community in the United States (one composed of prohibitionists, social purists, temperance reformers, and others) to press for more federal-level social control over Americans. Vice reform, from drinking to gambling to illicit sex, was a growing movement in the United States during the progressive era. A transnational coalition of moral reformers, including the Woman's Christian Temperance Union and the American Anti-Saloon League, saw in the reports and news coming from the empire the opportunity to build momentum for the prohibition movement that they had been building in the United States state by state for several decades. The campaign against the US military canteen that provisioned beer and light wines to soldiers provided the moralist coalition an opportunity to attempt legislation on the federal level. As so much of US-troop strength was overseas—the Philippines, Cuba, Puerto Rico, Guam, Hawaii—American progressive reform efforts became inextricably entwined with the island empire, and reformers constantly pointed overseas when bringing charges of immorality.[45] They argued that "the spectacle of Americans drunk awakens disgust in the Filipinos," and further, such behavior on the part of Americans was an affront to the "movement for protection of child races against the vices of civilization."[46] Prohibitionists grew their support in the islands, as civilian colonists bemoaned the sordid image that was coming to be associated with all US citizens in the Philippines. Colonialists worried that soldier behavior would not only incite ire from Filipinos but also diminish American prestige within transimperial circuits, particularly in nearby British colonial port cities, where US tourists often heard other Euro-imperial travelers denouncing Manila as a "hotbed of every vice."[47]

When the American prohibition coalition came after the military canteen, the federally appointed Second Philippine Commission, led by William Howard Taft, joined with the military to thwart the reformers' success by redirecting blame and culpability. In December 1900, the commission passed the Manila Liquor Licenses Act, a stopgap attempt to regulate who could sell liquor and what kind, as well as where saloons and bars could and could not be located. An attempt to place the blame for debauchery on local conditions rather than American soldiers, the Liquor License Act made it illegal to sell or give any native-made liquor to US soldiers within the city limits.[48] Redirecting reformers' gaze off of soldiers and the military and onto native-operated saloons and native-made alcoholic concoctions was the first step in the larger battle against prohibition.[49] When this lackluster concession to the moral coalition failed and the Anti-Canteen Law was passed later that same month, the indiscriminate and systematic vilification of Filipina sexuality became the de facto approach to its repeal.[50] US military officials heavily adopted the image of the Philippine prostitute as a graver danger to the body and body politic than beer or whiskey.[51] Thus, it was out of both habit (the longer history of the domestic empire) and necessity that American officialdom in the Philippines largely subsumed the diverse social and economic world of women in the islands under the derived umbrella of the sexual vice industry. Pointing the finger at sexually licentious nonwhite women as the real locus of debauchery in the Philippines instead of healthful glasses of beer allowed military surgeons, officials, and rank-and-file soldiers to deflect the criticism against their institution and still align with imperial dictates.

Support for the reinstatement of intoxicants in the canteen came mostly from within the military ranks, including soldiers, officers, doctors, and chaplains, as well as from wives and other groups that favored reform versus prohibition.[52] A large portion of the reports that assessed the outcomes of the Anti-Canteen Law came from the Philippines and were largely damning, citing the widespread increase of bars and saloons just outside military garrisons. Other complaints described increased desertions, increased destruction and theft of private property by soldiers, and decreased troop morale. Additionally, a common concern expressed was that the young American soldier, now driven to drink outside the regulatory watch of the US military, was becoming overly familiar not only with local alcohol and intoxicants but also with native women. Americans who wanted the prohibition bill repealed mustered the imagery of dangerous intercourse as a way to shift narratives and direct outcomes. Military officials thus painted native-owned saloons and bars, whose increase after the Anti-Canteen Law passed was purportedly astounding, as gateways to the potentially graver danger of illicit sexual relations with foreign women (largely Filipina). These sites, with their native-made intoxicants capable of driving white men to insanity or death, were the entry point to the worse evil of interracial sex with "native clandestine prostitutes."[53] This was an issue that Americans on both sides of the Pacific could find compelling. A simple can of beer provided in the military encampment, canteen supporters argued, would serve as a powerful prophylactic.

The increased desperation to drink now that they had been cut off within the barracks, officials reported, made American "boys" more susceptible to the lascivious advances of "vile" Filipinas.[54] As troops left the base in search of drink and diversion, they fell into the clutches of the Filipino saloon keeper and, consequently, into the arms of "disreputable women."[55] While some officers only alluded to this concern, others had no qualms about reporting on this indelicate topic. One major, reporting on conditions in Iloilo, believed that the connection between drinking and sex was so universally understood that he need not elaborate on how one results from the other, simply stating, "The native drinks being cheaper, and now more easily obtained than beer, have injured men morally and physically, especially in the matter of venereal diseases."[56] The saloon is treated as a space of multiple contagions, the primary health concern being the loss of sound mind and vitality due to the drinking of inferior types of liquor, and the secondary being the exposure to and possible sexual contact with Filipina women and others who worked within the sexual vice economy. Although the contraction of venereal diseases by American soldiers had been a problem since the first troops landed in the islands, it had previously not been connected to saloons and bars in the explicit way that the two had now come to be entwined.[57]

By painting the saloon and the Filipina as the source of soldier immorality, military officials simultaneously cast the canteen (and the larger military institution by extension) as a force of temperance in the tropics. In many reports, for example, military officials praised the canteen for producing a moral homosocial environment where men could go for diversion and drink. "The man who drinks beer in a canteen, where the traffic is regulated," stated an American captain stationed in Calamba, just outside Manila, "is much less liable to be thrown in contact with people whose conduct and talk will suggest a fall from a reasonable decent moral plane." The proprietors of such "low dives," he continued, will not only provide liquor but also happily provide "women of loose moral character."[58] In positioning "poisonous" vino and non-army bars as gateways to sexual licentiousness, opponents of the alcohol ban could attempt to rehabilitate the prurient reputation of the military by presenting its canteen system as moral and temperate and its infrastructure as one that protected the troops from the danger of brown bodies. Captain Edward Munson, assistant surgeon in the US Army, provided testimony to Congress commending the canteen for just that. According to Munson, who would later go on to write an influential handbook on hygiene methods for the US military in campaign titled *The Practice of Sanitary Tactics*, described the canteen as "instrumental" in preventing the abuse of liquor and other vices. The wider Anglo imperial world, he claimed, was indebted to the military canteen and the restorative beer it provided. From British troops stationed in Jamaica to Americans garrisoned in Manila, the medical community agreed that the "improvement shown in the figures for venereal diseases and alcoholism . . . was due to the establishment of a canteen."[59]

The white American solider, it seems, was more susceptible to and in danger of interracial intercourse than any other American population in the islands. More so than tourists, civilians, and other more casual observers of empire in the Philippines, and even more so than white women—who would arrive in more significant numbers toward the end of the decade—these men needed protection from nonwhite bodies. Beer in canteens offered that protection and assured temperate, virtuous, and non-diseased soldiers. Take it away and the soldier would be compelled into the waiting arms of immoral saloons and Filipina women, ultimately resulting in the ineffectiveness of the military due to incapacitation by venereal disease. As the American medical community both inside and outside the Philippines called for the reestablishment of the canteen in order to create a "safe" and homosocial environment of beer-swilling prophylaxis, the connection of the saloon with illicit interracial sex and of Filipinas with prostitution was solidified in the minds of many colonists.

While military and medical personnel cast white soldiers as innocents in need of sanitary diversion and blameless for their actions in the tropics, the assessment of Black soldiers was the opposite. Though Black soldiers also participated in the sometimes illicit and sometimes regulated sex trade in the islands, they did not have the presumption of innocence that white troops did. Sexual deviance already characterized how white colonists understood the segregated troops and the broader Black American population more generally, and Black-Filipino intercourse signified different dangers to colonial and military officials than did white-Filipino intercourse.[60] In particular, colonial officials believed that Black overfamiliarity with Filipinas was a corrupting influence on the impressionable "wards," a concern that materialized in the heightened regulation of Black troop movement through the islands to prevent liaisons with local populations.[61] The two Black volunteer units assembled specifically for the Philippine-American War, for example, were sent home in mid-1901, before the United States had even declared the war over. Their contracts were shorter than the regular two-year term for most other volunteer regiments, largely due to the fact that the US government could not decide if it was a good idea to muster Black volunteers for the Philippines. Detractors argued that Black soldiers would be overly sympathetic to Filipino "insurrectos" and further questioned their discipline and bravery.[62] Thus, it was largely white soldiers whom colonial officials and reformers alike saw as the potential prey of local women and disease, despite the fact that pre-deployment medical inspections revealed that significant numbers of soldiers had some type of venereal disease prior to arriving in the Philippines. Nevertheless, they were permitted to deploy to the islands.[63]

The high rates of syphilis in particular throughout the Philippine-American War bolstered ideas about Filipina women as disease vectors and the dangers of intercourse with the local populace. The medical community in both the United States and the Philippines was one of the most significant developers of these ideas. In September 1900, sexually transmitted infections reportedly constituted 8.97 percent of all sicknesses among the troops stationed in the Philippines, rising to a staggering 20.42 percent only seven months later. In 1901, the assistant surgeon general of the US Army, Charles Greenleaf, reported to Washington that the prevalence of venereal diseases "furnishes ground for the greatest apprehension, and is an item not exceeded in importance by any other affecting the health and efficiency of the army in the Philippines."[64] Doctors and surgeons linked the prevalence of venereal diseases to Filipinas and the sexual economy with all the authority of medical "objectivity," like the chief surgeon of the Second Division of the Eighth Army Corps who reported in 1899 that troops had "become habituated to the repulsiveness of the native women." According to him, the result was "a notable increase in venereal disease."[65]

The medicalization and vilification of Filipinas continued well after the war and throughout the colonial period, even when it was clear that the repeal of the Anti-Canteen Law was a failed prospect, attesting to the durability of dangerous intercourse as an adaptable tool for the evolving conditions of empire. After the war and into the second decade of US rule in the Philippines, as venereal disease rates in the islands grew to surpass the rates recorded in the contiguous United States, medical personnel persisted in characterizing dangerous intercourse as a medical condition emanating from the unwholesome bodies of Filipinas. They blamed "the abundance of native prostitutes," the "cheapness" of said women, and "the prevalence of venereal diseases among them." The Philippines, as well as "other countries 'east of the Suez,'" were referred to as places where "there ain't no ten commandments."[66] Even those few Americans who openly challenged the popular medical discourse about diseased Filipina women could not move beyond depicting them as sexually available and thus as potentially dangerous to the health of American men. For example, one medical officer noted in 1902 that venereal disease rates in the islands would be much higher were it not for the Filipina women, "who, as a class, I do not hesitate to say, are fully as virtuous as their American sisters."[67] However, he went on, describing the Filipina as "the dusky hued senorita who sells [the American soldier] bananas, and engages his fancy by the shy way she accepts his compliments, and the bewitching manner in which her full rounded breast peeps out from beneath her pinna chemisa, with never a suggestion, perhaps, as to the troubles *she* [emphasis in original] might bring him."[68] The medical endorsement of Filipina virtue and the "shy" Filipina maidens was not without the simultaneous suggestion of their sexual availability and, ultimately, the way that this availability could "trouble" the military garrison. The medical field's use of dangerous intercourse maintained the moral imperative and legitimacy of the US occupation through the prism of objective science and created a solid foundation for the development of the notorious rest-and-recreation system that solidified later in the World War II Pacific theater, a system that continued to understand Filipinas primarily as prostitutes.

The discourse of dangerous intercourse that irrevocably entwined Filipinas with the sexual economy insisted on the erasure of the broader social world of women in the islands. While military officials, surgeons, chaplains, and others spilled much ink on constructing a Philippine porno-tropics, their enumeration of military-adjacent saloons highlight an altogether different fact of Filipina participation in the vice industries. As the War Department requested status reports from all military outposts on the liquor problem and the effect of the Anti-Canteen Law, many reported back with the numbers of new saloons opened in the vicinity of their garrisons, who was operating them, and how the prohibition had affected troop discipline and morality. According to the responses, many of the proprietors of the saloons and drinking establishments that opened following the shuttering of canteens were Filipina women. Filipinas were engaged as entrepreneurs, running and tending shops and bars that provisioned American troops with the various liquors made illegal for distribution to troops within the Manila city limits.

Indeed, the mention of Filipina saloon- and storekeepers was simultaneously consistent and liminal in these reports, appearing frequently but never being remarked on, perhaps because elaborating on their presence might have betrayed the dominant narrative being proffered by military personnel. In other words, the military narrative of Filipinas as prostitutes was incompatible with the fact that Filipinas actually made up a large part of the entrepreneurial class that was provisioning troops with beer and alcohol. Further, the idea of Filipina prostitutes fit neatly with the imperial logic that the United States needed to uplift a debased Asiatic people in need of civilization; monied Filipina entrepreneurs, shopkeepers, and market vendors fit less neatly. Alongside the mostly American, Spanish, Chinese, and Filipino men who accommodated the liquor demands of the military, Filipinas found ways to make the canteen prohibition work for them.

In some outpost locations, women made up nearly half or more of the individuals listed as operating drinking establishments or selling intoxicants outside the military garrison. For example, in Abgao, Cebu, seventeen of the forty-two listed proprietors of "tiendas and native saloons" within a mile of the post were Filipinas. In Bacon, Sorsogon Province, Maxima Dalot, Luscia Viscaya, Margarita Garcia, Silvina Duaso, and other Filipinas appear alongside a handful of Filipino, mestizo, and Chinese men licensed to sell liquor. In Bay, Laguna, Victoria Apolinario sold liquor within a mile of the US military barracks alongside two Americans, W. A. Stegner and F. Shaw, as well as one Filipino, Daniel Timog. In Bogo, Cebu, Filomena Rubio and Filomena Mansueto were listed as parties who owned and operated "cantinas" that sold beer, whiskey, and wine. Their fellow entrepreneurs/competitors are described as Mariano Salazar, Chinaman Cinco, Eduardo Ferrer, and Miguel Sanchez, along with "a number of stands at the market" where similar drinks could be purchased.[69] Most market stands, too, were operated by women. As one American lieutenant stationed in Santa Mesa described in a letter to a friend back in New York, "The grog shops around our forts are usually kept by women."[70] The evidentiary dissonance I point to here—imagined unnamed Filipinas being prominently depicted as diseased prostitutes while actual Filipinas who appear by name as liquor vendors and shopkeepers are willfully ignored—points to the resoluteness of American ideas about Filipina sexual deviance. Americans who understood Filipinas primarily as prostitutes did not need supporting evidence to maintain the fiction, and Filipinas who appeared in other capacities were determinedly overlooked. This is not something that has changed much in the past hundred years.

That Filipina women would be well represented as part of the enterprising class that provisioned American troops with liquor is consistent with pre-existing norms. Filipinas had long contributed to household incomes throughout the Spanish period, often in occupations that Americans and Europeans did not tend to associate with women's labor.[71] Upon visiting local markets in the Philippines, for example, foreign colonial-era travelers would have been surprised to see that many, if not most, of the native tiendas, or shop stalls, were operated by local women. As one British woman noted of her visit to the market, "The wares were laid out on flat rush trays—bananas, maize, horrible-looking toffee, native fruits, and tumblers of pink tuba—a drink made of the sap of the palm tree coloured red. The stall-keeper was invariably a little brown native woman."[72] Additionally, travelers could find vegetables, fish, betel nut, woven fabric, and any number of commodities to haggle over. It was not uncommon for even well-to-do doñas (landed female heads of household) to run lucrative *sari-sari* (assorted goods) stores from the ground floors of their homes. John Taylor, an American military official tasked with keeping tabs on revolutionary momentum in the islands and keeping the US government apprised, reported this fact: "Young women of wealthy families frequently open small shops which they manage, and manage profitably. . . . They do not do it because of necessity nor do they consider such occupation in the least unbecoming." The ability to take part in public life, he reported, was common, and part of the reason that some revolutionaries had proposed that women be allowed to vote.[73] Large numbers of women found regular wage employment in the numerous cigar factories around the islands, as domestic servants in the homes of the more affluent, as weavers, or as agricultural workers. Others were employed as teachers or were themselves attending school, while others worked as propagandists by launching local newspapers that catered to a female readership.[74] They took part in the revolution against Spain and continued their support of the movement when Americans filled the empty shells left by the Spanish. Local women, from lowland Filipinas to Indigenous women to newer migrants from the Asia-Pacific region, were prominent in most every part of public life in the islands, although you would not know it from reading the reports of the occupying US military government. To more openly acknowledge that so many women not only ran businesses but took part in public life in a variety of ways would complicate the prurient narrative used to defend the canteen as well as the larger imperial project. As American men, mostly discharged US soldiers, were also well represented among the new liquor sellers across the archipelago, elaborating on the vendor demographic might also jeopardize the narrative of the innocent and imperiled troops at the mercy of immoral Filipino liquor peddlers. Deploying dangerous intercourse to bolster military control over the new colony insisted on subsuming these realities.

The alternative narrative embedded in these records not only highlights the discrepancies between American fantasies about lascivious Filipina women and what many women were actually engaged in doing but also gives a sense of how the everyday actions of Filipinos were, whether intentionally or not, playing a role in undermining US military control of the islands. As we have seen, military officials feared the debilitating effects of colonial sociality on the troops due to the canteen system giving way to saloons and stores selling intoxicants outside the garrison. It seems that their fears, although groundlessly fixated on Filipinas, were not unfounded, as the War Department began receiving reports detailing increased numbers of courts-martial for such crimes as rape and burglary in many if not most of the outposts around the archipelago. Trials by summary court for drunkenness, absences without leave, and desertion were also on the rise. As soldiers patronized local shops and saloons and became inebriated, they would "occasionally lie out of quarters," miss their regular inspections in the barracks, and be charged with dereliction of duty.[75] Filipinas (and other sellers) plying soldiers with drinks, then, could and did increase the visibility of sordid American behavior and military ineffectiveness by taking men out of combat readiness in real and significant ways. Anti-imperialists, temperance and moral reformers, and Filipino revolutionaries alike quickly turned this visibility to their own causes. Soldier drinking, one of the most ubiquitous and visible acts that mediated Filipino attitudes toward the American presence in ways that troubled imperial stability, was largely perpetuated by Filipinas.[76]

For Americans concerned with troop strength, saloons and bars were dangerous gateways to more illicit dangerous intercourse, while for Filipinos, these spaces of colonial sociality were gateways to broader possibilities in terms of economic stability in a shifting imperial landscape. Filipino men and women demonstrated their intent to make the most of the influx of soldiers by disregarding the colonial government's open hostility toward native-made intoxicants like vino and tuba. The 1900 Liquor License Act made it expressly clear that the colonial government disapproved of locally made intoxicants, especially when sold to American soldiers. The "sale, gift, or other disposal to soldiers of the United States army of any of the so-called 'native wines,' such as 'vino,' 'anisado,' 'tuba,' etc.," was declared unlawful within the city limits of Manila. While Filipinos could still sell locally made intoxicants, the law stated that they could not do so in first- and second-class bars, restaurants, or hotels, and a separate native liquor license was required to sell at more lowly drinking establishments. However, the stipulations of the law were often disregarded; in 1904, for example, seventy-seven people in Manila were charged with violating some part of the liquor law, and four others were charged with selling in proximity to an American military garrison. As an overwhelming majority of those charged with criminal offenses in the city were Filipinos (14,369 out of the 17,046 charged), it is likely that many if not most of those in violation of the liquor law were Filipinos.[77] Outside Manila, the sale of tuba and vino to soldiers was not prohibited, despite the attempts by some American commanding officers to make it so. Filipinos did not attempt to show deference to the desires of military or colonial state officials by stopping the sale of locally made intoxicants. Captain William Johnston of the Seventeenth US Infantry complained about this to colonial officials in Manila. He described witnessing the "violence, insanity, and suicide" among his men after they drank native liquor. He further suspected that Filipinos were introducing and addicting men to opium smoking. After petitioning the civil governor of Manila to stop issuing licenses for native liquors, Johnston received the reply that local municipal councils—made up of mostly Filipino representatives—were the governing bodies that made such decisions. Johnston went on to complain that several of the municipal council members in Cauayan, Isabela, where he was stationed, were themselves the proprietors of saloons and were thus not likely to hamper their own businesses by restricting the sale of native liquor to soldiers.

For the Filipino community, participation in the liquor business did not have the same stigma associated with it as it did for Americans. Filipino storekeepers and sellers, like those on the municipal council of Cauayan, were able to cultivate or maintain affluence and could even be from respected families and religious backgrounds. In Bay, Laguna, for example, Daniel Timog—one of two Filipino shopkeepers listed as a proprietor of a liquor establishment (the other being Victoria Apolinario)—was, by the 1920s, a municipal council member and landowner.[78] In Bogo, Cebu, Filomena Rubio, one of the operators of a cantina in the town, was part of a trio of philanthropic sisters who, in 1936, founded a religious school to help care for poor and orphaned girls in the community. Originally the Escuela de la Sagrada Familia, the school still operates under the name St. Louise de Marillac College of Bogo.[79] Rubio provided the capital to erect some of the buildings that make up a portion of the school. The Rubio sisters were landed elites, involved in the lucrative sugar business in Cebu. For Filomena Rubio, selling liquor to US soldiers would not be the last time she would have to adjust her economic world around the new American occupation. By 1939, she and her sister Raquel were among the first sugar doñas to attempt diversifying the agricultural outputs on their haciendas by growing other high-demand crops in response to the new sugar tariffs imposed by the United States.[80] For many Filipinas, selling intoxicants was part of the preexisting social and economic world in the Philippines, and the large influx of soldiers simply provided a larger consumer base. In selling liquor vilified by the American government, Filipina women and men—along with Spaniards, Chinese, and many Americans as well—used these suspected sites of dangerous intercourse to advance their own agendas and desires, often flouting imperial policies and preferences. Their actions, in turn, had debilitating effects on military effectiveness and, indeed, wider imperial stability.

While drinking played a large role in both Filipino and American criticisms of the occupation, it was hardly the only enabler of soldier behavior. Enlisted men in the tropics also acted out of feelings of racial and cultural superiority and expected deference from Filipinos.[81] These feelings of racial superiority existed with or without alcoholic lubrication. Additionally, through the regulation of the sexual economy in towns and cities where large troop strength resided, such as Manila, soldiers became accustomed to available sexual outlets without significant consequences.[82] That they should freely partake of the sexual environs provided to them was a clear message that troops received from their military institution, as well as from the business community in the islands. This was a durable message. After the war, as foreign commercial prospects in the Philippines took firmer root, American entrepreneurs continued to target the omnipresent soldier population. The Manila Merchants' Association, first established in 1902, targeted soldiers as a significant consumer population. In collaboration with the US Navy, the Manila Merchants' Association (which would become incorporated in 1920 as the American Chamber of Commerce in the Philippines) distributed a free tourist guide to the arriving men of the fleet, advertising American-owned businesses and suggesting sightseeing trips both in and outside Manila. The *Navy Guide to Cavite and Manila* appealed to the known tastes of the military element, with many an ad showcasing bars, dance halls, cockpits, restaurants, and other amenities. The Maypajo Road House, a dance hall and saloon, encouraged soldiers to "spend a very pleasant evening with your little brown sister." Pabst beer, another handbook announced, was available for purchase "everywhere."[83] Even if the wartime public-facing message of the US military was temperance and sexual morality, it was not one that was heeded or long lasting. As soldiers were discharged from service and took their leave, many chose to remain in the islands as part of the first American entrepreneur class, opening hotels, restaurants, and bars that catered to the new Western clientele. These American soldier-tourist-entrepreneurs, who had come to understand the local women primarily through the lens of dangerous intercourse, continued to reproduce this understanding as they played a foundational role in the early creation and maintenance of a recreational tourist industry, one that prioritized, marketed, and encouraged interracial intercourse. Dangerous intercourse was (and continues to be) a primary way that Americans understood the Philippines and its people.

Conclusion

For Filipinos and Americans in the first few years of the US occupation and military rule, real and imagined dangerous intercourse was an important tool in the pursuit of oppositional outcomes of empire. Filipinos like Clemencia Lopez and Emilio Aguinaldo could use the specter of dangerous intercourse as a peacetime and wartime tactic to inspire nationalism and garner support for immediate Philippine independence. In doing so, they often revealed the limits of inclusion into the Philippine nation, as gendered ideologies favored only some expressions of femininity and masculinity over others. In many ways, Filipinos' use of dangerous intercourse as a pro-independence tool was a response to American depictions of lewd and immoral native sexuality. By highlighting American wartime atrocities like the rape of women, Filipinos rejected the colonial discourse about native immorality by pointing the finger the other way. Ideas of elite Filipina womanhood were also strengthened by this nationalist rhetoric, and the idealized Filipina woman at risk of violation from the Americans—beautiful, Europeanized, but still traditional, moral, and civilized—stood in for the imagined motherland and belonged to Filipino men. The specter of sexual violence was all too real, however, for the vulnerable and marginalized populations of poorer and working women that bore the brunt of sexual violations and bodily intrusions, women who lay outside the bounds of idealized womanhood. The desire of revolutionaries and pro-independence nationalists to showcase and define the nation in moral and heteronormative ways that contradicted American projections of immorality has had a long-lasting impact on the Philippines, currently one of the last nations in the world with no legal divorce procedures outside the lengthy and arduous church annulment process.

Americans, too, mustered dangerous intercourse to their own purposes during the Philippine-American War. The US military, as the largest institutionally sustained American population in the Philippines, laid the foundations for interracial intercourse between Americans and Filipinos in the islands in ways that continue to reverberate and impact bilateral relations to this day. The US military and those who made up the rank and file shaped ideas about American and Filipino sexuality in ways that were long lasting and served the moral imperative of the empire. Americans stepped off the boat in the Philippines armed with ideas about Filipino sexual deviance, as such ideas about nonwhite peoples had long been instrumental in US settlement across the continent and Western Hemisphere, as well as overseas in the unincorporated territories. Transnational prohibition efforts played a large role in the painting of Filipina women as coarse and diseased. The predominant way that both the US military and transnational prohibitionists positioned and understood Filipinas was through the framework of prostitution and its adjacent vice industries. On the other hand, Filipinos and their understandings of Americans were shaped by interactions with the ubiquitous US military presence. Drunk servicemen provided fuel for anti-imperial critique and dissatisfaction with the US presence. American troops also constituted a very large, very loyal consumer group for Filipinos eager to advance their own economic agendas. Despite the issues that arose for the US military as a result of widespread prostitution, including high rates of ineffective soldiery due to venereal disease, prostitution was still understood to be an integral part of military success. With access to regulated and "sanitary" intercourse, Americans reasoned, soldier urges could be satisfied in ways that would keep troops combat ready. The abhorrence of Americans to interracial sexual relations with "repulsive" Filipinas was not enough to reign in the sexual appetites of soldiers. For Filipinas who worked within it or those Filipino elites who sought to regulate it, the sexual vice economy (and its adjacent liquor industry) offered ways to undermine US imperial rule and negotiate their own positions in the changing political climate. Both Filipinos and Americans tried—in vastly uneven ways—to shape narratives about gender and sexuality and to control interracial intercourse in order to see their vision of the Philippines emerge.

Chapter 2

Colonial "Frontiers"

Empire Building and Intercourse in the Northern
and Southern Philippines

It was not so much luck that had put German expat Otto Scheerer in the path of the American commission to the Philippines—the US governing body in the colony after the transition from military to civil rule. Sheerer arrived in the Philippines in 1882 and proceeded to make a name for himself among the business community in and around Manila. He set up his own cigar factory, La Minerva, a few years after his arrival and acquired residential properties in one of the commercial hubs of the city, allowing his Filipina common-law wife, Margarita Asuncion de la Cruz, to reside in one of them.[1] His financial success brought him into the same circles as some of the local Filipino elites who railed against the Spanish government and who would later oppose the American occupation. By the time Dean Worcester was traveling the islands with the First Philippine Commission in 1899, Scheerer's economic investments also included a coffee plantation in Benguet, northern Luzon. His residence in the mountains among the various Indigenous peoples located within the Cordillera region was both off-putting and fortuitous for the Americans looking to make inroads into the North, especially Worcester. A trained zoologist, Worcester had also made a name for himself. His zoological expeditions to the islands collecting flora and fauna prior to the Spanish- and Philippine-American Wars marked him as someone potentially useful in building the American colonial state in the Philippines. Despite his supposed expert knowledge on the islands, Worcester needed Scheerer to help him remain relevant to the commission. As someone with a Filipino family, connections to both elite and non-elite local populations, and knowledge of landscapes and languages, Scheerer could help Worcester broaden his "expertise" on the Philippines. Worcester requested Scheerer's invaluable services as a mountain guide and translator, as he was reputedly the only white person to reside in Baguio (then a small mountain town within the Benguet Province) at the time.[2]

Scheerer's familiarity with both the land and the people made him a vital intermediary between the local Indigenous communities in the mountainous Cordilleras and the official American traveling party. As Worcester turned his attention and camera away from plants, animals, and minerals to instead focus on people, it was often Scheerer who convinced the locals to take part in his photographic study.[3] The resulting ethnographic photo collection that Worcester generated from his guided excursion into northern Luzon was one of the most persuasive exhibits he presented before the American government that testified to the need for prolonged American occupation of the islands. The thousands of photos depicting the Indigenous people of the North were proof to Worcester and many other imperialists that the Philippines, peopled with the so-called non-Christian tribes, was in the infancy of civilization and not yet ready for independence. Interestingly, Scheerer and his mixed-race daughter Graciana were included in Worcester's ethnographic photo survey (see fig. 2.1).

Worcester also photographed Graciana by herself, describing her as an example of a "German mestiza girl, type 1."[4] Worcester's time spent cataloging the people of the Cordilleras was for him, time well spent, and in 1901 he was appointed secretary of the interior of the Philippines. This position oversaw many of the newly erected bureaus of the colonial state, including the Bureau of Non-Christian Tribes, modeled after and affiliated with the US Bureau of Indian Affairs and tasked with the study of the "pagan and Mohammedan tribes of the Philippines."[5] It was not just Worcester who owed Scheerer a debt; the wider American colonial enterprise had been aided by the intermediary status of the German expat, whose familiarity with local languages, people, and terrain had helped concretize the US foothold in the region.

Scheerer was one of many white settler intermediaries in the colonial Philippines who helped colonial state-building processes. American officials often recognized men like Scheerer as vital go-betweens, who were essential in the project of solidifying US control over the disparate regions of the Philippines. White settlers were the preferred interlocutors of American agents, whether they were European like Scheerer or, later, discharged US soldiers who had established themselves in areas where white settlers were

Figure 2.1. The caption included in Worcester's catalog of racial types labeled this image as "German mestiza girl, type 1. Standing with her father. Full length front views." Though Graciana Scheerer was the more compelling subject for Worcester, Otto Scheerer also merited inclusion in his catalog of racial types. Image courtesy of the University of Michigan Museum of Anthropological Archaeology.

few and far between. As English- or European-language speakers, white settlers were understood by those who sought their services as part of a shared
Anglo-European imperial world and distinct from the local population, regardless of whether or not these intermediaries saw themselves the same way.
At the same time, the fact that most of these white intermediaries were married to local women and often well connected to local communities marked
them as outside white respectability and therefore potentially dangerous.
Most Americans held as truth that "going native," or choosing to live outside
white civilizing influences, was sure to bring Anglo-European people "down
to the level of civilization that surrounds them."[6]

From the northern mountainous Cordilleras to southern Mindanao, this
chapter explores the role of dangerous intercourse in empire building in areas where the physical American presence was less pronounced. Colonists
understood the Indigenous communities in the North as facsimiles of Native
Americans in the United States and sought to document, catalog, preserve,
and analyze them. Colonial missionaries saw in these "non-Christian tribes" a
population to uplift and civilize via religious and educational reforms. Colonial state-builders also classified the predominantly Muslim population in
southern Mindanao as part of the non-Christian tribes, the region and its
people signifying to them the necessity of US tutelage. Neither the North nor
the South had been incorporated into the Spanish imperial regime in the same
way that the central regions of Luzon and the Visayas had been. While the
physical distance from the colonial capital played a role in this (as did the
mountainous landscape of northern Luzon, which made Spanish access difficult), the populations of both locales also consistently opposed Spanish claims
to the land.[7] In the North, the Indigenous Igorot people attempted to regain
land in the lowlands by raiding Spanish settlements. Spain sent frequent punitive expeditions north, which were largely thwarted until the latter half of the
nineteenth century, when larger military expeditions gained more ground and
concessions. However, most of the compromises made by the local Igorots
were symbolic gestures, offered until other methods of resistance could be
carried out.[8] Likewise, in southern Mindanao and the Sulu Archipelago,
where most Muslims in the Philippines resided, local communities resisted
Spanish attempts at conversion and settlement for over three centuries, raiding and attacking colonial coastal outposts with regularity. As scholars of the
Philippines have described it, the South was within the geography claimed
by Spain but largely lay outside state control.[9]

A study of interracial intercourse in these regions in particular allows us to
draw questions of settler colonialism more closely into the discussion of US

empire in the Philippines. The cases of the northern and southern Philippines demonstrate the continuities and breaks between settler colonial processes in the United States and the outlying new possession as American colonists adapted tried-and-true methods of dispossession to the Pacific. American imperialists pointed to the populations of the North and South to claim that the Philippines was not a nation of homogeneous European-approximating individuals capable of self-rule but rather a land of "pagan and Mohammedan tribes" that needed the colonial government to rule "in behalf of these uncivilized people."[10] At the same time, the colonial outskirts tantalized many Americans with the prospect of business opportunities to be sown (plantations in the South) and dug (gold in the North) from the earth. For American colonists trying to bring all seven thousand islands under US rule, the heterogeneous populations and geographies of the Philippines required different efforts and strategies, especially in the so-called colonial "frontiers"—locales that colonists imagined as more dangerous and uncivilized than the more familiar Christian lowlands.

Looking at geography and intercourse together illuminates the contours of colonial state responses to dangerous intercourse, where the farther afield regions often opened up possibilities for American men and local women to live unregulated and discreet lives, even as mixed families and relations simultaneously buttressed colonial aspirations for each region. Though the Philippine commission painted the picture of "dissolute, drunken and lawless Americans" dispersed through the islands "who [were] willing to associate with low Filipino women," and though there was undoubtedly a stigma against those who engaged in interracial intercourse (especially long-term and committed relationships), the colonial government needed white settler intermediaries to navigate the regions that were "unmapped and unexplored . . . hardly penetrated by white men."[11] White intermarried settlers in places like Manila had few opportunities to advance their socioeconomic positions, prompting many to keep their relationships secret. Intermarried colonists who lived outside dense American populations and social surveillance could often still advance their careers and livelihoods, especially as intermediaries between local populations and American colonial agents. Local women too, especially elites, could maintain and build their status through dangerous intercourse. Ultimately, dangerous intercourse on the edges of the colonial state was essential in the consolidation of regional colonial control, strengthening the US empire in the islands. Unlike in Manila, where reformers and moralists easily policed sociosexual segregation, "frontier" intercourse was characterized more by the ways that it could be put to use in the service of the empire, with or without the consent of those involved.

A Contingent Colonial Capital

The 1918 census of the Philippines listed 5,774 American residents of the islands. Of those, approximately half resided in Manila, while the other 2,858 lived outside the capital, scattered across the archipelago.[12] Solitary regiments, miners, and farmers outside large cities lived for months at a time in their regions without seeing other Americans or Europeans. This isolation from other white people worried many Americans, who believed that the influences of a white community were needed to prevent moral degradation resulting from proximity to the corrupt ways of the natives. Others, however, found the remoteness from American populations desirable in that it offered a reprieve from the judgments of the community and freer license to pursue the types of amusements and companionship that reformers were policing more and more in places like Manila.[13] This is not to say, however, that provinces outside Manila were entirely free of colonial discipline. In fact, concerned American colonists in Manila understood that the actions of their compatriots scattered across the islands reflected on the US population as a whole. Colonists often hoped for favorable press descriptions of the Philippines, as negative press might jeopardize investment and interest in the colony. Dangerous intercourse almost certainly generated bad press.

In March 1908, the *Manila Times*—the most widely read newspaper made by and for Americans in the Philippines—reprinted an article that appeared in the *Iowa State Register* titled "Degenerate Americans."[14] In the reprint, an American contractor, W. E. McVicar, described the time he spent in the Philippines: "This country (the U.S.) has never before sent out such a worthless, low class of people to any place as the Americans that I met in the Philippines. . . . You get away from Manila and every American you meet is a discharged soldier." The *Times* provided editorial commentary that lamented the truth in McVicar's assessment of the provinces: "Americans fall into the 'costumbre del pais' (custom of the land) and take a consort without the usual marriage ceremony."[15] Even though McVicar had not mentioned interracial cohabitation, the editors of the newspaper understood the subtext of his complaint. Homer Stuntz—the leader of the Methodist Episcopalian mission to the Philippines and a future Methodist Church bishop—similarly described his embarrassment of American transgressors: "Concubinage is a terribly common sin among Americans." Though he largely blamed the Spanish Empire for laying the foundations of cohabitation without marriage, he chided that the situation was "sufficiently shameful to cause us to blush for the influence exerted by scores of Americans who have been reared to know better than to live in open sin."[16] The prevalence of interracial sexual intercourse did not project a desirable image of the United States in the islands, but controlling dangerous intercourse in the Philippines, where anti-miscegenation laws did not follow the flag, was complicated. While behavior could be policed more vigorously in extralegal and social ways, policing intermarried settlers in the interior or outlying regions was difficult and risked ostracizing the intermediaries, whom the colonial state desperately needed.

A non-Manila-centered framework for examining the US-occupied Philippines highlights the ways that practical necessity shaped interracial relations, often more so than did imperial ideology. Local conditions also shaped both imperial strategy and dangerous intercourse, often creating conditions for mixed relations and families to flourish. The case studies of southern Mindanao and the northern Cordilleras also highlight the contingency of Manila's primacy as the colonial capital and seat of power. As the main American hub and port city that stood as the face of benevolent American rule, the possibilities of this model city were inextricably tied to what was happening in the farthest reaches.

Northern Philippines—the Cordillera Central

The Cordillera Central mountain range north of the Manila capital was and continues to be home to many Indigenous ethnolinguistic groups. The Cordillera Administrative Region of the Philippines today comprises the provinces of Apayao, Kalinga, Abra, Benguet, Ifugao, and Mountain Province. This configuration largely follows the 1908 boundaries set by the Philippine legislature (consisting of the American commission and the newly formed Philippine Assembly), which combined the various Cordillera provinces under one jurisdiction known as Mountain Province.[17] Americans and Filipino political elites thus affixed imposed borders and organizational terms on the inhabitants of the North, similar to the previous Spanish occupiers who largely referred to all the peoples of the Cordillera as "Igorrote" (Igorot). For the most part, Americans did not see the Indigenous groups in the landlocked mountain range as threatening to the American occupation in the same way as the lowland revolutionaries or the Muslims of the southern region. In fact, the opposite was more often true of US understandings of and responses to the people of the Cordilleras. Tribal groups in the North presented imperialists with an opportunity to drive home the idea of a civilizing imperative—that is, that the

US presence was necessary amid the backward native peoples. While Americans classified Muslims in the South as "semi-civilized" because of their system of leadership under ruling Datus, their practice of a recognized religion, and their more covered mode of dress, Indigenous tribes in the North were seen as "non-civilized" due to their practice of pagan and animist beliefs and their less covered mode of dress.[18] Many of the academic set who traveled to the Philippines as part of the imperial mission took to the familiar task of "salvage anthropology," believing that the inhabitants of the Cordilleras were, like the Native Americans of the United States, a disappearing race.[19] This academic wing of the colonial occupation believed that expansionism spelled the end of most Indigenous peoples, a natural progression, and so took pains to document their cultures before they supposedly vanished. Other Americans felt a paternalistic affinity with the "wild men" of the Cordilleras, finding them more honorable and noble than their lowland counterparts in Manila, whom they believed held too many vices passed on by the Spanish.[20] Some Americans admired the reputed "headhunters" of the North for their resistance to Spanish domination, idealizing them as "noble savages," and felt these populations needed protection from unscrupulous lowland Filipinos until they could be shepherded to their true potential through US tutelage.[21]

The position and status of women in their respective communities also played a role in how colonial intervention and intercourse took shape in the North, as family structure, courtship, and other social and sexual institutions were different from those in the southern and central Philippines as well as from the heteronormative social practices and family formations idealized by Americans. American academics and colonial officials were fascinated by the local practices of divorce and trial marriage in the North and documented them with a lurid obsessiveness, forming ideas about the Mountain Province as a place conducive to "going native," particularly because of the perceived sexual possibilities.[22] At the same time, control over interracial sexual relations with native women in the Cordilleras was less of a priority for Americans trying to assert control over the region than it was in places like Manila or even in Mindanao and Sulu in the South. The looser gender norms in the North aligned with American men's desire for sexual recreation, and these factors merged into an economic system of sexual trade that many Indigenous people and Americans found mutually beneficial. The concept of trading sexual services for money or other items was not unheard of in the North, so in many ways the American desire for sexual recreation fit within already established sociocultural frameworks of some of the native groups. Many American men quickly picked up on local nuances, offering to trade yards of cloth, food, or money in exchange for sexual companionship. Some towns in the Cordillera region garnered infamous reputations among Americans for their open and accessible sexual economies, and these towns drew American and European men alike. Cambulo town in Ifugao Province, for example, was well known and infamous, all the way to Manila.[23] Though Americans entered into preexisting sexual economies in the North, the influx of American money and goods undoubtedly influenced how widespread the sexual economy became, as it did throughout the islands.

It was not just academic observation that alerted the new colonizers to perceived sexual possibilities in the Cordilleras. The ability of casual travelers and observers to gaze on the bodies of Indigenous people in the Philippines was a liberating experience for American men and women, who often expressed their titillation in journals and letters. Many men, for example, wrote unabashedly about the pleasantness of coming across bare-breasted Igorot women on their travels through the mountain region. One American teacher wrote of his encounters with "topless" women working in the rice paddies in Bontoc Province: "In seeing these near nude and often beautifully formed bodies, one at first had startled eyes only for the magnificent breasts. . . . One got used to the lovely display."[24] An American military officer reminisced poetically about the unclothed bodies of the so-called mountain nymphs in the region and concluded that these encounters proved "not hard on the eyes."[25]

White women travelers, too, took note of the sparsely covered bodies of some of the northern peoples. Nanon Fay Worcester, who traveled north with her husband, Dean Worcester, in 1909, reveled in her ability to take part in such sights. Upon arriving in Bontoc in Mountain Province, she fixated on the body parts of the men and women, taking note of the "beautifully formed" people whom she likened to "bronze statues." Despite this positive appraisal, the near nudity of the men, "not one in twenty with a stitch of covering except his 'gee' string," affirmed her belief in their inferiority, as she concluded, "One certainly does get used to the naked savage here."[26] Her ability to view colonized bodies and, further, write home about them did not scandalize her respectability as a woman but rather shaped her sense of herself as an adventurous, liberated "new woman" who was improving her worldliness through experiencing the colonial empire. Indeed, her presence on the excursion trip north with her husband was one she fought for, as most in the traveling party (almost exclusively male) had discouraged her from coming along. When she did not slow down the traveling party on a particularly steep stretch of terrain, as they initially believed she would, she took pleasure in chiding the men and reminding them of their attempts to exclude her. Like so many American women who sought out empire as a means of liberation at the turn of the century, Nanon Worcester was able to escape, if only temporarily and incompletely, the confines of strict gendered expectations, crafting an identity for herself as capable and modern against the terrain and "savage" people of Mountain Province.[27]

Gendered assumptions and expectations not only formed the basis of American colonial identities like Worcester's but were also the foundation for how Americans approached relations with the local Indigenous populations. Because of the American tendency to project their "knowledge" of Native peoples in the United States onto the inhabitants of the Cordilleras, gendered diplomacy was the modus operandi. American expectations and assumptions about how gender functioned within Indigenous communities in the North, however, often did not align with how local communities conducted their affairs. For example, while Americans often held as sacrosanct that the presence of Indigenous women and children at diplomatic meetings meant that tribal communities meant no harm, this expectation was not always shared or understood by the highland people. This disjuncture between American expectations and actual local practices was exemplified in a 1911 disciplinary hearing involving Frank Walter Hale, the American lieutenant governor of the Kalinga Province, and some of the Kalinga inhabitants of the Guinabal district. According to the disciplinary report, the district had yet to be pacified to the extent that American officials desired, and Hale began a punitive expedition that resulted in the deaths of several inhabitants of the district, including two men, a woman, and a child. Hale was accompanied by members of the Philippine Constabulary (the native military force trained by Americans that also included some Americans as officers) and some Kalinga men who had demonstrated a degree of loyalty to him. While some American colonialists described Hale's actions in Guinabal as a condemnable onslaught of "hordes of armed warriors" intent on razing the district, others characterized the killing of people and livestock, as well as the burning of homes, as a necessary means of inducing peace in the region.[28] The subsequent mediation between the Kalinga leaders of the Guinabal district and Lieutenant Governor Hale demonstrated the in/significance of women's presence at such power-brokering sessions.

The meeting was mediated by the secretary of the interior, Dean Worcester, who listened to Hale's account of the events, which was essentially a lengthy chastisement of the Kalinga people for failing to heed American threats. According to the stenographer's report of this meeting, there was no space allotted to the Kalinga representatives to tell their side of the story or express grievances, and their input appears only as brief interjections during Worcester's comments. Serving as adjudicator in the meeting, Worcester conceded no fault on behalf of Hale, instead saying to the Kalinga representatives, "We have had a little trouble with you this last year and it was your fault. . . . Sometimes strong medicine is good for people but they usually do not like it very well. I hope you will not have to have any more medicine of that kind."[29] He urged them to accept American rule and described the guns and cannon that could be brought to Mountain Province from Manila if the "little trouble" continued, and he encouraged the Kalinga representatives to "bring more women" to the American outpost at Lubuagan. He had apparently noticed that only one woman was in attendance and spoke of the various other tribes that had brought numerous women and children with them on their visits to the American outpost. Worcester and his contemporaries believed that the willingness of the Kalinga people to bring women and children to visit the American camp indicated peaceful intentions as well as a willingness to concede to US rule.[30] He continued to press the matter of women's participation in diplomatic affairs: "People who have come a great deal farther than you have come this year have brought their women with them. You don't have to bring your women if you don't want to. . . . You don't need to be afraid to bring them; you can see that there is nothing to be afraid of over here. The first time Lubo came in there only brought one woman. This year there were a lot of them. I don't think Mañgali brought a great many women the first time."[31] Worcester further warned the delegation: "If [their] women hear from the other women what a good time that they had over here they will want to come and will blame their husbands for not bringing them." Worcester and his colleagues, like Hale, also impressed the idea of native women as markers of peace on other Americans traveling in the region, like Nanon Fay Worcester. In her journal (written two years before the mediation at the Lubuagan outpost), she is perceptibly aware of the presence or absence of native women and what each supposedly meant. She was often told, "It is usually a sign of trouble when the women are not around."[32]

Though Americans believed that Indigenous women's presence meant peaceful intentions, it is less clear that the Kalinga representatives at the hearing had the same ideas about diplomacy. At the conclusion of the meeting, for example, the leaders expressed their desire to avoid hostilities in the future. As if to emphasize this point, one man stated, "The reason that our women did not come this time is that they have to do the work."[33] Another representative (or perhaps the same representative, as all the Indigenous voices in the transcript are identified only as "one of the chiefs") offered, "When we come back next year we will bring some women of our people." The Kalinga leaders seemed to have only just recognized that there were gendered expectations for the conduct of diplomacy with Americans and offered to meet these expectations at the next meeting. Worcester's own account points to other Kalinga districts (Lubo, Mangali) that did not bring women to the American camp, suggesting that the "tradition" of such gendered mediations and diplomatic gatherings was a projected American understanding of native peoples, not an Indigenous habit.

A settler colonial apparatus that translated with more efficacy to the Philippines, especially in Mountain Province, was the creation of imperial interlocutors via intermarriage. Anglo-European men who married Igorot or Filipina women were potential assets to the American colonial government as cultural bridges and intermediaries. The American community commonly referred to these intermediaries as "squaw men," a pejorative racial slur that was commonly applied to white men in the American West who married or had sexual relations with Native American women.[34] In essence, American administrators overlooked the fact that these men "went native," especially when such interracial relations aided the successful pursuit of regional control. In 1901, for example, the Second Philippine Commission relied heavily on the assistance of Otto Scheerer and other intermarried men and their wives to navigate, find accommodations, and do the work of translation on their travels through the mountains. James LeRoy, secretary of the commission, described some of these men in his extensive chronicling of their 1901 travels. The large group trekked up the winding mountain trails with Scheerer and his young mestizo children, all of whom were fluent in Spanish and familiar with several of the local languages spoken throughout the Cordilleras. Scheerer's familiarity with Filipinos and Indigenous people was at once desired and reviled by the American colonial government. Though he was an indispensable guide, military officials in particular distrusted his loyalty to the new American order because of his intimacy with the highland peoples. One colonel stationed in the North referred to Scheerer's habit of wearing an Ifugao *bahag*, or loincloth, as evidence of his diminished whiteness and, correspondingly, his untrustworthiness.[35]

In the wake of the US commission inroads into the Cordilleras, more and more American colonialists sought out the respite of the northern mountains, where the elevation made the temperature more alpine than tropical and where men like Sheerer continued to aid them. Lodgings, for example, were often preferred in the homes of other Americans. If travelers could not find American hosts, Spanish or Spanish mestizo homes with amenities most suited to Western tastes and standards were the next best option. The home of Guy Haight was one such sought-out retreat in the region. Haight, a former American soldier who had remained in the Philippines after his discharge, married an Igorot woman from Suyoc in Benguet Province and opened Haight's Place, an American-style lodge that catered to mostly white travelers on their way to Baguio. Haight's Place was an American mainstay in Mountain Province, offering quaint and familiar accommodations as well as food prepared by Haight's wife, Susie.[36] Travelers were enamored with the unfinished pine board lodge and the panoramic views that reminded them of an "old-fashioned farm-house back in the mountains of Virginia or Kentucky."[37] Susie made a reputation for herself as an exceptional cook of American-style food, and some travelers seemed to understand the role she played in the success of Haight's Place, noting with more than a little derision that "the woman, whom he had purchased in marriage, according to the native custom, proved of great assistance as soon as he could talk to her."[38] This interracial relationship eventually incited the ire of Bishop Brent, the Episcopal bishop serving in the Philippines. Brent insisted that the couple stop living in sin and formally sanction their union with the church. He eventually officiated their marriage in 1908.[39]

Brent's agitation was likely fueled by the phenomenon of Anglo-European men in Mountain Province marrying local women according to local marital rites and custom rather than through what he considered to be more legitimate and moral channels. Though Brent was no believer in this type of amalgamation, even preaching from his pulpit that the races should not intermarry, he saw formally recognized marriage as the only moral option if such relations could not be prevented. On this matter, the church and the colonial government agreed. Though interracial marriage was not illegal, as it was in many US states, the colonial government largely frowned on it, although it preferred marriage to less formalized intercourse, the latter of which was seen as emblematic of corrupt Spanish rule. The military sought to dissuade dangerous intercourse by threatening deportation if soldiers were found to be cohabiting without a marriage contract, telling soldiers that such marriages required the approval of the ranking military officer.[40] While prostitution was largely engaged in openly by soldiers, longer-term and more committed relations tended to be more secretive, and confessing such relations to a commanding officer for permission to marry was a risk to one's social and career prospects. The message was clear: avoid committed entanglements with local women, but if that proves impossible, keep it hidden or face binding marriage/deportation. In places with fewer Americans, like the Cordilleras, American military men could circumvent these unofficial US policies and safeguard themselves and their careers by using what they knew of native marriage practices and culture. Stationed in isolated mountain outposts, even commanding officers without the watchful eyes of higher ups or moralists participated in long-term liaisons in the open, suffering little long-term consequences. Filipinas, for their part, came to understand that intercourse with Americans (and indeed Anglo-Europeans more generally) could provide a degree of financial support or perhaps even a house, as the salaries of enlisted men or constabulary officers, while not very large, were enough to support a local wife or mistress.

The career of William Dosser, an American serving in the Cordillera region police constabulary, illustrates how interracial intercourse was essential to US rule in the region as well as the freer intercourse that valued interlocutors could engage in. Dosser's sexual liaisons with native women in the Cordillera region are best illuminated in a series of interviews done by historian Frank Jenista. The interviews were conducted with many women and men from Cordillera Central in the late 1970s and early 1980s, and the interviewees, including a few of Dosser's former common-law wives, spoke candidly about their relationships with the constabulary official.[41] Many accounts noted Dosser's bravado as he openly sought woman after woman, often using lower-ranking constabulary officials to broker deals with those he desired. Many noted that he was a generous gift giver to his sexual companions. Several of his liaisons resulted in marriage, which were conducted according to local rites.[42] The interviews also point to the rational motivations of local women in engaging in relations with Americans. For example, Guinamay, of the Amganad village in Banaue, recalled that she could "pretend to cry to get anything [she] wanted" while married to Dosser.[43]

To procure companionship with women, Americans performed the customary marriage rites, which typically included a prayer ceremony, the sacrificing of certain animals, and the giving of gifts to family members. The Indigenous communities recognized these marriages, although they were not necessarily recognized by American law unless the couple filed the required paperwork with a local colonial office or authority.[44] American men could thus find and keep female wives/mistresses during their stay in the northern Philippines with relatively little fear of reprisal from American officialdom while satisfying local customs. This circumventing of binding American marriage laws was especially important among the constabulary officers, because the constabulary preferred to hire single men and also threatened deportation for those found to be in unsanctioned relations with native women. Men like Dosser, who secured long-term companionship, could abide by local rites but ultimately not feel beholden to them, as many Indigenous communities allowed for the dissolution of marriages and separation of spouses. Dosser's marriage to Guinamay, for example, ended as abruptly as it had begun. Upon returning from a long trip to the United States, Dosser was stung to find that Guinamay had moved on with someone else. Guinamay, it seems, was very aware not only of the potential benefits of intercourse with Americans, but also of the fleeting nature of these relations. In Dosser's absence, she allegedly solicited a relationship with a different American constabulary official before engaging in a relationship with a local Bontoc man. In her separation from Dosser, she kept a house and some agricultural lands he had "given" her.[45]

While Dosser's long-term marriages were to native Igorot and Ifugao women, in the end he chose to legally marry—according to American legal procedures—a lowlander Filipina mestiza in 1919.[46] This marriage, unlike his previous ones, would be harder to sever. The colonial government had only passed a law for divorce in 1917, and only under very specific and limited conditions.[47] Despite the elite status of Dosser's wife's family, Americans in Manila and among the growing American community in the Cordilleras shunned Dosser and Rosario "Charing" Madarang.[48] In the later decades of US rule beginning in the 1920s, white Americans in the north more tightly enforced a rigid white–nonwhite social divide, which even powerful men like Dosser could not overcome. As the cool weather of the mountains drew more American and European vacationers from Manila, the small town of Baguio quickly transformed into a summer playground for white people in the Philippines. The colonial government envisioned the "city of pines" as a place where sick Americans could convalesce and regain the health that had been sapped by the heat of the lowlands. The influx of colonists made the once more open climate for interracial couples look increasingly like the racial climate of Manila, where the ostracism of such couples was common. In one of Jenista's interviews, a white American woman who had moved to Baguio after Americans established it as their "summer capital" described the social stratification; Dosser and his Filipina wife, she reported, were "not in our circle of friends." Of Dosser she stated, "In my day we used to call them all squaw men."[49]

Though Dosser was outside the boundaries of polite American society because he was married to a Filipina, the colonial government valued his knowledge of Mountain Province and its people. In 1929, the American governor-general promoted him to governor of Mountain Province, an opportunity that would have been less likely to materialize for him in a place like Manila. His decision to marry (according to US legal standards) into an elite Filipino family also played a role in his advancement, as other men who married poorer or widowed Filipinas often did not receive such promotions in the constabulary, which kept track of who entered into marital relations with local women.[50] Indeed, higher-ranking constabulary officials often took into consideration the marital status of American men, especially if they were known to be intermarried, when deliberating on promotions and position requests.

In 1905, for example, George Hally applied to rejoin the Philippine Constabulary as a third lieutenant. Several American officials reviewed his application for recommendation. In the negative review by commanding colonel of the constabulary Harry Bandholtz, Hally was described as having "married a Filipino widow with a number of children." Bandholtz further questioned whether Hally had much to offer the constabulary, as in his estimation, Hally's situation had not improved since the time of his earlier resignation. The two subsequent endorsements by other constabulary officials read only "not favorably considered" and "attention to preceding endorsement." Needless to say, Hally was not reinstated. Taking matters into his own hands, Hally wrote an angry letter to Bandholtz saying he did not appreciate his "family affairs" being a factor in the consideration of his employment. He further stated that he knew of many other constabulary officers who had Filipina wives but did not face such retribution. A few weeks later he received a curt reply from Bandholtz stating it was his duty to relay the details of Hally's "conjugal relations" to his superiors and reassured him that these "relations" were not being disparaged nor were they the reason that the superior officers denied his request. Bandholtz further claimed no discriminatory feelings toward Hally's Filipina wife, not toward "her sex or nationality, for whom collectively and individually I have only the highest admiration and respect."[51]

Colonial agents who were outside the military, and fewer in number, could advance their careers through intermarriage, especially if the colonial government found their work valuable. Anthropologists, geologists, botanists, agriculturalists, and others who apprised the colonial government of the islands' resources were vital agents of empire. For these academics, connections with local communities were essential if they wished to know the bounty of the land and people. So it was for Henry Otley Beyer, a young American academic who traveled to the Cordillera region of the Philippines as part of the Philippine Ethnological Survey in 1905 under the US Department of Education (fig. 2.2). Like Worcester, he conducted research on the

Figure 2.2. H. Otley Beyer, right around the time he went to the Philippines. Image courtesy of Charity Bagatsing Doyl, great granddaughter of H. Otley Beyer and Lingayu Gambuk Beyer.

various Indigenous peoples in the North. He left the islands briefly in 1908 for ethnological work around the globe and to pursue more advanced anthropology training at Harvard University, returning to the Philippines and Mountain Province in 1910. He soon married Lingayu Gambuk, the daughter of prominent Ifugao tribal leader Cadangyan Gambuk.[52] She was much younger than Beyer, as was typical of many American-Filipino relationships, about sixteen years old at the time of their marriage. His relationship with this prominent Ifugao family opened doors for him within the community.

As a result of his ties to the Indigenous people of Banaue, Beyer accumulated vast geological and ethnographic data on the region. He wrote many articles dealing with the legends and myths of the Cordillera people, theories on early migration, and speculations as to the origins of the famous Banaue rice terraces, now a UNESCO World Heritage site. In 1921 he wrote a general guide appended to the national census detailing his purported knowledge of the peoples of the Cordillera region and beyond, titled *The Non-Christian People of the Philippines*. Later academics recognized his work as the definitive scholarship on not just the people of Banaue but the Indigenous peoples of the Cordillera central more broadly. In 1914, he was one of the founding members of the University of the Philippines Department of Anthropology, where he taught mostly lowlander Filipinos about Cordillera customs and culture until his retirement in the early 1950s. Americans and Filipinos alike lauded him as the father of anthropology of the Philippines. His work bolstered the colonial state's aims of building American-style education as well as teaching an American perspective of Philippine history and culture. He often praised the Ifugao people of Mountain Province in particular (the community that Lingayu belonged to) and admired them for their hydrological innovations in rice terrace farming. He spoke highly of what he perceived as their systems of private land and property ownership and of their values of "personal dignity, individual rights and liberty, applied equally to both sexes." Though he often expressed fondness for Lingayu's people and extolled their "culture of high development," he, like many academics of the time, understood the people of the Philippines as different racial types, ranging from "primitive" to "semi-civilized." He believed that many of the former were on the road to extinction, while the latter, like the Ifugao, could "survive the civilizing process" and become contributing members of a modern Philippine society.[53] In his view, this process of improvement was one Americans were helping along.

Through his marriage to Lingayu, Beyer gained not only cultural capital in the form of insider access to the Ifugao people and Mountain Province in general but also economic capital, as his studies of the people of the Cordilleras were his source of income and livelihood. Through dangerous intercourse, Beyer forged a prominent career. The American colonial government viewed him as an important agent of empire and often sought his advice on matters concerning the Cordillera region and, eventually, the Philippines as a whole. In 1965, colleagues organized a symposium in his honor both to mark his eighty-second birthday and to celebrate his work as dean of Philippine anthropology at the University of the Philippines. Though he died a year later, his impact on Philippine education continues. A memorial written for Beyer upon his death in 1966 describes him as "*the* giant in Philippine pre-history. . . . He was Mr. Anthropology. . . . Early in his career in the Philippines, he married the daughter of a prominent Banaue Chieftain. The establishment of this kin relation provided Beyer a lasting bond between him and the Filipinos. In 1966 the Ifugao gods took him to dwell with them forever in their heavens."[54] Unlike most of Beyer's obituaries, which left out any mention of his Ifugao family, this tribute to Beyer (written by a Filipino and fellow academic) delicately acknowledged that he owed much of his success to his "kin relation" through marriage to Lingayu. Beyer himself had notably said as much to a colleague that knew of his Ifugao family, giving him the advice to "get next to the chiefs and datus" if he wanted to get ahead in the Philippines.[55]

Lingayu and her family also benefited socially and economically from this relationship. Henry Beyer, the grandson of Beyer Sr. and Lingayu, described the prominent societal position occupied by his grandmother, who was the first female council member of her town (see fig. 2.3): "Because of her marriage to my grandfather, actually when they were organizing local government officers, she [couldn't] read and she couldn't write but she was the first councilor woman in the whole mountain province and the whole cordillera! She was appointed, so it was a [higher] status to be married to Dr. Beyer. . . . She was more accepted. . . . She stayed there [as councilor] for one term, which was two years at that time . . . but yeah I think she has a privilege as a council woman."[56] Henry described the deference with which others in the community treated his grandmother: "She [would] still walk to town, it's about one and a half miles, U.S. length[,] and she always strapped [on] her revolver. . . . When she was a council woman, you know, everybody that she meets, they have to give way [because] she doesn't want to give way. . . . So all these poor guys, they move aside instead of her giving way, she doesn't want to give way."[57] Lingayu had already possessed the high social status of being the daughter of an Ifugao leader, and this status only

Figure 2.3. A young Lingayu Gambuk Beyer wearing what might be a baseball uniform top, along with her gun belt. Descendants of Lingayu Gambuk Beyer have surmised that perhaps she chose to wear something martial looking as part of her role as a Barangay captain. Image courtesy of Charity Bagatsing Doyl, great-granddaughter of H. Otley Beyer and Lingayu Gambuk Beyer.

Figure 2.4. Portrait of Lingayu Gambuk Beyer, circa 1950s or 1960s. Image courtesy of Charity Bagatsing Doyl, great-granddaughter of H. Otley Beyer and Lingayu Gambuk Beyer.

grew through her association with Beyer, which was illustrated through her subsequent prominence in local politics. (see fig. 2.4).

To this day, the relationship between Henry Beyer and Lingayu Gambuk continues to have an impact in the Philippines. The family still holds a position of prominence in Banaue, and many people in the local community are aware of the family's history. Henry Beyer, who collects and sells local antiquities from the Cordillera region, credits his grandfather with his own interest in historical artifacts and ephemera:

> I learned a lot from him. Usually after when we would go to dinner, especially in the evenings, he talks and I would pay attention when he's getting [receiving] people, just people from Europe and Americans coming over to discuss their works on excavations in Indonesia, Egypt, . . . and when they ask my grandfather, I always pay attention when my grandfather is talking so I am a little bit of an expert on the recognition of the pieces. So it sort of caused an interest in me so after I graduated, actually I was into aeronautical engineering in the beginning but when I stayed with him in the hospital I lost track of my going back to school. When I went back I took up business instead, because I have to earn some money to work on some research of my own!

Because of time spent with his grandfather, Henry realized that there was a market for native-made curios and heritage items, such as handmade wooden spoons with Indigenous deities carved on the handles. Henry began bartering with the local community to obtain sought-after pieces and selling them at higher prices to tourists and collectors:

> So I make it into a business . . . because people buy these curios [and] stuff. . . . What I do is I buy metal spoons and I exchange them for the wooden spoons, old wooden spoons with figurines, really old ones that they [the local Indigenous communities of the Cordillera region] actually use. I barter with them and then I sell [the spoons] for five pesos to tourists[,] but when my father buys them for the shop, because we had a curios shop, he only pays me fifty cents! [laughs] But anyways, I was making business. . . . I just started in the early fifties . . . but now[,] you know, one spoon . . . costs about five thousand dollars, a real good one.[58]

Henry described how his grandfather disapproved of his business, advising him to instead keep and preserve such heritage artifacts.

Henry also spoke of Beyer's great love of and pride in his wife, Lingayu, and the many refused invitations for her to live with him in Manila, though he did not recall ever having seen a photograph of the two of them together. Archival accounts from Beyer's Manila colleagues diverge somewhat from Henry's description of his grandparents' relationship. From these accounts, it seems that Beyer kept his marriage and his Ifugao family an open but guarded secret. Filipino and American friends alike recounted never hearing of or meeting Beyer's wife, and how Beyer lived mainly in Manila, away from Lingayu and their son, William, in Banaue. One Filipino colleague wrote of Beyer in an obituary, "In his official record, it appeared he was a widower," and though he had seen Lingayu's backside "twice in postwar years," the funeral was the first time he had met her face to face. Once, he recounted, when Lingayu came to Manila to visit, Beyer "drove me off."[59] A close American friend described his shock upon meeting Lingayu and Beyer's infant son for the first time when the two were traveling through Mountain Province: "He had never breathed a word to me about this before."[60] This concealment was likely strategic on Beyer's part, as ostracism from the well-to-do American and Filipino communities was common for those who intermarried, and even more so if the offending partner was part of the non-Christian tribes. Lingayu's refusal to live with Beyer in Manila suggests that perhaps she did not feel comfortable leaving her home or living predominantly in the company of Americans, or that the arrangement of living apart was one that suited her expectations of their marriage. This disconnect in accounts—between my interview with Henry and accounts from Beyer's contemporaries found in the archives—also speaks to the differences in how interracial relations were viewed by lowland elites (Filipino and American) and Indigenous peoples. As Henry elaborated, "People here saw it as a good thing that Americans wanted to marry the women. . . . It made them feel good about themselves, that they were good enough."[61]

For their help in the cause of empire, colonial officials did not disparage men like Scheerer, Haight, Dosser, or Beyer to their faces about their personal relationships with local women, even if they did shun them socially, outside practical and colonial state matters. The services they offered to the colonial government were invaluable and would not be risked by making slanderous judgments about the men that literally led the way in Mountain Province. That did not mean, however, that these individuals' private lives were not open for public discussion. As one American reported on intermarried interlocutors in the Philippines:

> A number of Americans have married Filipina women; and, as one of our hosts was of that number, it may seem ungracious to criticise the custom. . . . American members of the Philippine Commission have set the stamp of their disapproval upon the querida system on the east—a European or American man living with a native woman without a marriage ceremony. While they do not encourage mixed marriages, they feel that even these are better

than the evil practice which helped to make the name "European" offensive in the Philippines.[62]

The colonial government, while giving its official stance on interracial marriage and sexual relations, had its own reasons for limiting involvement in the marital affairs of American men. American administrators and military officials tended to privilege practical necessity over racial ideology in the case of dangerous intercourse, often selectively ignoring transgressive relations for the longevity of colonial rule and the facilitation of US affairs in the Philippines.

The Southern Philippines and Amalgamation

Colonial policy in the southern Philippines differed from that in the North, especially in the first decades of the American era. There were, as in the North, few existing Spanish colonial infrastructures for Americans to build from, and many local Muslim leaders did not see themselves as part of the burgeoning independent Philippine nation that was embroiled in the revolution against Spain. This proved to be an obstacle for American officials sent to the South to secure US interests because they could not use the same pretense of assisting the revolutionary army in its anticolonial movement. With the outbreak of the Philippine-American War, the US military was busily engaged in fighting Filipino revolutionaries primarily in Luzon and the central Visayas. Colonial officials wanted to prevent the possibility of having to simultaneously engage the Moro people of the southern islands, at least, that is, until the bulk of the fighting with Filipinos in the central islands could be resolved.[63] As such, an informal policy of collaboration and accommodation with the Datu leaders of Mindanao was the rule during the Philippine-American War. In addition to formal acquiescence (on both sides) in the Kiram–Bates Treaty of 1899, which allowed some autonomy of the sultanate in exchange for the recognition of American rule, the US military pursued other stopgap measures deemed necessary to maintain the delicate balance of power in the southern Philippines.[64] More often than not, the course pursued by the United States in the South was tied to the knowledge Americans purported to have about Muslims in the Philippines, much of which consisted of transposed notions of slavery and harems. Americans acquired their understanding of Islam and its practitioners long before the military came to occupy the southern shores. From early American interactions with the naval privateers of the Barbary States of North Africa to the well-known Indian mutinies faced by the British East India Company, Americans had long sensationalized and mischaracterized Islam and other non-Christian religions, and this knowledge seeped into how military officers organized their garrisons in the southern Philippines.

Today, many people from Mindanao and the Sulu Archipelago use the term "Moro" (or "Bangsamoro") to identify themselves as part of an Islamic ethnolinguistic group outside the legal authority of the Philippine government, although both Spanish and American colonizers also used the term to different effect. The Spanish occupiers labeled the Muslim inhabitants of Mindanao as "Moros," or Moors, understanding them to be the equivalent of the Muslim populations they were familiar with from northern Africa. The term was one that placed many different ethnolinguistic groups under the same umbrella. American colonizers followed suit, dubbing the large island of Mindanao and the smaller Sulu islands that stretched out to neighboring Borneo as Moro Province.

The US military's occupation of strategic outposts in the South initiated interracial intercourse between Americans and Moros. Just as Americans found the company of local women in other parts of the island, so too did they in the southern region. According to military reports, however, local systems of prostitution had to be engaged in ways that would not incite the ire of the Muslim population. American fears about Muslim savagery and murderous tendencies played a role in the establishment of strictly regulated and segregated prostitution establishments that sought the exclusion of local Moro women in favor of recently arrived foreign women. Military leaders in Mindanao and Sulu were particularly concerned with the maniacal violence that supposedly characterized Muslim societies more broadly. Colonialists fears over Islamic ritual suicide—"juramentado," as the Spanish described it (literally "one who takes an oath"), or "running amuck," as American papers dubbed it—pervaded American notions about the peoples of the region. As individual acts of juramentado increased with the solidification of American control through the South, the image of the crazed Moro attacking infidels indiscriminately with bolos and other instruments of decapitation imbued military and civilian depictions of the dangers of Moro Province. This type of irrational violence, Americans declared, was characteristic of Islamic populations and represented a regional-specific danger, not to be found in other parts of the Philippines.[65] Local forms of intercourse would have to be adjusted as a result.

The characterization of Muslims in the South as explosively violent was part of how Lieutenant Colonel Owen Sweet justified his acceptance of the well-regulated brothel system that served the Twenty-Third Infantry under his command in the town of Jolo, on Sulu island.[66] Sweet, like many other American colonists, took much of his understanding of the inhabitants of Moro Province from the accounts of juramentado martyrs left by the Spanish as well as from the pages of British imperial history. He had taken over command of the garrison at Jolo in late September 1899. Two and a half years later he found himself under investigation for the charge of illegally maintaining "houses of ill-fame" for the express use of the US garrison.[67] The accusations originally came from an enlisted member of the Army Hospital Corps who had also served in Jolo and from representatives of the Woman's Christian Temperance Union. In their demands for an investigation, they painted a picture of debauched immorality in the Jolo outpost that went on not under the noses of the commanding officers but with their blessing. Three houses of prostitution, the accusers relayed, were under the protection of the US military. The thirty-five or forty Japanese women who occupied the three brothels received regular medical inspections from US military doctors, and armed military sentries were posted at the entrances. Apparently, so amiable were the relations between the Japanese women and the US military that they gifted Sweet with an expensive watch, valued at around $200, prior to his departure from Jolo.[68]

Once the investigation into these charges began in earnest in 1902, Sweet was already back in the United States, convalescing in Hot Springs, Arkansas. He attributed his poor health, consisting of "mental and physical nervous strain and overwork," to his time spent in Moro Province, where he claims to have suffered from dealing with the constant threat of "bloody fanatical war with the Moros" and the "detestable conditions" of immorality that surrounded him. Sweet and other officers denied the charges that the US military ran the brothels, and many fell back on the trope of irrational Moro violence to defend what they claimed was the "least objectional form" of prostitution and one that best ensured the "common good and safety" of the US troops. According to Sweet, he had been appalled by the immoral conditions he found upon his arrival in Jolo, where drinking, gambling, and prostitution were constitutive of the "harem-kept institutions of the Moros." He swiftly acted to eradicate all vice industries in the town, including prostitution, but when complaints came in from Moro men about "impure proposals to their women by the soldiers," there was no choice but to allow some sexual recourse to remain accessible. Rather than arouse the enmity of the Moros by insulting their wives and daughters, and to avoid any "terrible slaughters and butcheries," such as those committed by the "Mohammedans in India" against British imperial troops, Sweet made the decision to allow a group of Japanese prostitutes to continue their trade.[69] According to Sweet, these women were the glue that held together the flimsy Moro-US relationship, which had the potential to ignite at any moment.

Japanese women constituted a large portion of the workers within the sexual economy throughout the archipelago, and in some brothels, they trailed only local Filipina women in their representation. The decision of Sweet and his contemporaries to direct intercourse toward the newly arrived Japanese women reflected the ethnic distinctions that American colonialists made in the islands. Local Filipina and Moro women, they determined, were "universally affected with venereal diseases."[70] According to one major, a particularly "virulent form of syphilis" found in the islands might have been transported back to the United States had soldiers not been directed toward foreign women like the Japanese, who were deemed "less dangerous than those about Jolo."[71] American troops that shipped out from the presidio in San Francisco were already familiar with East Asian brothel workers (more so than Filipina and other Southeast Asian women) and likely felt more knowledgeable about and comfortable with this group of women than the local women. Because Japanese women were understood by the US military as "the cleanest" and least troublesome in relation to local women, their trade was allowed in order to protect the troops and the United States from foreign contagion.[72] As historian Paul Kramer has noted of this interlude in Jolo, body politics were imperial politics.[73] In this case, US soldiers' sexual access to certain bodies and not others was deemed a matter of national imperial importance, even if the Moro calamity that military officers warned about was not likely to materialize.

The idea of dangerous Moros running amuck was so deeply embedded in how Americans understood the population in the South that it was not just Jolo's sexual economy that was organized around this guiding factor. Throughout the towns of Mindanao and the Sulu islands, similar measures of directed intercourse were enabled and approved by ranking military officials, if not entirely sanctioned by the US War Department. Military officials allowed, for example, the same arrangement of the sex economy on Siasi island in the Sulu Archipelago. Japanese women were permitted for the stated purpose of avoiding an outbreak of hostilities with the local population, who, "being Mohammedan, deeply resented any tampering with their women by Christians."[74] Despite the restrictions on intercourse, the Jolo investigation brought to light that some enlisted men still formed relations with Moro women despite having orders not to cohabit with them, and Moro and other non-Japanese women continued to operate outside the military-approved sexual economy.[75] By the second decade of US rule, the regulation of a segregated system of prostitution in the South was common medical knowledge. The annual report of the surgeon general of the US Army for 1911, for example, showcased that the year's hospital admission rate for venereal diseases in Mindanao was only 189, compared with 291 admissions for Luzon and 368 for the Visayas. The report speculated that the 189 admissions would likely have been lower were it not for the Moro and Filipina prostitutes who continued to flout the regulated system and were reportedly "impossible to control."[76] Regardless of the efficacy of the Mindanao-Sulu sexual economy in preventing a second front of the war in the Philippines, military officials felt it prudent to prevent dangerous intercourse between Americans and Moro women by encouraging what they believed to be a safer (for both the physical body and the political body) form of intercourse. This directed economy was later held up by American medical personnel as a model worthy of emulation throughout the colonial state.

Americans continued to understand Mindanao as a powder keg throughout the colonial period. While most of the Philippines went from military to civil rule after Theodore Roosevelt declared the war over in 1902, Mindanao and the Sulu Archipelago remained under military control until 1913. As historian Katharine Bjork has noted regarding American administration of the region, "The Muslim south was Indian Country."[77] It was far from the colonial capital and overt American authority. Like American notions of the "frontier" in the US West, colonial officials imagined the possibilities of Moro Province but lamented the presence of its current occupants. As the United States sought to rein in the southern region more fully, most of the Muslim inhabitants did not concede to outside rule, just as they had not conceded to the previous Spanish occupiers. The perceived intrinsic violence of the Moro people and the unstable status of the region as a contested part of the larger Philippines more often than not meant that Americans treated the people of Mindanao and Sulu as subjects that could only be brought into the imperial fold via militarized violence. Once freed from most of the active fighting of the Philippine-American War in the central and northern islands, the military government launched a series of punitive wars against the Moros, many led by the same men who were valorized for their service fighting punitive wars against Native Americans in the United States.[78] The military governance over the region ended in 1913 and supposedly marked the end of the so-called Moro rebellion, although violence between Americans and Moros and between Filipinos and Moros became a mainstay.

Despite the prevalence of militarized violence, Americans had early on made plans for what to do with Mindanao. The Zamboanga branch of the American Chamber of Commerce called for a complete removal of Mindanao from the Philippines to use as an American colonial plantation similar to the US South. Other stateside imperialists urged for the settlement of undesired American populations there, including recent immigrants to the United States and Black Americans.[79] The American government in and out of the Philippines thoroughly considered many of these ideas, although most were never implemented. A constant in many of these plans for the future of Mindanao and for the extension of tighter control over the region was the necessity of disempowering the local Muslim rulers and population in general. As in the United States, the punitive campaigns against the local population were followed by larger-scale land settlement and assimilation plans.[80]

Settler colonization of Mindanao, colonial officials hoped, would help to integrate the Muslims with the Christians of the central and northern islands. They saw agricultural colonies in particular as a potential solution to the Moro problem. Muslim inhabitants could become tied to individual tracts of land and, in so doing, become accustomed to the US administration and its authority. If Christian Filipino and white American settlers went to Mindanao, it could alleviate population-density problems in Luzon and the Visayas and create a larger labor pool in the South. Further, Moros would mix with Christian populations, eventually becoming a nonthreatening and pliable population. The first civil governor of Moro Province, Frank Carpenter, touted in his 1914 report to the Philippine commission that the agricultural colonies were already bringing about these desired ends. As he stated, the colonies had fostered "increasingly amicable relations" between Christian and Muslim colonists. This type of friendliness, he continued, was "of prime importance, for its aim is the amalgamation of the Mohammedan and Christian native population into a homogeneous Filipino population."[81] The amalgamation approach to the incorporation of the South was, in many ways, nothing new for American policymakers who had sought to "assimilate" Native American populations for decades. Nor were the settler colonial plans for Mindanao new to the region. The previous Spanish occupiers, too, saw the South as a potential dumping ground for those who troubled social stability or were unfit to inhabit the empire proper.[82] The Spanish crown often forced vagrants, soldiers, and criminals from Mexico and Spain to go to the Philippines. Once in the islands, the Spanish colonial government deported many of these so-called undesirables to Mindanao. These longer and more global settler dimensions are essential to consider when thinking about the long historical memories of those subjected to colonial intrusions from outside powers.

By 1902, the US colonial government passed the Public Lands Act, outlining who could obtain land and how to buy, lease, or homestead. The large island of Mindanao was a prime location for settler possibilities. The homestead provisions of the act largely mirrored the US Homestead Act of 1862, wherein settlers could obtain "free" land, build farms, and then, after a period of five years of "improvement," apply for legal ownership of the land from the government.[83] Unlike the original 1862 Homestead Act, which gave only citizens or intended citizens the opportunity to acquire land (thereby barring most Indigenous people and people of color), the homesteading provisions in the Philippines were open to Filipinos and those classified as belonging to the non-Christian tribes, as well as American citizens.[84] Colonial administrators classified most land parcels throughout the archipelago as so-called public land, open and available for individual ownership. They reasoned that there was so much available land because "Filipinos have not tried hard to get land of their own." Apparently, Filipinos did not have the pioneering spirit of "the early settlers of America."[85] By the early 1920s, farming digests in the islands heavily encouraged hardy young men to take up the pastoral life on southern land that was "practically untouched." Extolling the virtues of the frontier, advertisements asked, "Why not start at once and take a hand in the great game of converting these natural advantages into positive wealth?" "Young man, go *South* where your talents will have free play."[86] These calls for homesteaders and investors ring with the familiar language of the US frontier, imploring Christian Filipinos and Americans alike to head to the internal frontier of Mindanao and settle agricultural colonies. The colonial government offered loans and transportation to further incentivize relocation and settlement.[87]

For all the extolling of the virtues of the pioneer and the muscular working of the land, the US colonial government thought little of the many homestead applicants. In 1907, reports on the status of public lands indicated that a majority of the applicants who attempted to get land titles were "the more ignorant Filipinos."[88] Likewise, colonial administrators did not highly regard the American population targeted for homesteading in the "wild" South. A case study of the Momungan agricultural colony in Lanao del Norte, a colony created for and settled by interracial American-Filipino couples, highlights some of the slippages between the laudatory language of settlement and the underlying colonial vision for Mindanao. Momungan was a project of the Mindanao Colonial Association (MCA), an organization of

Americans with economic interests in the South. The leaders of the MCA petitioned the governor-general of the Philippines, Francis Burton Harrison, to aid in the relocation and settlement of hundreds of mixed-race families. The government was amenable to the idea and allocated resources to help the MCA colonize Mindanao under the direction of the Bureau of Agriculture. The first settlers arrived in the northern Mindanao colony in 1914. Almost ten years after Momungan was founded, the Bureau of Agriculture declared it a failure, at which point the Bureau of Non-Christian Tribes took over its supervision.[89] By 1927, only sixteen or seventeen of the original American settlers remained in Momungan, with those who left citing "difficulties and lack of government support."[90]

While the Bureau of Non-Christian Tribes no longer designated Momungan an agricultural project of the state, Filipino homesteaders and farmers continued to settle there. The relative stability of the colony, despite the early departures, continued to aid in the process of amalgamation and non-Muslim settlement, and by the 1930s, Momungan possessed the largest Christian settlement in the larger Lanao province. American officials recognized this feature of the colony, and in 1935 the American provincial governor of Lanao described it as an "opening wedge for homesteaders who are slowly pushing southward."[91] Not only was the Momungan colony useful to the colonial government for aiding in the settler colonization of Mindanao, but it also played a role in promoting the respectability politics of the colonial state by hiding the presence of dangerous intercourse. As Jacob Lang, president of the MCA, described in his original 1914 petition for the creation of the colony, a special place for mixed-race families was needed to alleviate the hardships they faced. Intermarried men were socially ostracized in places like Manila, he noted, and the process of Filipinization deepened the financial instability of mixed families. The Wilson administration, which was eager to relieve itself of possession of the Philippines, had begun the process of Filipinization, whereby the colonial government replaced most low-level American civil servants in the islands with Filipinos as a way to train civil servants in preparation for independence. This undertaking, according to Lang, disproportionately affected intermarried American men. Many low-level civil servants who remained in the Philippines into the second decade of US rule had stayed because of attachments to Filipino wives and children. Lang and the colonial government agreed that these men, now unemployed in addition to being social pariahs, deserved aid.[92] If they could remain useful in the service of empire, all the better.

While Lang and the MCA noted in their documentation of Momungan that many of the settler men were "honorably discharged" regulars or volunteers in the US Army and therefore deserving recipients of governmental aid, other descriptions reveal the more common colonial attitudes toward intermarried white men. Early reports on the colony written by Americans rarely failed to point out the interracial demographic, many of which described the men as undesirables with native wives. A 1917 report on the colony stated of the settlers: "Quite a number had married Filipino women and had no desire to leave the country. The condition of these men was pitiable. There is no place in the social and economic organization of the country for Americans of that class[,] and the government . . . established them on public lands . . . where they will have an opportunity to work out their own salvations under the control of the bureau of agriculture."[93] Written by Charles Elliott, an American judge in the Supreme Court of the Philippines, this characterization of the Momungan settlers was markedly different from later accounts, especially those written by Filipinos. In 1930, Ludovico Hidrosollo, the Filipino director of the Bureau of Non-Christian Tribes, wrote a memorandum to the colonial government on the history and status of agricultural colonies. He made no mention of Momungan's settlement by interracial families, although he hinted at his knowledge of this. Hidrosollo was appointed director of the bureau in 1925 by American governor-general Leonard Wood, and like many Filipinos, he likely viewed interracial intercourse differently than did his white counterparts and perhaps not worthy of mention in his report. He did note, however, that "many of these Americans, if not all, lacked experience in agricultural work. They went to Momungan because they were convinced that they could go nowhere else. Having suffered setbacks during the first year after their arrival at the colony, and taking into consideration the fact that they were men unexperienced in agriculture, the result was clear: failure."[94] In fact, Hidrosollo seems to be making a pointed critique not of the settlers of Momungan but of the American colonial government, which hatched the idea for the colony. His assertion that the failure of the agricultural colony was a foregone conclusion because the settlers had no agricultural experience placed blame on the shoulders of American officials, not necessarily on the intermarried men. While Hidrosollo's account hints at the ostracism faced by the settlers, Elliott's description clearly understood the homesteaders as economic and *social* outcasts.

Despite how most Americans thought about intermarried settlers, they could still be made useful to the empire. Intermarried settlers facilitated the colonial government's amalgamation scheme, and some of these settlers, like C. J. Walker, could be deployed as useful propaganda to entice white and Christian settlers south. The Bureau of Agriculture, for example, touted Walker as a frontier success story, and described his homestead in its popular mouthpiece, the *Philippine Farmer*. In 1917, Walker went to Momungan with his Filipina wife and daughter (fig. 2.5). The article described Walker as a "man who made good in Mindanao," and his story typified the ideas of the American bootstrap work ethic and frontier "free labor." He obtained a small parcel of land and farming implements with loans from the US government. With this initial investment, he leased more land and eventually produced enough crops to be the first Momungan settler to clear his debt. This, the article stated, was done through his "hard work and strict economy, the two virtues essential in pioneering."[95] Not mentioned in the story is how a family of three could manage thirty-two hectares of land (about eighty acres, or just over sixty contemporary football fields) without the help of local labor. Surely there were more hands involved in the production of "315 caravans of corn" and "five tons of camote" than just the Walker family and their three mules. The story also does not consider the labor of Walker's Filipina wife and mixed-race daughter, who likely played important roles on the farm, perhaps using their language and agricultural and cultural knowledge to aid in their integration into the wider community.[96] This depiction of pioneer success glosses over Walker's engagement in dangerous intercourse to focus instead on his masculine and industrious frontiersmanship. It was a story that potential American settlers would find familiar, and the bureau likely hoped that Walker's success would promote further settlement of Mindanao by non-Muslims.

Another account of Momungan points to the differences in how Americans and Filipinos viewed interracial marriage. In 1933, a Filipino journalist praised American settlers for turning the former wilds of Momungan into a thriving paradise, declaring that one sure sign of the endurance of the settlement was "the fact that the American settlers have intermarried with native women."[97] The author did not explain why he believed this to be the case, but like many other Filipinos, he likely understood Americans who legally wed Filipinas and stayed in the islands as a better class of colonist than those who cohabited with or married local women, only to abandon them (and any children) upon their return to America. One would certainly be hard-pressed to find Americans during this time who would similarly attribute their countrymen's success in pioneering to their marriage to Filipinas.

An even later Filipino account also praised the colony and its racially mixed population of Americans, Filipinos, Japanese, Moros, and others. The writer described the cosmopolitan nature of the American mestizo children as a testament to the colony's racial harmony. The mixed-race American Filipino kids could "speak the local dialect like nobody's business . . . and mix freely with the Moro, Bisayan and Ilocano children in the colony." Interracial

Figure 2.5. The caption from the *Philippine Farmer* reads, "Mr. C. J. Walker, the first Momungan colonist, who has cleared his account with the Government, and his Filipina wife and daughter." Mrs. Walker and her daughter are unnamed in the article. Image courtesy of the American Historical Collection, Ateneo de Manila University.

marriage, like other forms of interracial intercourse, was a litmus test for many Filipinos looking to gauge American receptiveness to socioracial equality. In fact, interracial marriage was probably, for many Filipinos, one of the clearest indicators of such receptiveness. The attitude of the reporter toward the American pioneers reflected this understanding as he admired the convivial integration he witnessed: "In no other place in the Philippines today, perhaps, is the real spirit of brotherhood so faithfully observed as in Mumungan where all live in peace, love and honest labor." With Philippine independence only a few short years away, the reporter concluded that these old-timers would not leave like all the other Americans: "They like the place so much that they'll stick to it—make it the last real American frontier in the Far East!"[98]

Despite the praise heaped on the interracial settlement of Mindanao, Americans and Filipinos continued to understand the South as a place suited to undesirables and, in fact, a place where dangerous undesirables already existed. Through the decades, the prevalence and persistence of Islam in the South continued to conjure notions of wild and lusty sultans, lascivious harems, and ruthless raiding and slavery.[99] A poem written by a former Spanish-American War soldier and published twenty years after the founding of the Momungan colony titled "A Darky's Mournful Wail" told the fictional tale of a "Dixie colored man" named Mose Faggin.[100] As the poem goes, Faggin, a Black man, went to Jolo island to meet the sultan. While there, Faggin converted to Islam, apparently swayed at the prospect of having his own harem, and became the husband of four wives. "Now dis may soun' good, but it ain't so fine / 'cause yoh ain't see'd dem women folks ob mine / dey is allus' quarrelin' an fightin' ober me / Till I don't know if I'se a husban' or a referee."[101] The poem characterized the Moro women as knife wielding and sexually inexhaustible. Eventually, Faggin could no longer "keep on luvin' dem lak a good Moham" and returned to the United States, where he aimed to be "a one-wife husban'—the cullud Methodis' kind." The anonymous author, likely a white expatriate, wrote Faggin in the American minstrel tradition typical of the time.[102] The juramentado fame of the South also persisted, with the women depicted as armed with the instruments of decapitation.

"Mournful Wail" painted Mindanao as a place that accepted racial Blackness. The sultan and natives quickly accommodated Faggin, and his marital prospects were abundant. Dangerous intercourse could run rampant in the South, where women in particular had lurid libidos and carnally associated with Black men. Published in a Manila periodical that catered to the needs and concerns of self-professed "old-timers"—those Americans who arrived in the Philippines during the early days of US colonization, mostly men and former Spanish-American and Philippine-American War veterans—this poem underscored a strange irony in that a large proportion of the periodical's readership were themselves married to or cohabiting with Filipinas. The predominantly white readership likely enjoyed a good laugh after reading "Mournful Wail" and were reassured of the superiority of their own white/monogamous interracial relationships. The tale of Faggin and his harem discursively reinforced what types of dangerous intercourse were more acceptable than others. American old-timers could differentiate their own relations from that of a worse evil—interracial polygamy.[103] Published just months before the commonwealth period was inaugurated in 1935, wherein an elected Filipino president finally replaced the American governor-general, the poem also points to how white old-timers continued to understand their presence in the islands as a positive influence and one necessary to combat the backwardness of the local population. Lastly, the resolution of "Mournful Wail" suggests the commonplaceness of leaving a wife behind in the islands. The blot of dangerous intercourse could easily be wiped away upon returning to the United States. Faggin, like so many Americans who left behind women and children in the Philippines, could find a *real* wife back home.

Americans understood the southern Philippines, like the US West, as potentially productive and dangerous, overgrown with the possibilities of wealth but laced with dangerous natives, diseases, and immoral entrapments. Though many colonial officials in the Philippines lamented the coarseness of American frontiersmen, especially those with native wives, Filipino accounts of these same pioneers painted a decidedly different picture. For Filipinos who dissociated from the Moro populations of the South, American homesteaders and their interracial families did the work of national unification, incorporating Mindanao and making it productive in the best spirit of socioracial equality. The remoteness of Mindanao from larger American populations along with the flimsiness of US control over the region offered interracial couples opportunities to be homesteaders outside direct colonial castigation.

While some Americans and Filipinos "work[ed] out their own salvations" on agricultural colonies or engaged in sexual relations more freely than in Manila, these relations also served the imperial goals of the colonial state. The US empire's amalgamation plans directed at the Muslim inhabitants of the South benefited from interracial intercourse, with or without the approval of those settlers who crossed sexual color lines. In the case of Lieutenant Colonel Sweet's campaign, some types of interracial intercourse were promoted and other types were prohibited in an effort to appease the purportedly violent temperament of Moro men. Relocation to the frontier was an appealing option for those Americans who floundered in the wake of Filipinization efforts but also served the colonial state's aims of hiding miscegenation in Manila. The colonial capital could then more closely approximate a place safe from the dangers of racial mixing, a bastion of positive American influence in Asia. Governmental bureaus called on homesteaders as examples of "Americans that made good" by their "little brown sisters," examples that demonstrated the difference between Spanish conquest and American benevolence, or Spanish queridas and American marriages.[104]

Conclusion

Looking at intercourse and region together demonstrates that the practical needs of empire often outweighed its ideological justifications, and though that practicality opened up possibilities for intercourse between American men and local women, the broader work of dangerous intercourse in these regions solidified colonial and local elite structures of power. Especially in the first two decades of the US occupation, the North and the South and the intercourse that prevailed in each locale held make-or-break possibilities for the colonial government. Though imagined by colonialists as frontier zones of the colony, these sexual geographies were in fact central to the constitution of American power in Manila and across the archipelago. In Mindanao, the regulated system of prostitution was heralded by the colonial medical community as an example of successful sanitation practice in the tropics. Further, agricultural homesteads for mixed families satisfied two colonial administrative goals: peopling the South with more non-Muslims and removing American-Filipino couples from more densely populated American communities. Likewise, in the Cordilleras, intermarried white men were vital intermediaries, providing surveyors, administrators, academics, tourists, and others with access to Indigenous communities, which imperialists then pointed to as the prime beneficiaries of benevolent American tutelage. Americans like Beyer were considered experts on the Philippines and their people through their marriages to Indigenous women, strengthening the US empire by growing colonial knowledge.

Though opportunities arose for American men to engage more freely in interracial sexual relations without consequence and elite local women to maintain or advance their social status, most were less lucky. Like George Hally, whose hopes to rejoin the constabulary were thwarted because of his interracial marriage, more marginalized men and women saw little permanent improvement in their lives. Igorot women often faced abandonment and the severing of marital ties, as with Dosser's string of Ifugao wives who were ultimately left for a "legitimate" spouse. Moro women saw the restriction of their movement and, for some, their livelihood. Though women already in privileged positions might find their status more secure or improved, like Lingayu in Banaue or Rosario Madarang, dangerous intercourse did not ultimately provide local men and women the opportunity to radically transform their lives, colonial conditions, or local systems of power. While local women understood that they could earn incomes or material benefits (often temporary) via dangerous intercourse, these livelihoods were often dictated by the colonial regulations that allowed medical staff to violate their bodies and left women open to abuse, aspersion, and abandonment. It is difficult indeed to weigh the possible economic mobility of local women against the firming up of the military occupation of the islands. It cannot be overstated that the possibilities of negotiating power through dangerous intercourse were often overshadowed by the myriad and diverse ways that US imperialism profited from such connections and, in many cases, continues to do so.

An exploration of the sexual geography of the Philippines beyond Manila during this period foregrounds the nature of US imperialism in the islands as one that relied on the familiar policy of settler colonialism. Though the US occupation of the Philippines is not often understood as a settler colonial project, a consideration of the disparate sexual geographies reveals how settler colonial processes were nonetheless an integral part of the occupation. In the Philippines, mixed-race rather than white families often made up the settler population, and they were ostracized from both the US body politic and proper American society in the colony. The American settler society in the Philippines demonstrated who could and who could not come home after a stint in the islands, as intermarried men with Filipino families could choose to either abandon them (as most did) or remain indefinitely in the islands, where their interracial marriages were not considered crimes. Few chose to take their foreign brides and children home to America, where most states had firm anti-miscegenation laws.[105] Eventual absorption into Philippine society also marked these settler families. Though they were inflected with American culture and values and in many ways lived Asian American lives, interracial settler families tended to live outside larger

American populations and were more often accepted into Filipino communities. While this push to the borders of colonial American society did further the imperial aims of obscuring dangerous intercourse and growing the American presence further afield, it also created what it sought to prevent or regulate, giving rise to different sexual geographies of interracial intimacy.

Chapter 3

Colonial Sociality and Policing Dangerous Intercourse, 1898–1907

The well-to-do American women of Manila were scandalized. A member of their own ranks had transgressed one of the more inviolable social pacts of white womanhood in the tropics. Alberta Torres (previously James), a prominent young white American woman, had married a Filipino. Adding insult to injury, both the US and the Philippine presses were splashing their romance around in their headlines, especially since Alberta decided to go to Manila with her husband, Antonio Torres, who was a member of William H. Taft's traveling party to the Pacific colony. The couple met in 1903, when Alberta was attending a Catholic preparatory school in Washington, D.C., and Antonio was a law student at Georgetown (fig. 3.1). Two years later, in 1905, they married at St. Patrick's Catholic Church. Torres was following in the footsteps of his father, who had a close association with the US colonial government and was currently serving as a justice of the Supreme Court of the Philippines. Despite her husband's wealth and position in the Philippines and despite the legal sanction of her marriage—as opposed to the less formal relations most American men had with Filipinas—Mrs. Alberta Torres's interracial relationship was judged by many Americans in the Philippines as irredeemable. When the couple arrived in the Philippines with the Taft party, they received a frosty reception from the many American moralists who deplored interracial intercourse.

US and Manila newspapers sensationalized the Torres marriage, publishing articles about the arrival of the couple and the "coming ostracism of this little lady by the American women in Manila."[1] One social event hosted for the

Figure 3.1. The *Washington Times* captioned this picture of Alberta and Antonio Torres "Filipino and his American bride." The local Washington, D.C., press kept track of their story and two months later ran an article describing how the couple was departing for Manila with William H. Taft's 1905 diplomatic entourage bound for Asia. The same photo was included with the story and was captioned "The groom an Americanized Filipino and his wife a bright Washington girl."

visiting Taft party in particular—a festive ball given by prominent Manila businessman Mariano Limjap—was depicted by the press as a hotbed of American snobbery. According to the *San Francisco Argonaut*, the atmosphere of the party was tense, as American women made hostile remarks about Mrs. Torres, saying that she should be "properly snubbed," and "[indulged] openly in depreciatory remarks about the Filipino people in general, though at the moment accepting the hospitality of a wealthy Filipino with a fine house."[2] Taft, the ranking American official in the colony, took it on himself to defuse the powder keg by making a show of interracial intercourse. He called for a rigodon (a popular formal quadrille line dance) and danced first with the Filipina lady of the house and then proceeded to dance with "all the leading ladies of each of the provincial towns." He then "took particular pains to lead out for a waltz the little American girl from Washington . . . the bride of Antonio Torres."[3]

Though the press blamed white American women for the racial animosity that was boiling over in the colonial capital—a fact conspicuously visible upon the arrival of Alberta and Antonio Torres in Manila—it was, in truth, a widespread problem for the American colonial government in the Philippines. As Americans settled in and made themselves at home in the islands, working and living alongside Filipinos, they expressed more and more concern over what types of relations with the colonial wards were appropriate and which were not. The underlying concern for many was that these friendships would transgress unwritten social orders, spilling over into the realm of sexual/romantic engagement. Colonial sociality, especially in sites imagined to be interracial gateways, was particularly troubling for concerned Americans in the Philippines because there were no formal barriers or laws preventing or outlawing interracial sexual relations. Anti-miscegenation laws could not follow the flag; to legally prohibit marriage and interracial sex between Filipinos and Americans would have undercut US professions of magnanimity and commitment to social equality. At the same time, overt American racism against Filipinos prevented the colonial administration from maintaining stable relations with local elites. Smoothing over the everyday acts of Americans proved a difficult task for which colonial officials were unprepared, especially as they often shared the racist attitudes of their civilian and military counterparts. The project of American benevolence was one that needed constant reaffirmation. Taft was one of the best performers of colonial intercourse, and he pressed other Americans to follow his lead. Under an imperial occupation that purported to be open to social equality, colonial sociality was perhaps the most significant arena of diplomacy, as it constantly tested the sincerity of the new regime.

Colonial sociality encompassed a broad range of interactions and relations taking place in the overseas possession. Social interactions occurred in a variety of locations and situations, such as markets, public parks, parties, clubs, and private homes. Relations between Americans and Filipinos most often took shape in ways that reflected the dramatic unevenness of the colonial society. Colonial sociality also served as an arena of negotiation, wherein daily interactions were heavy with the sociopolitical implications of imperial rule. The bars and saloons frequented by American soldiers and other gateways troubled colonial stability because the sexual always threatened to spill into the social. For most Americans, colonial sociality had always been bound up with ideas of deviant Filipino sexuality and possible sexual contagion, but there were some sites that especially unnerved Americans. Such locations aroused in colonists heightened anxieties about "social vice" and "immorality," as they imagined dances, parties, and cabarets as places of romantic or sexual possibilities or places where libertine behavior was more acceptable and common.[4] Dancing was one such area of colonial sociality that quite literally closed the distance between Americans and Filipinos in ways that many colonists found uncomfortable, threatening, and salacious. In the absence of legal prohibitions that policed social and sexual color lines, vigorous methods of extralegal policing emerged in the colony. Enforcing sociosexual segregation became the duty of the moral police—concerned moralist Americans and some Filipinos—rather than that of a governmental mechanism or branch.

But moral reformers were not the only ones policing politically charged gateway spaces. Colonial officials faced public relations nightmares because of the everyday acts of racism that colonists proffered in an effort to draw the color line. How to address, for example, the problem of white women refusing to dance with Filipino hosts at high-profile events became an important matter of state, discussed at the highest levels of governance in the islands. Filipinos, whose ostentatious displays of wealth at social functions were arguably about more than simply being hospitable and fashionable, pushed officials to address such slights, pointing out that the racial animosity of Americans was not winning the confidence of the local population.[5] The multiple ways that people understood, engaged, and sought to control gateway spaces was integrally tied to competing visions of and aspirations for the future of the colony. The sites examined here, namely the baile and dance halls/cabarets, were charged with these competing visions of the colony and have been treated seriously by scholars as legitimate political arenas.[6] These dances and festive events—especially during the first few years of the colonial period—were spaces where Americans and Filipinos could employ interracial sociality to prove or discern loyalties, build relationships that could translate into political collaboration, and delicately contend for power in a shifting colonial order. Interracial intercourse was central to this politicking, although for Filipinos, sociality that verged on the romantic or sexual held vastly different meanings than it did for Americans.

Unlike many of the Americans who shared gateway spaces with them, Filipinos generally did not express the same anxiety over racial mixing or relations that might move beyond the platonic. Rather, Filipino attitudes about gateway locations like bailes—integrated social balls or parties—were often informed by how those spaces functioned historically before the American occupation, as well as by local understandings of racial mixing. Filipino attitudes toward and approaches to gateway spaces, as we will see, were also shaped by anticolonial desires and aspirations for flexibility, mobility, and the stability of socioeconomic positions within the new regime. This alternative understanding of gateway locales highlights some of the different attitudes of Filipinos and Americans about interracial intercourse.

Centuries of experience with outsiders, namely Spanish colonists and Chinese settlers, colored much of the Filipino outlook on interracial intercourse. Spanish colonists and Chinese settlers had openly engaged in relations with the local populations of the islands, forming connections ranging from illicit extramarital affairs to formally sanctioned relationships. Indeed, many of the powerful and influential Filipino families and individuals with whom American officials engaged politically had Spanish or Chinese ancestry.[7] Filipinos themselves disclosed to American officials that having European ancestry through a Spanish friar, for instance, was often a mark of pride rather than a disgrace, as friars held religious authority and further provided their liaisons and children with some financial stability. As one Filipino explained to an American surveyor, the relationships friars had with Filipina women "became so common that [they] passed unnoticed."[8]

Unlike in the United States, where a drop of nonwhite blood would legally prohibit access to resources and privileges, being mestizo in the Philippines—the Spanish classification for a local *indio* of mixed race—often did not preclude such ascendancy. While ascendancy to the very highest rungs of the socioracial hierarchy that placed Europeans from Spain at the top might be generally inaccessible, mixed-racial heritage historically afforded individuals' loftier positions than those classified as full *indios*. Accordingly, many Filipinos who were accustomed to interracial sexual intercourse expressed less concern about the romantic or sexual possibilities ascribed to gateway locales than did Americans. As we shall see, in the case of bailes and dance halls, Filipinos were less concerned with crossings of the sexual color line than with how they were perceived and treated in these spaces and how such interactions supported possibilities for sovereignty. The battle to gain and maintain legitimacy over the islands was not only being fought between colonial officials in the Philippines and American reform groups at home, back and forth across the Pacific Ocean through courts, executive orders, and telegrams. The project of benevolent assimilation also required a degree of support from Filipinos themselves. Friendly posturing and overtures of social equality were necessary to stem resistance to and critique of the occupation. For Americans invested in segregation, maintaining racial boundaries while trying to highlight the social inclusion of Filipinos was quite often a complicated dance of skirting around issues, strategic displays, and pageantry. The convergence of racism, social intercourse, and the specter of interracial sexual intercourse was not easily navigated in the colonial Philippines. Spaces of amity and friendship became suspect and dangerous. While efforts to win Filipino approval began with a bloody war that resulted in the deaths of over four thousand Americans and over twenty thousand Filipinos, both sides tried to start over with a dance.[9]

Festive Sociality and Diplomacy: A Delicate Dance of Power

In 1902, Eva Johnson, an American girl living in the Philippines with her father, wrote to a girlfriend back home, describing her life in the tropics. "You asked me if I had been to any dances, or boat riding," she started. "It seems to me these people are giving 'bailes' and dances all the time. There is hardly a week passes that I don't go to some party. And often times during the 'fiesta' times, three and four balls are given a week."[10] A few months later she wrote to the same friend, joyfully detailing that the colonial government had given her father a new post as a judge in Manila, explaining, "We will have a better time socially."[11] Affluent Filipinos and high-ranking colonial officials attended the posh society affairs that young Eva was enticed by, and rank-and-file American soldiers and teachers working for the empire, whose colonial whiteness superseded their modest socioeconomic status, also usually had access. The elite hosts of more lavish affairs, however, typically denied admission to Filipinos of more modest means. Americans often wrote of how frequently they received invitations to bailes, both in cosmopolitan centers like Manila and in smaller provinces and villages.[12] Since the Spanish period, bailes and fiestas were mainstays of the Filipino social scene. They continued to be an ever-present reality across the islands, where Americans and Filipinos came together socially to eat, drink, and dance into the early morning hours. Aside from the American colonial governor living in Malacañan Palace, it was usually Filipino elites who hosted festive bailes.[13] Besides the entertainment that these events provided, they functioned as spaces where Americans and Filipinos made first impressions, welcomed guests, exchanged courtesies, and sorted out intentions.[14] More importantly, the space of the baile was saturated with Filipino aspirations for influence and independence, and American contempt for and incredulity at confronting wealthy, European-facing Filipinos.

While Americans often mistook festive events as evidence of Filipinos' openness to friendship or as symptomatic of local hospitality and native indolence, elite Filipinos saw these spaces as integrally tied to their prospects for independence, spaces where they could gauge American receptiveness to socioracial equality. The differing understandings of festive events speaks to the larger disjuncture in how Americans and Filipinos understood the occupation of the islands. For visiting American commission members, for example, their frequent invitation to bailes signified Filipino eagerness to welcome Americans and their tutelage. For Americans unable to see beyond the framework of the islands as a new and indefinite American possession, bailes became a quaint bauble that colored their first impressions of the islands and their people. While these festivities were often the first or last encounters with Filipino hospitality, they were also spaces where Filipino elites could demonstrate their own power and status. Lavish decorations, sumptuous food, and ostentatious displays of wealth through finery were mainstays at bailes in Manila and farther afield. In the face of popular American understandings of the supposed savage, uneducated, and impoverished Filipino, the hosts of bailes presented an oppositional narrative. As wealthy, influential, and gracious hosts who were well acquainted with European customs and trends, they were, in many ways, presenting themselves as more closely associated with Western culture than their American guests.

The US commissions to the Philippines often involved a whirlwind tour around the archipelago, during which American members of the party were whisked from province to province for the purpose of reporting back to the US president on the state of their new possessions in the East. James LeRoy, secretary to the 1900 Taft Commission, wrote profusely of the bailes and festivities planned by the Filipino community that dominated the itinerary. From Baguio to Iloilo to Negros and back, Filipino hosts who were often members of the local elite invited the commission members into their homes. In fact, so numerous were the invitations to parties that the commission turned down many offers in order to stick to their itineraries and complete their fact-finding mission in a timely manner. In the towns near Iloilo, for example, LeRoy described "a great deal of rivalry over entertaining the Commission, Iloilo, Jaro and Molo each wanting to give a banquet and a ball. In the arrangements, Jaro was to have only a 'breakfast' on Friday, and the people of that town were considerably disappointed and wanted the Commission to stay for them to give a ball."[15]

LeRoy took particular note of the ostentatious appearance of Filipina women. He wrote of one baile, "The best gowns of Iloilo also soon appeared, in a large turn-out of ladies, who made quite a show of jewels." At another party in Negros, Filipina women attended in all their finery, "with painted skirts and jewels galore."[16] In 1906, an article in the US-based *Independent* recounted the immense wealth of the mestizo families who often threw parties in Manila, detailing the considerable "comfort and luxury" of their lives. "Their houses are large. . . . They have carriages, in some cases automobiles, jewels and lavish wardrobes. One or more members of a family have usually travelled abroad, and perhaps lived for some time in Europe."[17] The relative wealth of Filipinos versus Americans was put into sharp contrast at bailes and balls, as Filipino elites often invited not just US colonial officials to their parties but also military officers, American schoolteachers, and other American civilians.[18] Though American civil servants had incomes sizable enough to place them on a higher socioeconomic rung than many Filipinos— salaries that could purchase amenities in the Philippines that would be out of reach in the United States—the wealth that their Filipino hosts enjoyed would have been a stark contrast.[19]

While Americans described the Filipinas in these accounts as ornamented as well as ornamental—pleasant scenery at bailes as well as within the broader landscape of the Philippines—Filipinas were not the one-dimensional baubles colonialists imagined them to be. We can understand something of the desires and intentions of Filipina hostesses by considering their ostentatious displays at bailes. In donning expensive and often imported clothing and luxurious jewelry, Filipinas participated in a time-honored method of demonstrating rank and stature: dressing for dinner. They showcased their wealth, sophistication, and consumption of European culture through modes of appearance and presentation. As scholars of gender and empire have shown, dress and appearance were modes through which the affluent, from the monarchy to nobility to imperialists, conveyed their presumed superiority.[20] Elites in the Philippines were well aware of the racist ideology that imbued American understandings of their society. Conspicuous consumption was a way to redirect or challenge this narrative.[21] Embodying their wealth and status while presenting their homes, replete with lavish decorations and feasts, disoriented ideas of Filipino barbarity and lack of civilization. That the fiesta was a common social function during the Spanish period as well— marking religious holidays, the political and royal achievements of Spain, and seasonal harvests—highlighted the connection of Filipino elites with European society and culture.[22] Furthermore, as commission members traveled throughout the archipelago, they often conducted state business, such as appointing local governors in the towns they visited. This was done either by commission appointment or by community consensus. As such, local displays of hospitality and pomp were also ways through which Filipinos could attempt to secure positions of power for themselves within shifting imperial realities. We misunderstand Filipinos apparent zeal to host colonial officials if we classify it (as many Americans did) as simply hospitality or as gratitude for aiding the ouster of the previous Spanish colonizers. Instead, we must understand these spaces as sites of defiance, where women played a large role—both as organizers of bailes and as symbols of them. Bailes muddied American justifications of empire in the islands, creating conditions whereby US officials were hosted as guests in the homes of their new colonial wards, whose fitness for self-rule was being questioned. In this reversal of roles, Filipinas revealed the irony of the US mission in the islands. In their lavish homes and through their displays of fashion and generosity, Filipinas demonstrated that in these islands, it was they who constituted the elite and wielded authority and power.[23]

The Filipino pushback against imperialism through bailes troubled many American colonial officials, who understood what such demonstrations of wealth and culture meant for American authority in the islands. For example, Harry Hill Bandholtz, chief of the Philippine Constabulary, lamented what he viewed as the misinformation about "the true Filipino character" that Americans encountered in the social life of large cities like Manila. Bailes, with their requisite dancing of the rigodon, wearing of finery, and consumption of ample food, did not impress Bandholtz, who viewed these events as sites of superficial posturing. His disdain for bailes and what he understood as the false image of Filipinos depicted during them highlights his understanding of these spaces as important locations for political maneuvering. As he stated in a letter to Major General W. H. Carter, assistant chief of staff to the US Army, visiting dignitaries and American military personnel in the Philippines should travel outside Manila "incognito," if possible, avoiding the "gauntlet of flower girls" and "the descriptions of the angelic virtues of the progressive Filipinos as pictured in acrobatic immediate independence speeches." Bandholtz reasoned that Americans should observe the local people outside the social world of Manila to get a true estimation of the Filipino. This would show them, as it had apparently shown him, that Filipinos were not ready for independence. Interracial sociality, according to his estimation, was dangerous for the longevity of the US presence, as it challenged American notions of Filipino backwardness. He continued his critique of baile pageantry, describing his experience of "suffering through a 'banquete' of twenty-seven courses of chicken and twelve of carabao lubricated with a liquid supposed to be claret but properly called 'tinto.'" In this recollection, even the wine, or "tinto," masqueraded as civilized.[24] Bandholtz's denigration of Filipino cuisine and of his Filipino host's alleged attempts to pass off local red wine made from nipa palm alcohol as French claret illuminates the broader American understanding of Filipinos as deceptive—that is, as imitators of culture rather than possessors of it.[25]

Americans and Europeans alike passed judgment on the omnipresent baile in ways that showed their discomfort with the alternative narrative that emerged from these festive spaces. Many whites in the islands reconciled their belief in Filipino socioracial inferiority with the lavishness of fiestas by understanding their hosts' zeal for entertaining as frivolous and indolent. Americans wrote much on the topic of bailes thrown by Filipinos, judging these parties to be a reflection of the native love of leisure and idle pursuits, furthering the racist notions that native peoples of the tropics were lazy and disinclined to work. One of the most detailed accounts of the social environment of bailes comes from the letters of Mrs. Campbell Dauncey, an English woman who spent nine months traveling in the islands. A supporter of Anglo-American imperialism but a skeptic of America's ability to emulate the British model, Dauncey's chronicle derided Spaniards, Americans, and Filipinos alike, although she held the brunt of her disdain for Filipinos. Like her contemporary Bandholtz, she described what she considered the derivative nature of these events and painted her hosts as self-important divas who did not truly possess culture but only poorly imitated it.[26]

Dauncey recounted one baile in the smaller city of Iloilo in a letter dated January 8, 1905. The popular rigodon dance she wrote off as dull but entertaining because she was able to "really see the people, and they were well worth the trouble of turning out after dinner to look at." Her voyeuristic evening continued as she described the Filipina and mestiza women present, who wore "the native muslin camisa . . . always worn with European skirts of appalling colours and cut. One little brown woman had on a long train of scarlet plush, with huge white lace butterflies fixed across . . . which made one burst into perspiration merely to look at it." For Dauncey, the clothing of these "brown women" was impractical and garish. It was not just the dress of Filipinas that Dauncey disapproved of but practically everything about their self-presentation. When a "mestiza" and a "Eurasian" woman performed a song and piano accompaniment, she was appalled by the "ghastly grey-white" face powder of the singer as well as the performance, which she deemed "so bad that you feel all hot and ashamed." Dauncey described the Filipina singer, who "faced the audience with the aplomb and self-confidence of a prima-donna," as fanciful and lacking self-awareness. In this Englishwoman's estimation, Filipina wealth and worldliness was nothing but pitiable self-aggrandizing mimicry.[27]

Dauncey recounted another ball, given at Malacañan Palace. Luke Wright, the American-appointed governor-general of the Philippines, was the host of this particular "gubernatorial party." American governors of the Philippines quickly adopted the baile as a political tool, inviting crowds to the palace for dinner and dancing. Once again, Dauncey revealed her understanding of Filipina sociocultural inferiority through what she judged as inappropriate or ostentatious dress: "'Manila at a glance' included one or two who looked like gentle-folk, and there were certainly a great many pretty dresses, which, I am told, the wearers import from Paris recklessly."[28] The festive attire of Filipinas became a topic of gossip among the Anglo-European baile attendees, hinting at the discomfort of some white women, like Dauncey, with Filipinas who imbibed and consumed elite European cultural forms. Faced with Filipinas who possessed the means to import gowns from what was and is largely still regarded as one of the fashion capitals of the world, white women turned affluence into frivolity and recklessness. They understood Filipina embodiment and performance as cheap, imitative, and even embarrassing. These characterizations reflected common colonialist attitudes toward Filipinos in general, ideas that stressed civilizational immaturity and lack of fitness for self-rule.

Interracial Gateways: Transgressive Intercourse at Bailes

Bailes also exposed the tenuous nature of white-Filipino colonial sociality because of the sociosexual possibilities that the integrated space provided. Comparing festive sites of colonial sociality (bailes) with the more vilified saloon underscores that for most Americans, any site of colonial public comingling—whether reputable or not—was haunted by the possibility of interracial sexual contact. While this possibility constituted a dangerous ambiance for some Americans, others found the romantic prospects to be found at bailes a quaint part of life in the tropics. It was largely American men who were drawn to the amorous interludes they imagined occurred at bailes, and their depictions of alluring native women validated ideas of white virility and masculinity while also promoting ideas about Filipina romantic inclination toward the new occupiers. One American, for example, reported on a baile hosted for "Manila's 400," or elite set, in May 1899. He described the "pretty senoritas," whom he suspected may have "designs on the hearts of our 'American chappies.'" He added, "If the glances which I saw going from great brown eyes toward a pair of shoulder straps are any indication, I am afraid some of our girls at home are going to lose their soldier-boy sweethearts." Such reports framed romantic possibilities in the tropics around the martial masculinity of the Spanish-American and Philippine-American Wars, both of which broke out only a few months prior to this event. While the author suspected that the "charmingly courteous" ladies were "concealing any slight ill-feeling they might naturally have had over the recent victory of the Americans," the violence of the war was assuaged by the perceived attraction of Spanish and Filipina women to American soldiers.[29]

Other accounts were much less enthusiastic about the romantic possibilities created by the integrated space of the baile. Mrs. Campbell Dauncey, for example, summarized the sentiment of a large swathe of Anglo-American society in Manila in her assessment:

One can see from a glance, at any gatherings, where the people of various shades of white and brown keep very much together. Some of the Eurasian women are quite pretty, but they spoil their little round faces with thick layers of powder over their nice brown skins. . . . The white men are friendly with many of the Mestizos, and dance with their pretty daughters, and are even occasionally foolish enough to marry the latter; but white women keep quite apart from the coloured folk, and it would be an unheard-of thing to dance with one; while as to marrying a Filipino, no woman one could speak to would ever dream of such a horrible fate.[30]

This account highlights the gendered dimensions of colonial sexual possibilities for Anglo-European men versus women. While the *Freedom* newspaper writer described the attraction of local women to American men, Dauncey highlighted the eagerness of white men to pursue nonwhite women. The assessment of "Eurasian" women's attempts to appear attractive can be read as Dauncey's perception that local women were also openly courting interracial romantic possibilities, but she pointed explicitly to American men as "friendly" toward nonwhite women and "foolish" in their attempts to woo them. In her estimation (and no doubt in the estimation of many white women in the colony), it was white men who opened the door too widely to racial integration in their immodest overtures to nonwhite women.

Dauncey's characterization of white women's abhorrence at the thought of intimate physical contact with Filipinos also speaks to why it was more often American men, rather than American women, who participated in "fiesta politics."[31] Filipinos and American colonial officials alike often pointed to white women's bigotry and "race prejudice" for inciting the ire of the

Figure 3.2. Taft's entourage traveled around the Philippines, attending various social and political events. Here, Taft (center side view in dark jacket and pants) and Alice Roosevelt (facing Taft in white jacket) are exchanging words amid a group of gathered Americans and Filipinas.Image courtesy of the Freer Gallery of Art and Arthur M. Sackler Gallery Archives. Photograph by Burr McIntosh, The Alice Roosevelt Longworth Collection of Photographs from the 1905 Taft Mission to Asia, FSA A2009.02, Gift of Joanna Sturm, granddaughter of Alice Roosevelt Longworth, 2009.

local population and causing tension at social events. The disdain of many American women toward their Filipino hosts presented colonial officials with diplomatic headaches. One flashpoint event that brings to focus the tensions surrounding colonial sociality and American racism was the 1905 visit of Alice Roosevelt, daughter of then president Theodore Roosevelt, to the Philippines. The first daughter accompanied Secretary of War William Howard Taft on his diplomatic tour of Asia and acted as a visiting dignitary in the countries they toured (fig. 3.2).

On their stop in Manila, her presence in the islands brought to a head the racially fraught issue of who was fit to entertain whom. So sought after was the opportunity to host the young celebrity that the Manila press nicknamed her "Princess Alice." Her visit and questions over her hosting were so incendiary that American commission members found themselves scrambling as

Filipino elites accused them and other white colonialists of racial bigotry. Secretary of the commission James LeRoy recounted a heated debate that transpired between American diplomats and Filipino governors of various provinces at an official government dinner held at the Hotel Metropole in Manila on August 7, 1905.[32] Eighteen provincial governors attended, many of whom were Filipino, along with several US congressmen, members of the US commission, and several elite Filipino politicians. Not long into the dinner, Filipino representatives brought to the table complaints of American bigotry and racism. Arsenio Cruz Herrera, a Filipino politician, began an unexpected and long-winded (according to LeRoy) tirade against American governance on the islands. His complaints were numerous, and he concluded that the colonial government had "lost the confidence of the Filipinos." According to LeRoy, the Americans present and even some Filipinos disagreed with Herrera's depiction of the current administration under governor-general Wright, dismissing the complaints as a tiresome "harangue" and "plainly beyond reason in its violence."[33] When the Americans attempted to refute Herrera's charges and reassure him that American perpetrators of violence and other abuses against Filipinos would be dealt with, Herrera brought up an issue that was harder to explain away: American bigotry as demonstrated through social segregation.

In particular, Herrera accused commission members of not entertaining Filipinos in their homes and further complained that "Filipinos were elbowed out of the entertainment program for the visiting congressmen."[34] Voicing the complaints of Filipina women as well, Herrera brought up American women's feelings of superiority, describing how they excluded Filipinas from the planning of entertainments for the visiting Alice Roosevelt. American women further made Filipinas feel that they were "not wanted to have anything to do with the reception of American ladies." In particular, he accused the wife of the current American governor-general, Luke Wright, of being racist and excluding Filipina women.[35] The realm of formal entertainment, while most often seen as a sphere of women's influence, was also often a top concern for men, both Filipino and American. Elite Filipino men like Herrera, who often dealt with American colonial officials, shared the sting of rejection with their wives and other Filipinas who were left out of the event planning for visiting dignitaries from the United States. They further shared in the interests of Filipina women by reminding their American guests that among the native population, they were the elites.

Filipinos were not the only ones to point to the problem of white racism made visible through social exclusion. Americans sympathetic to Filipino

concerns and sensitive to how overt racism threatened to subvert US colonial interests criticized their compatriots as well, both men and women. In
early 1906, for example, the US-based newspaper the *Independent* published
an article written by self-proclaimed feminist and pacifist Elsie Parsons, wife
of New York congressman Herbert Parsons, both of whom were also members of Taft's entourage on his 1905 mission to Asia. In her article, Parsons
admonished the "snobbishness," or racial animosity, of Americans toward
Filipinos, as evidenced by their disdain for mixing at bailes and festive
events.[36] She began by describing the gulf between the "native aristocracy"
of wealthy and cultured Filipino and mestizo families in Manila and the
Americans: "It is not difficult to see at once that this barrier is raised up by
the Americans, and, moreover, the American women." As far as she understood and according to the Filipinas with whom she had contact, "not a single Filipina lady was invited to meet Mrs. Roosevelt or the ladies of the
party at any of the dinners given in their honor."[37] She further reported on
the racism apparent in the American press in Manila, as one outlet published
its hopes that the first daughter would not be seen dancing at parties with
any "gugus" while visiting.[38] In her description of bailes, Parsons recounted,
"No resident American women danced with Filipino partners except in the
case of one square dance, where the ranking American woman present was
officially bound to follow Secretary Taft's example, he dancing with the hostess and she with the host." Parsons's criticism of American racism in the
colony was in line with her critical opinions about the social conventions of
the time, especially as they related to contemporary racial ideologies and ideas
of proper women's roles.[39]

Bailes and other festive events quickly became sites of discipline. White
American women disciplined brown bodies and white men through their
unwillingness to dance and mix socially. Using social spaces and informal
networks of "gossip," white women could express their disapproval of interracial intimacies and shun from polite society those who transgressed what
they believed to be proper racial boundaries. Filipinos, colonial officials, and
visiting representatives in turn disciplined white women who they believed
endangered the fragile amity between the new occupiers and the native population.[40] The US commission in the Philippines was acutely aware of the
mounting racial tensions over intimacy at bailes, and officials took it on themselves to match their professions of benevolence to their actions.[41] The concerns brought up by Filipinas and Arsenio Herrera, far from being "plainly
beyond reason," as some commission members suggested, were in fact taken
very seriously by American officialdom. Taft, for example, advised mem-

bers of his high-profile entourage to be mindful of their behavior. As Alice Roosevelt described in her travel journal, Taft "remonstrated" with her on the matter, saying, "he did not want the feelings of our hosts to be hurt."[42] To address the animosity that had been ignited by the dignitaries' arrival in the Philippines, Taft invited the Filipina society ladies to host a baile for Princess Alice, an event that he and Mrs. Wright attended. Taft made sure to dance with the Filipina hostess, while Mrs. Wright—presumably having been disciplined and asked to adjust her public behavior—danced with one of her Filipino hosts.[43] American imperialists wielded the tool of dancing, and the superficial overtures of racial liberalism it conveyed, to literally and figuratively close the gap between colonizer and colonized.

Though these accounts point to the racially segregationist attitudes of white women in the colony, it would be a gross mischaracterization to conclude that they were simply more racist toward Filipinos than were American men. After all, both men and women upheld racial segregation in most other spaces of American colonial sociality, such as the American Club, the Baguio Country Club, and the Army Navy Club, as well as churches and golf courses.[44] What the explicit calling out of white women's racism by Filipinos and Americans alike does demonstrate, however, is the different set of sociosexual standards to which white women, as opposed to white men, were beholden to. That fewer America women married and had intimate sexual or romantic relations with Filipinos than American men did with Filipinas was less a reflection of different racial attitudes than of different gendered expectations and stakes. For men, sexual access to colonized women was an institutionalized part of US empire, not only in the islands but also throughout US history. Advertising encouraged American men to become friendly with their "little brown sisters" in dance halls.[45] The military regulated brothels and red-light districts for "sanitary" sexual encounters. White women, on the other hand, aside from the visible realms of social politicking, did not receive the same encouragement.

What Dauncey, Parsons, and others really highlighted, then, was the double standard in sexual norms and respectability that white women faced, both inside and outside the colony.[46] In this equation, white men could participate in the imperial goal of expressing friendship and social equality through intercourse, while white women were much more limited. This double standard created a gendered disparity in terms of who was and who was not able to advance imperial agendas through "fiesta politics." Sexual and marital relationships between white women and Filipinos, like that of Alberta and Antonio Torres, further highlighted this double standard. While men who engaged in interracial intercourse were institutionally supported but often socially shunned, women who crossed sexual color lines were doubly shamed and shunned.[47] The figure of the aforementioned Mrs. Torres, for example, became a lightning rod for white American women concerned with sexual and racial propriety in the colony, as one of their own ranks had betrayed the sanctity of white womanhood and demonstrated herself to be a deviant through her relationship with a Filipino man.[48] Taft was indeed disciplining white American women into compliance with the larger goals of the colonial enterprise by publicly dancing with Mrs. Torres and the rest of the Filipinas at the party. The commission secretary noted this in his journal, describing Taft's decision to dance publicly with Mrs. Torres as a purposeful attempt to "show that he disapproved of the race prejudice now being displayed here more strongly even than in the full days of military rule."[49] This act effectively turned the racist actions of white women and their disapproval of interracial intercourse into isolated incidents of women's idle gossip and pettiness, obscuring the fact that ideas of Filipino racial inferiority formed the basis of US imperialism in the islands, a logic that most American men as well as women supported.

Policing the "Social Evil"

Bailes were not the only sites of dangerous intercourse that observers and participants policed and that came to have amplified political significance. In the latter part of the first decade of US rule, as the population of Americans in the islands expanded to include more teachers, families, entrepreneurs, missionaries, foreign tourists, and other travelers mixed in with the ever-present military population, efforts to turn Manila into a shining example of American benevolence intensified.[50] For many, this vision of Manila was one in which interracial social intercourse was best kept superficial, and interracial sexual intercourse had no place at all. The social police in the islands—composed of American and Filipina women's organizations, church groups and clergy, moralist Filipino officials, the Young Men's Christian Association (YMCA), and others—never lacked for a cause to take up. Reformers especially wanted to eradicate prostitution, in addition to drinking, drugs, and gambling. But many of the relations that reformers opposed fell outside what was legally policeable. Police could only target areas of sexual transgression that were illegal, such as adultery or unlicensed prostitution. Other types of interracial sexual transgressions fell under the "jurisdiction" of what Filipino constabulary officer Emanuel Baja called the "morals police."[51] The morals police lumped most interracial sociosexual relations, including cohabitation, marriage, the querida system, and even "too familiar friendships," under the catchall of "social evils" that plagued the colony and needed surveillance.[52] Since bailes were widely considered a respectable venue for entertainment despite the possibilities for interracial intercourse, the morals police were squarely concerned with reining in venues more closely associated with vice and immorality. Though the moralist coalition was not able to drastically reduce American men's sexual privileges in the colony, they nonetheless shifted the atmosphere of Anglo-European men's sexual unaccountability and privilege, which marked the first few years of the occupation. And though there were moments of collaboration between Americans and Filipinos in policing socioracial boundaries where sex was concerned, motivations for and interest in policing such boundaries—as with bailes—often reflected competing visions of the future of US empire in the islands. As is usually the case when elites grapple for political power, here under the cloak of morality, it was the already marginalized Filipina women at the heart of dangerous intercourse who shouldered most of the consequences.

In February 1907, the largest American newspaper in the Philippines, the *Manila Times*, debuted a regularly running column titled In Woman's Realm, a testament to the growing number of American women and families who settled in Manila and attempted to create a US simulacrum in the tropical soils of the islands.[53] In this column, women discussed various topics, including how to cook American foods using local ingredients and how to dress for the tropics, as well as their opinions on contemporary issues. High on the list of disconcerting issues for these American women was the prevalence of interracial intimacies between Americans and Filipinos. Though many colonialists had previously ignored interracial intercourse, exploited it, or allowed it to continue unhindered for the good of the colony, the local press now publicly discussed and debated such relations in ways they had not before. This is not to say, however, that the arrival of white women disrupted the formerly halcyon interracial colonial paradise signaled by the commonplace interracial sexual intercourse between white men and native women.[54] As we have seen, a sexualized racism characterized how even those with progressive attitudes for the time thought about Filipinas. Interracial intercourse in the islands had always been marked by racism and violence, but now more people in the colony were speaking out about such relations. Unlike the colonial government, which used bailes and other forms of superficial intermingling to showcase its supposed openness to social equality, many of the American morals police were open about their desire for segregation, especially in sexual matters.

White American women and American religious organizations took up as their greatest concern the well-being of young white men serving in the US military. Like the military doctors and chaplains who tended to the sexual ailments of white American men in the first few years of colonization, these new reformers framed their white countrymen as innocents thrust into the lion's den. Though moralists considered the men who visited red-light districts and had Filipina mistresses a rough class of American, they still sought to intercede on behalf of these groups and made excuses for their behavior. For example, many members of the morals police claimed that immorality was largely due to "tropical neurasthenia," a disease in which the tropical weather of the islands made vigorous American men weak and "feebleminded." This, they believed, made otherwise moral Americans susceptible to lascivious native women.[55] Many colonialists affectionately dubbed the young men of the military "happy-go-lucky" young "boys" and understood them as above reproach, despite their sexual folly in the islands.[56] American church and women's groups took it on themselves not to chastise these young Americans too harshly for their indiscretions but instead to provide alternative wholesome amusements in the company of their own countrymen *and* countrywomen. Sexual congress, it seems, was not off-limits or immoral if it occurred between compatibly raced individuals.

Bishop Charles Brent was one such moralist who believed young American men needed alternative outlets for their social and sexual energies in the Philippines. Brent was a moral crusader and segregationist who served the Episcopal community in the Philippines from 1902 to 1917.[57] He created the Columbia Club, a religious organization that provided sporting events, liquor-free dances, and other amusements to "provide for the social and moral welfare of young men in Manila."[58] The club amenities and activities were intended for the white community only. Brent, like many imperialists of the time, believed that Filipinos were unfit to rule themselves and that their inferiority marked them as undesirable marriage partners for white men and women.[59] Brent often spoke out against interracial marriage from his pulpit. He even crafted a special twelve-page sermon titled "Othello Preaches," in which he detailed the evils of marrying outside one's race, drawing largely on his time spent in the Philippines and what he knew of colonial India.[60] Believing the "tragedy of Othello [was] a piece of real life," Brent used the ill-fated interracial marriage in the Shakespearean tragedy to outline his—and hence the Episcopal church in Manila's—stance on intermarriage.[61]

Apparently, in Brent's time abroad proselytizing in Asia, he observed that intimate relationships between those from "the Eastern and Western hemispheres" were not suited to marriage, "especially if the Westerners be from the temperate zone and the Easterners from the Tropics."[62] Framing his beliefs within church doctrine and drawing from the Shakespearean tragedy, Brent preached the following:

> It remains true that "real differences of race never lose their separating force." They will always say, "Thus far, and no farther." Community of interests, natural or developed from capacity inherent in both parties, is the necessary foundation of all fellowship, intimacy or union of whatever sort. . . . Intuitively, one might say, men, as a general rule, make their selection of life partners from a restricted group, the delimitations of which run in concentric circles, the outermost being racial; within lie the national, the social and the religious. . . . Love, in one sense, moves along the lines of least resistance. Hence it is normal and healthy that they who marry should make their selection from among those whose race, nationality, education and environment, social and religious, is akin to their own.[63]

Brent's idea to host Columbia Club dances in order to provide white men with romantic possibilities drawn from the white community was inspired by his belief in racial segregation more generally. Indeed, Brent also attacked social intercourse as a gateway to illicit sexual liaisons:

> To promote social intercourse is to promote marriage. Society is the hotbed of young love, and whoever is admitted on terms of equality may not be faulted if he count himself eligible for the highest prize. . . . There is on the part of various earnest persons, though seldom among those who have lived in the Orient, a desire to promote close social intimacy between foreigners resident in Oriental countries and the natives. Many who advocate this would deprecate the thought of intermarriage. But freedom in the former promotes freedom in the latter, especially where young life is concerned.[64]

A large portion of the well-to-do American women in the islands shared Brent's vision of a socially and sexually segregated colony, and they frequently teamed with him in the pursuit of these goals. In February 1907, the Women's Auxiliary of the YMCA took up the charge of addressing the needs of the young white men of Manila, discussing the need for "systematic efforts to supply home influences" to this target population.[65] The Women's Auxiliary gathered statistics on the living arrangements of many young American men in Manila, finding that only one in six were living in a setting they believed had proper American influences. Most lived in military barracks, with Filipino families, or with their Filipina wives or mistresses. "This is a picture that needs no comment," the Women's Auxiliary declared; men's isolation from Americans was morally dangerous. Legal forms of policing segregation and miscegenation could not be reproduced in the Philippines, but that did not prevent members of the Women's Auxiliary, many of whom saw themselves as the best suited to enforce morality, from teaming up with the YMCA to expand influence over young men who had "gone native."

The presence of these moral crusaders was undoubtedly felt by the US male population in the islands, as some eventually began to self-censure their behavior (at least publicly) in the presence of white ladies. For example, public flirtation with Filipinas was discouraged at the Paco Fire Station in Manila, as "American ladies are always passing to and fro," and the fire chief did not wish to give the appearance of a scandalous establishment.[66] Having earlier been overlooked, catered to, and generally allowed to go on with little consequence by the American colonial government, the intimate and sexual practices of American men in the Philippines were now under the local jurisdiction of the morals police. In time, American and Filipino groups of moralists in Manila came to work together to contest immorality in general, their broader constituencies garnering more public attention and concessions, even if their interior motives did not always align.

Skirting the Issue: Dance Halls and the Divergent Interests of the Morals Police

Twelve years after William Taft led Alberta Torres out onto the dance floor as a superficial show of support for Filipino-American interracial mixing, colonial sociality via dancing once again made headlines. This time, however, pageantry would not be enough to appease the offended parties. This was largely because the dancing in question did not happen at bailes but at public dance halls, where patrons could pay to dance with Filipina *bailarinas* (dancers). As reformers argued, such public entertainments were breeding grounds for illicit interracial sexual transactions, immoral at best and, more concerning, possible fronts for regulated prostitution. Both Filipinos and Americans protested the operation of dance halls, and they consolidated their efforts to form an interracial moral coalition. These efforts led to one of the first widespread and sustained disruptions of white men's sexual prerogative in the colony. At the same time, the move to dismantle the sexual privileges of American men in Manila came at the cost of Filipina *bailarinas'* bodily and economic autonomy, leaving many of them in positions more precarious than before.

Legal and extralegal policing coalesced in April 1917, when the Filipino mayor of Manila, Justo Lukban, along with a broad constituency of reformers, made it clear to the local press that they intended to do everything in their power to shut down public dance halls in the city. Lukban, a conservative Protestant and member of the Nacionalista Party, whose brother had been a general of the revolutionary army, expressed the opinion of the morals police when he stated that "most dance halls now operating in the city are centers of immorality."[67] Similar to the taxi-dance halls in the United States, where Filipino men could pay to dance with white women in residence, dance halls in Manila flourished, only here, American men paid to dance with Filipinas.[68] Some of these businesses operated as a combination of cabaret and dance hall. Patrons could dine and watch a performance but also take to the floor with an available partner for a small fee. Lukban and his constituents set out to prove that many of the women dancers also sold sex for money, often to their dance hall patrons, and they sought out medical information to bolster their efforts.[69] Prompted by the mayor's office for data, the Philippine Health Service and the Philippine General Hospital reported that many of the *bailarinas* they had previously examined had tested positive for venereal diseases. They also shared how the efforts of some municipalities to regulate dance halls by mandating the frequent examination of *bailarinas* was ineffective, as the women would share their "VD-free cards" so that their friends would not be prevented from working. In light of these facts and the desire of moralists to eradicate rather than regulate the sexual economy, the YMCA, the Women's Auxiliary, several church organizations, and others collaborated on a campaign to shut down the dance halls.[70] The mayor and other reformers sought out respectable American and Filipina women as natural allies in the crusade, as they were widely understood to wield moral authority as keepers of the domestic realm.

The issue of shuttering dance halls drew a large moralist coalition in part because such establishments were so commonplace. Some catered to mostly Filipino crowds, some entertained a mixed group and drew many American military men, and other, fancier cabaret dance halls drew the elite of Manila—both white and Filipino. And while it was predominantly the Filipino- and soldier-patronized establishments that drew the initial criticism, it was eventually the more elite clubs, owned and patronized by Americans, that captured

Figure 3.3. The large dance floor of the Lerma Cabaret is featured on this postcard, likely printed in the 1920s or 1930s. Image courtesy of Pinoy Kollektor.

the attention of white moralists and prompted a coalition of morals police to action. In July 1917, a few months after Mayor Lukban attempted to close down the first of the dance halls, Elwood Brown, the physical director of the Manila YMCA, solicited the Women's Club of Manila for support in his campaign against the American-owned Lerma Park cabaret and dance hall (fig. 3.3). The Women's Club was an integrated organization that elite Filipina women took part in shaping, especially after the club elected its first Filipina president in 1918. In his letter to the Women's Club president, Brown wrote:

> The young Men's Christian Association desires, through you, to call the attention of the members of the Women's Club to the following fact—that largely by reason of the patronage and recognition given it by the American and European women of this community, the Lerma Park dance hall has come to have a certain air of respectability which the conditions there do not warrant. The members of your club probably do not know that many of the dancing girls employed at Lerma are women of ill fame; that it is definitely known that some of these women are a prolific source of venereal contagion; that many of the American and European young men who form the habit of visiting Lerma because it is "made respectable" by the presence of respectable women, wait until these women have gone . . . and straight

away fall into temptation—not only to excessive drinking but to immorality as well.[71]

Brown implored the women to see the dance halls as a threat to their own
respectability. If upstanding white and European women like the members
of the Women's Club patronized the dance hall, they added to its "air of respectability," while women of "ill fame" were surreptitiously plying their
trade under their noses. His approach worked, as the club membership of
elite American, European, and Filipina women readily agreed that they did
not want to be associated with any business suspected of being an after-hours
site of illicit relations, even if they themselves had only visited Lerma Park
for dinners or shows on the cabaret side.

It is harder to determine, however, if the Filipina members of the club
(many of whom had Spanish ancestry) felt slighted at Brown's suggestion that
the presence of American and European women at the Lerma—and hence
not the presence of Filipinas, however elite they might be—lent the club an
air of respectability. While it is likely that many of the Filipina members
identified to some degree as European because of their Spanish ancestry, most
Americans did not consider even the most elite and mestizo segments of the
Filipino community to be socioracial equals. This sentiment of racial superiority undoubtedly existed in the early years of the Women's Club, as evidenced by the solely white presidents of the society until 1918, when the
club inaugurated its first Filipina president, former Manila Carnival queen
Pura Villanueva.[72] Whether Filipinas had the same concerns as white
American women when they decided to support the YMCA in boycotting
the dance halls is debatable. Did the Filipina members share the concerns of
Elwood Brown (and their Anglo-American club sisters) for the moral welfare
of young American boys tempted into boozing and interracial sex, especially after Brown left them out of his assessment of who constituted the
"respectable" element of Manila society? Did they similarly understand
Filipina dancers through the myopia of prostitution and disease, or did the
dancers incense them for other reasons, if at all? It is likely that while the
mixed-race constituency of the Women's Club of Manila joined men like
Brown and Lukban in their support of dance hall closures, they had divergent interests in the moral issue, interests that were reflected by their racial
and colonial positions within society.

For example, though Brown's description of susceptible white men easily
seduced by nonwhite women was certainly why many white members of
the Women's Club got involved in the campaign, it is doubtful that Filipina

women shared the same degree of concern for the moral well-being of white colonialist men. This is not to say that Filipinas did not care to police the sexual economy. The reputation of the Lerma as a place where otherwise virtuous young white men were corrupted by the supposedly disease-ridden Filipina *bailarinas* was likely morally offensive to the elite sensibilities of Filipina women in the organization. Further, elite Filipina club members may have cared little for and identified even less with the working-class women who danced for a living in cabarets and dance halls, preferring to distance themselves from the notorious *bailarinas* and other Filipinos who they believed reflected poorly on the merits of Filipino society. At the same time, however, that Filipinas would have been overly concerned with the bodily integrity and virtue of American soldiers and other colonial occupiers is doubtful. What is more likely is that elite Filipinas logically understood that public denigration of Filipina *bailarinas* had consequences for them as well. The durable association of Filipina women with the sexual economy did no favors for Filipino aspirations for independence, self-rule, or even social equality. It had long been a strategy of elite Filipinos to distance themselves from the populations in the islands that American occupiers pointed to as the uncivilized beneficiaries of US rule. For example, elite Filipinos objected to the "primitive" Igorot village display at the 1904 St. Louis World's Fair, believing it to be an inaccurate representation of the people of the Philippines and understanding the role it played in advancing imperialist visions for the islands.[73] Joining the campaign against those establishments primarily owned and patronized by Americans and now associated with prostitution also critically drew attention to and challenged imperial edicts of white moral superiority. Whatever the impulses of elite Filipinas in this matter, it is not a stretch to conclude that they were more interested in limiting the visibility of "diseased *bailarinas*" and redirecting the American narrative about Filipinas as women of loose morals than in saving white men's virtue. Additionally, here was a chance to draw attention to the dissonance between American imperial claims of moral superiority and the American fueled sexual economy growing in the islands. Joining a campaign to shut down American dance halls patronized by Americans looking for sex was a smart move for the Filipinas of the Women's Club. It likely troubled them and their coalition little that it meant putting Filipina dancers out of work.

The Women's Club of Manila resolved to "heartily cooperate with any movement having for its object the correction of the evils set forth in the letter aforesaid" and pledged to write to the provincial governments where such dance halls were located, such as Rizal, Santa Ana, and Caloocan (all on the outskirts of Manila proper), asking that "steps be taken to suppress resorts having an unwholesome influence upon the community."[74] The club members agreed to a boycott of the Lerma Park cabaret and dance hall and also resolved to press for the removal of any markers of American or European nationality from these businesses. The Women's Club would not tolerate the use of white national emblems to attract clientele into immoral dance halls, so the members contacted the Philippine chapter of the Daughters of the American Revolution and the "consular representatives of the allied powers" to let them know about the improper use of their flags.[75] This desire to disassociate white national insignias and signs from the cabarets and dance halls was in line with the imperial understanding of Americans as bearers of civilization to the islands. Both American and Filipina women considered empire in their pursuit of dance hall closures but likely had different outcomes in mind.

Not everyone in the colonial capital was as keen as the morals police on eliminating dance halls, as the male-dominated press quickly pointed out. The boycott called for by the Women's Club—particularly targeting the American-owned Lerma club and the Santa Ana Cabaret—was praised by some and lamented by others. Many op-eds and letters to the editor filled the American papers after the Women's Club declared its intention to boycott Lerma Park, a testament to the influence that the club members had in Manila's colonial society. The *Manila Times*, for example, published a statement in support of the dance halls, especially the "better class" of businesses such as Lerma Park and the Santa Ana Cabaret. The paper clearly opposed the morals police and outlined a defense of the dance halls that recalled the medical community's support of provisioning beer in the army canteen:

> We believe the dance hall and the cabaret fill a legitimate need in this community. The dance hall furnishes amusement which can be made innocent, to hundreds of men who might find their pleasures in other resorts far more dangerous to the welfare and health of the community. . . . If it is at all possible to maintain a dance hall which does not present a menace to the community, the TIMES believes the institution should be maintained. There are hundreds of soldiers and sailors who find their only clean amusement in public dancing. Closing the dance halls is driving them to some other amusement far more perilous to the community.[76]

The *Times* writers continued to mount a defense, describing in very great detail the interior layouts of both clubs and how some reorganization could make respectability more transparent. Their intimate familiarity with the establishments was apparent in the minutiae. The Santa Ana Cabaret, the author outlined, was designed to separate those who were attending a cabaret show from those who went to dance with *bailarinas*. The layout, the author determined, was a much better structural device to keep the riffraff away from the respectable clientele than the interior of the Lerma club. In the latter, the separation of the two types of patrons was more porous, as the dance hall was separated from the cabaret by only a line of potted plants. It was more possible, the paper speculated, for the Santa Ana to keeps its well-to-do patrons away from scandal due to the segregated spaces, but not out of reach for the Lerma club to do so as well. For the *Times* writers, the specter of interracial prostitution was not enough to warrant the destruction of "innocent" interracial intercourse through dancing. In fact, it was the specter of prostitution, they argued, that necessitated the survival of the cabaret and dance hall. Without them, the young soldiers and sailors would be "driven" to more immoral haunts. Ironically, men who supported dance halls played on and used the fear of interracial sexual intercourse to endorse businesses that fostered such relations.

Other patrons and supporters of the dance halls wrote with similar concerns for American men who might be driven to worse entertainments, questioning the logic of the YMCA and the Women's Club. One writer criticized the boycott, insisting that if fewer women of good reputation visited the Lerma or the Santa Ana, there would be fewer good women with whom men could socialize, further exposing men to "the lure of the bailarina." He further stated, "If I were striving for the uplift of Lerma Park I should preach boycott to the bad bailarinas, not to the respectable women."[77] Other men wrote to the papers defending their patronage of Lerma and Santa Ana, saying that they visited these places only for the dancing, not for any immoral or "filthy" purposes.[78] Others wrote to defend *bailarinas*, objecting to the way moralists typified them as "loathsome" and "diseased." Many such writers also demonstrated their personal familiarity with the Filipina dancers in their descriptions of jovial and chaste *bailarinas*. For example, one man wrote of how white male patrons often propositioned *bailarinas* for sexual favors, only to be refused by the more virtuous women. These patrons, he claimed, offered thirty or forty pesos in the hope that a *bailarina* would accompany them home for the night. "Why not get after some of the men who are constantly besieging some of the girls with improper proposals?" he asked.[79] Another editorial also pleaded for the fair treatment of *bailarinas*, describing many of the dancers as "wholesome" and non-diseased. Eventually, however, the American owner of the Lerma Park cabaret and dance hall, A.W. Yearsley, feeling the pressure to defend his business from ruin, made a public appeal directly to the Women's Club of Manila, not the mayor or the YMCA, demonstrating the degree to which women's influence in the sphere of morality could affect lives and livelihoods. Yearsley attended a meeting of the Women's Club to see how he could make things right and win back the approval of "every respectable element of the city."[80]

This outpouring of support for dance halls from the white male community of Manila reveals a distinct gendered and racial divide not only in what types of amusements were deemed acceptable but also in who was more concerned about the effects of dangerous intercourse. While most Americans, both men and women, agreed in theory that miscegenation with native Filipinos was undesirable and did not believe in true socioracial equality, many of these same men had no problem forming temporary intimate relations or having casual sexual relations with Filipinas. With the greater presence of reformers and social purists in the Philippines, and the success of American-Filipino reform coalitions, many white men found their sexual and social privileges threatened. Though men protested restraints on their privileges, most did so anonymously, signing their letters to the newspapers with pseudonyms, not wanting to be publicly known as miscegenists or "squaw men."

The momentum of the morals police in Manila continued into 1918, when Justo Lukban—building his reputation as *the* anti-vice mayor of Manila—set his sights on another arena of interracial intercourse: the infamous Gardenia red-light district. Lukban, like the Filipinas in the Women's Club, was driven by more than simple opposition to immorality. In cooperation with the American police chief of Manila, Lukban organized a quarantine of the red-light district between October 16 and October 25. On the night of the twenty-fifth, police rounded up 170 women from the Gardenia district, forced them aboard two steamers, and deported them to Davao, a city in southern Mindanao. Apparently, between the sixteenth and the twenty-fifth, Lukban worked with the Bureau of Labor to organize the details of the deportation and the receipt of the women in Davao as laborers. After a three-day shipboard journey, the bureau presented the women to the mayor of Davao as contract laborers. Just days after the raid, friends and family members of the deported women began putting together a case against "the Iron Mayor," which eventually found its way to the Philippine Supreme Court.[81]

Understanding Lukban's decision to deport some of the city's most vulnerable women requires a recognition of how Filipinos understood the implications of interracial intercourse. As one biographical anecdote about

Lukban explains, his momentous decision to shut down Gardenia was spurred when the problem of prostitution hit too close to home. As the story goes, Lukban was investigating the spread of prostitution outside known vice zones to more public places of recreation, like the Manila Bay area facing Luneta Park. It was there he witnessed his own *lavandera* (laundress) in flagrante with an American sailor in a kalesa.[82] The truth of this account is not necessarily as important as why this particular story proliferated as a means to explain Lukban's hasty deportation of almost two hundred women. Though the islands were in the midst of Filipinization, and the American colonial state was replacing more and more American civil servants with Filipinos, the sociocultural climate in the capital, one that gave American's easy access to Filipina women with impunity, vividly demonstrated that it was still Americans who were in charge. For Lukban, to see a woman "of his household" consorting with an American sailor would have been reminiscent of the lechery of Spanish friars. Anti-imperial resentment toward both the Spanish and the Americans surfaced and ignited Lukban to action.[83] Much like the revolutionary government's regulation of the sexual economy as a means to showcase Filipino capability for self-rule, it is likely that Lukban's actions were a way to redirect authority in the city and narratives of Filipino immorality to instead highlight Filipino resolve against immorality. Indeed, even the nationalist Filipino newspaper *El Ideal* lauded the morality campaign and goaded the "American press and colony" to accomplish their reform task, saying, "It would be a pity indeed if this beautiful attempt were not to produce the desired results, leaving only half done a moralizing campaign." Such failure, *El Ideal* continued, would benefit rather than hinder immorality in the colony.[84] *La Vanguardia*, another Filipino-run paper, described how dance halls lured virtuous Filipina women away from motherhood and other domestic pursuits, pointing to the corrupting influence of the American institution on the local population.[85] Lukban, the Filipino newspapermen, and their contemporaries turned the dance hall issue into an anticolonial grievance. Certainly Lukban's actions in cutting off men's access to Filipinas and other women in the sexual economy was a move more decisive than any the US colonial government had ever made. American officials paid lip service to vice eradication but intervened sparingly. That the now mythologized tale of Lukban witnessing his household laundry woman with an American sailor circulated for so long also attests to the power of collective memory to proliferate alternative histories in the face of colonial epistemologies, as well as a deep common investment in reframing imperial narratives about Filipina hypersexuality.

Lukban's attempts to cut off American men's access to interracial sex and redirect the discourse about Filipina women and immorality, however, should not be confused with a corresponding concern for the well-being of the women working within the sexual economy. In his (and his contemporaries') estimation, these women imperiled prospects for Philippine independence. Lukban's actions suggest that he was not worried about the consequences of his deportation order. Even when the local court ordered him to bring the women back to Manila, his efforts were half-hearted. And though families of the deported brought a case against him that went to the Supreme Court, some of the justices expressed their approval of Lukban's coup. One Filipino justice, in the dissenting opinion, opposed the sentencing and punishment (nominal as it was) that the court handed down to Lukban—a 100 peso fine and a charge of contempt. Justice Florentino Torres believed that the charges should be dropped. He described how Gardenia had been "for years a true center for the propagation of venereal diseases and other evils." Torres further asserted that the deported women, like lepers or cholera patients, were not guaranteed constitutional rights because of the sanitation-related dangers they posed, in addition to their "free practice of their shameful profession." Other justices, however, believed that Lukban got off too lightly. The slap-on-the-wrist punishment, Justice Manuel Araullo argued, set a bad precedent for the aspiring nation. He concluded, "In the Philippine Islands there should exist a government of laws and not a government of men."[86] It was over the bodies of vulnerable women that Lukban, Torres, and the others attempted to define or push certain understandings of the nation and its people while under the watchful eye of the American colonial government. Vying for power in the colonial state via control over women's bodies, which often stood in for the nation, is a common thread in the history of occupied nations. The women in this case, as colonial scholar Lata Mani has asserted about Indian women under the British empire, were the foundation from which various ideological battles were waged over the future of the colonial state.[87] As such, those waging these battles were not necessarily interested in the desires, perspectives, or welfare of the women at the center. To maintain their weak hold on power in the colony, Lukban and Torres, in particular, actively engaged in disavowing and eradicating the liberties of women within the sexual economy.

In the end, the majority opinion of the court commended the efforts of Lukban to eradicate vice and clean up the red-light district but found his methods unlawful. Even though he essentially dismissed the court order to retrieve the women from Davao, and the court subsequently charged him with contempt of judicial rulings, many of the justices as well as the moral reform community heralded him as a hero. Some of the women managed to come back to Manila of their own volition and resourcefulness, others married and settled in Davao, and others were never tracked down. Americans critical of Lukban's actions—many who partook in and benefited from the sexual economy—quickly painted his actions as an example of Filipino autocracy and despotic rule, an accusation Justice Araullo seemed to predict in his court opinion.[88] The victories of the morals police were often short lived. Though the anti-vice campaign drew a wide range of supporters, including many from the Filipino community, such as members of the Manila Board of Directors, judges, and other important officials, their efforts to shutter the dance halls did not stop the success of some of the larger American-owned establishments, nor did prostitution come to a halt.[89] By the 1930s, for example, the Santa Ana Cabaret had reached new levels of success, advertising itself as "the largest cabaret in the world" and hosting scores of US sailors prior to the Japanese occupation of the islands during World War II, only waning in popularity in the post-independence years (fig. 3.4).[90] Prostitution in the city also continued to thrive, a testament to both the resistance of colonialist men to relinquish their privileges and the resoluteness of the women employed in the sexual economy. Ultimately, we must consider the efforts of the morals police as bound up with the imperial order, in which Americans feared challenge to their moral authority, and Filipinos contended with the continued insistence by Americans that they were immoral and incapable of self-rule.

Conclusion

For many Americans, colonial sociality in the Philippines was always and already intertwined with ideas of deviant Filipino sexuality and immorality, a consequence of which was the strained relationship of the colonial state with its new so-called wards. As the primary point from which Americans could demonstrate a commitment to some form of social equality that aligned with professions of benevolence, the day-to-day was suffused with political meaning and interaction that more often than not betrayed such professions. Gateway locations like bailes and dance halls were hot spots for colonial tensions, as ideas of interracial intercourse were easily mobilized by both Filipinos and Americans in attempts to control the direction of colonial rule. While Americans used bailes as a space of pageantry to demonstrate openness to social

Manila's Finest

for
PARTIES
BANQUETS
CELEBRATIONS

〜〜〜〜 The Largest Cabaret in the World 〜〜〜〜

SANTA ANA CABARET

JOHN CANSON
Proprietor

SPAGHETTI DINNER
Our Specialty

Figure 3.4. Advertisements like this promoted the Santa Ana Cabaret as the "largest cabaret in the world." Filipina dancers, or *bailarinas*, danced with customers on one side of the dance floor, while the other side was reserved for the more elite and "respectable" patrons.

equality, Filipinos used the space to demonstrate fitness for self-rule, elite socioeconomic status, closeness to European customs and traditions, and hospitality. All these things flew in the face of popular American ideas about uncivilized Filipino subjects. Toward the end of the first decade of US rule, as the morals police increased in numbers in the colony, the intimacies of white American men with Filipinas could not be passed off as socioracial openness and would be more openly challenged and condemned by the wider Anglo-European community in the islands. Moral coalitions found ways to promote de facto segregation in the colony without formal measures to prevent interracial intercourse. Filipinos in the moral coalition against dance halls and red-light districts, more deeply aware than their erstwhile white moralist allies that American insistence on Filipina immorality yoked the nation to US rule, thought of empire at every turn. Their hopes to challenge and redirect such ideas that formed the foundation of the US occupation, though, thought little of the women at the center of these tensions or their well-being.

All the examples of colonial sociality that verged on the sexual (or, in the case of the red-light districts, were explicit sites of interracial sexual contact) demonstrate the complex nature of social proximity and reform efforts in the colonial Philippines. By opening our inquiry to include not only prostitution but also sites understood as gateways to interracial intercourse, as well as examining the integrated nature of reform, a more complex sociopolitical picture of colonial Manila emerges. So much of the scholarly work on colonial moral reform is focused on white women and religious groups and their proselytizing in nonwhite colonized countries, saving white men from the dangers of interracial sex and saving colonized peoples from barbarism. The efforts of the integrated moral police in the Philippines shifts our understanding of such reform and its rootedness solely in notions of white supremacy and imperial logics. Filipino men and women also agitated for changes in the realm of interracial intercourse, but they did so according to their own objectives. For some, dangerous intercourse was about contagion and the deviance of nonwhite peoples; for Filipinos, it was symptomatic of the tyranny of colonial rule and inspired anticolonial resistance.

The Filipino men and women who attempted to control "social evils" in the islands were more concerned with illegal acts of prostitution and spaces broadly understood as immoral. Bailes and even marriage and cohabitation did not concern these reformers in the same way that they did Americans. For many American colonizers, to engage socially with Filipinos was opening the floodgates to moral depravity and integration. For Filipinos, with their long history of colonial interracial intercourse, prostitution was more damaging to the reputation of Filipino society than were reputable (or at least legal) marriages. Vice economies reflected not only on Filipina women but on Filipino society as a whole. The local population understood this and sought to change this association. The discourse perpetuated by American occupiers that vilified the "diseased" *bailarina* was one that people like Lukban and the Filipinas involved in the Women's Club of Manila attempted to mediate in ways their power would allow, often at the expense of more vulnerable Filipina women. Challenges to the sexual economy—most often initiated by American women and elite Filipino men and women—did what the US colonial government did not favor: restricted the sexual exploitation of Filipina woman and the sexual privilege of white American men. The sexual frivolity of white men in colonial outposts could become lightning rods for anticolonial nationalism.[91] Mutual collaboration on reform efforts around vice and social evils, then, only thinly veiled competing interests for the future of Manila. For moral coalitions to work, Americans and Filipinos had to dance around the issue of exactly *who* was being unseemly and immoral.

Chapter 4

The Trials of Intercourse

Criminality and Illegitimacy in the Colonial Courts

In 1907, a scandalous murder case involving lies, infidelity, and interracial sex rocked the colonial American community to its core, causing ripples in the press for months to come. "Manila's Case of Dementia Americana" headlined the *Manila Times* on the morning of Thursday, June 13, and detailed the slaying of an American named Charles A. Pitman by fellow American Chester A. Davis. Davis, the papers reported, was a former member of the Seventeenth Artillery turned Manila firefighter who had recently married a young Filipina, Inez Davis (formerly Barios). During the trial, Manila newspapers reported that Davis found out about his wife's infidelity and, in a fit of jealous rage dubbed "Dementia Americana," shot and killed her rumored lover.[1] The trial of Chester Davis turned into a public spectacle, pulling in the rapt attention of the Manila public. Much of the media attention, however, focused on Inez rather than on the murder, going over the details of her supposedly sordid life before and after she married Davis. It was clear that the American public sympathized with the two white men involved in this crime, even though their willingness to take up with Filipina women spoke volumes about their perceived morality.

Other crimes involving interracial sexual relations similarly brought the scandalous sexual behaviors of American men in the Philippines before courts and juries, although none of them quite captured the attention of the American public like the Davis case. The outcomes of these "trials of intercourse" often illustrated the common pitfalls and deficiencies of the colonially constructed legal system to administer justice and equal treatment before the law.

The courts often handed out disparate sentences determined less by the severity or gruesomeness of the crime and more by the race and gender of both the perpetrator and the victim. For example, the typical punishment in cases of murder ranged from twenty years' imprisonment to death by execution.[2] Though Davis killed another white man in the colony, he received only a life imprisonment sentence, with the judge stating that the "extenuating circumstances" of the case "offset the aggravating circumstances."[3] In other words, though the court found Davis guilty of murder, the extenuating circumstances that became known during the spectacle of the trial—that is, the supposed sexual debauchedness of his unfaithful Filipina wife—counterbalanced the crime, affirming the idea that Mr. Davis was also a victim and not solely responsible for his actions. A few months later, the Supreme Court of the Philippines commuted his sentence to ten years' imprisonment.[4]

The testimonies given at the trial and the press coverage of the spectacle revealed how the American public at large thought about Filipinas. The proceedings lambasted Inez Davis, the woman at the center of this tropical romance gone bad, as sexually promiscuous, immoral, childlike, and threatening to the health of white men in the islands, dramatizing how Americans understood Filipina women largely through a prism of deviant sexuality and prostitution.[5] The *Manila Times* of June 13 described Mrs. Davis as "notorious" and stated that "her reputation was known to every member of the force both American and Filipino," implying that she had sustained illicit sexual relations with numerous men. The press even misidentified her previous surname as "Torres," before correcting this in their June 14 coverage, and took to calling Inez Davis simply "the woman," "girl," or "bride," further anonymizing her and limiting any sympathy that she might garner (fig. 4.1).[6] While Chester Davis was also undoubtedly excoriated as an immoral man and a degenerate, his public denigration was much more tempered, his poor behavior contingent on outside stressors and factors that drove him to immorality, namely his Filipina wife. In addition to foregrounding Inez's deviance, the press quickly speculated as to Chester's sanity, spreading rumors that he possessed some sort of mental incapacitation such as tropical neurasthenia, a made-up pseudoscientific condition wherein white people lost their vitality in inhospitable climates. This, the newspapers mused, could explain why an otherwise good American man degraded himself with local women and was driven to murder. Reporters dug up details about the circumstances of Inez and Chester's wedding, and these too evoked sympathy for Mr. Davis. Apparently Chester had been threatened by his future

Figure 4.1. The American-run press in Manila portrayed Inez Davis as simultaneously a child and a seductress. The *Manila Times* ran this photo alongside details of her court testimony on its front page with the subheading "Her life of Shame."

mother-in-law to marry Inez (who was then reportedly six months pregnant) or face charges of seduction. This narrative presented Davis as an American who "did right" by marrying his Filipina lover despite his aversion to the union. "The morning of the day they were married," the *Times* reported, "Davis either was or acted as if he was despondent and desperate at the thought of having to marry the girl, and while telling his troubles to Deputy Chief Samuelson he handled his revolver in such a way as to intimate that he might use it on himself."[7]

Moralists, racial segregationists, Filipino elites, and Filipina women in relationships with Americans all had a stake in the Davis murder trial. For those who sought to police dangerous intercourse to a greater degree in the colony, the legal system offered an avenue for recourse, airing hidden immorality and igniting reformist fervor. Though American men faced no formal barriers—like anti-miscegenation laws—to forming sanctioned or unsanctioned relations with Filipinas, the legal system was still a very useful tool for those looking to enforce racial-sexual boundaries and shape the colonial social world. An exploration of legal cases involving interracial intercourse also helps to flesh out the differences in how colonizer and colonized thought about crossing the sexual color line. Filipino newspapers and judges, for example, often had very different things to say about the trials of intercourse than did their American counterparts. Moreover, as interracial relationships with Americans became a day-to-day reality for Filipinas, so too did the consequences of this intercourse: abandonment, abuse, and even murder. Many local women navigated the colonial legal structure to push back against the dangers of such intercourse, and though they often won their cases, their experiences navigating the system overwhelmingly mirrored that of Inez Davis. Though Filipina women and their mixed-race children could seek recompense through the courts, the colonial legal system was one that rested on and amplified American ideas of Filipino inferiority. Once in court, Filipinas often found themselves fighting against charges that they were unfit mothers, prostitutes, or illegitimate members of American families. Though Filipina litigants could win child custody, claim the right to inherit property, or seek spousal support, it often meant subjecting oneself to intense scrutiny and public defamation.

Filipinas' legal efforts highlight their expectations and desires regarding marital outcomes, and their understandings of interracial intercourse, made legible through the legal archives, tell a different narrative from the one described in American colonial recollections and sources. Americans were largely preoccupied with the imagined dangers posed by intercourse, and even those men who engaged in relations with Filipinas shared the racist attitudes of their countrymen and envisioned themselves as pioneers braving the unknown. Filipinas, on the other hand, were concerned with real-world strategic issues concerning socioeconomic stability and the preservation of their families. The cases explored here also underscore the different stakes for Filipinas versus Americans of entering into interracial relations. Unlike most of the men, Filipinas were vulnerable not only to abandonment by spouses but also, in some cases, to meeting their deaths at the hands of American lovers or husbands. These different stakes in interpersonal relationships mirrored the treatment one could expect from the colonial court system, a system that, like the larger imperial umbrella, was rooted in American notions of moral imperative that depended on ideas of Filipino immorality and deviance. Colonial officials, for example, believed Filipinos to be incapable of making moral and just decisions outside American guidance and prevented them from fully leading the high court. Instead, the American-established Philippine Supreme Court was composed of seven justices—four Americans and three Filipinos—all of whom were appointed and approved by the US Senate and president.[8] Despite these institutionalized measures to deny Filipino capabilities and shore up ideas of inferiority, women still used the court system to subvert or challenge American notions of Filipina sexual depravity and point instead to American sexual impunity and abuses toward women.

Despite the pitfalls of the uneven and biased legal system, it was still a site where Filipinos could debate the nature of interracial intercourse in ways that undermined US imperialism. American men could be beholden to their legal marriages and to Filipinas in ways that they did not expect to be. Filipinas found courts receptive to their claims of inheritance and child custody, often to the displeasure of the American claimants on the other side of the courtroom. At the same time, these cases show the limits of the legal system in terms of rendering fair and impartial judgment and punishment. Filipinas were often slandered publicly, and Black Americans on trial received much harsher punishments than their white counterparts. While the court system was one colonial institution that provided the possibility for self-determination and anticolonial outcomes, it was still a system meant to validate and support US interests in the islands.

Crimes of Passion and American Criminality

The legal proceedings of the Davis case created opportunities for extralegal social policing and proselytizing by the American moralist segment in the islands. American residents of Manila were soon writing to the public opinion section of the *Manila Times* to vilify interracial marriages, prompting defenders of these relationships to write in, urging readers not to take the

Davis case as law. While some, like the anonymous Mrs. Lingo Lyon, quickly used the Davis case to argue that miscegenation was a social evil that should be eradicated, others, mostly men married to Filipinas and even one Filipina married to an American, wrote to the paper of their happy interracial marriages.[9] Of the men who wrote to the paper to defend their marriages, however, only one signed with his actual name.[10] The closeted nature of interracial intimacies in Manila prevailed, with even those who would speak out in its defense not wanting to divulge their identities or acknowledge their own relationships in public for fear of being labeled a degenerate. They had good reason to be fearful.

As witness testimony revealed more details in the Davis case, one of Chester Davis's coworkers at the fire station was outed as a "squaw man." Despite not being connected to the crime, Frank W. Schenck, a witness for the defense, found himself on trial for immorality. The defense team asked Schenck, a low-level civil servant, to divulge information regarding his own relations with Filipina women during his testimony as part of an orchestrated strategy to defame Inez Davis. As the paper reported, "Schenck told the court that he had sustained illicit relations with Inez Davis prior to her marriage. . . . During the cross examination Schenck admitted that he was a married man, or, as he put it, 'as good as married under the Spanish law.'" After his testimony, the judge lambasted him and proclaimed, "Men who run with prostitutes are as low as the prostitutes themselves. . . . A man that will associate with prostitutes does not deserve any protection. Men who behave need have no fear of the courts."[11] This self-incriminating testimony not only sealed Schenck's reputation as a degenerate within the colony but also confirmed the suspicion of many Americans. Inez Davis, they concluded, was indeed a lewd woman, or, as stated by the judge, a prostitute. The day after Schenck gave his testimony, his superiors at the fire station suspended him from his job pending a review, on account of "rule 12 of section 6 of the civil service manual, which makes immorality sufficient cause for dismissal from the government service."[12] One month later, after Schenck aided the defense team in making Davis seem more innocent, he was fired.[13] Men like Schenck, who cohabited with Filipinas outside sanctioned marriage and held more vulnerable and expendable government positions, could be made examples of in this way. The social climate of hostility to interracial relations no doubt contributed to why many men chose to keep their queridas a secret. The trial in many ways became a public forum for outing known and suspected transgressors of sexual mores, as other men called to the stand in the Davis trial revealed that they too were guilty of being "immoral" in their nocturnal habits, one witness even pleading with the prosecuting attorney to shield his identity "for the sake of his wife and children."[14]

The Davis scandal offered American moralists a way to extend social policing into the legal realm. The murder of one white man by another was also concrete proof for many in the American community of the dangers of interracial intercourse. White men degrading themselves by having relations with Filipinas was one thing; white men turning on each other to the point of murder over the sexual ownership of Filipina women was the culmination of the myriad dangers of the tropics. It was significant that Davis killed another white man, as the American community was hardly interested in cases with Filipino victims. For example, in 1917, an Irish man murdered his Filipina wife of ten years. James Kelly, the perpetrator of the crime, married Praxedes Velasco in 1907, when he was twenty-five and she was fourteen. By 1917, they had four young children who would go on to shoulder the brunt of Kelly's violent crime. A religious orphanage took in the three daughters, Anita, Mildred, and Irene, while Jim, the second youngest, went to live with one of his mother's relatives. All four would carry the blurry memories of what happened to their parents with them throughout their lives, as well as the stigma of having a father who was a known murderer. Their lives would be so altered by this course of events that in 1978, Margot Pimental, the daughter of Mildred, took it on herself to find out what had transpired that summer of 1917, eventually finding the archival truth of the murder in a dusty Manila library.[15]

According to the scant newspaper coverage, the husband and wife engaged in a "violent quarrel," which was not out of the ordinary for the couple except for the fact that this fight would be their last. Kelly stabbed Velasco seventeen times with a butcher knife and, shortly after, turned himself in to the local authorities in Manila and confessed what he had done.[16] The stabbing murder of a Filipina by a European expat, a man who Americans considered part of the broader Anglo-European "old-timer" community, was of little interest to the expatriate community. There was no media spectacle over the crime, even though it was arguably a more violent murder than the shooting involved in the Davis case. Indeed, Kelly's repeated and violent stabbing of Velasco with a butcher knife was less interesting to the American press than the concurrent debates about whether or not dance halls in Manila were immoral. The disinterest in the Kelly case was also reflected in the open-and-closed nature of his trial and sentencing, as the local Manila court arraigned and sentenced him within the same morning, the day after the murder of his wife. According to the *Manila Times*, the couple had quarreled often for the past several years and separated for brief amounts of time but always reconciled, as neither wanted to give up custody of their four children. During his testimony, Kelly described the day of the murder, saying his wife was irrationally "moody and ill-tempered." Scared she was going to leave him and not return, he sent his children to visit with a nearby relative of hers, believing she would not leave the vicinity without the children in hand. As Kelly confessed, "She then told me she didn't care where I might send the children and even went so far as to say that she wouldn't care a bit even if I threw them into the Pasig river, and that if she went away she would go to some other place. Then she spoke of the loss of her affection for me. This made me mad. I lost my self-control and consciousness, took a knife—and don't know what happened next."[17] Kelly's final characterization of Velasco in his confession, a woman he had murdered just hours before, was as an unfit mother. Her indication that she did not care about the fate of her children, if indeed she had actually made those statements, may have reflected less a lack of concern about her children and more her frustration with her husband and her desperation to leave him. Ultimately, Praxedes Velasco told her husband—according to his testimony—that it was *him* whom she had no more affection for. This, according to Kelly, is what "made him mad" enough to kill her. Kelly pleaded guilty to the charges, and "in view of his confession to the court that he committed the crime while he was enraged, he was given a term of 14 years, eight months and one day in Bilibid prison, and ordered to pay an indemnity of P1,000 to the heirs of the deceased."[18] Despite the nature of the crime as demonstrating more intent to kill (which typically warranted heavier punishment) and being more gruesome (seventeen stab wounds as opposed to a single bullet in the case of Davis), the court and the press treated Kelly's case as if it were less horrific. His sentencing was more lenient, and the public interest was almost inconsequential.

Another difference in the cases of Kelly and Davis, in addition to their disparate sentencing for the crime of murder and the amount of attention paid by the American community, was in who passed their sentences. In the 1907 Davis trial, a white American judge presided and sentenced him to life imprisonment, which the Supreme Court later reduced to ten years. In the 1917 Kelly trial, Vivencio del Rosario, a Filipino judge, presided. Rosario had served in the Philippine civil service since 1902. It is difficult to say why Rosario sentenced Kelly to only fourteen years' imprisonment when the punishment for murder typically ranged from a twenty-year prison sentence to death by execution. Whether he possessed nationalist leanings or cooperated with and accepted American rule is difficult to discern, and the lines between the two sides were often complicated and blurry, especially as it concerned interracial sexual intercourse. While one could attribute the relatively lenient sentencing to Kelly's cooperation and confession, it may have been that Rosario sympathized with Kelly, as he, unlike the many Anglo-Europeans who had sexual relations with Filipinas, actually stayed in the islands and married. On the other hand, given the impunity that generally insulated the white community, the sentence of fourteen years for the charge of homicide might have seemed substantial to the judge, especially when handed down by a Filipino. Rosario also might have wished to not appear overly strict with Kelly, having his own career in mind, as the governor-general (the highest-ranking political office in the islands) and many other high-ranking officials were still white Americans. It could hurt his career if they believed he was guilty of legislating anticolonial nationalism from the court bench or identifying too closely with the Filipina victim. What is clear from the sparse coverage of this trial is that this Filipina murder victim was less important and interesting to the American community than the white male victim in the Davis case.[19] In the end, Kelly served little of his fourteen-year sentence, not because of a pardon or appeal but because he died, likely a result of suicide, shortly after his imprisonment.[20]

While the lives of white Americans like Davis and other Anglo-Europeans like Kelly were often safeguarded even though they had committed murder, other Americans could not rely on their race to protect them. The case of Augustus Hicks, a Black American charged with the murder of his Filipina mistress, demonstrates the discrepancies in legal treatment. Hicks lived in Cotabato, a town on the southern island of Mindanao. Between 1902 and 1907, he and Augustina Sola, a Christian Moro woman, lived together in a common-law marriage. In November 1907, Sola ended the relationship and went to live with a nearby relative. According to court records, she "contracted new relations with another negro named Wallace Current, a corporal in the army," only a few days after her split with Hicks. The characterization of Sola's new relationship as "illicit" and "contracted" highlights that, similar to the example of Inez Davis, the court understood Filipinas in interracial relations largely as prostitutes. One evening in late December, Hicks and a companion called on Sola and Current at the home of Sola's brother-in-law. Hicks and Current argued and then scuffled. At some point, Hicks took out a revolver and fired a single bullet at Sola. She died within the hour. The provincial court found Hicks guilty of murder and sentenced him to death by execution. He appealed this decision to the Supreme Court of the Philippines, but the court upheld the decision.[21]

As with Davis and Kelly, the dissolution of Hick's relationship with a Filipina woman preceded the murder. Unlike these other cases, however, the court sentenced and upheld the death penalty. Hick's crime resembled the murder committed by Davis; both men went to the home of their victim with a firearm and inflicted a single fatal gunshot wound. Davis's whiteness helped cast him as more innocent, victimized by his prurient wife. Hicks did not have the benefit of whiteness working in his favor, and he paid with his life. Even his nationality as an American was not enough to spare him. This was typical of the in-between status of Black Americans in the service of empire in the Philippines. While Black soldiers and civilians in the Philippines found some privileges extended to them that they were not privy to in the segregated United States, access to imperial perks and the same type of impunity as their white counterparts was tenuous at best. For example, many American imperialists argued against sending Black military regiments to the Philippines and claimed such troops would be an immoral influence on impressionable Filipinos. The idea that Black men were immoral and sexually licentious was not a new one, and this notion made its way into imperial rhetoric. For Black troops in the islands, these racial logics meant more frequent rotations and the early withdrawal of regiments from the islands. In 1902, Governor-General Taft organized Black troop removal and rotation, claiming that these units got along "too well with the native women." This over familiarity was apparently "demoralizing" for Filipinos.[22] So while the colonial government often intentionally neglected or even catered to white men having sex with Filipinas (as in the case of military-regulated brothels), it sought heavier regulation of Black sexuality in the islands.[23]

Imperialist fears over Black soldiers and Filipinas forming relationships also emerged out of long-standing ideas about interracial solidarities and the threat that such solidarities might pose for American expansionist efforts. In the years during and after the Civil War in particular, many white Americans came to fear the solidarities formed by Black and Indigenous peoples and what such alliances might mean for US continental expansion. These white American fears flowed into discussions on overseas expansion as well, especially as prominent Black American academics and Africans in the diaspora who had long been critical of Anglo-European colonial expansion, built international anticolonial alliances.[24] Two years before Taft's comments on the dangers posed by Black troops in the Philippines, for example, the 1900 Pan-African Conference—the precursor to the Pan-African Congress, first held in 1919—met in London to organize around issues of Black emancipation and anti-imperialism, disseminating its appeal to world leaders.[25] Anticolonial revolutions led by free and enslaved African populations in places like Haiti were well known to people in the United States, and these movements informed how white Americans largely feared Black emancipation and the role this population might play in empire building. For all these reasons, military officials in the Philippines were constantly preoccupied with desertions and dereliction of duty, especially committed by Black troops.

The possibility of Black soldiers eschewing their military duties had a different meaning attached to it than white soldiers being absent without leave. Even though Black desertion rates in the Philippines were unremarkable, they were often slightly higher than those in white regiments, and fears over Black ex-soldiers' interethnic alliances with Filipinos captivated Americans in the United States, especially as sensationalized stories about David Fagen, a Black deserter turned general in the Philippine fight against the Americans, appeared in the US press in 1900.[26] Though newspaper coverage of Fagen declared him a "vile traitor" and depicted him as inept and lazy, Black soldiers he served with in the Twenty-Fourth Infantry described his poor treatment by white military officials prior to his desertion. Fagen aided revolutionaries in their attempts to persuade other Black soldiers to fight for Philippine independence rather than participate in what many people of color and Filipinos alike understood as a race war. Fagen, who was rumored to have married a Filipina (some accounts point to this relationship as the catalyst for his desertion), managed to evade capture for several years, thoroughly embarrassing his erstwhile American commanding officers and straining the military pacification efforts on the islands. American audiences read about Fagen with rapt attention as the press sensationalized his exploits in the Philippines as well as his elusiveness. Some even reported that he had made his way back to the United States and was spotted in California. Though even Black newspapers lamented Fagen's betrayal of the US Army, they, like other newspapers in the United States, assumed that Fagen was moved to join the revolutionary Filipino army out of a sense of shared racial oppression. Fagen's ultimate fate is still a question of debate. When his Filipino regiment surrendered to the Americans, Fagen was not among them, and his revolutionary compatriots refused to give him up because they did not believe he would be treated justly as a war prisoner but rather be summarily executed. They were right to fear this, as the US military soon offered up a $600 reward for the capture of David Fagen, dead or alive.[27] Eventually, in November 1901, a Filipino hunter brought a decomposed head and some of Fagan's personal effects to US authorities, and the US military quickly declared their final victory over the American "traitor." Contemporary scholars, however, speculate that the military speedily closed the Fagen incident as a way to quash the public's attention on the failure of US officials to capture him. Sightings of Fagen continued well after he was declared dead.[28]

The transnational obsession with David Fagen was symptomatic of how Black desertion particularly unnerved and troubled US military officials. Black military units and much of the Black community in general—both in the United States and in the Philippines—expressed their growing discontent with all forms of American racism in the aftermath of the Cuban campaign. Black troops returning from the Caribbean often found that the possibilities for fuller American citizenship through martial masculinity did not materialize in the ways that they had hoped. Violence erupted frequently between whites and Black regulars in Texas, Tennessee, Georgia, and California. These incidents were well known to military officials, as was the growing anti-imperial rhetoric and critique among Black regulars in the press. White Americans so feared rebellion from the segregated troops that they suspected any Black soldiers who expressed even marginal sympathy with the Filipinos of aiding the revolutionaries. And even while actual troop desertion was relatively low and defection to the Filipino cause was even lower, it was Black rebels who faced the harshest punishments for aiding Filipino revolutionaries. For example, of the twenty defectors (both Black and white) who were sentenced to death in the Philippines in 1901, all but two had their sentences reduced by then president Theodore Roosevelt. The two who did not receive commuted sentences and paid with their lives were Black soldiers formerly of the Ninth Cavalry.[29] Ultimately, the largely imagined problem of armed Black resistance in the occupied Philippines was more or less resolved with the removal of the four segregated regiments from the islands in 1902.[30] While US military officials treated Black defection in the Philippines very seriously, the public face of this concern diminished and dismissed Black anti-imperial, antiracist sentiments and revolutionary participation as unpatriotic, bumbling, or symptomatic of Black immorality in general.

Recently, scholars have asserted that Black colonists in the Philippines benefited from the more relaxed racial attitudes necessary in the colony due largely to Filipino demands for socioracial equality. While it is true that many Black civilians in the Philippines, including teachers, missionaries, and entrepreneurs, could access resources and positions mostly out of reach to them in the United States, the way that the colonial government treated Black troops they believed susceptible to rebellion highlights the limited nature of such racial flexibility in the Philippines. As Cynthia Marasigan points out in her important study of Black soldiers and colonists in the Philippines, racism was deeply felt by these populations in the islands. Many Black settlers who married Filipinas and chose to stay in the islands, for example, often opted to live outside areas with large white American populations and mostly interacted with Filipinos.[31]

Taft's allusion to interethnic romances between Black soldiers and Filipinas as "demoralizing" for the new colonial wards must be understood as part of the broader historical and contemporary issues that threatened the stability of US imperialism in the islands. Despite not warranting much attention by the moral police in the same way that white-Filipino intercourse did, white imperialists understood Black-Filipino relations as posing a different sort of danger. Though white men who engaged in interracial intercourse were accused by their countrymen of "going native" or "being Filipinist," they were hardly thought of as susceptible to the revolutionary and anticolonial aspirations of their Black counterparts. Moralists deemed white-Filipino intercourse unsavory and detrimental to moral and physical health but understood Black-Filipino intercourse as seditious and treasonous.[32] In proclamations such as Taft's and the military measures to heavily regulate Black troop movement in the islands, US officials obscured the history of interethnic solidarity and transnational/transpacific Black resistance to racial and imperial violence, relying on the stable and enduring ideas of Black immorality and sexual licentiousness to do so. The court sentencing of Augustus Hicks reflected the broader Black experience under US empire. Unlike the cases of Davis and Kelly, in which white American men got away with murder, Hicks paid with his life.

The case of Captain Boss Reese, an American military commander of the Philippine Scouts, further reveals the contours of white sexual impunity in the colony. In late 1910, Reese was accused of sexually molesting and abusing numerous Filipino scouts under his charge. Testimonies from the courts-martial trials accuse Reese of sodomy from as early as 1901, although a bulk of the charges brought against him were for acts committed in 1909. In the early months of the Reese scandal, American military officials tried to protect Reese at every step, hoping to stamp out the issue before it even began, and they were largely successful. The US and Philippines presses never caught wind of the same-sex sodomy details of the trial, and outlets only reported vaguely on his drunk and disorderly conduct and his "brutal treatment" of subordinates. Military higher-ups kept the story secreted away because of how damaging the evidence mounting against Reese was, both for the army and for the colonial government, which justified its presence in the islands by proclaiming moral authority and benevolent intent. Even when

Reese attempted to resign after his accusers brought the first charges, his superiors did not accept it, seeing a hasty resignation as essentially an admission of guilt. Reese instead went to trial, where many of his colleagues attempted to prove that the charges of "unnatural" and dangerous intercourse were incompatible with what they understood as his "normal" masculinity. This approach initially worked, and the military court dismissed the charges of sexual abuse and only convicted Reese of drunk and disorderly conduct. While military authorities protected Reese, they silenced those who brought the charges of sodomy and sexual abuse in the first place. First Lieutenant J. I. Thorne, a military doctor who brought charges and testified to hearing sexual "voices and groans" coming from Reese's quarters and seeing Filipino scouts leave afterward, was honorably discharged.[33] Captain Julian De Court also brought charges against Reese. De Court first joined the New York Infantry Volunteers in 1898 and by 1901 was a commissioned officer with the Philippine Scouts. After the trial, he was court-martialed by US military authorities for bringing false accusations and convicted of insubordination.[34]

Nevertheless, Filipino scouts and other concerned American military personnel did not heed the message to stay silent and not make trouble, and they continued to accuse Reese of sexual abuse. In August 1911, almost a year after the first court-martial trial, he was once again charged, this time with conduct unbecoming an officer and a gentleman, a catchall violation that covered and continues to encompass sexual crimes including rape and sodomy.[35] With the testimonies of numerous Filipino soldiers and male domestic staff who served under Reese, the court found him guilty of seven out of nine specifications of conduct unbecoming, in addition to multiple specifications of drunkenness on duty, disobeying orders, and "conduct to the prejudice of good order and military duty." The court recommended dismissal from the military and fifteen years of confinement and hard labor, but Reese never served out this sentence.[36] The military sent its findings and recommended punishment to the White House for approval, and though every other guilty verdict was approved, the seven guilty verdicts for sodomy (under Article of War 61, dealing with conduct unbecoming an officer and a gentleman) were not. In addition, the executive government did not approve the hard labor and prison sentence, approving only dismissal from the military. Reese ceased to be an officer of the army on September 10, 1912.[37] Barely a month later, on October 6, Reese was dead.[38] He died in the Philippines, where he was buried as a civilian.

The fact that military officers (successfully) covered up the dangerous intercourse at the heart of the trial and that the executive branch of the US government refuted and overturned the charges of sodomy points to how Americans understood the "unnatural" dangerous intercourse at the heart of the trials as particularly threatening to the colonial endeavor in the islands. Unlike the ubiquitous dangerous intercourse between American men and Filipina women that was considered "normal" and tolerated to the extent that it was not legislated against, Reese's actions—in the eyes of colonial state officials—could not serve the professed imperial message of socioracial equality (as interracial marriage often did), nor could they support the claim of moral ascendancy that justified imperialist claims to the islands. That the crimes were perpetrated by a military authority, someone who was supposed to embody heteronormative imperial masculinity, made it all the worse. At the same time, however, the outcome of the military trials and the discourse produced around them point to the ways in which Reese's acts were not as far out of line with US claims of moral authority and superiority as they might initially seem. As cultural studies scholar Victor Mendoza's thorough account of the Reese saga highlights, the US military was, at this point, largely unprepared for and inexperienced in dealing with criminal charges regarding same-sex intercourse within the ranks. The crime of sodomy came and went from the Articles of War that governed the US military in the first quarter of the twentieth century as revisions and amendments were made, reflecting the extent to which categories of difference relating to sexuality were still being debated and formed. During the trials, the American officials attempted to make sense of Reese and his crimes, and his manliness and "normalness" were destabilized by the charges of his "unnatural" acts. Although the charges against Reese derailed his identity as a manly and respected military officer, this identity was continuously being set back into place by the stronger and more stable assertion of Filipino deviance and immorality.

In fact, with the general public kept out of the proceedings, the military trials were less a vehicle for reckoning with Reese's crimes and more a platform for military and colonial officials to solidify their notions of Filipino perversion. Though the Scouts and others directed their accusations at Reese, American military officers and court officials treated the Filipinos as if *they* were the ones on trial. Ultimately, the American court of opinion understood the Filipinos embroiled in the trials as unequivocally at fault, liable for the actions of their American commanding officer. As the court documents from the 1910 trial reveal, military prosecutors wanted Filipinos punished regardless of the sentence Reese received; if he was found innocent, Filipino accusers would be court-martialed for presenting false accusations and evidence, and if he was found guilty, Filipino accusers would be similarly disciplined for allowing Reese to use them "as women."[39] The logic was clear: Filipinos were either scheming liars or effeminate "degenerates." The indictment of Filipinos as unnatural and deviant was nothing new for Americans and very much in line with the logics of deviant gender and sexuality that were at the core of the occupation. That Reese's abuse was directed at Filipino men versus women was thus not necessarily at odds with imperial notions of native sexual availability or American manliness. While Americans went back and forth debating the nature of Reese's sexuality—perverse or normal—and though he was found guilty of sodomy in his second court-martial trial, in the end it was his "normal" masculinity and sexuality that stuck. American ideas of Filipino sexual degeneracy undergirded the Reese trials, just as they undergirded the more numerous interracial relations occurring between American men and Filipinas and the larger project of colonial occupation more broadly.

The similarities and differences between the Reese case and the aforementioned civilian court cases highlight several important distinctions regarding interracial intercourse in the colonial Philippines. Most obviously, these cases demonstrate how white men in the islands could count on clemency and preservation from the worst consequences of their criminal behavior. All these cases threatened the projection of US moral superiority, and in each sex-inflected scandal, the danger to white people and white authority was tempered by the bedrock fantasies about Filipino sexual proclivities and availability. The entrenched American belief in Filipino deviance/immorality could even lead to absolution, in the case of Davis, who got away with murder. All these cases speak to the cheapness of Filipino life and dignity in the American colonial state, from the supposed disreputability of Filipinas like Inez Davis, for whom aspirations toward marital "respectability" were impossible, and Praxedes Velasco, whose life was adjudged to be worth less than the lowest typical punishment for murder, to the worthlessness of Filipino grievances against sexual violence.

The differences in each of these cases also allow the cleavages of the American colonial social order to more fully emerge. Moralists, colonial officials, and well-to-do Americans in the Philippines considered low-ranking American civilians, like Davis, Schenck, and Kelly, more or less expendable in the imperial pecking order. While their whiteness insulated them from harsher judgment and stricter punishments, they were confirmed miscegenists and degenerates to their American compatriots who deplored interracial intercourse. Their attachment to and close association with Filipina women—whether or not those relations were based in equity and mutual satisfaction largely made no difference—marked them as outside respectable American society. Americans lamented the fact that their countrymen made permanent or semipermanent commitments to Filipinas; the fact that they killed over these associations was unthinkable. Augustus Hicks was even more disposable. As a Black American in the colony, Hicks could not rely on public sentiment and whiteness to mitigate his case. His Filipina ex-lover and victim, like Inez Davis, was depicted by the court as a prostitute. White Americans and even the elite Filipinos that had joined the ranks of the US-led Supreme Court understood Hick's life as simply more immoral.

The case of Captain Boss Reese, in comparison, involved a respected and relatively more powerful imperial agent, and though his engagement in deviant dangerous intercourse was potentially more explosive for the stability of US empire, Americans who knew of his crimes understood him more as a degenerate rather than a "squaw man." In the eyes of most other Americans, Davis, Kelly, and Hicks had all "gone native," attempting to possess and form long-term liaisons with Filipinas that approximated heteronormative courtship/family practices. Though contested by moralists and white supremacists, there was privileged space for these relations in the colony, similar to how dangerous intercourse had been a disdained but integral part of domestic settler colonialism. There was likewise privileged space for those colonialists who had informal relations with Filipinas in the sexual economy. American officials, especially within the military, had more tolerance for white men engaging in sex with prostitutes than the act of "going native" via intermarriage or engaging in longer-term relations. Though Reese's sexual abuse of Filipino bodies was in line with wider-scale imperial practices such as rape and prostitution, American officials deemed it more dangerous in many respects because it called American martial masculinity into question, a cornerstone of US imperial identity and key justifying logic of the occupation. The discourse surrounding his case, for example, reflects that American officials were not just concerned with understanding Reese's sexual habits but also worried about the moral reputation of the US regime in the face of growing demands from Filipino nationalists, who, as officials described in their correspondence related to Reese, were "daily becoming more loud-mouthed and blatant in their demands" for independence.[40] Colonialists also had the very practical interest of keeping the colonial Filipino army functional, as many Scout captains threatened to resign en masse if Reese was not dismissed from military service.[41]

The disciplining of Anglo-American men in the colonial Philippines reveals the contours of what Mendoza terms "colonianormativity," or the "sometimes coercive, sometimes mild regulation of bodies, populations, identities, comportment, acts, behavior, affects, attachments, and desires into modern racial, sexual, and gendered conventions that accorded with the optimization of compulsory heterosexuality, white supremacy, and overseas colonial expansion."[42] All the cases of dangerous intercourse examined here both supported (and were supported by) and troubled the colonianormative imperial project in the islands. Reese's violent engagement with Filipino Scouts, and the relations of Davis and Kelly with their Filipina wives, were very much in line with the imperial logics of Filipino immorality and sexual availability. Anglo-American men's sexual access to Filipino men and women was in many ways a heavily advertised perk of empire, predicated on notions of white masculine superiority and compulsory heterosexuality. Even the relationship of Augustus Hicks toed the line of colonianormativity, as Black troops in the islands who participated in the militarized occupation found some of the perks of white imperial masculinity available to them, especially in the form of access to local women. At the same time, these highly visible criminal cases of dangerous intercourse (or semi-visible in the case of Reese) highlight the precarity of colonianormativity as an ideal that had to be constantly reaffirmed and upheld through disciplining both Americans and Filipinos. The threats emanating from dangerous intercourse were numerous, from the semi-incorporation of lascivious Filipinas into white families to the possibility of queer "unnatural" white sexuality. When the circumstances of dangerous intercourse spilled into the criminal, court outcomes were damage control for the preservation of Anglo-American empire in the islands.

Reports of American abuses involving Filipina wives and mistresses were common features of daily life across the archipelago, from Manila to Mindanao.[43] Like the cases detailed here, American newspapers shored up ideas of nonwhite sexual deviance in their coverage of American abuses. All these cases point to the limits of colonial justice, especially in cases dealing with dangerous intercourse, in which Filipino immorality and criminality were often the baseline for how Americans understood the crimes committed by their countrymen. The design of the colonial courts affirmed this assumption. In such a scheme, white American culpability could never be fully acknowledged or realized. Though the colonial courts did not often demand answerability from white Americans, they were not necessarily void of the possibility of recourse. Filipina women and mixed-race American mestizos, for example, frequently squared off against a legal system that was skewed against them to advance their own agendas and desires. Against the odds, they often won.

Women Take On the Courts

In August 1935, *Woman's World* magazine offered legal advice to Filipinas in their regularly featured advice column titled "The Filipina and the Law." Written by Nieves Umali Makalinao, an affiliate of the College of Law at the University of the Philippines, the public legal forum mostly offered advice dealing with family law. The readership, it seems, hungered for an informal education about the legal system and their rights within it, an education that could help them navigate such issues as abandonment by a spouse, rights to conjugal versus paraphernal property (owned by both spouses jointly vs. owned by the wife only), and divorce. In her August 1935 column, the author included a scenario involving an interracial marriage between a Filipina and a US Navy man. Makalinao likely based the advice column's hypotheticals on her real-life experiences dealing with common types of family law cases or on questions sent to the magazine from its readership. Either way, the overrepresentation of family law scenarios reveals how Filipinas actively looked for legal pathways to better their domestic situations for themselves and their children, especially when they felt that they had been wronged by spouses.

The hypothetical case involving interracial intercourse laid out a story familiar to women in the Philippines in 1935 as well as today. As the case study goes, Josefina, a Filipina, is abandoned by her American military spouse. The nameless husband apparently heard "bad rumors" about his wife's character, rumors that caused him to abandon his wife and kids. The rumors mentioned in the story likely alluded to sexual immorality or infidelity, vices that Americans commonly associated with Filipinas, especially those who engaged in interracial intercourse. Makalinao's narrative dismissed the "bad rumors" as false and baseless, pointing instead to the American husband's irrationality. His abandonment of Josefina, the story continued, was symptomatic of his tendency to act "without listening to reason." He did not heed Josefina's insistence that "there [was] no truth" in the rumors regarding immorality, and instead of listening to his wife, he moved out, although he continued to send a small amount of money (about 50 pesos per month) to Josefina for support. The question the fictional Josefina posed to the advice column was whether there was any legal way to compel her husband to return to her and their two daughters. Makalinao informed her readership that unfortunately there was no such law. She did, however, suggest a different and practical course of action to those who might find themselves in Josefina's shoes: "Josefina still has a remedy and that is to bring an action for support against her husband. By support is understood all that is necessary for food, shelter, clothing and medical attendance. . . . Certainly the amount of fifty pesos does not satisfy to the extent of the term *support* inasmuch as the husband earns more than two hundred pesos. The two daughters being minors, are entitled to education, included in the term support, so they can continue their studies and maintain their former social standing."[44] With this advice, Makalinao made clear what all the Josefinas reading the column likely already understood: marriage was a contract recognized by the law that entitled wives and children to socioeconomic support. Though Josefina ideally wanted her American spouse to be present, sharing in the duties of raising their children, any additional support obtained through legal pathways was welcome.

The dubiousness of the colonial legal system did not prevent Filipinas from fighting for what they believed they deserved or were entitled to. Some women fought transpacific court battles to mend the damage done to their esteem and reputations by abusive American spouses, while others took their claims for autonomy and self-determination all the way to the Supreme Court of the Philippines. The cross section of cases presented here demonstrate how Filipinas refused to let American spouses and lovers impugn their character and rob them of their children and resources. Equal treatment before the law may have been impossible, but this did not prevent women from challenging popular American notions about Filipina sexuality and deviance and, in doing so, calling into question the moral imperative of US imperialism in the islands.

Filipinas who participated in trials of intercourse often found themselves there because others rejected their legitimacy. Because American ideas of Filipina/o promiscuity and immorality were foundational not just for the courts but for the entire colonial project in the islands, legal cases between Americans and Filipinas in matters of dangerous intercourse most often operated from the assumption that Filipinas and mixed-race children were illegitimate claimants. From the legitimacy of their marriages to their legitimacy as next of kin to the legitimacy of their having custody over their own children, illegitimacy framed Filipina and American mestizo experiences in the colonial courts. Even though trial outcomes often favored Filipinas, their experiences nonetheless reflected how colonial courts understood them as illegible claimants of or to American families. The difficult position of Filipina litigants stemmed not only from how most Americans regarded them but also from the typically tenuous and informal nature of many of their relations. It was the rule rather than the exception, for example, that most American men cohabitated with, rather than legally wed, Filipinas. As one American lawyer in Manila recounted in his memoirs, many American men in long-term relations with Filipinas sought out legal marriage only in their old age. Old-timers could ensure that their surviving spouses and children would inherit pensions and assets even if the guarantee was secured from their deathbeds, although many Filipinas did not even have this safeguard.[45] The legal rights of Filipinas in informal relations were already precarious without the additional burden of being seen as unfit mothers and spouses. For women like Maria Bancosta, these factors co-conspired in ways that threatened to take her daughter away.

In 1923, Maria Bancosta filed a petition with a lower court in the large province of Cavite, just southwest of Manila, for the custody of her daughter, Ina Bancosta. At the time of the petition, Ina lived with an American, P. C. Due, and his wife. Due was not Ina's father—at least, he did not present himself to be so to the court. Rather, Due claimed he acted on the authority of Ina's father, Jack Hamilton, a shipkeeper for the US Navy. Hamilton was not present at the lower court trial brought by Maria Bancosta because he was ill and convalescing in Baguio, which was several days' travel north. Because Ina's father was not present to claim custody, and the only proof of paternity was the testimony of P. C. Due on behalf of Hamilton, the court found in favor of the only verifiable birth parent present, Maria Bancosta. Due brought Ina to the local sheriff, who then delivered the child to her mother. It was, however, a short-lived victory for Bancosta, as just three months later Due appealed the decision to the Supreme Court of the Philippines on the grounds that he had not had sufficient time to collect evidence of paternity or other testimony from Jack Hamilton. In the Supreme Court trial, Due's primary evidence was a letter supposedly written by Hamilton that outlined his wishes for the custody of his daughter, including placing her in Due's care. If Due did not want to care for the girl, Hamilton asked that she be "[turned] over to the Society for Protection of American Mestizas" in order to ensure her "a better future than she could possibly have if placed in the care of her mother."[46] One section of the letter mentioned Hamilton's inheritance in the United States, which Ina Bancosta would inherit in the event of his death. Due made sure to emphasize this inheritance as proof of Hamilton's paternity.

Although the letter only alluded to the mother's unfitness, stating that Ina would be better off in an orphanage, Due took it on himself to injure Bancosta's reputation before the court in the hope of strengthening his claims. According to the court report, he claimed Bancosta was immoral and sexually licentious, "living maritally" with another man and already responsible for five other children in addition to the girl in question, all apparently from different men. He asked the high court's permission to depose several witnesses who could testify to Maria Bancosta's behavior, which he claimed was "short of being exemplary." By accusing Bancosta of sexual impropriety and prostitution, Due used a successful strategy that aligned largely with how many Americans already understood Filipinas in mixed relationships. In this case, however, Due's charges fell flat and the court denied his request for additional depositions. While the court agreed to hear his charges of sexual immorality, the justices considered the issue of paternity to be the more crucial factor in the case, superseding considerations of Maria Bancosta's fitness as a caretaker. They ordered Due to obtain a deposition from Jack Hamilton to give further evidence that he was Ina Bancosta's father rather than gather witnesses who might speak to Bancosta's supposed immorality. This, Due reported, was impossible, as Hamilton died shortly after the first trial with the lower Cavite court. Without the additional testimony from the supposed father, and without evidence to substantiate Due's accusations of immorality, the court affirmed the original findings of the lower court and granted custody to Bancosta. Unlike the parental claim of Hamilton, Bancosta's claims over her daughter were "a fact established, and not disputed by the parties."[47]

P. C. Due's intense investment in the custody battle of Ina Bancosta speaks not only to the depths of American belief in Filipina sexual licentiousness but also to how Americans easily fell back on this trope in order to access sociolegal protections unavailable to their colonized wards. Despite Hamilton's association with Bancosta, an accused prostitute, his fitness as a father met no challenge in the available court records. Even though he requested that his daughter be put in the custody of the colonial state, in an orphanage that, according to historical records, did not even exist, the court based his fitness as a father solely on his ability to produce offspring, while it based Bancosta's fitness as a mother on her sexual past, present, and future. The court's willingness to entertain Due's charges of sexual immorality affirm this. In filing a petition for the issuance of a writ of habeas corpus for the safe return of her daughter, Maria Bancosta rejected the illegitimacy ascribed to her. Indeed, in filing a habeas corpus case, a type of case reserved for unlawful imprisonments and detention,

Bancosta pointed instead to the illegality of Hamilton and Due's actions in taking her daughter away from her. Despite the efforts of Americans to portray intermarried Filipinas as unfit wives and mothers, most, like Maria Bancosta, did not abandon their mixed-race children (unlike their American husbands), as evidenced by the relatively small number of American mestizo wards in orphanages as compared with the overall numbers of American mestizos enumerated in census records.[48] Rather, they fought, as Bancosta did, to keep their families intact while demanding accountability from delinquent husbands. It was then, as it is now, well within their rights to do so.

The same presumed illegitimacy that marked Filipinas as being outside legal American families also extended to their mixed-race children. American plaintiffs often challenged the legitimacy of American mestizos as legal heirs and inheritors of white wealth and property. Even when mestizos were acknowledged by their American parents, which was a rarity in the colonial period, their legitimacy was still unstable and open to scrutiny and examination. Like their Filipina mothers, American mestizos defended themselves in the courts as their erstwhile distant relations attempted to strip them not only of material wealth but also of their membership to white American families. Like their mothers, mestizos often found success in the courts, as in the case of the Johnson-Ibañez family. On February 4, 1916, in Manila, Emil Johnson, a naturalized American citizen, passed away, leaving behind a large Filipino family. Luckily, Johnson left a will to provide for them in the event of his death. Though Philippine law typically required three witnesses to cosign wills, the local Manila court deemed Johnson's two witnesses as sufficient to advance the will to probate, the legal reasoning being that the documents met all the requirements for probate under the laws of Illinois, his state of citizenship in the United States. With the will approved and admitted to probate on March 16, 1916, the court began the process of parceling out the estate to the named benefactors. The five Johnson-Ibañez siblings were set to inherit a majority of the assets in the will without a hitch until a white American half sibling, Ebba Ingeborg Johnson, challenged the validity and probate of the will a few months after the court declared it legal. Ebba's initial petition to the court to invalidate the will was denied in February 1917, but she was not deterred. She brought her case before the Supreme Court of the Philippines shortly thereafter, and the case went to trial. According to the court record, Ebba was born a few months after her father, Emil Johnson, left for the Philippines in the summer of 1898 as a member of the US Army. In her father's absence, she was raised by her American mother in Chicago and later by her paternal grandparents in their home country of

Sweden. In 1902, Ebba's mother, Rosalie Johnson, obtained a divorce from an Illinois circuit court on the grounds of desertion, as Emil Johnson never returned to his family in Chicago after his discharge from the army. Like so many others, the young soldier had found other opportunities in the Philippines, and though he visited Ebba in Sweden at least once in early 1903, he already had another child on the way in Manila. The evidence presented in the summary of the trial points to limited if any contact between Emil and Ebba after this visit.

Johnson returned to the Philippines after seeing his daughter in Sweden, and a few months later, in May 1903, his mestizo daughter Mercedes was baptized, followed by another daughter Encarnacion in 1906, and a son named Victor in 1907. Johnson's Filipina wife, Alejandra Ibañez, was likely part of the reason he chose to remain in the islands following his discharge from the military. He had two other children, Eleonor and Alberto, with a Filipina named Simeona Ibañez, who was likely his wife's sister or other close relation. While his will named Ebba as a beneficiary, set to receive 5,000 pesos of his 231,800 peso estate, this amount was modest in comparison to the amounts he left to his Filipino family. He left Alejandra and Simeona, for example, monthly allowances of 75 pesos and 65 pesos each, respectively, on the condition that they remain single. Considering that Emil Johnson was only thirty-nine years old upon his death, and that Alejandra and Simeona were likely many years younger than him, a monthly allowance over the course of several decades would amount to more than 5,000 pesos. Additionally, Johnson left the remaining half of the 231,800 peso estate (after the shares willed to his brother and parents in Sweden) to his five mestizo children. According to the Supreme Court, if Ebba successfully invalidated the probate of her father's will, the estate would enter intestate administration, or administration where there is no will present to delimit the wishes of the deceased. The court recognized that this would "prepare the way for the establishment of the claim of the petitioner as the sole legitimate heir of her father."[49] Ebba, the court surmised, was trying to claim the entire inheritance as her own and, in the process, pauperize her not-so-distant relations.

Without any court transcripts, it is difficult to know the trial's exact contours, but the recognition of the judges that Ebba Johnson wanted to be the sole beneficiary implies that her father may not have been legally married to Alejandra Ibañez, as was common of so many mixed "marriages" in the colonial Philippines. In typical intestate cases without legally approved wills, inheritances usually passed to legal spouses or children from legal marriages. While the lawyers for Ibañez identified her as Johnson's wife, naming her as

Alejandra Ibañez de Johnson, and the will regarded her as his (primary) wife, nowhere in the record did the court refer to her as his legal wife. Instead, the court summary stated only that "he appears to have entered into marital relations" with her. The rest of the summary refers to her as Alejandra Ibañez, without the Johnson surname. Because the court's task was to determine whether or not the lower court was correct in their validation of the will based on Illinois law, considerations of the validity of the marriage were outside the scope of the case. Nevertheless, the Johnson–Ibañez family's legality was the underlying current of the proceedings. Even though the marital status between Emil and Alejandra Johnson should have had no bearing on the trial, Ebba's petition to the Supreme Court was grounded in the widely accepted notion that Filipinas and their mixed children were impossible members of American families. Thus, even though the Johnson–Ibañez family was fortunate that Emil acknowledged them and made legal provisions for their care, the prevailing thoughts and opinions of other Americans regarding who was fit for incorporation (into both the personal and the political family) had the potential to dramatically shift their fortunes. In other words, even with the protection of white fathers, dangerous intercourse still meant dangerous precarity for Filipino families. Regardless of whether or not Johnson and Ibañez were legally married, Ebba Johnson's petition, if successful, would have triggered an investigation into their domestic arrangement. This is likely what she hoped would happen. Ebba couched her goal of becoming the sole inheritor in the presumed illegitimacy of Filipinas and mestizo children, a move that highlights the experiences of many Filipina women and children involved in trials of intercourse. Their positions were flimsy and always in danger of being challenged by outsiders, especially by those whom they might otherwise count as family. Ultimately, however, the high court found no fault in the lower court's approval of the will to probate. The judges agreed that the will of Emil Johnson, a naturalized citizen of Illinois, was in accordance with state laws. In an outcome uncharacteristic for most Filipino families left in the islands, the Filipinas and mestizos in this case inherited the majority of monetary assets, as well as shares in Johnson's lucrative rope manufacturing business.

Without a legal will, legitimacy as heirs was almost impossible, even with substantial corroborating evidence. In 1936, Mike and Violetta Gitt, the mestizo children of American William Gitt and Filipina Juana Malayto, enjoyed a short-lived victory in a lower Philippine court but were not as fortunate in the final outcome of their litigation as the Johnson–Ibañez family. Mike and Violetta wanted the court to recognize them as the legal heirs of their father, William Gitt, who passed away in 1916. The lower court found in their favor and named them the sole heirs of the deceased, set to inherit his shares in the Philippine-based Benguet Consolidated Mining Company. Many American colonists, like William Gitt, were quick to invest in the extractive gold mining developments in the Philippines, and the lure of mineral wealth anchored expatriates in the islands. After Gitt died in 1916, Kathleen Grace Gitt, the legal American wife of William Gitt, inherited the mining stock as the sole beneficiary of his estate. It is unclear if Kathleen knew of Mike and Violetta when she took possession of the mining stock, but she certainly did by 1936, when in response to a case brought by the Gitt siblings she claimed that they were not acknowledged children of the deceased and therefore could not inherit. When the lower court decided that Mike and Violetta were the sole heirs, she brought her own case before the Supreme Court of the Philippines.

Kathleen Gitt and Mike and Violetta Gitt clearly had competing interests in whether or not the latter two were indeed the acknowledged children of the deceased. According to the Supreme Court summary of the initial trial, William Gitt and Juana Malayto lived together "as husband and wife" for six years in the Philippines, although they never formalized their relations and remained unmarried. Mike was born in 1905, and Violetta in 1907. In 1908, William left Juana and the children to legally marry Kathleen Gitt. Over the next five years, William sent money to Juana, Mike, and Violetta, even after he left the Philippines to reside in the US territory of Hawai'i. Upon his departure from the Philippines, William entrusted an American business associate still residing in the colony to continue allocating money to his abandoned family. When William passed away in 1916, Mike was eleven years old and Violetta was nine. Twenty years later, Mike and Violetta Gitt continued to grapple with their marginal legal status as abandoned American mestizos.

In her appeal, Kathleen Gitt sought the overturn of the lower court ruling on the grounds that the Gitt siblings had not proven themselves to be the acknowledged children of the deceased, even if the court conceded that they were, in fact, his children. The Philippine Civil Code made the distinction that not all "natural" children were necessarily "acknowledged" children. The latter required proof in the form of birth certificates, a will, or some other legal document. Thus, for children to inherit property from their parents, they needed proof that the named parents legally claimed them as their own, an act that few American fathers of mestizo children did. Though the name "William Get" was listed as the father on Violeta's birth certificate, Gitt's corroborating signature was absent, meaning that the document was not sufficient to prove acknowledgment. Further, Kathleen Gitt's lawyers asserted that if the siblings wanted to claim the legal status as acknowledged children of William Gitt, who died when they were minors, they should have filed a petition within four years after turning twenty-one, the legal age of majority, as laid out in article 137 of the Civil Code of the Philippines. Since both siblings were past the four-year limit—Mike was thirty-one at the time of the first trial and Violeta was twenty-nine—there was no legal way for them to be recognized as acknowledged children. The deadline for the legal system to acknowledge what the Gitt siblings had always known but neglected to formalize was in 1930 for Mike and 1932 Violetta, years before they brought their claim. It is likely the siblings only learned of the inheritance after the deadline. The supreme court ultimately found in favor of Kathleen Gitt. In its majority opinion, the justices declared that the lower court "really erred in declaring Mike Gitt and his sister Violeta Gitt heirs."[50]

Despite the clear stipulations of the civil code, the lower court had ruled in favor of Mike and Violeta and declared them the sole legal heirs, even though being an heir automatically necessitated being an acknowledged child. Understanding how and why the lower court "really erred" in their decision, considering that the litigants had presented little legal evidence that their father legally recognized them, partly falls within the realm of speculation. Mike and Violeta did not ask to be recognized as the acknowledged children of the deceased in their original 1936 petition but rather to be recognized as heirs. It is plausible that they were aware that the statute of limitations on filing for legal acknowledgment had passed and did not want to draw attention to this fact when they brought their inheritance suit. In any case, when the lower court ruled that they were the sole heirs of William Gitt, it was also (purposely or unwittingly) by default, granting Mike and Violeta the status of acknowledged children. Mike and Violeta only had their narrative of their father financially supporting them and their (unsigned) birth certificates, not enough to prove recognition from a parent. At most, the Supreme Court surmised, this evidence might have been enough to compel the father to recognize them were he alive but did not satisfy the stipulations of the civil code. Was the lower court attempting to remedy some of the social injustices and hardships that the Gitt children had endured? Given that the inheritance was stock in Philippine gold mines—gold that supplied the US treasury and carried the stigma of American greed since the first decade of the US occupation—perhaps the judges wanted to see some of that wealth, upon the birth of the commonwealth period, put back into the hands of Filipinos.[51] Perhaps the lower court simply failed to consult article 137 and overlooked the fact that the siblings had no proof of acknowledgment, as the petition was for the purpose of being named legal heirs, not a paternity suit.

I am inclined to think that the lower court was not guilty of gross negligence, as the Supreme Court justices asserted, but was perhaps reasserting its own power in a period when formal US control over the nation was waning and hopes for self-rule were high. Finding in favor of the Gitt siblings benefited two out of the thousands of mestizo children whom Americans had abandoned, and might best be understood as a way that lower court judges were refusing imperialism and white supremacy in a nation on the eve of independence.[52] The dissenting opinion of two out of the five Supreme Court justices that heard the case supports this inclination and highlights how Filipino public servants across the spectrum, from lower court circuit judges to justices of the highest court in the land, attempted to steer the nation in a different direction from the one laid out by the previous American occupiers, a direction that benefited Filipinos. "There is not the least doubt that the applicants-appellees Mike Gitt and Violeta Gitt have been in continuous possession of the status of natural children of the deceased William Gitt," wrote Justice Manuel Moran. In his dissent, an impassioned Moran described how the Supreme Court had in the past handed down opinions stating that a person claiming to be an acknowledged natural child need not present an application to be legally declared so. Moran's description of children impoverished through no action of their own gestures to the realities of most American mestizos. As the appellees were themselves American mestizos, Moran undoubtedly reflected on those broader realities and how they resulted from the decades of US control in the islands in penning his opposing opinion:

> The provisions of law relative to the acknowledgement of natural children should be construed liberally in their favor. . . . Those children of distracted love, who were brought into the world without their consent and under disadvantageous conditions, at times bordering on cruelty, are deserving of all the equitable considerations within the power of the courts to dispense, which courts would undoubtedly be acting in consonance with the spirit of the times if, instead of applying the rigors of the law in all their crudeness, they were to facilitate them the means, compatible with the interests of justice, to improve their lot or condition. It is not at all offensive to public

interest for this court, once in a while, to temper the severity of justice with effusions of generosity.[53]

Unfortunately for Mike and Violeta, the majority opinion upheld the "crudeness" of the civil code, denying them the legal status that Moran believed they were entitled to. The Gitt siblings ultimately did not share in the mineral wealth of the islands as their father and erstwhile stepmother had.

The ruling likely relieved many Americans still living in the islands, especially those men who had also abandoned their mixed-race children in the islands. That Filipina women and mixed-race children would be entitled to the property and assets of Americans was a jarring reality for many colonists. In fact, Americans were used to the impossibility of such inheritance, an impossibility assured by the many state-adopted anti-miscegenation laws in the United States. No such laws followed the flag to the Philippines, however, and the jurisprudence of the islands forged ahead in creating new precedents that often did favor Filipinas and their mestizo children. In 1939, a case involving interracial marriage and inheritance in the Philippines made transnational news when a lower Manila court determined that Kentucky state laws regarding intermarriage did not apply to the overseas commonwealth. The case in question involved the inheritance of an estate by a woman described in the US press only as a "Moro woman named Mariang."[54] Upon the death of her husband, a white American named David Staples, Mariang inherited half of his $50,000 assets. Charles Staples, the brother of the deceased, contested her inheritance on the grounds that Staples's home state of Kentucky "does not permit marriage between white [people] and members of the colored races."[55] By this logic, he believed, the marriage was illegitimate and hence the right to inherit was also null and void. Unfortunately for Staples, the Manila court did not agree and found Mariang's marriage, reportedly performed by a "Mohammedan priest" in 1913, to be legal. The judges in the Staples case concluded that in determining the validity of Mariang's marriage, it was the laws of the Philippines, rather than Kentucky, that held.

Charles Staples did not pursue the matter further, so the case was never heard before the Supreme Court. If it had been, it is unlikely that the justices would have reversed the original decision of the lower court. By 1939, Americans no longer held appointments as justices on the Philippine Supreme Court. In February 1936, the last remaining American members resigned, and the first Filipino president of the new commonwealth government replaced them with appointed Filipino justices.[56] By the time Charles Staples contested Mariang's inheritance, most lower court judges were also Filipinos.

While in the past, both lower courts and the Supreme Court had upheld US state laws or considered them when making decisions (as in the case of Emil Johnson and the validation of his will according to Illinois state law), anti-miscegenation laws were simply incompatible with the realities of Americans and Filipinos living in the Philippines, not to mention highly offensive to many Filipinos who considered these cases in court. Interracial relations between Americans and Filipinas were ubiquitous in places like Manila, where many Americans resided. Even if white American men tried to hide their relations, the sexual economy and vice-adjacent recreational outlets, such as the cabarets and dance halls that facilitated such liaisons, were very visible parts of local life. The reality whereby Americans abandoned Filipinas and mestizo children with impunity informed the everyday experience of Filipinos throughout the occupation, a fact that judges, politicians, and other civil servants frequently reminded their erstwhile American benefactors of when it suited their political goals. For example, in 1930, Manuel Briones, a Filipino delegate to the US House of Representatives, reminded American politicians of their soldiers' and sailors' debauched behavior in Philippine ports of call. The hearing that Briones attended was one that debated the merits of Filipino exclusion from immigration to the United States, a measure he opposed. If US representatives were dismayed by Filipino "immorality" in the metropole and sought their exclusion, Briones suggested a reckoning with the sexual economy built by American men in the Philippines.[57] Likewise, for a Filipino judge in Manila to hear a case in which an American petitioner sought to deprive a Filipina widow of an inheritance on the basis of an overseas white-supremacist law would have been exasperating to say the least. That the American plaintiff would choose to bring the anti-miscegenation petition during the post-1935 commonwealth period, a transitional time that many Filipinos heralded as the formal beginnings of an independent nation, would have been a slap in the face of the Filipino elites now running the government. Mariang's case is the only one I have found that tested the applicability of US anti-miscegenation laws in the islands. The US media that covered her trial lamented the final ruling. The Filipino judges, they claimed, "established a precedent" in Mariang's case.[58] It would be decades before anti-miscegenation laws in the United States would be deemed similarly irrelevant.[59]

Even when courts found in favor of Filipino/a litigants, much of their experiences within the legal system were shaped by the imperial state's denial of Filipinos as part of legitimate American family units. Though the colonial government openly recognized and tacitly accepted Filipinas and mestizos within illegitimate American family units—common-law marriages, the querida system, the sexual economy, abandoned children, and so on—these illegitimate families were largely contained within the Pacific possession and, though they made the US colonial government prostrate before Filipino criticism, they posed little real threat to American wealth and property. The workings of the socio-legal justice system largely reflected broader US imperial claims that Filipinos were, as yet, unworthy to inherit the gift of American-wrought civilization, unfit members of the family of modern nations, and incapable of raising the islands to full nationhood. The United States strategically and consistently framed the Philippines and Filipinos as subordinate family members: a dependent ward, a maligned little brown brother or sister, and a sometimes willing and sometimes unwilling marital partner.[60] Despite years of American pontification about the familial relationship between the United States and the Philippines, the reality within the colony, as these legal cases reflect, was that Filipinos were most certainly not members of the American family, not even diminutive members.

Conclusion

Trials of intercourse revealed the unruly nature of interracial relationships in the colonial Philippines. Dangerous intercourse prompted Americans not only to murder one another but, more often, to murder Filipinas. Interracial relations created legal transnational conundrums. Dangerous intercourse in the colonial Philippines blurred the lines between the sexual economy and "legitimate" sexual relationships. Participation in dangerous intercourse opened some possibilities for Filipinos to legally benefit from the wealth Americans tore from the shores and mountains of the islands, though inheritance was never a foregone conclusion, even in the most respectable or legal arrangements. The colonial justice system delineated not just who was guilty or innocent but also what constituted a family and what did not. Although there were no laws preventing or criminalizing interracial intercourse, the colonial state still understood and treated those who transgressed sociosexual color lines as criminals, as the cases of Schenck, the discharged firefighter; Mariang Staples, the Moro widow; and Maria Bancosta, the defamed mother, so clearly demonstrate. The American practice of socially policing interracial intercourse bled into a colonial legal system built on bedrock ideas of Filipino unfitness and criminality.

In truth, the legal justice system in the colonial Philippines was—like many justice systems, especially those that form part of colonial infrastructures—a socio-legal justice system. Its primary purpose was to protect the varied interests of the colonial state and its values, not necessarily to ensure justice and equitable outcomes for all. The social, racial, and gendered logics of US imperialism informed every aspect of the legal system, from its creation and composition to its operation and findings. Filipinas' and mestizo children's experiences within this socio-legal system were thus informed by the white supremacist logics that posited Filipinos as subordinate or illegitimate members of the body politic, even though courts often found in their favor. Respectability as legal spouses was out of reach when even the recognition of these marriages were always and already questioned or under suspicion. American mestizos constantly had to prove their status as acknowledged offspring of Americans, even when American family members left ample legal documentation meant to protect them. For Filipina wives and American mestizo children across the socioeconomic spectrum, dangerous intercourse might have offered some social mobility, but it also brought with it a precarious legal position wherein membership to one's own family (and the American body politic) was always in question. Even when Filipino civil servants were sympathetic to Filipinas and mestizos and understood them as legal beneficiaries, as in the Gitt case, the colonial foundation of the legal system still ensured that Filipinos remained largely outside legitimate American families, and thus forging a divergent path from US empire was difficult. Not much has changed in the past hundred years. As the entangled and asymmetrical relationship of the Philippines and the United States continues, Filipinas and mixed-race American Filipino children are still unstable members of both personal and political family units, guilty until proven innocent.

Chapter 5

Depicting Dangerous Intercourse

Sam and Maganda on the Pages of Empire

Abraham Van Heyningen Hartendorp was shocked when the calls came for his deportation. It flew against his sense of self and the carefully crafted persona he had built in his almost fifty years in the Philippines when, in 1964, Filipino senators accused him of being anti-Filipino and asked the Philippine Deportation Board to begin proceedings for his removal as an "undesirable alien."[1] Hartendorp had written a series of editorials in the past few years criticizing the nationalization and "Filipino-first" efforts of the recently independent Philippine government, calling such legislation "insane," "discriminatory," and akin to stealing from non-Filipino nationals.[2] He characterized nationalist and Filipino-first slogans as "the cry of the dispossessors who, through government financial and other economic controls, pant after usurping the place and seizing the hard-earned wealth of others with no show of right other than that they are 'Filipino'" and was particularly critical of governmental efforts to limit businesses owned by non-Filipino nationals.[3] His polemic also garnered unwanted public criticism of his employer, the Philippine branch of the American Chamber of Commerce, the executives of which began to censor his editorials.[4] Despite the reproach, he still felt well within his right to make such characterizations. Hartendorp first came to the Philippines in 1917, and like his US-based settler forebears, who turned to the civil service as a way to participate in empire building and national life, he transformed his educational averageness in the United States into a thriving colonial career in the Philippines.[5] He started out as a teacher with the US civil service and then joined the literary world as a magazine editor,

eventually gaining prominence in the field. When the deportation proceedings began, he used his literary platform to refute the accusations leveled
against him, writing an extensive autobiographical sketch detailing his life
in the Philippines. In his concluding remarks, as if to drive home his indig-
nation at being characterized as an anti-Filipino imperialist, he flaunted his
current and former Filipina "wives" and numerous Filipino descendants.[6]
"With all this behind me, with seven children, seventeen grandchildren, and
three great-grandchildren, all Filipinos . . . how could I ever 'insult,' as I have
been charged with doing, the Filipino people who have become my own
people and my kin?"[7] For Hartendorp, his Filipino family was the most vis-
ceral and convincing evidence of his commitment to the nation.

It would take more than a blended family, however, to convince Filipino
politicians, many of whom had been fighting for Philippine independence
since the turn of the century, that old-timers like Hartendorp were anything
more than American imperialists, especially when these expats continued to
openly question the capacity of Filipinos for self-rule. As the US-Philippines
relationship shifted and the colony's status changed to commonwealth in 1935
and then to independent nation in 1946, so too did the position of longtime
American settlers. Hartendorp was one of the Manila Americans who had
been in the islands since the "empire days" and whose elite position in the
nation was unsteadied by the policies and priorities of the newly independent
government.[8] As American old-timers—a self-selected endearment meant to
convey both longtime residence in the Philippines and deep familiarity with
the nation and its people—reflected on US empire amid the geopolitical
changes taking shape around them that threatened both their sense of self and
their elite status, they, like Hartendorp, leaned on dangerous intercourse for
stability, often doing so through the realm of the literary.

As the relationship between the United States and the Philippines shifted,
so too did American and Filipino cultural representations of this relationship. Turn-of-the-century American cultural productions that depicted US
involvement in the islands relied on the trope of Filipino immorality (sexual
and otherwise) and backwardness to legitimate the annexation of a peoples
who had just won their independence from Spain. Representations of sexual
relations between colonizer and colonized likewise espoused the idea that
intercourse was dangerous, primarily for the sanctity of white racial purity
and the moral constitutions of white men.[9] Filipino writers, too, consistently
wrote interracial intercourse as symptomatic of the uneven relations between
the United States and the Philippines, and much wartime propaganda in the
early 1900s depicted American occupiers as lecherous rapists of a virgin

motherland.[10] By the 1930s, however, it was the eve of independence, and prominent Americans in the Philippines, many who had lived in the archipelago since the time of the Philippine-American War, shied farther away from earlier portrayals of dangerous interracial intercourse. Instead, their writings painted these relations—and their participation in such liaisons—as nostalgic and romantic and, more importantly, a testament to their own deep commitment to and familiarity with the nation. The changes in American imperial fiction were not coincidental, nor did they simply reflect a corresponding shift in American attitudes toward Filipinos and US empire in the Pacific. Rather, as this chapter highlights, the softening apparent in American writings on interracial relations followed the waning of the formal American presence and American power in the nation. Filipino representations also shifted, but much of the characterization of dangerous intercourse coming from Filipino writers was very different from the literature produced by Americans. Interracial intercourse did not form the core of the Filipino community in the islands as it did for Americans. Indeed, dangerous intercourse depicted in Filipino literature continued to be just that: dangerous. While turn-of-the-century depictions of lurid occupiers that defiled women were largely gone, many of the Filipino reflections on empire during the commonwealth and early independence era still used interracial intercourse to point to and criticize the asymmetrical relations between colonizer and colonized. Though many Filipinos understood formalized interracial marriages in the colonial period as indicative of American openness to socioracial equality, even this sentiment lost its robustness, especially as the postindependence US military buildup throughout the archipelago continued to shore up the ever-growing sexual economy, and liaisons contracted through this economy were the dominant form of dangerous intercourse in the islands. Thus, American depictions of Sam and Maganda from the colonial to the commonwealth eras were more mercurial because older unhesitatingly racist depictions of Filipinos no longer sustained but threatened the beneficial positions of old-timers now living in a foreign country versus a US colony.[11] Filipino characterizations remained relatively stable largely because Filipinos continued to contend with American empire and its detritus, even after formal independence. The increasingly visible and normalized sexual economies in the islands, for example, continued to be emblematic of US dominance, as much of the Filipino literature from the commonwealth and early independence era made clear. Settler careerists, on the other hand, did what settler societies have always done. They literally rewrote the history of dangerous intercourse and, in so doing, reimagined a violent imperial past as a wistful romantic interlude.[12] In their writings, they showcased themselves as pioneers at the forefront of American efforts to modernize and civilize the Philippines, their lack of race prejudice attested to by their relations with Filipina women. A commonality between the writings of both Filipino and American authors who debated US empire with pen and paper was that their debates often played out over the bodies of vulnerable Filipina women.

Drawing from Christina Klein's idea of "global imaginaries," this chapter understands the literary productions of US empire in the Philippines as local/transnational imaginaries, or imperial fiction. In Klein's assessment, Americans created "global imaginaries" in their plays, poems, books, and other productions that depicted Euro-American empire as a way to understand contemporary geopolitical relations. These imaginaries shaped popular consensus about local and global affairs and also reflected how people experienced such interconnections. Similarly, the texts examined here were not fiction or fantasy in the sense of being false or recounting things that never happened. Rather, understanding the American texts in particular as imperial fiction recognizes how authors often refused to comprehend the colonial realities of unequal relations, as well as the perspectives and desires of the Filipino people they claimed to be so familiar with. Like the constructed settler origin narratives of the United States, Australia, Hawai'i, and so on, the "imaginaries" created by old-timers provided them with a "stable sense of individual and national identity" as well as an emboldened sense of manliness and virility, though that self-assuredness relied on static and orientalist understandings of Filipinos.[13] Upholding such static notions relied on American writers either interpreting Filipino expectations and desires in ways that validated their own sense of idealized self or ignoring such pushback altogether. In framing the cultural texts herein as imperial fiction or fantasy, this chapter necessarily attempts to recover those buried Filipino voices. Filipino authors also produced local imaginaries of their own, although they more accurately comprehended the unevenness of the sexual economy and understood interracial relations as rooted in the exploitative colonial relationship of the Philippines and the United States. Filipino writers were decidedly not nostalgic or romantic in their depictions of American-Filipino intercourse. The sentiment Filipino writers conveyed in their stories about dangerous intercourse was more often one of remonstration rather than wistfulness. For Americans, settler life in the islands largely depended on romantic attachments to Filipina women as a way to claim belonging, and these relationships were often centered and romanticized in their reflections. Taken together, these poetics of empire help us to understand how Americans and Filipinos alike made sense of the commonwealth and immediate postindependence years, and how interracial intercourse was a prevailing lens through which they understood the historical relationship between the United States and the Philippines.

From Color Line to Colorful Past: Imperial Fiction, Settler Fantasy, and Nostalgia

By the 1930s, self-described American old-timers were a dwindling population. Geopolitical developments and age contributed to the declining number of old-timers, as many began to leave the Pacific in anticipation of the coming war, and others simply passed away in the islands. The colonial relationship between the United States and the Philippines also took a turn after the passage of the 1934 Tydings-McDuffie Act. This legislation changed the colonial status of the Philippines to commonwealth and laid out a ten-year path to independence. Upon the inauguration of the commonwealth, an elected Filipino president replaced the American governor-general as the new chief executive of the islands. Many American settlers were troubled by these changes, as they had been by the Filipinization efforts of the earlier decades, and the promise of independence on the horizon unnerved old-timers who wrestled with how to maintain their relevance and privileged way of life. The struggle of these settler careerist "pioneers" to make sense of their place in the islands often played out in the realm of the literary and, moreover, typically involved the rewriting of the history of dangerous intercourse in the Philippines.

Such was the case with the 1937 publication of an anonymous poem titled "Brown of the Volunteers" in the *American Oldtimer*, a monthly magazine created by and for longtime American expatriates in the Philippines. The poem recounted the travails of Private Brown, formerly of the US Volunteers during the Philippine-American War. As the narrative goes, Brown took his leave from the military and decided to stay in the Philippines. He soon became accustomed to liquor and the company of women. Brown soon became "color-blind" and wed a Filipina. All was not paradise, however, and soon his wife's extended family moved in to his home, and Brown took to commiserating with his fellow Americans at the local watering hole. The characterization of Brown's life reads as part admonition, part jest. The forum of the *Oldtimer*—a magazine whose American readership was largely intermarried to Filipinas themselves—suggests that this poem was included in the issue as an inside joke, a lighthearted commiseration about the shared experience of being intermarried in the Philippines. This version of "Brown of the Volunteers," however, was not the first version of the syllabic poem. Originally written sometime between 1908 and 1920 by Frank Cheney, an American civil servant in the Philippines, the 1937 version differed from the earlier one in several significant verses. The editorial changes made to the Cheney poem reflected the broader sociopolitical changes that were happening in Manila in the 1930s and what those changes meant for those who had engaged in dangerous intercourse in the islands.

Frank Cheney first came to the Philippines as a teacher in 1908 and wrote frequently for the *Manila Bulletin*, an American-run daily newspaper. In 1916 he was promoted to superintendent for the Manila Trade School. He likely wrote "Brown of the Volunteers" during his time in the Philippines before he returned to the United States in 1920. While much of the 1937 poem was the same as the original, Cheney's version is more explicitly a cautionary tale that advised against interracial miscegenation in the Philippines. The shift in the tone of the poem is most clearly apparent in the first quatrain:

Numberless shades of color mix
In language, religion, and politics,
and a man must stick, if he hopes to win

To his color and kind 'til he cashes in.

—"Brown of the Volunteers"
Frank Cheney (1908–1920)[14]

Colors innumerable mingle, and mix
In language, religion and politics
And a man must choose if he hopes to win

And stick to his choice until he cashes in.

—"Brown of the Volunteers"
American Oldtimer (1937)[15]

As the Cheney version stated, "a man must stick, if he hopes to win / To his color and kind 'til he cashes in," while the later version was altered to read, "A man must choose, if he hopes to win / And stick to his choice until he cashes in." The revised poem erased the explicit anti-miscegenation message of sticking to one's own "color" and transformed what was a clear rebuke of crossing the sexual color line into a laughable parable about sticking to one's "choice" with conviction. Other edits similarly shifted the message of Cheney's poem, softening the more racially explicit or offensive parts to paint a more sanitized, although still racist, picture of intermarriage in the Philippines. For example, Cheney's original version described the Filipina wife of Private Brown as a woman "whose skin was black," while the new version amended it to "a woman less white than black."[16] The updated poem still denigrated racial Blackness, but it made the distinction that Filipinas were not Black but somewhere in between white and Black. The purposeful changes to the *Oldtimer* version were not just a matter of stylistic choice; rather, they reflected both the political shift in the US-Philippines relationship and the changing contours of the old-timer community that remained in the islands.

Many American old-timers in the later decades of the US occupation sought to foreground what they believed to be the pro-Filipino, or "Filipinista," trajectories of their colonial careers as a way to set themselves apart from the more explicit racism of the previous decades. In the earlier colonial period, most Americans would have shunned the label "Filipinista," a term imperialists applied to those they believed placed Filipino interests above those of their own countrymen. The term also carried the disparaging sexual implication that someone had "gone native" and marked one as outside the realm of the socially/politically acceptable.[17] However, in the commonwealth period, to be dubbed a Filipinista—a true friend of the Philippines—was a designation that many old-timers embraced, especially when it came from Filipinos.[18] While Cheney's original "Brown of the Volunteers" was in line with stateside US policies like anti-miscegenation and exclusion laws meant to deal with both the "negro problem" and the mounting "yellow peril," the subtle softening of the poem by the *Oldtimer* was a necessary move in the reimagining of the American footprint in the islands.[19] Unlike in the US metropole, where Indigenous dispossession and eradication eventually paved the way for large-scale white settlement and territorial incorporation for which settlers did not have to justify their presence, the much smaller settler population in the Philippines and the transition of the colony to independence made it imperative for old-timers to highlight their kinship with the nation and people. Thus, it was important for longtime colonial careerists to distance themselves from the empire days, a time of heavy-handed and more visible American control of Filipino affairs, even as they longed for a return to those days. Old-timers had to differentiate their relationships with Filipinas from the more defamatory stereotypes and depictions popularized by Americans in the preceding decades as a necessary part of this reimagining. Cheney's anti-miscegenation stance in "Brown of the Volunteers" was less compatible with American settler goals in the commonwealth period. Being singled out as anti-Filipino was bad for business, and it also challenged old-timers' sense of themselves as more racially liberal. At the same time, even though the American settler population had shrunk, those remaining had formed a tight-knit and insulated community, one that could read the updated "Brown of the Volunteers" in the pages of the *Oldtimer* and be assured that it would be shared largely among other American expats and would not necessarily draw the ire of the growing number of pro-independence Filipinos.

Despite their small numbers, American old-timers continued to wield disproportionate influence and capital in the Philippines. In addition to their mixed-race families, they often had assets, careers, and influence that kept them anchored in place.[20] These settler colonial careerists left behind a voluminous literary archive describing their lives in the Philippines, their thoughts on US imperialism, and their objections to Philippine independence. Interracial intercourse features prominently and was most often used for self-promotion or to advance the interests of US empire. Just as intermarried men were integral to the early incorporation and control of various parts of the Philippines, old-timers continued to parlay their relations with Filipinas into long-lasting careers that were vital to the perpetuation of American power and influence in the islands, especially in a period of waning formal US presence.[21] As self-appointed tastemakers, political advisers, and businessmen, their cultural productions took on more weight as the texts they left behind, largely read by other disproportionately empowered Americans, continued to shape how later expats understood Filipinas, the Philippines, and the sexual possibilities available in the islands.

Turn-of-the-century imperialists and anti-imperialists alike often thought of and depicted the Philippines and Filipinos as possible liminal members of the American family, from "little brown brothers" and sisters to orphaned unruly children in need of guidance from their adoptive US parent. The image of the damsel in distress was also commonly used to perpetuate the idea that masculine American protection was needed in the Pacific. These representations were not new; the US press and politicians alike historically portrayed US relations with Latin America and encounters with Indigenous peoples in gendered terms of familial proximity.[22] Many political cartoons about Philippine annexation highlighted this continuity. It was not uncommon for caricatures of both Native Americans and Black Americans to appear alongside those of Filipinos in cartoons about Philippine annexation. Such depictions suggested that new Filipino subjects were the latest in a series of uncivilized wards that the United States was attempting to uplift.[23] US debates over annexation were also saturated with the metaphor of the Philippines as a sometimes willing, sometimes unwilling, romantic consort. As historian Kristin Hoganson has pointed out, the metaphor of marriage for annexationists implied consensual relations and "honorable intentions" but also highlighted adherence to gendered hierarchical relationships.[24] On the eve of Philippine independence, politicians still favored the marriage metaphor, though some, like Montana congressman Jacob Thorkelson, shed the pretense of honorable partnership: "We paid $20,000,000 for our oriental bride, and Congress approved and legalized the ceremony."[25] The trope of familial or marital proximity was essential to the narrative of American benevolence, a trait of the US empire that supposedly set it apart from other European empires. The imagery of interracial intercourse did not wane with the passage of time or with the eventual granting of independence.

The idea of marriage as a metaphor for imperial expansion was so popular and durable that many American men who stayed indefinitely in the Philippines with their wives or lovers fancied themselves as personifications of a pioneering Uncle Sam and actively engaged in reproducing the allegory of the sometimes licit, sometimes illicit, Philippine-American relationship. They, of course, had a personal stake in the perpetuation of such a narrative. Even though an uneven and enduring colonial relationship was all but assured by the foundations laid by US imperialism, old-timers were uneasy with the coming independence. In setting out to anchor themselves more firmly, they perpetuated the sacrosanct idea of US exceptionalism through ideas of interracial intercourse.

Many old-timers, for example, sought to demonstrate their continued importance to the nation by building personas as experts on the Philippines and Filipinos. In a marked shift from the days of largely closeted interracial liaisons, by the 1930s many old-timers were making interracialism and their transgressions of the sexual color line a prominent part of their identities, centering their participation in dangerous intercourse as proof of their commitment to the nation. The connection between interracial intercourse and claims to intimate knowledge of the nation and its people was vividly put on display in the fictional story "Chronicles of Sam and Maganda," written by old-timer Hammon H. Buck. Buck came to the Philippines with the South Dakota Volunteers and left the army in 1900. Like many former soldiers, he elected to stay in the islands and took a civil service job as a teacher.[26] The US Department of Education assigned him to a post in Cavite, just southwest of Manila, where he eventually met and married his Filipina wife, Dolores Angeles. They had six children together, and by 1906 he had been promoted to division superintendent for the neighboring province of Batangas.[27] Buck was a regular contributor to *Philippine Magazine*, a monthly English-language outlet for aspiring Filipino writers and artists. Edited by old-timer A. V. H. Hartendorp, the magazine was attuned to American interests, featuring business and political news relevant to expatriates. Buck published his serialized "Chronicles of Sam and Maganda" in the July and September issues of the magazine in 1927. In 1935, just a year after the passage of the Philippine Independence Act, he published the tale again as a stand-alone pamphlet in Manila, with some additions to the 1927 version to reflect the passage of the act.[28] In this fifty-page volume, Buck turned the old allegory of the US-Philippines romance into a narrative epic purportedly adapted from "Malayan folklore," one of his professed areas of expertise.[29] He was likely referencing the precolonial origin story of "Malakas at Maganda," although the similarities between Buck's allegory and the Philippine tale were practically nonexistent. According to some versions of the origin story, Malakas (strong) and Maganda (beautiful) emerged from a split in a giant bamboo plant. They had many children who populated the Philippines, and in some versions of the story, all modern-day peoples across the globe were descendants of Malakas and Maganda.[30] Buck took this story, which understood the Philippines as the wellspring of humanity, and turned it into a tale that promoted Philippine submission to imperial rule.

The cover image of *Chronicles* illustrates the US-Philippines relationship that Buck envisioned, with the supplicant Maganda, her sleeve torn and her hand extended toward Sam as he gazes down at her (fig. 5.1). The first chapter opens with the annexation of the Philippines, when Sam Brown, the "Western Youth, strong and vigorous by nature, good-hearted, blundering, and generous . . . withal a gentleman and anxious to do the right thing by the opposite sex," saves the "shy, eastern maiden," Maganda, from the "low-browed" Spain, who was "holding her by her long dark hair."[31] After wresting Maganda from the clutches of Spain, Sam, bedecked in the star-spangled garb typically worn by America's Uncle Sam, is hesitant to let her go along on her own path, despite Maganda's reassurance that she will manage fine on her own. Here Buck reimagines the Philippine-American War as a violent domestic disturbance, wherein "Maganda was the struggler. . . . Sam merely maintained his grasp on the maiden, all the time counseling patience and submission and promising to lead her along bright and pleasant paths."[32] Buck resolves this implicit rape scene with Maganda's submission. She quickly stops "kicking Sam's shins" in appreciation of the shoes, skirts, and face powder he introduces her to for the improvement of her appearance.[33] Sam encourages Maganda to partner with him in developing the agricultural and mineral resources of the islands, promising that they could become rich. Maganda responds with skepticism: "I am an unprotected maiden and if you want to, you can despoil me of all my treasure, including my reputation, but

Figure 5.1. The front cover of Hammon Bucks allegorical critique of Philippine independence, *Chronicles of Sam and Maganda*. Image courtesy of the American Historical Collection, Ateneo de Manila University.

you certainly can't expect me to help you despoil myself, at least not until you've declared your intentions." Buck continues his story for forty more pages, waxing poetic about the kindhearted nature of Sam, who, despite his willingness to control Maganda, cannot commit to the idea of marriage. Described as a "naturally chaste maiden," Maganda does not want the ambiguous position of an "oriental" mistress, although she has no trouble appearing romantically receptive and growing accustomed to Sam's money.[34] Buck's long-winded allegory sought to demonstrate Filipino unpreparedness for independence and was openly pro-imperialist. In his estimation and based on his "authority on things Filipino," Filipinos themselves did not truly desire a break with the United States.[35] According to Buck, the "little coquette" Maganda only feigned "a dislike of Sam's program which in reality she [did] not feel."[36] Instead of a "divorce," Buck proposed a "permanent union" between the United States and the Philippines, suggesting "some modified form of statehood."[37]

Buck's ability to make relevant political commentary depended on the presentation of himself as an expert on the Philippines. As he explained, only someone like himself, someone who was "intimately acquainted with her psychology," would know "her" interiority.[38] Chronicles, he stated, would "acquaint the reader with the changing relations that have obtained between the United States and the Philippines from the time of the occupation down to the present." Chronicles, however, was not a rare insight into Filipino nature but rather a reflection of the author's understanding of himself within the shifting bilateral relations of the United States and the Philippines. As Edward Said and other postcolonial scholars have demonstrated, the ruminations of Anglo-Americans on empire tell us more about how imperialists understood themselves in opposition to racialized others than they convey any truth about nonwhite colonized peoples.[39] In Buck's case, his ability to "understand" the conjugal US-Philippines relationship—one that mirrored his own marital status—was a reflection of his sense of self as a Filipinista.[40] Both old-timers and Filipinos embraced the label "Filipinista," as it seemingly affirmed racial tolerance and social equality. Yet even a cursory reading of Buck's Chronicles underscores not an affirmation of equality but rather an adherence to ideas of Filipino inferiority. Buck relied on the same tropes of Filipinos as childlike and naive that many imperialists relied on to justify annexation, and like those previous imperialists, he believed that he—rather than Filipinos themselves— knew what was best for the Philippines.

The racism and sexism that were foundational to the building and maintenance of the US empire in the Philippines were also foundational to Buck's narrative. At the same time, it was a narrative that was (according to Buck) only possible because of his deep intimacy with Filipinos. Buck's romance-rape fantasy fit neatly within broader cultural tropes of the Filipino as a subordinate relation (such as a brother or a child) as well as with the marriage metaphor so commonly used to express transnational connection but also subordination. For example, Buck describes Maganda as a "child of the orient," a "creature fashioned by nature to be petted," and immature. Further, Sam's attitude toward Maganda is not "parental" but "more compelling . . . and more all-embracing than is advisable or ethical on the part of a guardian toward his ward."[41] Even as Buck demeaned Maganda as a petulant Lolita who used her sexuality to get what she wanted, he simultaneously held fast to his belief that interracial intercourse was indicative of imperial goodwill and commitment to social equality. The American empire, he opined, was a better empire than other Anglo-European empires because of sociosexual intercourse, whereas "neither Dutch Hans or John Bull would care to be seen in public with their charges."[42]

Buck's allegory, like the revised "Brown of the Volunteers," tempers American expressions of racism toward Filipinos. Nowhere in the narrative was this more effective than in the scene in which Maganda considers her marital options. Indeed, Buck routed his affirmation of white supremacy most effectively through Maganda's character, rather than Sam's. In her appraisal of marriage prospects, Maganda rejects "John Chinaman," "Cousin Togo," and "Uncle Bombay," in favor of Sam. Buck attributes this "preference" to the tendency of women to "select for [their] mate the most perfect individual of the other sex that can be found in the neighborhood." Maganda, he concludes, has no "pride of race," as she is so "dazzled by Sam's glitter." In this depiction, it is Maganda, not Buck nor even the fictional Sam, who harbors white supremist sentiment.[43] With Maganda as his mouthpiece for expressions of white supremacy, Buck, like other old-timers who composed imperial fiction, characterized the preponderance of interracial intercourse in the commonwealth as a product of Asian women's sexual desire for white men, rather than as symptomatic of exploitative imperial conditions and the constrained but rational decision making of women under the thumb of empire. The longevity of this idea about Asian women's proclivity for white men has helped sustain and grow some of the most robust and notorious sexual economies in the world. By the time he wrote *Chronicles*, Buck was a successful landowner and agriculturalist living in Tagaytay, a city just a few hours south of Manila, which became a popular holiday spot for people looking to escape the city. Buck played a prominent role in the development of Tagaytay as a tourist destination. He also used his social influence to connect with Filipino elites and politicians, some of whom purchased parcels of his sizable Philippine landholdings.

Many Filipinistas like Buck espoused ideas of socioracial equality while promoting white and American supremacy, failing to understand how one idea was incongruous with the other. What made the ideas compatible for these old-timers was their participation in dangerous intercourse. Transgressing the sexual color line was so audacious, especially under the auspices of the moralist community in the Philippines, that it must mean (in their estimations) a transcendence of racial prejudice. A. V. H. Hartendorp likewise believed this to be the case, as he made clear in his deportation hearing.

Hartendorp's early life in the United States, like that of Buck, who hailed from South Dakota, was entangled with settler colonial projects. At the age of twenty-four, he left his family's Colorado homestead to pursue a career in colonial education abroad.[44] He embarked on his transpacific travels without a degree, hoping to work in the field of racial psychology and to "study the negritos," one of the Indigenous groups in the islands.[45] His interest in the study of "primitive" peoples first took shape in the United States amid the unfurling realities of Native American dispossession and genocide. A self-proclaimed colonialist who sought to advance American goals in the islands, he played an important role in the administration of eugenics-driven intelligence testing to Filipino pupils. His articles on the subject claimed that such testing had proven that "Philippine intelligence norms were only slightly below the United States norms, the difference being accounted for by the language difficulty."[46] After leaving the civil service, Hartendorp made a career for himself as a writer, working for various newspapers and teaching classes at the University of the Philippines. He later became the editor of *Philippine Magazine* (previously *Philippine Education*, a magazine published for the benefit of Thomasite teachers in the islands), a literary and cultural monthly, which helped launch the careers of various Filipino artists and English-language writers. During World War II, Japanese military forces deemed Hartendorp and all other Americans civilians—including American mestizos who could not pass as Filipino—as enemies and jailed them at Santo Tomas Internment Camp in Manila. He served as an informal adviser to President Manuel Quezon, the first Filipino president during the commonwealth period, as well as later president Sergio Osmeña. Many Filipinos and American expatriates saw Hartendorp as an expert on Philippine-American relations and on the Philippines in general. He left a prolific archival record of his life, not only in his published works but also through his self-published six-volume memoirs.

To this day, American old-timers and other Americans and Filipinos invested in Hartendorp's version of US-Philippine history praise his life and works as exemplary.[47] Most archival accounts remember Hartendorp as a great contributor to the literary world of the Philippines and as someone with a great "interest and love for the country and its people."[48] These accounts, like Hartendorp's own memoirs, never failed to mention his interracial marriage and his American mestizo children, all ostensible markers of his racial tolerance. Upon his passing in the late 1970s, one obituary described how "that part of Manila social life dominated by American women" shunned Hartendorp for being a "squaw man." The memoriam continued: "The scars left by the ostracism he for a time encountered . . . [help] to explain the depth of his identification with the Philippines, a commitment he shared with only a handful of Americans."[49] While the commemorations of Hartendorp's life omitted the more lurid details of his time spent in the Philippines, namely his various sexual exploits, his own memoirs painstakingly detailed and seemingly reveled in those moments of sexual experimentation.

Hartendorp's imperial fiction is important to unpack because of its sheer volume and disproportionate influence on how later American settlers (who also wielded undue influence and privilege in the islands) formed their ideas about the historic and contemporary role Americans played in the Philippines. Hartendorp framed himself as "not a tourist, a visitor, a guest, a beneficiary of the hospitality of the country," but as "a settler" with legitimate claim to the islands.[50] He was dismissive of charges that US imperialism was exploitative. For Hartendorp, being a settler (first in the US West and then in the Philippines) was not only unproblematic but something that he claimed with pride. His elevation of settlers as exceptional diminished the dispossession and violence that colonized people bore under the US flag.

Despite his commitment to his settler "belonging" in the Philippines, Hartendorp's identity as a Filipinista was not stable, especially as the nation was on the precipice of independence. The calls for his deportation attest to the flimsiness of expat status in the immediate postcolonial years. Filipinos challenged his self-proclaimed belonging and dedication to the nation. In doing so, they pointed to the curated nature of the Filipinista identity constructed by American expats and recognized dangerous intercourse not as a marker of individual racial transcendence but as symptomatic of Filipino subjugation. For many Filipino nationalists, participating in interracial sex and having a mixed-race family did not equate to antiracism or ownership over the nation. Though the Philippine Deportation Board ultimately did not evict Hartendorp from the country, and though many of his Filipino friends came to his aid to defend him, the incident seems to have troubled him deeply, as the charges of being anti-Filipino were so incongruous with how he understood himself and his life in the Philippines. His desire to rehabilitate his reputation as a friend and supporter of the Philippines and to defend what he understood as his contributions to the nation were likely part of the impetus for penning his six-volume memoir just a few years before his passing. Though Hartendorp never claimed to be Filipino—indeed, he painstakingly maintained his US citizenship, never naturalizing or even learning the local language, as did his compatriot Hammon Buck—he nonetheless sought to portray himself as racially liberated and as someone dedicated to the nation and its people.[51]

In the six-volume reflection, his belief that interracial sex equated to antiracism was front and center. Hartendorp, like many other American men, used the laboratory space of the Philippines to test his own sexual virility.[52] Indeed, his sexual experience mirrors the development of his career, moving from unsuccessful sexual advances in the United States to abundant sexual opportunity in the Philippines. Once abroad, Hartendorp quickly familiarized himself with the local sexual economy of Manila and began accumulating his "expertise." His first sexual encounter at the age of twenty-four bestowed on him, in his own estimation, an intimate knowledge of how Japanese women in the brothels of Manila felt about their trade, and he noted, "Prostitution among the Japanese was at that time an accepted social institution. . . . The women practiced the profession with no apparent feeling of abasement or guilt."[53] From here, his performance of white imperial masculinity became unfettered. This was a performance that depended on the refusal to comprehend the motivations and practical desires of the women involved in his liaisons, as doing so would have upturned his carefully curated sense of his own sexual prowess and socioracial broad-mindedness.

Like Hartendorp's unsophisticated understanding of the agency, economic vulnerability, and desires of Japanese women in the red-light district, he was similarly out of touch with the desires and realities of other women he encountered in the Philippines. For example, he often accompanied H. Otley Beyer, his colleague and mentor, on ethnological trips through Mountain Province. Hartendorp quickly acquainted himself with the women of the Cordilleras. In Baguio, he met Beyer's Ifugao wife, Lingayu Gambuk; their infant son, William; and many other individuals from the town. One young woman in particular was instrumental in Hartendorp's continued sexual experimentation and fantasy production. As he recounted, a sixteen-year-old girl named Dulimay caught his eye: "[She] wore a colored hand-woven scarf over one shoulder and breast. Perhaps that was what first attracted my attention, for most of the others were 'topless.' I considered what was hidden by that scarf!"[54] While Hartendorp's recollection begins with his own initial attraction to and desire for Dulimay, he goes on to construct their sexual relationship as one of mutual attraction and desire for sexual expression. Dulimay's perspective was not reflected on; rather, her presence was the jumping-off point for Hartendorp's fantasy of embracing "free love" and racial transcendence. He was titillated by what he perceived to be the sexual practices of the community. Like his contemporaries who surmised Indigenous peoples as being at an earlier stage of human evolution, one not yet affected by overconsumption and overcivilization, he embraced the "barbarian virtues" of the Ifugao people and happily embraced "going native."[55] The Ifugaos, he believed, were not moralistic in their approach to sex and were open to "young people getting together before marriage to test their love,—trial marriage." Hartendorp jumped at the opportunity to "test the idea." During his time in Mountain Province, he not only tested his imperial virility with Dulimay but also began building the foundations of his identity as a Filipinista. "The two of us so different from each other, had yet been drawn so closely together that invidious racial separateness had been nullified."[56] Racial divisions, he concluded, disappeared through dangerous intercourse.

To recover what might have motivated Dulimay to form a sexual liaison with a white American requires more than Hartendorp's base assertion of strong mutual attraction, though his memoirs offer some insight if one reads beyond his imperial fantasy. For example, Dulimay was friends with Beyer's Ifugao wife, Lingayu Gambuk, and this friendship informed how she understood relationships with colonialist outsiders. Though Lingayu's family was already prominent in their community, her marriage to Beyer secured them an even more advantageous position. Beyer's social and economic capital ensured his Ifugao family stability during the shifting colonial times. Dulimay and the rest of the community observed the benefits of Lingayu's relationship and were likely also familiar with the local trade in sexual companionship for commodities and resources, a trade that had been commonplace in the area since the Spanish occupation. White American soldiers or constabulary officers in the region commonly engaged in interracial cohabitation and sex with native women. The women, in turn, received money, clothing, or houses as part of their arrangements.[57] That Dulimay asked Hartendorp to purchase a house for her upon his departure from Baguio attests to her keen knowledge of how such arrangements worked and her logical understanding that she was owed remuneration. After looking at several homes of the "common type,"

Dulimay found one on sale, and Hartendorp paid about 25 pesos for a recently constructed one. Dulimay, he recalled, "was a poor girl and lived with her sister, the parents being dead[, and] was pleased with the gift and proud of now having a place of her own."[58] Though Hartendorp refused to comprehend their relationship as part of the broader regional sexual economy, believing that his "gift" was simply an act of his own generosity, Dulimay's understanding of their arrangement clearly drew upon her intellectual understanding of local sexual economies and their histories.

Reading Dulimay's request in this way illustrates that Hartendorp was not the only one testing certain social norms. Dulimay too entered into experimental relations to provide for herself and her family based on her knowledge of interracial intercourse. So while Hartendorp imagined their liaison as a mutual attraction and transcendent experience that ignored racial difference, it was actually racial difference—and all that interracial intercourse promised—that motivated Dulimay to become involved with him. Hartendorp's fantasy about Dulimay simply acting on her strong attraction to him was also not without graver consequences. Narratives about Indigenous sexuality, especially anthropological ones, reproduced a certain type of imperial knowledge about the Indigenous peoples in the northern Philippines. His description of sexually open Ifugaos and uninhibited sex with Dulimay validated American understandings of sexual immorality among the "savage" population of the islands. This supposed knowledge of the social and sexual practices of native groups in Mountain Province perpetuated the idea of a "porno tropics"—a sexually promiscuous and therefore uncivilized population—which helped enable the civilizing mandate in the islands.[59] Indeed, it was these ideas about racial differences and sexual immorality that enabled colonialist men to penetrate Indigenous communities—and Indigenous women—in the first place. Hartendorp's narrative ensured the longevity of this type of colonial knowledge.

A later encounter proved more dangerous for Hartendorp's colonial career as well as for the Filipina he became involved with. At one teaching outpost, he met a Filipina maid working in the home of a mixed Australian Filipino family he was acquainted with. The unnamed woman, he recollected, "seemed to look at me with interest."[60] She was dismissed from her position within the household after the family accused her of theft but was able to find janitorial work in a local government building, where Hartendorp kept his office. One evening, their relationship took a turn toward the scandalous when the young lady "crept" into his home "with the evident intention of staying the night." Hartendorp welcomed her visit and advances, letting her spend the night with him and giving her some money as a "gift" in the morning.[61] His refusal to understand her logical motivations for pursuing him had dangerous implications for his early career and spelled trouble for them both. The morning after their tryst, Hartendorp impressed on the woman his desire for discretion if they were to continue their "friendship." After she left his residence, she was apparently seen by onlookers "parad[ing] up and down the street" in a new hat and "gaudy" parasol (just purchased with Hartendorp's "gift"), proclaiming she was now Hartendorp's mistress.[62] Hartendorp was alarmed and did not want to be reported to the Bureau of Education for impropriety by any of the residents of the town. Filipinos often reported American teachers to the bureau, especially those who they felt were racially bigoted toward them. Because American teachers were low-level civil servants, it was easy for the colonial state to make examples of them and uphold the tenet of benevolence at the same time.[63] With the help of the Australian expat who used to employ her, Hartendorp got the woman deported back to her home province, dismissing the whole episode as "ludicrous" rather than the product of rational decision making by a vulnerable young woman. Her decision to buy a few luxury items with the money she received hints at what her material expectations of Hartendorp were. Unfortunately, her gamble proved more dangerous than enriching, and her deportation home likely restricted her options for work and financial stability even further.

Dangerous intercourse eventually sealed Hartendorp's fate in the islands when he learned that one of his liaisons, Cornelia Andrade (sixteen at the time of their courtship in comparison to his late twenties), was pregnant. Although he admittedly wanted to return to the United States after his teaching contract expired, not wanting to "get tangled up with any girl" and having apparently taken measures to prevent children, Andrade's pregnancy upended his plans.[64] Hartendorp revealed in his memoirs that he considered staying in the Philippines after the baby was born (prematurely), but even this baby, it seems, was not enough to cement his commitment to stay in the islands. As he recollected, "Abandoning the child would be unthinkable. Must I give up all thought of returning to the United States? Must I make the rest of my life in the Philippines? Many an American in the country has had to face that same situation."[65] Though he mused that he "was always quite free from racial prejudice," his qualms about the new direction of his life with a Filipina "wife" and mixed-race child made him reckon with his own sense of being racially open-minded. Though Hartendorp's writings often pointed to his "marriage" to Andrade as evidence that he was not anti-Filipino, the truth is that he never legally bound himself to her, even after having five children together. Like so many of the informal relations Americans engaged in, theirs was a common-law marriage. Hartendorp rationalized away the informality of this union in his assertion that a true marriage is one's heart and not necessarily "contracted before a priest or judge." Forgoing the marriage contract was a convenient way that many Americans circumvented social and financial responsibility for a legal spouse upon the dissolution of their relationship.[66] Thus it was for Hartendorp, who dissolved their relationship purportedly due to Andrade's propensity to gamble, though he was also displeased by her growing sexual distance from him.[67]

Hartendorp eventually married formally in 1953, and as with his previous sexual interludes, his reflection on this marriage reveals more about the changing US-Philippines relationship and shifting US foreign policy in the Pacific than it does about the author's self-styled racial liberalism and love for the nation. The nineteen-year-old Segunda "Gundie" Amoy first came to the home of Hartendorp as the caretaker of his grandchildren and was forty years his junior. Like many domestic servants working in the shadow of empire, then as well as now, she was vulnerable to the lurid intrusions of her employer. Hartendorp first spied on her while she was bathing, and the one-sided encounter fueled his desire for the young woman. The violation of Amoy's privacy would be followed by a public denigration of her intellect and later the violation of her bodily integrity.

Shortly after their marriage in 1953, Hartendorp published a wedding announcement in the *American Chamber of Commerce Journal*, a publication read primarily by Americans but also by some Filipino business leaders. In it, he publicly denigrated Amoy's intelligence: "She does not know anything about anything, except living, thank God. . . . I shall never have to hold intellectual conversations with her, dear girl."[68] Whether or not Amoy was aware of this announcement is unknown, but that Hartendorp published it in a journal read primarily by the American community speaks to the more open nature of interracial intercourse in the later postindependence period. As the American community contracted and became more insulated, many who remained in the islands were intermarried themselves, so the slight against Amoy would have read like a private joke among old friends. The openness about interracial intercourse helped remaining old-timers portray themselves as pro-Filipino rather than American imperialists. The characterization of Amoy as unintelligent also highlights Hartendorps inability to understand her interest in him as a smart and calculated move by a woman with limited financial options. Ultimately, the denigration of Amoy was softened by the

simultaneous announcement of matrimony. Marriage, as both a contract between two individuals and a metaphor for geopolitical entanglements, was
an institution that signified a close relationship but also allowed for and sustained abuse.

In 1961, Amoy flew to Okinawa with Hartendorp to undergo an abortion, one it seems that she did not completely desire. After having two
children together (in addition to the five children from previous "wife" Andrade), Hartendorp worried about his financial stability. After the failure of
their birth control methods, Hartendorp asked his adult son, who worked at
an American hospital, to find a doctor to give Gundie a D&C (dilation and
curettage). His son reported that none of the doctors would perform the procedure, as it was, and continues to be, illegal in the Philippines, but did
suggest a doctor in Okinawa, Japan, who was known to perform abortions.
Fortunately for Hartendorp, another adult son worked in the American Army
Clinic at Camp Kue in Okinawa and arranged their visit and appointment
with the Japanese doctor, who practiced off base.[69] Hartendorp accessed circuits of travel created by decades of US militarism and imperialism in the
region. These travel circuits connected current (Okinawa) and former (Philippines) US imperial sites and military installations, which were easily accessible by passport-holding Americans. Hartendorp and Amoy's experience
also reflected the gradual shift in US imperial policy that favored military
base accumulation and buildup over the annexation of territories, a shift that
began in earnest during World War II.[70] Because of these Asia-Pacific circuits, Hartendorp had the luxury of planning and controlling his family size
in a way that most Filipinos could not.[71]

Hartendorp tidily recounts in his memoir that a day after the procedure,
Amoy was up and about and "entirely recovered from the experience."[72]
However, a later entry sheds some light on Amoy's own desires regarding
children. Amoy enjoyed spending time with her grandchildren and great
grandchildren, and their presence prompted her to voice her desire for another baby, although Hartendorp concluded "she did not mean it too seriously." Amoy occasionally grew "wistful" and said things like, "If our child
had lived, he (or she) would be so-and-so years old now."[73] Despite Amoy's
expression of her desires, Hartendorp did not take seriously her aspiration
for more children. From Amoy's embedded narrative, it is difficult to believe that she was as determined for the abortion as her husband was, despite
his assertion that it was a mutually agreed on decision. She may have gone
willingly to Okinawa, but her choice was limited in many respects. Hartendorp was the main source of income for her family, making her free will not

as free as it would seem. If nothing else, Hartendorp's assessment that Amoy was "entirely recovered" from the procedure was not sensitive to the long-term emotional effects of abortion that many women experience, especially in a society where it was still widely condemned and in a situation in which the patient lacked broader options.

Throughout his memoirs, Hartendorp reflected on the Filipinas in his life in the same way that many colonialist writers did before. That is, he relegated them to a position of non-subjectivity, while he alone was capable of rational and intellectual transcendence. His liaisons offered him a thrilling chance to experiment and perform his own imperial masculinity, an experience that informed and inflated his ideas of his own manhood and sexual attractiveness. Meanwhile, the women in his narrative, those who best understood the confines of both a patriarchal society and a colonized one, and who made rational, strategic, and intellectual decisions to engage in interracial intercourse, were written as simply being infatuated with him. Colonialist memoir, as a literary genre, must be interpreted as a form of imperial fiction. After all, imperial power and privilege shaped the realities of colonists. Remembering and writing the colonial past is a form of constructing and shaping it, often for the benefit of those doing the recollecting.[74] These works were not simply nostalgic yearnings for youthful days past but romantic revisions of imperial history for the sake of sustaining an imperial future. In many ways, the settler narrative that old-timers perpetuated achieved just that, as figures like Hartendorp, Buck, and others are still well respected and remembered positively by many Americans and Filipinos in the Philippines. This extensive examination of an off-puttingly rich settler careerist archive also demonstrates that while much of the danger for American men who engaged in dangerous intercourse had dissipated since the decades of colonial rule, for many Filipinas, it remained.

Dangerous Intercourse and Anti-imperial Critique

From the colonial period through the commonwealth era, Filipino writers who wrote on interracial romances between colonizer and colonized largely did so as a way to express nationalist aspirations, critique American imperialism, or point to the gendered inequalities faced by Filipina women living under the American flag. While dangerous intercourse was understood to be an apt vehicle through which to discuss the US-Philippines colonial relationship by Americans and Filipinos alike, this is largely where the commonalities end. For Filipino writers who ruminated on empire, dangerous intercourse was, in a word, dangerous. It was dangerous for Filipinas, it was dangerous for the nation, and it could also be dangerous for the Americans who engaged in it. But unlike the revisionist settler fiction that many Americans produced, Filipino stories more accurately reflected the broader realities of interracial intercourse that played out across the archipelago. While Americans romantically rewrote dangerous intercourse as a way to forestall the loss of American power and prestige in the islands, Filipino writers laid it bare.[75]

Filipinos had long used the realm of culture as an outlet for nationalist aspirations. By the time of the American occupation, Filipino writers had penned many books, poems, and plays to voice their dissatisfaction with their previous Spanish occupiers.[76] The tradition continued into the American period, even after the Philippine commission passed the Sedition Act in 1901, making it unlawful to, "utter seditious words or speeches, write, publish, or circulate scurrilous libels against the United States." The act also made it unlawful for Filipinos to advocate for Philippine independence "orally, or by writing or printing or like methods," during the ongoing Philippine-American War.[77] To be sure, prior to the Sedition Act, rallying cries against the US occupation were common in various Philippine press outlets, and often dangerous intercourse was one of the most damning admonitions thrown against the new colonizers. After the American colonial government passed the Sedition Act forbidding written or verbal assaults against the US occupation, many artists and writers turned to allegory and symbolism to disguise the critiques that could land them in jail (or worse). American officials kept their eyes open for seditious plays and dramas that featured lecherous or greedy characters, which often symbolized US rule over the islands. These characters often sought to violate or abduct the Filipina heroine of the play (who usually personified Philippine freedom or independence) or thwart a romance between the Filipina and Filipino protagonist (who represented the Philippine nationalist or patriot).[78] For many Filipino writers who came after the revolutionary period of seditious dramas, interracial intercourse was still largely depicted as dangerous (for Filipinas and the nation) or, at best, as a problematic reality that was not likely to produce happiness for anyone entering into such a relationship.[79]

In the post–Philippine-American War decades, the revolutionary fervor that had inspired a host of seditious plays had softened somewhat, although scathing critiques of US empire continued. Filipinos continued to find new ways to steer the nation toward paths they—and not the colonial state—desired. This shift in Filipino approaches to the ongoing occupation was also reflected in the literature produced in the 1920s and the commonwealth period, in which Americans are depicted less as martial usurpers who violently rape local women and more as part of the larger backdrop of the population of the Philippines, albeit an out-of-place, problematic, or undesired presence, and one that made social inequalities under empire hypervisible. One such story that offered a more tempered rejection of interracial intercourse was published as a serialized short in a women's magazine in 1923. Written by Filipino writer and politician Tomas Alonso, "Little Pickanniny Girl" was a cautionary tale, one that depicted a regrettable interracial relationship that left neither party satisfied or happy. Alonso, like many Filipino politicians, had been a member of the Revolutionary Philippine Army that fought against the American occupation.[80] His long-standing opposition to US rule was reflected in his story. "Little Pickanniny Girl" was published in *Woman's Outlook* magazine, the "official organ of the National Federation of Women's Clubs of the Philippines." The magazine's editors, Trinidad Fernandez and Pura Villanueva Kalaw, were well-known Filipina suffragists.[81] *Woman's Outlook* often published news that apprised its primarily Filipina readership of their evolving political rights and promoted women's welfare more generally. Alonso's fictional account of a liaison between an American sailor and a Filipina *bailarina* reflected not only his own understanding of the asymmetrical Philippine-US relationship but also the broad appeal and continued usefulness of the interracial romance metaphor as a vehicle for anti-imperial critique.

The story was not so much a cautionary tale but a lamentation of dangerous intercourse in general. The American sailor, a clear personification of the United States, is named Sam, while the Filipina *bailarina* is simply referred to as "the girl." Sam was enraptured by the Filipina and called her his "little pickanniny girl" or his "wonderful little brownie lass." He monopolized her work time by buying multiple dances with her and made her promise to dance only with him. After a night of dancing, Sam asked the girl if he could take her home. The girl, understanding the sexual implications of the request, ran to her mother (who oversaw the girl's occupation as a dancer) and begged for a different job. The girl pleaded, "Let me scrub floors, launder clothes, or do anything else." Her mother, however, encouraged her to return to Sam, reminding her that the earnings from her "heaviest costumer" would help pay for a lawyer to get her brother out of jail. The girl returned to Sam and danced with him until the early morning hours and agreed to meet with him again the following evening. A drunk Sam returned home to his ship, berating himself when he realized he had not bothered to ask for the girl's real name but excited at the prospect of seeing her the next night.[82]

The narrator, presumably Alonso, as the story is presented as a firsthand account of Sam and the Filipina *bailarina*, concluded that "none of them cared for each other." Sam's amorous feelings stemmed from the "stimulating influence of White and Mackay's product" (liquor), and the *bailarina* had "an eye only on his money," which she planned to use to free her brother from jail. Once the falsely accused brother was released and could provide for the household, the *bailarina* hoped, she could return to school and "the virtuous path once more." The moralizing short story reflected the gendered norms and attitudes of the time, wherein even the suffragist editors of the magazine often framed their claims to political participation around ideas of feminine morality and virtue.[83] Even though the Filipina character was poor and forced to work in the sexual economy, she was someone whom the broader readership could sympathize with, even if they did not share her social class. Unlike the thinner and more scandalous depictions of Filipina dancers that were popularized at the time by the moralist-reformist set who sought to eradicate vice and close down the dance halls, Alonso fleshed out the *bailarina*'s desires and motivations.[84] Alonso's story did not romanticize interracial intercourse, nor did it depict Filipinas as willing and eager to partner with Americans. Instead, the story was attuned to some of the realities of poorer Filipinas, unlike in most of the fantasy reflections written by American old-timers. Published in a politically geared Filipina women's magazine, and written by a longtime proponent of Philippine independence, this story reflected some of the shared interests of the Filipina editors and readership, as well as Filipino politicians not content with colonial status. Namely, the story links some of the contemporary societal ills of the nation, like the sexualization and exploitation of impoverished Filipinas, to the larger issue of American rule.

Alonso's thinly veiled critique of American rule also turned on its head the concurrent anti-suffragist rhetoric in the nation that blamed Filipina women specifically for the continued paternalistic relationship with the United States because of their "susceptibility to everything foreign."[85] His depiction of a Filipina whose desire was to reject Sam, the symbol of the enduring American presence in the nation, was likely a welcome one for the Filipina suffragist editors of the magazine. Likewise, Alonso's use of "pickaninny" (a misspelling of the US pickaninny) as Sam's endearment for the Filipina dancer might have been meant to draw attention to the color line laid down and enforced by most Americans in the Philippines, one that positioned Filipinos in the Philippines within the same marginalized position as Black Americans in the United States. The pickaninny was a popular American and British cultural production, one that depicted Black children as cartoonishly ignorant, neglected, and, like white perceptions of Black and African people more generally, resistant to pain.[86] Similar to the minstrelsy depictions of the "dandy" or "sambo," the pickaninny was a cultural figure that supported and naturalized racial violence against Black people. Americans frequently used the derogatory and paternalistic slur as well as the image of the pickaninny to refer to Filipinos, adults and children alike.[87] While Alonso's use of the slur was likely a rejection of American racism, we must also consider that while some Filipinos formed close relationships with Black colonists, others attempted to distance themselves from racial Blackness in general, applying the ideas of racial inferiority not only to Black colonists but also to the poor, indigenous, and non-Hispanized populations in the Philippines.[88] For Alonso to apply the term to a poor Filipina *bailarina* in a women's magazine run by elite and well-educated Filipina women hinted at the class and race distinctions that Filipinos associated with interracial sexual intercourse.[89] The association of the *bailarina* with marginalized racial Blackness might have been an acceptable characterization to Filipino elites, who often differentiated themselves from those associated with immorality and sexual vice. Ultimately, Alonso and the editors of *Woman's Outlook* may have also been interested in shifting the narratives about immorality associated with Filipina women, if not to warn against too friendly relations between American men and Filipinas then certainly to direct the discourse about Filipinos—and Filipina women in particular—in a direction that was more useful for pro-independence and pro-suffrage agendas.

Alonso channeled his criticism of the US presence in the islands through both the cultural realm, as with the publication of this story, and the political realm. As a prominent representative from his home island of Cebu to the Philippine legislature, he used his political influence to promote anti-imperialism.[90] In the 1930s, he urged the Philippine legislature to push the United States on its promise of eventual independence by advocating a plan of "non-cooperation" and "resistance."[91] His proposal came several months after the highly publicized anti-Filipino riots in Watsonville, California, where an armed mob of predominantly white instigators burned Filipino establishments, terrorized the Filipino community (predominantly composed of young men), and ultimately killed twenty-two-year-old Filipino farmworker Fermin Tobera. The Watsonville riots were the culmination of years of anti-Filipino sentiment that had been building in connection to white fears over both the loss of jobs and the loss of white women to Filipinos. The riots incited anti-Filipino violence across California and other parts of the United States, and it did not dissipate.[92]

In the Philippines, Filipinos organized rallies and protests in solidarity with the terrorized farmworkers, the violence yet another reminder to Filipinos on both sides of the Pacific that they were second-class citizens of the US empire, even in their own homeland. Filipino politicians in the United States and the Philippines used the momentum of the Watsonville riots to push pro-independence agendas, the efforts of which ultimately culminated in the 1934 Tydings-McDuffie Act.[93] Though many Filipino politicians who advocated for the 1934 act—and the definitive timeline to independence it promised—heralded it as a victory, they also recognized the compromises spelled out in the new legislation. Namely, commonwealth status came at the cost of restricting Filipino immigration to the United States. Since the early years of the occupation, the US government had classified Filipinos as US nationals, meaning that they enjoyed restriction-free immigration to the United States and its outer lying possessions. With the Philippine Independence Act, they were reclassified as aliens and limited to a fifty-person-per-year immigration quota.[94]

While some scholars characterize the period of Filipinization in the second decade of US rule as a turning point from revolutionary hostility to American rule to one of accommodation and acceptance, the literature presented here highlights the continuity of Filipino nationalists' grievances against Americans, largely expressed through the trope of interracial intercourse as a symbol of imperial transgressions over the nation.[95] In the later decades of US rule, other writers also incorporated the figure of the white American colonizer, most often represented by an American sailor, into stories exploring Filipino desires and contemporary issues. Unlike many American depictions of intercourse as the foundation of positive American-Filipino relations, Filipino writers more often understood interracial relations as a site from which uneven power relations stemmed and therefore a useful site of critique. Paz Latorena, a prominent Filipina writer, used the trope of interracial intercourse in her 1928 short story "Desire" to highlight the elusive nature of companionate love as well as the sexualization of Filipina women. Latorena is widely hailed as an early pioneer in the realm of Filipina women's writings on gender and sexuality.[96] She accumulated literary prizes for her writing throughout her academic career, and "Desire" was named by another prominent writer, Jose Garcia Villa, as one of three best Filipino short stories of 1928. By 1934, Latorena had earned her PhD and was a faculty member at the University of Santo Tomas, Manila, where she taught short-story writing.[97]

Latorena's story revolves around the "homely" Filipina protagonist who lamented her "broad masculine forehead, the small eyes that slanted at the corners, the unpleasant mouth, the aggressive jaws." She also lamented the "beautiful harmony" that was her body, a body of "unusual beauty" that made her the object of men's lustful advances. The protagonist, horrified by the "unbeautiful light" that shone from men's eyes when they looked at her body, hid her figure under shapeless clothes and resigned herself to a loveless life. The unnamed heroine supported herself by writing short stories for newspapers and magazines, and her work eventually attracted the attention of a white American expatriate. While the man was described by the narrator of the story as "one of those who believed in the inferiority of the colored races," he nonetheless initiated a friendship with the Filipina protagonist rooted in his appreciation of her writing sketches, which he found to be like "those of the people of his race." The two struck up an unlikely friendship rooted in their appreciation of literature. Eventually, the heroine, someone who desired a "pure" love from someone who could see beyond her beautiful body, decided to test the waters with her new "friend" by wearing a shapelier dress to one of their outings. While first confident she had found a companion who liked her for herself, the American soon lustily expressed his desire for her body. When he saw her disappointment at this outburst, he promptly apologized, but it was too late. The disillusioned protagonist replied to her erstwhile companion, "You have just been yourself . . . like other men."[98]

Like Alonso's story, interracial intercourse was the conveyance through which Latorena expressed the unwanted sexualization of Filipina women. Both Filipinas depicted in the short stories had dreams and desires—one for an alternative livelihood and the resumption of her educational attainment and the other for genuine acceptance and love—that were at odds with the interracial relations they were engaged in. While Latorena could have chosen any nationality for her antagonist, her choice of a white American for the lascivious role was telling. Having come of age in the shadow of empire, it is likely that she had experienced her own unwanted encounters with American men, and by the late 1920s, the spectacle of US soldiers and sailors trawling the streets of red-light districts was almost cliché. It was a spectacle that Latorena would have been quite familiar with, if not through her own experiences then through the simple fact of living in a heavily colonized and militarized city. The imperial critique is more apparent when one considers that "Desire" was published in a newspaper known for frequently publishing anti-American articles and having a clear pro-independence agenda, the *Philippine Herald*. The *Herald*, often referred to by Philippine scholars as the organ of the Nationalista Party, was the first English-language Filipino daily newspaper and, by 1935, had the largest circulation of any of the Filipino-run daily papers.[99] Latorena's indictment of American men's lasciviousness toward Filipinas—an indictment used time and again by Filipinos hoping to point out the hypocrisy of American benevolence—was the type of fiction that *Herald* editors would have hoped to secure for publication. Latorena's work was also part of a growing literary nationalist trend in the 1920s of depicting Filipina heroines as *kayumanggi*, or brown-skinned, in opposition to the mestiza or light-skinned heroines held up as examples of feminine virtue in both the Spanish and the American periods.[100]

Even in Filipino representations that featured Americans as protagonists, authors continued to characterize intermarried Americans in ways that reflected the realities of the asymmetrical power relations between Americans and Filipinos or otherwise reflected the demographic realities of the colonized nation. In 1933, the popular women's magazine *Liwayway* (The Dawn) published a short story by writer Gregorio Coching titled "Puso ng Dios" (Heart of God). The story featured a downtrodden but virtuous Filipina named Virginia who is rescued from her life as a *bailarina* by a wealthy American named William.[101] William is a "mayamang Amerikano" (rich American), and his marriage to Virginia materially enriches Virginia's family and community. At the same time, William is depicted as something of an antihero, heavy-handed with Filipinos and used to getting his way. In one scene in which William is demanding that the local clergy perform the marriage immediately, Virginia fears and laments his imperious treatment of the priest, saying, "Hindi na ba nagbawa iyang kapusukan nang loob mo? Paskongpasko e magbubuhat ka na naman nang kamay, at hanggang dito sa simbahan ay ibig mo pa ring mangboksin" (Hasn't your brazen rashness diminished? It's Christmastime and you're manhandling someone, and even here in the church, you still want to go boxing).[102] William is an American sailor with the US military and a proponent of US imperialism. He thinks Filipinos are impressionable and prone to vice. Upon his marriage to Virginia, he urges her kin to mimic Americans: "Tanggapin ninyo ang makabagong pamamaraan sa pagunlad at ang masaganang karunungang ibinibigay sa inyo nang aming bansa" (Accept new ways of progress and the abundant knowledge bestowed on you by our country).[103] Coching's rags-to-riches fantasy story reflects the broader realities of the sexual economy that involved poorer local women and American men, and points to the expectations and desires of local women who engaged in dangerous intercourse. Though he describes his protagonist as fortunate to have left her life of hardship after her union with William, such outcomes from colonial intercourse in the real world were mostly fantasy and not without their own set of dangers for Filipinas.

Conclusion

Today there is a term, popularized by Filipino film and literature alike, that reflects the continued understanding of interracial intercourse as a site from which to critique the US imperial presence in the Philippines. "Hanggang pier lang" (Until the pier only) is a contemporary pejorative applied to Filipina women who become involved with American military men. The phrase expresses the idea that the romance will last only up until the pier, because once the GI returns to the United States on his military transport ship, his Filipina lover will be left behind.[104] Though this particular expression was popularized in Filipino postwar literature and films of the late 1940s, the sentiment behind the "Hanggang pier lang" representation—hostility toward the American occupation, insinuations of sexual immorality—were ideas that found expression in the cultural productions of both Filipinos and Americans since the early days of the annexation and through the postindependence period.[105]

Imperial fiction that depicted dangerous intercourse in the American colonial Philippines highlights the discursive strategies used by Filipinos and Americans alike to steer the direction of the US-Philippines relationship. As both groups reflected on empire and attempted to advance their own desires and aspirations for themselves and the nation, the realm of the literary was a productive space from which to wage campaigns or make critiques. Filipino depictions of interracial relations remained relatively stable. Dangerous intercourse largely represented continued Filipino subjugation to Americans, and the use of the interracial relations trope was a time-tested method of anti-imperial critique. From the seditious plays to Paz Latorena's "Desire," interracial relations between American and Filipinos were not represented as reliable paths to fulfillment, nor did they signify positive bilateral or interpersonal racial relations. Rather, they were most often presented as obstacles to Philippine independence or as relations that were symptomatic of the larger societal issues facing a colonized nation. Even in stories like "Puso ng Dios," in which a white savior "rescues" a Filipina, characterizations of Americans—as domineering, heavy-handed, and arrogant—often looked as they did at the turn of the century.

American cultural productions equivocated on dangerous intercourse as the political status of the Philippines shifted and old-timer positions became more unstable. American expats intent on maintaining their influence in the postindependence period capitalized on the idea of interracial intercourse as historically transgressive to carve out long-lasting settler careers from which they continued to promote the interests of the US empire. From Buck's allegory on US-Philippines history to Hartendorp's fanciful memoirs, intercourse was construed by old-timers as something that bestowed on them intimate knowledge of the islands and people. In supposedly eschewing the racial dictates of their home nation, they positioned themselves as true friends of the Philippines, evidenced most strongly (in their estimations) by their Filipina wives and mixed-race children. The refusal of American old-timers to fathom the more complicated and rational decision-making processes of the Filipina women in their lives upheld the fantasies that they constructed about themselves and of US imperialism. It is the hopes and desires of Filipinas written in the margins and absences of these settler texts that make studying these works more compelling. While Filipino writers were more in tune with the realities of dangerous intercourse throughout the islands and how such relations reflected the asymmetrical relations between the United States and the Philippines, the body of old-timer writings underscores the fact that settler careerists comprehended little about the people and place they claimed to be so familiar with beyond the fantasies that they constructed.

Chapter 6

Making Mestizos

Filipino American Mixed-Race Children and Discourses
of Belonging, 1898 and Beyond

In the summer of 1937, the murder of a prominent American rice planter and plantation owner, Percy A. Hill, captured the headlines of many American newspapers in the Philippines. The *Manila Daily Tribune* ran the headline "Gang of 10 Raid, Loot Hacienda, Murder Planter" and, like the other newspapers, initially characterized the event as a case of malevolence by a group of Filipino tenant workers.[1] As the press fleshed out more details of Hill's life and demise, the coverage slipped further and further away from the murder and, like a serialized soap opera, came to fixate more on the family drama revolving around Hill's illegitimate children from a previous Filipina lover. Ricardo Hill (or Richard, as he was alternately known), an American mestizo born to Hill Sr. and his former common-law wife, Martina Ramos, was the eldest of the six known living children of the deceased. The defense team in the legal case quickly fingered Ricardo as the prime murder suspect, despite there being guilty parties in police custody who already confessed. The only evidence needed by the defense to cast suspicion on Ricardo was his exclusion from his father's will. Percy Hill had children with three different women, first with Filipina Martina Ramos, then with American Helen Livingstone, and last with Filipina Caridad Hill. He had apparently excluded both of his children with Ramos from his will, leaving most of the Hill assets to his four legitimate heirs, three children from a marriage to his late wife Helen, and his youngest child from his current wife, Caridad. When Ricardo was questioned about his knowledge of the will, which disappeared during the robbery-murder along with other valuables kept in a storage chest, he stated that he knew nothing about it, nor the allegations that his father had disinherited him in favor of his legitimate half siblings.[2]

While suspicions about Ricardo's criminality eventually subsided with the charging of several others who confessed, the ease with which he was presented by the defense team as a person of interest in the case illuminates a major theme explored in this chapter, namely the insider/outsider status of American mestizos, the mixed-race children of American Filipino parentage.[3] The lawyers for the accused, faced with mounting evidence against their clients, including possession of Hill's stolen property and witness testimonies, attempted to steer the direction of the case toward a new suspect. Ricardo was an easy target, and they needed only to muster commonly held understandings of American mestizo immorality. Mixed-race children were often stigmatized by the presumed conditions of their birth and the association of their Filipina mothers with the sexual economy and prostitution. In the case of Percy Hill's murder, it was easy for the lawyers to play on these popular notions about mestizos as they presented Ricardo as a potentially dangerous threat to the "legitimate" Hill family, a possible mastermind behind the murder of his own father. Questions of whether or not he felt ill will toward Hill Sr. peppered the interrogation of Ricardo, reflecting the unease many colonialists felt about the large and growing number of American mestizos in the islands. Despite Ricardo's testimony that his relationship with Hill was amiable, the press, like the defense team, questioned his loyalty, his morals, and his "Americanness," even drawing attention to the apparent novelty of his colloquial designation of Hill as "my old man" by putting it in quotation marks.[4]

While the story of Ricardo Hill demonstrates the contours of American mestizo belonging in the Philippines, it is also a story that most mixed-race offspring in the islands would likely find novel. Ricardo's experience of closeness with his American parent—living only a short bicycle ride away, spending evenings with his father working on projects when the "legitimate" family was away in the city—was one that most mixed-race children of American and Filipino parentage did not have the privilege of enjoying. For most other American mestizos, a meaningful relationship with their American parent was rare, as most American fathers simply left their children and liaisons and returned to their lives in the United States. American mestizos were a population whose place in the US homeland as well as in the Philippines was one that was always and already questioned, a source of constant concern and even fear. The notion of dangerous mixed-race colonial subjects was not a new trope that emerged from the US empire in the Pacific.

Indeed, the idea of dangerous half-white dissidents and malcontents was an idea that the Anglo-European empires had been growing and shaping since before the United States existed. Like in British India, where mixed-race children of Anglo-Indian unions were understood by colonists as subversive but also "potential recruits" in the cause of empire, colonialists in the Philippines grappled with how to incorporate American mestizos.[5] American experiences with Black, Indigenous, and Latin American peoples in the Western Hemisphere—where free mixed-race people of color and Black-Indigenous alliances were deemed threatening to both the institution of slavery and settler expansionist policies—were also part of the broader US conception of racial mixing that American mestizos in the Philippines were now understood within.[6]

In the Philippines, however, a different set of racial experiences and histories existed. Historian Nicholas Molnar points out, for example, that the "one-drop" racial classificatory system of the United States, rooted in American slavery, was not necessarily compatible with the racial classificatory system of the Philippines. When Americans landed in 1898, they found that local understandings of race were predicated on the entangled histories of the Indigenous populations, Spanish imperialism, and the migratory patterns of Chinese, Malaysians, and other Asians.[7] Chinese and Spanish mixed-race peoples had existed in the archipelago for centuries, carving out livelihoods and families that helped integrate them into island life. New American occupiers and their mestizo children did not immediately fit local racial designations but would, like the populations before them, become incorporated in new and different ways. Colonialists often constructed the American mestizo population as one that was at once dangerous due to the threat they posed to ideas of white racial superiority and American prestige and in constant danger of falling victim to the supposed baser nature of their Filipino heritage. For many Filipinos, the general acceptance of American mestizos was in line with preexisting local attitudes toward racial and ethnic mixing, even as the new population was also set apart from Spanish and Chinese mestizos on the islands.

Spanning the early colonial years to the post 1935 commonwealth period, I trace the changing discourse about the mixed-race offspring of American-Filipino liaisons. From the colonial state's impulse to classify and understand different mestizo types—Spanish mestizos, Chinese mestizos, European/American mestizos—to the efforts of churches and small charity organizations to protect and provide for children of partial American parentage, Americans were preoccupied with the product of racial mixing in the colonial site. Progressive reformers, charity organizers, and others directed the discussions of American mestizos in ways that allowed US imperial professions of benevolence and moral superiority to coexist with the presence of thousands of abandoned mixed-race children. Rhetorically casting mestizos as "orphans" was the primary way that Americans were able to reconcile this equivocation. As philanthropic organizations came to characterize American mestizos as orphans, they recast this population from a symbol of American licentiousness and corruptness in the tropics to a symbol of the American impulse for humanitarianism and goodwill. The reality was, however, that while most American fathers left behind their children, Filipina mothers did not. Despite the fact that mothers and extended Filipino family members largely supported and raised their American mestizo children, one of the main components of American campaigns for Mestizo uplift was the denigration of Filipina mothers and Filipino influences. These campaigns largely glossed over the American men who fathered the "orphans."[8] At the heart of charitable efforts for the care of impoverished American mestizos was the foundational belief that not providing proper instruction under American auspices would leave these mestizos largely to the mercy of their baser "Filipino blood." The creation and control of a narrative about American mestizos and their parents was not coincidental or random but had very specific imperial utility. American charitable organizations discursively "made" mestizos in a way that tempered the danger they posed to imperial professions of moral superiority.

Charting the discourse surrounding this mixed-race population illustrates how Americans perceived a preexisting tolerance for mestizos in the Philippines, and how this understanding imbued colonialist thinking about the "natural" place for American mestizos, both within the physical boundaries of the Philippines and within the racial hierarchy of the islands. In the early years of the occupation, US officials relentlessly pursued information about the scores of mestizo children of Spanish friars, and this phenomenon colored American notions of what types of sexual behaviors and families were more or less common or tolerated in the islands. This, in turn, fueled colonial fantasies about how American and Filipino sexual mixing—and indeed potential children—might be tolerated and received in the new territory. This chapter also explores how American mestizos themselves understood their socioracial position within the Philippines, as well as how they pushed back against the colonialist characterization of mixed-race people as simultaneously dangerous and valuable because of their Filipino and American blood. American mestizos who were fortunate enough to have legitimate standing in their families—thus shielding them to an extent from the social and economic stigmas of being abandoned or from illicit relationships—attempted to circumvent popular discourses pertaining to mixed-race children of partial American parentage. Prominent mestizos came to view themselves in the context of a waning formal US colonial presence and formed organizations, like the Manila-based Daughters of American Veterans (DAV), to show their pride in being American. They could negotiate semi-privileged positions within the American community through their involvement in DAV, redirecting and rejecting the predominant narrative about dangerous, immoral, and orphaned mixed-race offspring. Ironically, in American mestizos' attempts to navigate belonging and social hierarchies in the colonial Philippines, they, like the charitable organizations that framed them as vulnerable "orphans," strengthened the colonial racial dictates that helped solidify a US imperial future in the islands, even after independence.

Friar Lands, Families, and Prurient Fantasies

In the year 1900, the US commission to the Philippines reported on the state of the new colonial possession in the East and described the ethnically mixed population of the islands. Chinese mestizos—those residents of the islands with one Chinese parent and one Filipino parent—were described as "intelligent men" but also "restless, scheming, and untrustworthy."[9] This characterization endured, and in 1925 a US newspaper reported that "in the life of the islands, Japanese and Chinese mestizos have taken a leading part," although not necessarily a positive or beneficial part.[10] Taking cues from eugenics, which reached heights of popularity in the early twentieth century, Americans in the Philippines took copious notes on the ethnically mixed population of the Philippine islands. Chinese and Japanese mestizos in the archipelago, they concluded, were inscrutable and wily, albeit slightly elevated above the native Filipino population, while Spanish mestizos were typically considered the most civilized population in the islands because they possessed European blood and because of their higher-class status. New American colonists often characterized Spanish and Chinese mestizos as superior to the native population, although still susceptible to the baser ways of the native because of their "Indian" blood.[11] Commission member and zoologist Dean Worcester, for example, included mestizo populations in his photographic documentation of flora, fauna, and people of the islands. He and other imperialists then used the photographs as "evidence" that the local inhabitants of the islands lacked civilization and hence needed American tutelage. In Worcester's 1905 index to his vast Philippine photograph collection, he organized the pictures of people according to whom he believed were the least civilized to the most, listing Indigenous groups such as the Ati, Aeta, and Agta as the first entries. Mestizos, on the other hand, were the last group to be listed in the index before he moved on to cataloging photos of animals, plants, and landscapes. Of the mestizo population, he noted in his introductory overview: "The most intelligent and highly educated and influential men in the Islands are Spanish mestizos. Many of the best business men are Chinese mestizos, and these two classes are numerically and in every other way by far the most important classes which exist."[12] When the mixed-race American offspring of dangerous intercourse became more and more apparent, colonists and Filipinos alike sought to place them somewhere on the spectrum of this already complex tapestry of race and ethnicity in the islands.

To be sure, the official colonial record is filled with many accounts describing the "differences" between mestizos and other racial groups in the archipelago. Even the elite Spanish and Chinese mestizo business leaders and politicians who hosted American officials were fair game for colonialists looking for anthropological subjects with mixed racial heritage to put under the microscope. The report of the first US commission to the Philippines (the Schurman Commission), for example, suggested how important American officials deemed the topic of racial mixing in the islands. In their attempts to understand the new possession and the local inhabitants, the commission conducted extensive interviews with Anglo, Spanish, Filipino, and Chinese local residents. Invariably, Americans would ask their respondents to describe the various ethnic groups in the islands, along with which groups made the best laborers, which groups were fit to have local governing responsibilities, and what types of citizens "half-breeds" made, among other things.[13] At the time of the Schurman Commission interviews, the US military was concurrently fighting the troops of famed revolutionary leader Emilio Aguinaldo, a Chinese mestizo. Aguinaldo, who also helped lead the charge against the previous Spanish colonizers, piqued American interest in the place of mestizos in Philippine society, especially as he was the leader of the burgeoning Philippine republic, a republic that the US administration did not recognize. Commission member Dean Worcester, for example, asked William Daland, an American broker who had resided in the Philippines for twenty years prior to the US annexation, "Which ones of the present leaders [of the Filipino Revolutionaries] are Chinese Mestizos?"[14] Daland named Aguinaldo as one with "Chinese blood."[15] The Schurman Commission interviews focused heavily on discerning local attitudes toward Chinese and Chinese mestizos, underscoring US concerns about labor demands and the possibilities for the capitalist exploitation of the islands but also how the Philippine population might respond to a Chinese exclusion policy similar to the one in place in the United States. While some respondents, like the Spanish mestizo Benito Legarda, described someone who was a "mixture of Chinese and the native" as "a very good citizen and a hard worker," others, like Daland, had more defamatory characterizations.[16] Often with white respondents like Daland, American officials let slip their own assumptions and attitudes toward the nonwhite population, as when commission member Charles Denby, former US minister to China, stated of the Chinese population rather than asked, "They have largely intermarried with the native women, and have produced the worst race in the country, known as the Chinese mestizo or half caste?" Daland responded, "Yes, they are the worst class we have. . . . They are treacherous and unreliable, but they are smart; the touch of Chinese blood seems to make them more cunning."[17] Even some of the Chinese interviewees had less than positive things to say about mestizos. The well-known and prominent Chinese merchant Chan Quiensien, who came to the Philippines from China at the age of fourteen and Hispanicized his name to Carlos Palanca upon his baptism, told commission members that while Chinese mestizos were some of the wealthiest people in the Philippines, they were not very intelligent. "With regard to very good intellects there are very few," he stated. They relied instead on "usurious" practices to make their money.[18]

While these early commission interviews were preoccupied with ascertaining general attitudes toward the Chinese and Chinese mestizo residents in the islands, a different survey conducted by the colonial government fixated on local understandings of Spanish mestizos—or, as some referred to them, Español Filipinos.[19] Conducted just after the Schurman Commission testimonies were gathered, the 1900 friar lands investigation focused instead on discerning how people felt about the many (primarily Spanish) religious orders in the nation. Capitalizing on the tensions between landless Filipino farmers and landed Spanish friars and the built-up animosity of local inhabitants against the Spaniards more generally, the United States launched an inquiry into the state of lands held for ecclesiastical use, with the stated intent of redistributing the land more equitably. The friar lands investigation was a useful source of information for US colonial officials. Like the Schurman

Commission interviews, the investigation into the religious orders outwardly seemed to reflect the US commitment to rectifying Spanish abuses as well as a benevolent interest in the grievances of ordinary Filipinos. Like many studies conducted by the colonial state, however, the underlying impetus was to gather information that would ensure the smooth transition from Spanish to American rule. Using local testimonies to understand local priorities and attitudes was also a way for Americans to forge their imperial path. And while the stated purpose of the friar lands inquiry was the redistribution of land to address growing agrarian unrest, the resulting 1904 Friar Lands Act did not drastically change access to land for tenant farmers and ordinary Filipinos. Instead, in 1902, shortly after the friar lands investigation, the Vatican sold around 90 percent of the lands in question to the United States for $7 million. Landed Filipino elites, as well as US corporations and individual colonists, ended up buying and leasing much of the land.[20]

Like the Schurman interviews, the friar lands interviews proved to be a useful intelligence-gathering tool for Americans, especially about the history of race mixing in the islands. American officials were keen to use these interviews to learn about local social practices and attitudes toward racial mixing. In particular, interviewers prodded respondents—mostly elite or landed Filipino men and clergy members—about the sexual lives of friars. Interviewers were also interested in what types of family formations were deemed more acceptable than others.[21] They directed many of these interviews, at one point or another, toward the topic of friar immorality, specifically as it involved sexual relations with local women, and how Filipinos felt about such behavior. American officials, for example, asked Don Felipe Calderon, a well-to-do Filipino attorney who was himself the grandson of a Franciscan friar, to speak generally about "the morality of the friars." Without hesitation, or so the transcript goes, Calderon described the commonness of encountering the children of friars: "No one ever paid any attention to it or thought if it, and so depraved had the people become in this regard that the women who were the mistresses of friars really felt great pride in it and had no compunction in speaking of it. So general had this thing become that it may be said that even now the rule is for a friar to have a mistress and children, and he who is not is the rare exception, and if it is desired that I give names, I could cite right now 100 children of friars."[22] When further questioned as to whether this breaking of religious celibacy vows by the clergy was "the subject . . . of great condemnation by the people," Calderon replied simply, "By no means." Calderon was at times dismissive of suggestions by the American interviewer that the Spanish friars were disliked because of their sexual proclivities, saying that the breaking of celibacy was merely an "infraction of the canonical law," and even going so far as to say the clergy "bettered our race." After double-checking that "the immorality of the friars is not the chief ground of the hostility of the people against them," the American interviewer moved on to other topics.

Similarly, in an interview with Jose Rodriguez Infante, an elite Filipino landowner in Pampanga, a province just north of Manila, American officials again asked questions relating to the sexual promiscuity of friars and the children that they fathered. Infante, like Calderon, described knowing a great many men and women who were the sons and daughters of friars, having several children of friars currently living on his estate. When asked if sexual immorality "was the ground of hostility against the friars," he too answered no, stating that he believed the antagonism resulted from the friars' political and financial control. Immorality, Infante continued, "had a slight influence, in the case, but it became so common that it passed unnoticed."[23] In another interview, Filipino lawyer and landowner Nozario Constantino stated that there was "no morality whatever" with regard to the friars. Pressed further by colonial officials, who were clearly interested in hearing more about mestizo children and transgressive sexual acts, Constantino divulged his observations about various clergy having concubines and many children, although, he added, speaking about the children specifically, "we do not look upon that as a discredit to a man." Continuing to press the subject, US officials asked if it was true that the people had "become so accustomed to the relations which the friars had with the women that it really paid little part in their hostility." According to Constantino, sexual licentiousness was part of why people disliked the friars but not in itself the cause.

American officials were so intrigued by the sexual transgressions of friars that they steered the interviews into topics that had less to do with the friar lands than with their own desires for information regarding sex. It is no coincidence that the matter of interracial sexual intercourse weighed heavily on the minds of colonial officials, as by the time of the friar lands inquiry in late 1900, complaints from American reform and religious groups about regulated systems of prostitution for the benefit of US military troops were numerous.[24] News of Uncle Sam's troops frequenting brothels and the failure of the colonial administration to shut down red-light districts had reached the ears of moralist groups and anti-imperialists in the United States, prompting calls for government action.[25] Around the same time that many of the friar land interviews were taking place—from July through November 1900—the Woman's Christian Temperance Union put together a petition for a formal investigation regarding the news of regulated prostitution and immorality in the islands. In October 1900, it submitted the petition to the president and the secretary of war.[26]

The Schurman and friar lands investigations produced information that Americans used to measure how their own rule in the islands was shaping up, as well as to anticipate what reactions Filipinos might have to the administrative, economic, cultural, and social changes that the occupation brought. With the help of these interviews, Americans could gauge how the local population would perceive licentious behavior and other types of American intrusions. As US military men in particular garnered a reputation throughout the islands for the liberties they took with local women, interracial sexual intercourse and attitudes toward mestizo children deliberately seeped into the friar lands talks. In fact, as commission members conducted their reconnaissance on sexual matters, they often explicitly compared US troop debauchery with friar licentiousness. For example, in the interview of Brigadier General James F. Smith that was included in the inquiry, commission leader William Howard Taft (soon to be the first governor-general of the Philippines) asked if US troops stationed in the central Visayan Islands had married Filipinas and further wanted to know about the status of "the social evil" (houses of prostitution) in the region.[27] Smith reported that while he did not know of any brothels in the region, he estimated that around 2 to 5 percent of the American soldiers had local "mistresses," and that an unaccounted number were likely secretly engaged in "temporary cohabitations." He added that the secrecy was due in part to local intolerance for relations out of wedlock: "The higher class of Filipinos, of course, won't tolerate immorality among their women. . . . They are about as strict among the higher classes as we are." During the course of their discussion about soldiers and interracial sex, Taft referred to an interview conducted previously with a clergy member in the western part of the Visayan Islands, stating, "I can't help remembering what the bishop of Jaro said about the temptation to which the young friar was exposed when he went out into a village like that. I think the temptations of a soldier are greater and the restraint less, 10,000 miles away from home, and east of Suez."[28] The connection for Taft was immediate; the sexual lives of Spanish friars and their many mixed-race children informed his thoughts on the transgressive sexual acts of Americans and likely also his considerations of how Filipinos might view these transgressions.

American men in the Philippine islands would go on to father countless mixed-race children with Filipina women. For all the interest colonialists had in setting the US regime apart from the Spanish—demonstrated here by the colonial administration's desire to see the friars vilified for their sexual liaisons—the American government in the Philippines did little to overhaul the sexual proclivities of troops in the islands and even less to hold men accountable for their offspring. According to one account, the stance of the Taft Commission was, "When it is known that an American employee of the Government is living with a native woman, he is told to bring a marriage certificate or present his resignation."[29] While the commission saw it necessary to warn soldiers away from cohabiting with Filipinas by threatening punishment, there is little evidence that points to any comprehensive state-sanctioned repercussions faced by American men who engaged in dangerous intercourse. When charges of cohabitation and paternity were so easy to deny, and the highest-ranking colonial officials (like Taft) expressed sympathy for the "plight" of young American men "miles away from home," these declarations were merely lip service.[30] Despite the abundance of Filipino testimonies denying that Spanish sexual proclivities were the main grievance against the former colonial masters, Taft and other colonial authorities still had interracial sexual impropriety in the front of their minds as they inflated the significance of interracial intercourse in damaging both Spanish and American prestige in the islands. Likely because they did not fully understand how race and ethnicity operated in the Philippines and fell back on understandings of the American "color line," officials emphasized their desire that "America [not] suffer the same reproach" as the Spanish due to transgressive intercourse. These pronouncements, however, were largely superficial gestures that aligned with the benevolent mission of US empire, and the colonial government did little to actually hold its citizens accountable.[31]

Although some colonists would begin to take notice of the growing American mestizo population within the first decade of US rule, it would not be until the 1920s that more formal recognition of US responsibilities for the children abandoned by Americans would take firmer root within the expatriate community in the Philippines. As we shall see, however, even efforts by nongovernmental charity organizations and religious groups to provide for American mestizos largely lacked any plans for seeking accountability from American fathers. Indeed, even when the children of dangerous intercourse were made visible for all to see, American men who left behind a "little family" in the Philippines still enjoyed a climate of impunity.[32]

Creating "Orphans": American Mestizos, Charity, and Discourses of Abandonment

> It is calculated that at the present time, 1911, there are between five hundred and one thousand American half-castes in the Philippine Islands, a large number of whom are illegitimate and abandoned by their reckless progenitors. Besides these children, who are the subjects of our solicitude, there is a large number of children of lawful marriages, who will be abandoned when their fathers return to America, as many of them will finally do.
>
> —Luther Parker, *Verses of the Philippines*

In 1911, Luther Parker, an American who traveled to the Philippines as a Thomasite teacher (Americans affectionately dubbed these teachers "Thomasites" because most came to the islands aboard the US transport ship *Thomas*), included these demographics in his book *Verses of the Philippines*. Parker sold his book, composed mostly of poetry, as a fundraiser to benefit American mestizos in the islands.[33] Published and sold in Manila, this volume provided one of the earliest known estimates of the number of American mestizos in the Philippines and was one of the earliest published works to appeal for charitable aid. The 1903 census did not enumerate American mestizos, but it did include a note indicating that a small number of American Filipino mixed-race individuals added to the "mestizo" population composed mostly of Spanish and Chinese mestizos.[34] By the 1918 census, conducted under US auspices, the total population of Americans in the Philippines numbered 5,774, along with an additional 2,820 "American half-breeds." This was a significantly large population when one considers that this number of mestizos was almost half of those counted as "pure" Americans.[35] Other accounts around the 1920s put the population of Filipino American mestizos at over 18,000, which, if accurate, would mean that this population was three times that of Americans enumerated as one race in the islands.[36] In contrast to this figure, the census of 1939 counted 8,709 Americans in the islands, with only 1,431 American mestizos. The census data collected from this period, however, can be quite misleading when one considers that the US military population in the islands—a population that well exceeded the civilian population for many years of the American occupation—was not enumerated in the census, nor were their families or dependents. Also, enumeration was often highly subjective, and census takers in 1939 were instructed not to count second-generation American mestizos as "mixed" but as "whichever race predominates."[37] Census workers likely enumerated many mestizos as "black," yellow," and "brown" rather than as "mixed" based solely on appearance, especially in cases where there was no American family member present in the household, which was the case for many mestizos left behind by American fathers. In all likeliness, the population of Filipino-American mixed-race individuals probably totaled more than census estimates, somewhere in the middle of these disparate estimates. I point out the problems of enumeration not just to pin down accurate numbers but also to highlight the politics of the colonial census. A lower estimate of American mestizos, especially in comparison to the previous census, might give the impression that Americans were more sufficiently warned away from dangerous intercourse or that the problem of abandoned American mestizos was declining.

As the philanthropic interest in the American mestizo population grew after the first decade of US colonization of the islands, so too did the burgeoning discourse about them. Most often, organizations that described American mestizos subscribed to the current popular ideas of eugenics. Mestizos were considered inferior to "pure" white people but perhaps, if afforded the right influences and tutelage, superior to native Filipinos. The growing visibility of American mestizo children throughout the archipelago inspired many different aid and charity efforts, as sympathetic Filipinos and Americans bore witness to the widespread reality of child abandonment by fathers from the United States. Though many church and aid groups felt the need to call attention to the plight of these mestizo children, they did not feel the same need to criticize the American men who shirked their responsibility for the children. In fact, it was the children themselves, as well as their Filipina mothers, who received the harshest indictments from those organizations that professed to be invested in their welfare. Philanthropic Americans like Luther Parker, as well as the civic organizations they formed to address American mestizo welfare, all contributed to the contradictory dynamic of calling attention to the many abandoned mestizos in the Philippines while blaming the children for their potential corruptibility. Organizations like the American Mestizo Protection Association (AMPA) and the American Guardian Association, established later in the 1920s (an organization that exists to this day), were, for the American community, the primary sources of information regarding mestizos. These organizations established transnational networks of support for mestizos as they solicited donations on both sides of the Pacific. Transnational progressive reformers shared much in common with their stateside counterparts, most notably their commitment to moral uplift and tutelage, especially for those they believed prone to racial "degeneracy."[38] While the colonial government was conspicuously silent about the growing numbers of fatherless American mestizos, these Manila-based organizations created discourses about mixed-race "orphans" that shifted attention away from the realities of American abandonment of children to instead highlight on American goodwill and responsibility for the downtrodden.

One of the earliest American attempts at organized fundraising for mestizos was in 1911, with the publication of Parker's *Verses of the Philippines*. Parker's book provides one of the earliest American characterizations of this population, along with an assessment of interracial sexual relations in the islands:

> The subject of miscegenation in the Philippines is one that must be faced and the problem of what is to be done with the abandoned children of Anglo-Saxon fathers and Filipina mothers must be solved by those great hearted members of our nation whose sympathies are aroused by a knowledge of the suffering and degradation that is to be the lot in a very few years of those winsome little half-caste girls who are growing up in ignorance, literally by the hundreds, all over the archipelago, from the land of the head hunters of Luzon, where some deserter from the army took to his shack a daughter of the wild man and later deserted her when the trail became too warm, to the land of the Moro of Mindanao, where white men, with no pride of race, have carelessly left to the future a problem in the harmonization of the Orient and the Occident that appalls the more conscientious with its terrible import.[39]

Parker contradicts his initial description of these children as the "abandoned children of Anglo-Saxon fathers and Filipina mothers" in his description of Filipinas: "Enough cases have been observed to make it evident that, as a usual rule, a Filipina woman when deserted by her American paramour or husband, as the case may be, goes to live with some Chinaman or Filipino who offers her a living for herself and children. Figure to yourself, reader, the future of such children, especially if they be female." Parker considers all mestizos "abandoned," regardless of whether or not they were still under the care of their mothers. After the departure of the American father, according to this description, all individuals in the life of the mixed-race child were disreputable and unsavory in character.

While Parker is quick to characterize the "Chinaman or Filipino" as pimps and generally immoral, his description of his own countrymen qualifies their behavior. Similar to the sympathy that Taft expressed for American soldiers succumbing to temptation in the tropics, Parker made excuses for American men who abandoned their children. These men, Parker suggests, were army deserters and miscegenists with no "pride of race." They were careless in their behavior but not generally immoral and lascivious like the Chinese or Filipino caretakers he later mentions. Though he describes these men as aberrant and perhaps deviant, they are not representative of the broader swath of Americans but simply "some deserter" or one-off offender. Later in his introduction, he was even more explicit in his sympathy for the American men who abandoned children: "For that ever-increasing number of Americans who are irreparably identifying themselves socially with the life of the Philippines the author has no censure, but a very great sympathy for the man. Cut off from home, friends and loved ones by ten thousand miles, who in his utter lonliness [sic] of spirit seeks companionship and love of whatever human being can break the unendurable monotony of existence in the tropics."[40] According to this characterization, Americans who disregarded social mores to socialize with Filipinos (and later abandoned their children) were really only guilty of loneliness.

Parker called on his readers not to judge too harshly the white men in the islands who had relations with native women. The first poem in his book, titled "The Squaw Man's Justification," was expressly intended to soften attitudes toward his countrymen, illustrating to the reader not familiar with life in the tropics how the local conditions—and local people—made it impossible to resist the allure of interracial intercourse for all except "only the most puritanical or those possessed of a great race pride." According to the poem, a large part of the allure that drew in helpless men was the eagerness of native women to partner with white men. Parker, like so many of his compatriots who wrote about miscegenation in the Philippines, represented Filipinas as not only sexually available but drawn to white men because they perceived them as superior.[41] In "The Squaw Man's Justification," a Filipina "dark-skinned maid" was willing to forsake her family in order to attain whiteness:

Small wonder, then, that the White's a god in the heart of a
dark-skinned maid,
In whom nature has softened the mark of Cain to a less repulsive shade.
The burning desire of every one of the daughters of Mother Night
Is to change the color that nature gave to the heavenly gift of white.[42]

Parker absolved white men who "went native" because, in his view, native women were so eager to form liaisons with them. In his view, it was the native women fervently pursuing interracial intercourse with the new "gods" who were mostly to blame for the behavior of white men. This absolution of American men was the standard way that most philanthropic efforts around mestizo children framed interracial relations in the Philippines. By excusing American fathers or discounting them as exceptional or nonrepresentative, white racial superiority and American claims of civilizational morality remained intact, even in discussions of left-behind mixed-race children.

In addition to selling copies of his book as a way to raise money, Parker ran public solicitations for donations in the local Manila newspapers. On January 19, 1911, the *Cablenews-American*, a Manila-based American newspaper, printed a letter from Parker that implored the readership to contribute money to a mestizo care fund. As the letter explained, the money raised would be used for the care of "half-caste" children and to secure for them a "place in life that their blood entitles them to." The philanthropic inclination of expatriates like Parker to uplift orphans was also marked by an investment in the value and sanctity of white "blood." It was this genetic material, most charity organizations reasoned, that made them deserving of welfare and conditions better than those of their Filipino caretakers. Parker's appeal in the *Cablenews-American* relied on this sentiment to sway feelings on the matter of American mestizos. He demanded that colonists invest in the welfare of mestizo children or else "the American community as a whole must stand convicted of holding the same attitude toward life in the Philippines as the transient soldier or civilian" responsible for fathering them.[43] This civic appeal to uphold the value of whiteness and American morality worked. Shortly after the call for donations, concerned individuals began to send money to the newspaper directly, and the "*Cablenews* Half-Caste fund" was established by Parker and his contacts at the paper. The newspaper directors held the money in trust and distributed it on a case-by-case basis. Ideally, Parker envisioned that enough funds would be generated for the eventual creation of an institution wholly dedicated to American mestizo welfare. Like the larger project of imperialism in the islands, notions of white racial superiority and American benevolence were the foundations on which charitable aid to mestizos was built.

In the wake of these early fundraising efforts, concerned colonists created the American Mestizo Protective Association and conducted one of the first formal surveys to assess the number of American mestizos and their living conditions in the islands in 1913. AMPA relied on often unresponsive provincial governors and volunteers for its census and, as such, received only representative numbers back (in AMPA's estimation) from the cities of Cebu and Iloilo, where a combined two hundred children were counted. From

AMPA's efforts, it was estimated that around fourteen hundred American mestizos resided in the Philippines, although it acknowledged that this was a rough estimate. Like Parker and the concerned Americans who responded to his solicitation, AMPA was invested in the "white blood" of mestizos. The organization's explicit purpose, according to its articles of incorporation, was the care and protection of "abandoned half-caste children of white American fathers and Filipino mothers." Though Black Americans also left children in the islands, these were not a priority for AMPA. The association eventually dissolved sometime during the course of World War I.[44] Several years later, a new organization emerged after yet another US mission to the Philippines to determine whether or not the conditions in the islands merited independence. The 1921 Wood-Forbes Mission to the Philippines was commissioned by newly elected US president Warren G. Harding. Harding, facing pressure from the previous Democratic administration to consider the immediate independence of the Philippines but also from his own party to restore some of the American power lost during the Filipinization efforts of the previous decade, was invested in receiving a negative prognosis on independence for the colony. Harding appointed his recent opponent for the Republican nomination, Major General Leonard Wood, to the post of governor-general of the Philippines and made him the leader of the fact-finding mission. Harding also appointed Cameron Forbes, who had served as governor-general of the Philippines from 1908 to 1913, prior to Filipinization efforts, as co-leader. Ultimately, the mission presented a scathing report to the US government in 1922, dashing Filipino hopes for independence.[45] It was from the activities of this mission that the newest iteration of American charitable aid to mestizos emerged.

During their several months of travel throughout the islands, Wood, as well as his appointee to the mission, Lieutenant Colonel Gordon Johnston, took note of the great many fatherless children of US servicemen and civilians. Wood took a special interest in American mestizos and, in November 1921, founded the American Guardian Association (AGA), with Johnston as its first president. The AGA, like its predecessor, AMPA, was the newest curator of the public discourse about American mestizos. Following the lead of previous progressive reformers interested in the white mixed-race population, the AGA held resolutely to the logics of white supremacy in its mission of helping children of partial American parentage, despite the more diverse constituency of supporters the AGA attracted when compared to AMPA. But because non-white and non-American charitable organizations and individuals were also interested in the mission of the new association, the foundational logic of needing to nurture the "white blood" of mixed children (which supposedly gave them untapped potential, unlike their Filipino peers) was one that had to be downplayed. After all, the Philippine press and other local Filipino religious and charitable organizations also lent their support to the new association. In 1922, for example, the AGA followed in Luther Parker's footsteps, publishing a cookbook—*Good Cooking and Health in the Tropics*—to be sold as a way to raise funds for the organization. The book was the work of the Ways and Means Committee of the AGA, which was composed of mostly well-to-do American and Filipina women. While the cookbook does not specifically note the "white blood" of the mestizo wards, whiteness is presumed and ascribed in other ways. The introduction, for example, describes the "freckles and clear-cut American features" of American mestizos, which "mark them out only too visibly." Additionally, the illustration that serves as the frontispiece of the book depicts a red-cheeked little girl with light brown hair and light skin (fig. 6.1). She stands on a dirt road beside a palm tree, and the caption reads, "The American Guardian Association will take care of me." There is a nipa palm dwelling in the background, the type featured prominently on souvenir postcards and zoological photographs alike as a "typical native house," perhaps meant to signal what the fate of this child might be without the generosity of the AGA.[46]

In addition to the new Filipino members and supporters for mestizo aid, the local Black American expat population made their support for the AGA known through their generous donations. The Colored American Community League (CACL), an organization formed by local Black veterans of the Spanish-American and Philippine-American Wars, was one of the most ardent supporters of the AGA. The CACL members conveyed to the AGA that they knew of many children throughout the islands whose fathers were from the Black military units that had been rotated through the islands during the previous decade and that they felt a responsibility to care for them. Black American contributors to the AGA, unlike most of the white members, understood American mestizos according to nationality versus race. This was a difficult thing for most white American members of the AGA to accept. Many did not view Black Americans as real Americans, and correspondingly Black American mixed-race children in the islands were completely outside their purview. Despite the generous contributions of the CACL, AGA philanthropic efforts continued to depict American mestizos as worthy of aid because of their proximity to whiteness.[47]

In the fall of 1925, the AGA took its moral crusade for mestizo "orphans" across the Pacific Ocean, soliciting for charitable donations in the United

Figure 6.1. The frontispiece illustration of *Good Cooking and Health in the Tropics*. The colorized image depicts a young girl with rosy cheeks and light brown hair. Image courtesy of the American Historical Collection, Ateneo de Manila University.

States. The presumed whiteness of American mestizos was apparent in the numerous descriptions of the blue-eyed, blond-haired, and fair-skinned "orphans" who awaited US aid in the Pacific. With the home base of their efforts located in New York, the AGA spent more than a year seeking the goodwill and dollars of stateside Americans, publishing frequent newspaper ads to tug at their heartstrings. With the help of noted financial campaigner Mary Frances Kern, the AGA hoped to raise $2,000,000 within the year.[48] It organized fundraising events in various US cities, asking women's clubs and religious organizations to host meetings for its members so they could pitch its cause. The ideas propagated by the AGA about American mestizos were heavily influenced by contemporary eugenics discourses. Developed in the latter half of the nineteenth century as a scientific field of study interested in the outcomes of crossbreeding among plants and animals, the eugenics movement quickly drew in those interested in the scientific explanations of observed human difference. In the United States, as in other geographies, scientific racism and eugenics came to be mutually constitutive as racist ideas shored up notions of "better breeding" while state and local governments turned to science in order to restrict or "fix" nonwhite or less white immigrants.[49] Eugenics supporters also sought to uphold institutionalized racism and protect against the mixing of white and nonwhite races, comparing "mulattos" to the sterile offspring of interbred horses and donkeys. The popular turn-of-the-century US imagery of the Philippines and its people incorporated the eugenics discourse, often featuring Filipinos with simian and apelike features. Cultural artifacts from the time, such as novelty postcards collected by soldiers and tourists and political cartoons weighing in on Philippine annexation, highlight the supposed racial differences between colonizer and colonized and speculate on the outcomes of interracial unions. Figures 6.2 and 6.3, for example, depict the offspring of Filipinas and white Americans as primates.

The 1920s was the height of the eugenics movement in the United States, and the AGA was clearly familiar with the language of the pseudoscience. Its advertisements often used the competing scientific ideas of hybrid vigor (that a mixed offspring could exceed the limitations of both parents) and hybrid degeneracy (that a mixed offspring would carry the worst traits of both parents) in describing the mestizo "waifs" across the sea. According to these solicitations, American mestizos possessed both good traits and qualities, attributed to their white blood (coded as "American blood" in the press), and negative qualities, attributed to their Filipino heritage. The AGA claimed that without intercession, the children would never know the benefits of their Americanness

Figure 6.2. *Life* ran this cartoon as its August 31, 1899, cover image. The caption read, "Three Years After. Corporal O'Toole, after leaving the army, decided to remain in the Philippines." The depiction of the Irish O'Toole and his mixed family reflects American fears over debased white men "going native" in the Philippines, as well as anxieties over mixed-race offspring. The child featured here, for example, has a simian-like gait and appearance.

but would fall victim to the baser natures expressed through their Filipino blood. If brought up properly, however, with American values and habits, the AGA believed that these unfortunate children could become outstanding citizens and future leaders of the Philippines, being American in all but name.

Despite the vigorous public airing of the United States' shameful record in the Philippines—with the AGA running fundraising advertisements and receiving press coverage in the *New York Times* almost twice monthly for over a year—the revelation of thousands of mixed-race American offspring

Figure 6.3. Postcards such as this made popular souvenir items for Americans. The caption reads, "Philippine Islands—Soldiers who have married wealthy Filipino girls, and the first born baby." The American tendency to compare Filipinos to monkeys is the basis of the apparent joke of the postcard, as one soldier holds a human baby and the other (center) holds a monkey. Image courtesy of Mario Feir Filipiniana Library.

in the tropics elicited little criticism from those reform groups previously so outspoken about liquor traffic and prostitution in the islands. This speaks to the success of the AGA in turning a dangerous story of American miscegenation in the tropics into a philanthropic opportunity, transforming biracial American children in the Philippines from dangerous malcontents in the colony into safely confined wards that possessed bright futures within the boundaries of the Philippines. The fundraising efforts showcased the AGA's understanding that American mestizos would always be non-US citizens, their true place in the world being prominent Filipino citizens who could potentially cultivate American interest in the tropics even after independence. For example, in one AGA advertisement in the *New York Times*, American mestizo children were described as "future citizens of this most Eastern possession of the United States."[50] Admiral Bradley Allen Fiske, spokesman for the AGA, expressed his objective that mestizo children in the Philippines "be educated to be good American citizens, so that they might not be deceived by the unrest of a few in the [Philippines]."[51] Fiske was speaking of a civic Americanness rather than a legal entitlement to citizenship, as the future he described for mestizos was a future in the colony.

The AGA also represented mestizos as socially and politically valuable American proxies in the Pacific, a population that was "destined to form a stabilizing element in the native population."[52] With the proper training and influences (made possible by charitable donations), these children could take up the mantle of American ideals after the end of formal colonization. "The American-Filipino children are certainly worth saving. They have imagination and initiative which is wholly lacking in the native. The boys, if properly brought up, should become leaders of the Filipino people. The girls, if educated, are particularly sought out as wives by ambitious and self-respecting men."[53] AGA founder Wood and former governor-general Forbes also bolstered the idea of American mestizos being a potential imperial force in the islands after the US departure. A solicitation for aid conveyed their stance that mestizos could introduce "salutary ideas of self-rule and administrative efficiency. Children of partial American heritage, they believed, "[would] be an invaluable means of commending progress to the other natives. When [colonial occupation] ceases, they will greatly increase the likelihood of carrying on effectively."[54] Neglecting to Americanize mestizos, on the other hand, might spell catastrophe for US empire in the islands. Do nothing for these children, one article speculated, and the United States ran the risk of fostering a new generation of Aguinaldos. The insurgent former first president of the independent Philippine republic, Emilio Aguinaldo, continued to be one of the most vivid representations of anti-American uprising in the colony.[55] The AGA was quick to play up fears of insurgency in their appeals for charity:

> Indeed, Aguinaldo, whose armed rebellion against the United States after the islands came under the American flag, a little over a quarter of a century ago, was a source of so much trouble, expense and bloodshed, was a mestizo, though with no American blood in his veins. It is therefore imperative that the new generation of mestizos, children born of American fathers and of native mothers, now numbering some 20,000, and who are pronounced by General Wood to be unusually bright, high spirited and comely, the American characteristics predominating over Malay traits, should be carefully trained, influenced and cared for, so that they may develop into a useful class of the population, instead of into a source of danger to the rule of the United States.[56]

The idea of dangerous mestizos in the Philippines and the possibility of their fomenting irrational, anti-American hostility was blamed on the influence of "Malay traits." Properly cultivated "white blood" was the solution. These depictions erased the culpability of American fathers and even suggested that the blood they left behind was a gift to the unruly and uncivilized nation. The idea of the "dangerous mestizo" would again be invoked in the 1960s by the Pearl S. Buck Foundation for Amerasians, playing on Cold War fears about anti-American sentiment in the third world.[57]

The AGA campaign also highlighted another concern that US officials had about the condition of American mestizos in the colony. The presence of hundreds of thousands of blue-eyed youngsters across the islands, many reportedly more destitute than native Filipinos, flew in the face of the prevailing ideas of white racial prestige and supremacy. Both ideas were at the core of US imperial ideology, and both were jeopardized because of the existence and visibility of white "half-castes" who were not in the proper place on the racial hierarchy, namely right underneath white American occupiers. Governor-General Wood expressed this concern: "We cannot, as a people afford to have American blood on a lower social level than the blood of other nations. But such will be the inevitable result if we fail in this humanitarian and social obligation."[58] General Wood's plea demonstrated that the concern was not necessarily for the children themselves or for taking responsibility for callous American acts abroad. White blood, coded as "American blood," and hence whiteness, was in danger. His statement made starkly evident the inseparable nature of the American "humanitarian" impulse, white supremacy, and empire. Transimperial considerations in particular weighed heavily on the minds of those progressive reformers thinking about the fate of American mestizos in the Philippines. As one fundraising advertisement stated, "Wood's appeal for funds in their behalf is just as much deserving of generous response as those in Great Britain receive in behalf of the sorely tried Eurasian elements in India and in King George's Malay possessions."[59] The message was clear: charity for mestizos was upholding white supremacy, and further, it was empire building.

The AGA constructed American mestizos in the Philippines as simultaneously dangerous for US international prestige and in danger of being absorbed into the local native population. Some mestizos, though, were more imperiled than others. For the AGA, the salvation of mestiza girls was of the greatest concern, and the narrative created around these girls was more urgent and scandalous than that created around their brothers. Descriptions of mestizas were rife with tales of sordid sexual danger and slavery if they were left in the care of Filipinos. Alva Hill, an American lawyer who spent thirty years in the Philippines, described in his memoirs his belief that American mestizas were especially in need of protection: "Many of them are physically very attractive. For that reason they are in great demand as recruits for houses of prostitution. . . . Occasionally the mothers of mestiza girls even hire them to the public for immoral purposes."[60] Luther Parker's early 1911 plea to Manila Americans published in *Cablenews-American* painted a similar scene: "The thought of meeting an American girl, barefoot, in rags and in poverty, toting rice along the muddy carabao trail in some barrio, with her owner and master trudging along behind, carrying an umbrella or rooster, is unbearable."[61] The 1922 AGA cookbook also told of an investigation into a grim but titillating scene: "Girls of twelve or fourteen [are] exploited and taught to lead immoral lives for the profit of their own mothers. The number of girls, mere children, so engaged is appalling." According to this last account, the investigation included a sting operation in which a US congressman tested the ease of obtaining as property a young mestiza, going through with the transaction as far as "the verge of completion."[62]

The AGA did not hold back these vivid accounts in their US-based fundraising efforts either. They presented to the public the belief that the peril faced by girls was much greater than that faced by boys. Most American mestizos, they claimed, were in danger of going the "evil ways" if left without the proper influences; however, "this is even more true of the girls than of the boys." Progressive-era ideas of forced prostitution, or "white slavery," tinged the descriptions of compromised mestizas. White slavery narratives proliferated across the nation in the decades prior to the AGA campaign, arousing the ire of many Americans as they thought about poor white women and girls forced into sexual slavery. In 1910, the federal government passed the White Slave Traffic Act to criminalize the sexual traffic of white women. The AGA's fundraising campaign was shaped by the Progressive Era fascination with sexual immorality, and it capitalized on the popular image of vulnerable white waifs forced to live depraved lives. The mission to "shield the girls from a life of debasement or from sale into marriage not far removed from slavery" was not just charity work; it was also preemptive vice reform work.[63] Local churches and religious institutions also took part in the care of mestiza girls in particular. The American Union Church of Manila, for example, built a church hall specifically to house and educate half-Filipina girls deemed in need of assistance by the AGA, while the Santa Domitilla Vocational School offered to care for twenty American mestiza girls "free of charge" (figs. 6.4 and 6.5).[64] The idea that mestizas were more prone to the

Figure 6.4. "Wards of Union Church Hall." Image courtesy of the American Historical Collection, Ateneo de Manila University.

Figure 6.5. "Primary grades in the Santa Domitilla Vocational School." According to the *American Oldtimer*, some of the children pictured here were beneficiaries of the American Guardian Association. Image courtesy of the American Historical Collection, Ateneo de Manila University.

lascivious nature of their parents was even factored into the cost of their up-
keep and training; $12.50 a month, the AGA reported, was sufficient for
providing for a mixed-race boy in the Philippines, whereas a girl apparently
required $15 a month to be saved from infamy.[65] The campaign organizers
worked to acquaint the US public with the storied mestiza, even having two
young girls, "both children of mixed marriages," do a "native dance" before spectators at fundraising meetings.[66]

For the most part, the AGA and other American organizations that supported its mission wrote American men out of their charity narratives or
treated them with sympathy. Some supporters, like the Reverend Frank Laubach of the Union Theological Seminary at Manila, even exonerated the
abandoning fathers completely. Laubach expressed his belief that "one of the
greatest contributions America is making to the Philippine Islands is the min-
gling of blood of the two peoples." Americans had used the rhetoric of
"improving" nonwhite nations/people through racial mixture in the recent
past, especially in discussions of relations with Latin America, Indigenous
nations, and the free Black population in the aftermath of the Civil War.[67]
The AGA campaign depicted Filipina mothers, on the other hand, as depraved prostitutes who were willing to sell their light-skinned daughters
without hesitation. With this denouncement of Filipina mothers and their
immoral nature, it is no wonder that the local Filipino community in New
York sought to distance themselves from the picture being painted of immorality in the Philippines. Dr. Jose Ramirez and S. C. Villegas, prominent
Filipino community leaders in the United States, indicated their support for
the AGA's drive, saying that they were "deeply interested" in the cause, but
they also saw fit to express their disapproval of intermarriage: "We urge
among our own people marriage among our own kind. We believe that each
race has its own peculiar place in the universal plan."[68] Marriages and relations between primarily Filipino men and white women in the United States
had spurred racial violence in states like Washington and California since
the 1920s. Even earlier, at the 1904 World's Fair in St. Louis, a race riot
erupted when white men attacked Filipinos who were seen socializing with
white women on and off the fairgrounds.[69] By the 1930s, anti-miscegenation
laws in several states were amended to include "Malay" or "Filipino" as races
that could not marry whites.[70] Villegas and Ramirez were acutely aware of
American hostility toward Filipinos who fraternized with white women and
likely wanted to distance themselves from such scandal. Their statement can
also be read as an adherence to respectability politics, in which they are declaring their own fitness for residence in the United States.

Other responses to the AGA fundraising drive would not be so tempered in their treatment of American abandonment of children in the overseas empire. Prominent Black academic, civil rights activist, and Pan-Africanist W. E. B. Du Bois, for example, did not miss the chance to indict US imperialism abroad. Having seen the AGA's "delicately worded appeal for funds," Du Bois used the fundraiser to draw critical attention to the gendered dimensions of US empire in the Philippines:

> What is all this about? In plain, cold English, the American people in bring-ing peace and civilization to the Philippines, have left 18,000 bastards in the islands! Isn't this fine work? Can you not see the Godly White Race struggling under the Black Man's Burden? Can you not see how Americans hate social Equality with brown women? Why is America asked to support these illegitimate victims of white men's lust? Because the United States gov-ernment, the War Department and Govenores Wood, Taft and Forbes have somehow let American skunks scuttle from the islands and leave their help-less and innocent bastards to beg and perish, and their deserted mothers to starve or serve as prostitutes to white newcomers.[71]

While much has been written on the sometimes supportive, sometimes am-bivalent, and often oppositional stance of Black Americans to US empire in the Philippines, most has focused on Black Americans' and Filipinos' recog-nition of shared racial oppression. Du Bois's condemnation also draws in gen-der disparities. In his aptly titled "Philippine Mulattoes," he acknowledges that the AGA rhetoric was much like the "tragic mulatto" tropes that pro-liferated in American literature since the mid 1800s. In white- and Black-authored stories alike, mixed-race characters were mostly portrayed as maladjusted outsiders to both races, ultimately left in poverty or doomed to early and unhappy deaths.[72] Du Bois's article, unlike the other voices that chimed in on the mestizo fundraising campaign, not only called out the re-sponsibility of American men and the US government but also called atten-tion to the hypocrisy of US professions of benevolent empire.

The "tragic mulatto" archetype was most often applied to mixed-race women and played on white fears about miscegenation, especially in situa-tions where the ability of the mixed character to pass as white helped lure unsuspecting white men into marriage. The AGA's mestizos, however, did not present this danger to white family formation in the United States because they were always and already relegated to a life in the Philippines. Though the AGA's depiction of mestizos drew from the mulatto trope, the fundraiser rhetoric differed in that it presented the mixed-race "orphans" as dangerous only if they did not receive American tutelage and charity. Du Bois concluded his admonition of the aid drive by ridiculing the AGA's campaign, calling instead for collective action against US imperialism. "Send, in God's name, America, two million dollars . . . and send simultaneously . . . two million protests to Washington to lambaste the heads of Congressmen who permit the holding of the Philippines as a house of prostitution for American white men under the glorious starts and stripes." The criticism might have taken a different form or perhaps may not have materialized at all had the AGA actively conveyed its interest in caring for both white and Black American mestizos in the Philippines. Du Bois would have had to contend with the culpability of Black soldiers who also left behind children in the Philippines. Instead, the AGA's characterization of mestizos as unequivocally semi-white invited the comparison to white sexual violence against Black women in the United States.

Ultimately, it seems that the United States public was less interested in the cause of needy "half-castes" than in earlier reformist campaigns against drunk soldiers, military-regulated brothels, or white American women found to be employed in prostitution in the Philippines several decades earlier.[73] In fact, the AGA and its US constituents failed to win the widespread support it sought from the public. One campaign advertisement in June 1926 suggested that the efforts to raise $2,000,000 were not going as hoped.[74] The ad chastised Americans, saying that the appeal for funds by General Wood had thus far been "practically unheeded." "Has our slogan become: 'Millions for foreigners, not one cent for Americans?'" At one AGA meeting in the United States, many in attendance questioned the legitimacy of the mestizo children, perhaps put off by these youngsters not being the product of legal unions or implying that if fathers did not claim them, then they were not necessarily an American obligation. Colonel Peter E. Traub, an AGA supporter and spokesperson, misled the crowd with his response that "most of the children were born in wedlock," though he also conceded that "the foundlings" were equally needy. Traub further retorted that "relief organizations for other nationalities . . . did not ask questions about the legitimacy of charges."[75] For all their efforts to secure aid from the American public, it seems that the AGA's portrayal of immoral Filipina mothers—women who may have tricked and seduced good American men—may have inadvertently closed, rather than opened, wallets.

"Girls of Exceptional Usefulness": The Daughters of American Veterans

The information conveyed about American mestizos and their mothers by the AGA may have played a role in the disappointing yield of this particular fundraising drive in the United States. Nonetheless, the image of the destitute mestizo prone to sexual vice (especially girls) was resolute in its longevity. That is not to say, however, that such tropes of morally corruptible mestizos went unchallenged. In fact, around the same time as the AGA created narratives of noncitizen, vice-prone "orphans" in the Pacific, other groups developed their own ideas about American mestizos. One such organization, the Manila-based Daughters of American Veterans, contested the discourse around mestizos. First formed in 1928, several years after the formation of the AGA, the mostly mestiza members of the DAV attempted to negotiate belonging within the American community in the Philippines, often through celebrating and ascribing to heteronormative gender roles and ideas of proper femininity. As an organization founded on the glorification of American veterans of the Spanish-American and Philippine-American Wars, the mestiza members claimed their own Americanness and presented themselves as dutiful and accomplished daughters with filial respect for their valiant fathers. They reminded the American expatriate community of their own familial ties to the United States and presented themselves as respectable society women. This self-presentation served as a way to distance themselves from the prevailing rhetoric about mixed-race children, particularly mixed-race girls. In embracing their Americanness and proclaiming their respectability, they negotiated positions of prestige and status for themselves in the islands. In doing so, their platform also obscured the uneven nature of American-Filipino relationships, most of which did not resemble that of their own nuclear families. In their unproblematic celebration of their American fathers, the DAV advanced the claims of empire, portraying their progenitors to be heroes of a just war, rather than colonial subjugators and imperial settlers.

The DAV was not interested in addressing the abandonment of mestizos in the Philippines. Rather, its goals included remembering and celebrating American veterans, and supporting the endeavors of its membership. The organization regularly held formal dinners and dances and, in most ways, conformed with the rules and etiquette of other American society clubs in Manila. While many of these clubs during the colonial period—such as the Army and Navy Club, the Manila Yacht Club, and the Cotillion Club—

were exclusively for white members, the membership of the DAV was unique in that it was largely composed of American mestiza women. The membership roster of the DAV was brimming with names that reflected the mixed American and Filipino backgrounds of the women involved. Consolation Anderson, Ceferina Witte, Trinidad Holmes, Conchita Hill, Felicidad Peck, Remejia Peck, Cresencia Renner, Amparo Schober, and Rosario Van were some of the first members of the organization.[76] Anglicized names, too, were just as common for mestiza women in the Philippines. The newspaper coverage of the club highlighted the mixed-race nature of the membership. A special old-timers edition of the *Manila Bulletin*, for example, announced the formation of the DAV alongside other news items featuring the mestizo sons and daughters of American residents of the Philippines. The old-timers insert featured headlines about the mestizo children of longtime American residents who had made good in their careers and education or were otherwise showing promise as upstanding members of the community. Such spotlights painted quite a different and more flattering picture of mestizos and their settler fathers than did the various publications of the AGA.

To be sure, the women in the DAV were not the targeted beneficiaries of the AGA's philanthropies. Though the AGA did not differentiate between elite American mestizos and those who lived in poverty, casting the entire population as needy orphans, the members of the DAV were neither fatherless nor destitute. Indeed, the basis of the DAV organization was that its members had legitimate ties as acknowledged children to American veterans. As such, the members had significantly different lives than those of the "orphaned wards" whom the AGA fundraised for, mainly reaped through the benefits and privileges that their American fathers had access to, largely via old-timer networks, military pensions, and their privileged status as American colonizers. Elite mestizos could use their social class and proximity to the American community to advance their goals and negotiate elevated social positions for themselves.[77] Some elite mestizos also inherited elevated social class positions from their Filipina mothers. As recalled by Mary Bowler, the mestiza daughter of an American Thomasite teacher and a Filipina from a prominent family, her mother's family objected to their daughter marrying a poor American teacher, his socioeconomic position being well beneath theirs.[78] With their settler fathers in their lives, the DAV mestizas could distance themselves from the stigma of being invariably associated with the sexual economy and prostitution. This widespread association of mestizas with sexual immorality might well have been one of the main factors that motivated the young women to create an organization that emphasized paternity and marital respectability. Whatever the individual circumstances of their families, the DAV members were proud enough of their heritage to openly celebrate it, which was not the case for the thousands of other mestizos who grew up quite differently.

While the relatively affluent DAV membership was not necessarily interested in uplifting poor mestizo "orphans," this did not mean that they were obtuse to the social ostracism that mixed families and mestizos in particular faced in society. Their membership advertisements hint at their experiences of being outcast from polite society. The foremost goal of the DAV was to "give honor and respect to all American Veterans living, and to honor and perpetuate the names of those that are dead, and to show them all loyalty at every opportunity." They also wished "to bring together all daughters of American veterans and to aid and encourage those who need friendship, encouragement and assistance . . . , to establish a business bureau and a reading and rest room in the city, and to encourage any marked talent in art, music and literature among its members, and lastly . . . provide clean and wholesome amusements for its members, such as socials, excursions and picnics."[79] The stated goal of forming a common community, cultivating friendships, and giving "encouragement and assistance" to one another suggests that social isolation was something that many of its members felt deeply.

The goals and structure of the DAV mirrored other social clubs in Manila at the time, many of which held similar social events and established clubhouses in the city center. For mestizas to mirror other elite women's clubs, however, they needed to project their elevated social class but also a refusal of the traits typically ascribed to mestiza women. In highlighting their kin relations to American veterans, the members of the DAV claimed an American identity that set them apart from both the native Filipino and the poorer/abandoned American mestizo population of the islands. In addition to stressing filial loyalty, "Americanness," and pride, the DAV was concerned with showcasing the accomplishments and reputability of its members. Art, literature, and music were considered respectable pursuits for young women looking to marry similarly respectable (or more respectable) men. The DAV's emphasis on providing "wholesome amusements" for its members highlights a concern with morality—again, a distinct refusal of the popular association of mestiza women with the sexual economy and immorality. In adhering to ideals of proper femininity and Progressive Era morality, the DAV was much like any other proper women's social club of the time. The DAV also sought to spotlight the accomplishments of its members, "[hoping] to show a group of girls of exceptional usefulness and progressiveness."[80] By touting their "usefulness," especially within the realm of what was considered proper femininity, these mestizas further demarcated themselves from the popular ideas of degenerate, impoverished, and immoral mixed-race children. In crafting its public facing identity, the DAV reminded those who might look down on them that they, unlike other mestizas, possessed a status that afforded them leisure time for picnicking, sports, and artistic expression. In other words, the members of the DAV used heteronormative ideas about proper femininity and womanhood to express themselves as contributing members of society and as socialites on par with the socialites of the many other women's groups in Manila.

The DAV also rejected the idea that its members were potentially dangerous malcontents, dissatisfied with American rule over their nation. Their strict adherence to Americanness and exemplary womanhood necessitated the downplaying of their Philippine heritage. This was done primarily through the excising of Filipina mothers from their self-produced public image. In a group that espoused such ideas of womanhood, press depictions of the DAV conspicuously lacked any mention of the women who had likely done most of the work of raising these proud American daughters. In some cases, the absence of Filipina mothers in the press that followed the DAV was glaring. In its reporting about the DAV inaugural ball, for example, the *Manila Bulletin* stated that the members were hard at work on the final preparations and that "all veterans, sons and daughters of veterans are cordially invited."[81] In fact, nowhere in any of the press about the DAV are the mothers of these women mentioned or photographed. The closeting away of Filipina mothers, whether intentional or not, further strengthened the DAV's public personification as proud Americans, distancing them from the so-called vulgarities of their Filipino blood. The nondisclosure of Filipina mothers on the part of the DAV was consistent with the discrediting discourses about Filipina mothers generated by the AGA.

Though they might have downplayed their own Filipina mothers, they apparently sought out solidarity and council from white women role models, particularly the Daughters of the American Revolution (DAR). According to Ruth Bradley Sheldon, DAR state regent of the Philippines (1927–47), the DAV modeled itself after the prominent lineage-based American women's organization. The DAR had formed a Philippines chapter in 1913 primarily to support the education of Filipina nurses.[82] According to Sheldon's annual report to the DAR, two mestizas and a prominent Filipina, Mrs. Sofia De Veyra, visited her when she was living in Manila to inquire about her organization. De Veyra was a widely known member of the Women's Club of

Manila, and her husband, Jaime De Verya, was a politician and former Philippine commissioner to Washington.[83] As Sheldon recalled, the Filipinas had observed the DAR both in the United States and in Manila and "wished to form an organization along similar lines and for similar purposes," so she gave them a copy of the by-laws and constitution for their reference. Shortly after, she concluded, the DAV was formed, and the mestiza members were "a credit to themselves and to those after whom they patterned, whom they imitated."[84] Both Sofia and Jaime De Veyra were Nacionalistas and used their platforms to push for Philippine independence. Sofia did so through her charity work and contributions to the Women's Club of Manila, where she worked to show Americans on both sides of the Pacific that the Philippines was modern and that Filipinas had many social and professional possibilities open to them. Like many elites who desired a leading role in the governance of the nation, she was vexed by the popular depictions of Filipinos as "naked savages who eat dogs" and understood that such representations stood in the way of independence.[85] Her interest in forming a mestiza club in the vein of the DAR was in line with her priorities of carefully curating a modern and industrious image of the Philippines and its people, an image that showcased the historic intercourse between the two nations. Highlighting elite mixed families with American veteran patriarchs was a politically expedient move.

Though some of the mestizas likely understood their positioning of the DAV as a way to negotiate both their own marginalized status in society and the colonial status of the Philippines, they also aligned themselves with the narrative of benevolent US imperialism, which understood American soldiers as liberators rather than colonial subjugators. Not only that, but in seeking out the DAR as a model, they also validated the longer settler colonial history of the United States. Both organizations created and maintained their own respectability at the expense of others: the dispossessed, the Indigenous, the poor. The respectability and validation that mestizas could claim through their fathers, who stayed in the islands with their mixed-race families, also went both ways. American fathers could also accumulate sociocultural capital from the accomplishments of their mestizo offspring and thus differentiate themselves from the disdained "squaw men," who went native in the Philippines. Unlike the maligned Americans who did not contribute to American prestige in the islands, these old-timer fathers could point to their respectable children, raised with American values. As the old-timers newspaper boasted, "It is evident that the DAV's are to be a real power in the land."[86] Like the AGA, American expats envisioned that those of their children who made good could be leaders of the nation.

Ironically, despite the emphasis the DAV placed on their Americanness, many of them were likely not formal citizens of the United States. Citizenship laws, as they concerned Americans in mixed marriages and their children, were complicated and have conflicting accounts. For example, the 1938 census stated that the children of an American father and Filipina mother who were legally married would receive the citizenship of the father. However, of the children counted from these American-Filipino marriages, only 626 are listed as having American citizenship, compared to 1,334 who hold Philippine citizenship. Another table from the same census reported the same number of American mestizos with Philippine citizenship and only 97 with US citizenship. The five-hundred-plus discrepancy in the census report is telling. Though the two charts were consistent in their reporting of the 1,334 mestizos with Philippine citizenship, the confusion seems to have arisen with determining who was American. The haphazard process of enumeration was conceded by the Bureau of the Census: "Many difficulties arose in connection with the determination of citizenship and the interpretation of the data. . . . Most of the difficulties arose in connection with the classification of those whose fathers and mothers belong to different races."[87] Enumerators were told to count only children of legitimate American-Filipino marriages as US citizens. However, they were also told to count those American-Filipino couples consensually living together without a marriage contract as married. This was likely confusing to both census takers and those being counted. Additionally, the rights of citizenship, even in legal marriages, were not automatically bestowed, unless, for example, a mestizo was applying for legal documentation, such as a US passport. From the reported numbers, it seems that many mestizos went without this formalization. As one old-timer recounted in a 1937 editorial, many American men did not realize that their mixed-race sons and daughters (born outside marriage) were not US citizens until they tried to obtain American legal documents for them and were denied.[88] It is likely that people simply reported their citizenship as whichever community they felt more a part of, with more mestizos choosing Philippine citizenship over American, having made their lives in the islands.[89]

Through the celebration of a comparatively few heteronormative and affluent mixed families, the result of American men not abandoning their Filipina wives and offspring in the Philippines, the DAV perpetuated a misleading picture of interracial relations. In rejecting the demeaning narratives about American mestiza women in the Philippines, they were able to negotiate their own marginalized identities and status within the colonial racial hierarchy. Elevating themselves, however, also reified the American conquest and occupation of the Philippine islands, institutionalizing the romantic idea of benevolent American involvement in the islands. In doing so, they, like their fathers before them, were the latest in a long line of participants in and supporters of American imperialism in the islands.

Conclusion

> With the severance of the political ties will come also a severance of another type of American-Filipino relations—the intermarriage of Filipinos and Americans. The severance of these ties, however, will not end the problems created by such marriages. For more than thirty years Filipino and Americans have inter-married, two cultures and two races have blended, until we have today thousands of children of mixed blood in the Philippines. For those who are interested in these marriages, the chief concern is not whether the Americans and Filipinos have lived together happily . . . but whether the children of these marriages will be an asset or a liability to the Philippines—whether they will be Filipinos or the most forlorn of all creatures, half-castes who do not know how to feel at home in any environment.
>
> —Mrs. Winifred O'Connor Pablo, 1935

The parental advice by Mrs. Winifred O'Connor Pablo on the topic of how to properly raise American mestizo children appeared in the popular Philippine magazine *Woman's World* in May 1935. In the article, Mrs. Pablo, a white American woman married to a Filipino man, described how she raised her mixed-race children and how she believed all such children of interracial unions in the Philippines ought to be raised: as proud Filipino citizens. Parents who tried to raise their mestizo children as American, she believed, would ultimately fail and doom their children to misery. Mrs. O'Connor Pablo, however, did not believe Americanizing mestizos would fail because of their base Filipino proclivities or because she believed racially impure mestizos could never be truly American. Rather, her advice was more practical, diverging from the narratives of the AGA and the DAV alike.

Mrs. O'Connor Pablo's stance was simple. If an interracial family has chosen to make their lives in the Philippines, their mestizo children should be taught to embrace and connect with the culture and people around them. She characterized the mestizo (a word that she disliked) raised to be an American as an outsider in the Philippines, one that "insists on his difference, and

I fear, his superiority." These feelings of superiority, she elaborated, were the result of training a child to value their American heritage over their Filipino heritage. One should not teach a mestizo child who neither "looks nor speaks" like an American that the US culture is better than that of the country they reside in. She chastised those who made disparaging comments to their mestizo children about Filipino food or customs. "Because American culture is different does not mean that it is superior, and fine though the culture is, it is not the culture that is going to make[the] child happy in the Philippines." She further commented on the kindness of Filipinos, many who welcomed her and her mixed-race children into their communities.

While her ideas about mestizo children being raised in the Philippines as Filipinos were in line with much of the prevailing sentiment of the time, which saw no place in the white racial homeland for mestizos, Mrs. O'Connor Pablo's stance demonstrates a different entry point into the discussion. As an American woman in the Philippines married to a Filipino, O'Connor Pablo likely faced ostracism from the American community. She made clear her appreciation for Filipino friends that welcomed her and her children but did not mention American friends with similar attitudes. Her interjection into the mestizo debate did not berate Filipina mothers, question the capacity of mixed-race children to be moral, or proclaim any sense of proud American nationalism. Rather, her appeal seems to be one of redress, almost an apology to the Filipino people for the attitudes of her American compatriots and, indeed, some of the mixed-race children convinced of their own "superiority."[90] The Filipina editors of *Woman's World* may have appreciated the divergence of her comments from the more popular discourse about mestizo children, which, as this chapter has demonstrated, was not kind to the Philippines or Filipino people, particularly Filipina women.

The long history of American mestizos in the Philippines is one that most scholarly literature positions as a post–World War II phenomenon, often noting the presence of colonial legacies but rarely looking at the colonial period comprehensively.[91] A postwar approach to American mestizo history is not only inaccurate but also effectively mitigates the history of US imperialism.[92] It is within the formal colonial period of US-Philippines relations that American mestizos first become constructed as a population precluded from American citizenship and, indeed, from American responsibility. In 1949, after Philippine independence, the AGA changed its name to the American-Philippine Guardian Association. In 1979, the leadership of the organization decided to change the name again to the Philippine American Guardian Association (PAGA), in recognition of the greater involvement of Filipinos in the organization than Americans. PAGA exists today, but the group of expatriate Americans attempting to care for mixed-race children in the Philippines has dwindled significantly, reflecting the postindependence reality of leaving Filipinos to handle the fallout of American occupation. While between 200,000 and more than 500,000 Filipino Amerasians are now estimated to be living in the Philippines, little has been done in the past hundred years to institutionalize American responsibility.[93]

Conclusion

"My Filipino Baby," Absolution, and the Aftermath
of an Imperial Romance

In 1946, amid waning US involvement in World War II, a popular song called "My Filipino Baby" reached the number two spot on the American country music singles charts. Sung by Country Music Hall of Famer Ernest Tubb, the lyrics reminisce about a man's time spent in the Philippines with a special Filipina, and the sadness American soldiers felt as they sailed away from the islands:

> All the sailors' hearts were filled with fond regret; / Looking backward to this island where they spent such happy hours / Making love to every pretty girl they've met / Well up stopped a little sailor with his pride eyes all aglow / Saying take a look at my gal's photograph / Then the sailors gathered round him just to look upon her face / And he said, "I love my Filipino baby."[1]

The many World War II sailors who were stationed in the Philippines, like the generation of war veterans who had been stationed there forty years earlier, found Filipina babies of their own to love and then leave, no doubt a factor that influenced the popularity of the song at this particular moment in time. The American soldiers and others who listened to "My Filipino Baby" in the United States may not have known it, but they shared the song in common with the previous generation of veterans from the Spanish-American and Philippine-American Wars.

Released originally as sheet music in 1898 and reprinted in 1899 and again in 1901, "My Filipino Baby" turned interracial romance and overseas imperialism into parlor entertainment, just as the 1940s version allowed veterans to take their romances with Filipinas back home with them in a sanitized form.[2] Originally titled "Ma Filipino Babe," the earliest sheet music drew on the blackface minstrel tradition, its lyrics similar to popular "coon songs" of the period.[3] The more obvious minstrelsy-influenced parts of the 1898 version—the original speaker was a "colored sailor lad," and the lyrics described "shiny faced" and "blackfaced" Filipinas—were removed or altered, reflecting a changing American self-image at a time when the United States was supposedly fighting fascism and imperialism overseas. While the original song domesticized the post-1898 island empire using the comedic romance of two similarly matched undesirables (a Black sailor and a "blackfaced" Filipina), the made-over song similarly and differently used romance to commemorate tender feelings of time spent in the tropics. Both versions sanitized and misrepresented the reality of sexual relations between Americans and Filipinas, relations that were exploitive, unequal, and rooted in the white supremacist logics of imperialism. But while the original song relied on a white supremacist comedic spectacle to help justify empire and make colonial wards seem in need of rescue and containable, the 1940s version, also laudatory toward the US presence in the Pacific, relied on the romantic incorporation of submissive tropical women into American hearts, if not the body politic. By the 1940s, the very imperial origins of the song, as well as its blackface minstrelsy template, had been erased, and instead the themes of romance and nostalgia were foregrounded.

The history and longevity of "My Filipino Baby" demonstrate what this book has argued, namely that real and imagined sociosexual intercourse in the colony served the liberal justificatory logics of empire in ways that still reverberate today. The colonial state managed, read, and imagined the dangerous intercourse between Americans and Filipinos in whatever ways were most beneficial and practical for the empire. American colonialists often used sociosexual relations between colonizer and colonized as a way to showcase supposedly positive, or exceptional, bilateral relations between the United States and the Philippines. Even the dangers that interracial sexual intercourse posed to US colonial rule—wherein prostitution and rape threatened the imperial claims of racial and moral superiority—were tempered by various means. By bringing a feminist critique and analysis to the relations studied here, we see how social and sexual intercourse served the empire when Americans and others reframed it from dangerous to beneficial. As the US empire worked to reframe or strategically manage dangerous intercourse, it effectively turned racism, imperialism, and exploitive asymmetrical relations into romance and intimacy. US imperial exceptionalism thrived through the fantasy of the intimate, in which the sociosexual incorporation of some colonial wards via intercourse stood in for actual socioracial equality and respect. This fantasy sustained the longevity of the US imperial presence in the islands well after formal independence.

The idea that social and sexual interracial intercourse is a sign or symptom of positive racial relations—an idea espoused by contemporary ideologies of multiculturalism and neoliberalism, especially in discourses of mixed-race identity—is not a new one.[4] As this book has illustrated, the same logic that many have used contemporarily to immortalize the landmark case of *Loving v. Virginia* as a national multiracial holiday—the logic that interracial intercourse equals tolerance and equality—was used at the turn of the century to ensure the legitimacy and durability of overseas American imperialism.[5] Indeed, the hegemonic power of empire to reproduce itself without the formal structures of colonial rule is largely facilitated through the debris, or what is left, of colonial state building projects commonly understood to have been beneficial for the occupied country. Systems of education, sanitation, and missionary institutions that colonizers erected in the Philippines are easy to point to as solid examples of the benevolent intent of Americans. In the same way, most types of interracial intercourse, especially the long-term and formal, may seem to signify benevolent intent and openness to social equality. Indeed, some scholars of empire have made exactly that argument. Though many imperial projects of the colonial state were seemingly positive, all colonial state building is rooted in notions of white supremacy and the baseline understanding of colonial subjects as uncivilized, subordinate, and inferior. With the cover of being a "positive" outcome of imperialism, some colonial institutions are more difficult to draw into critical engagement with and critique of US empire. This is dangerous and lends credence to the narrative of exceptionalism.

Prominent American cold warriors of the 1950s, 1960s, and 1970s understood the power of sociosexual intercourse wrapped up as intimacy to win over local nonwhite populations to the side of the free world. Perhaps the most prominent among them was CIA strategist Edward Lansdale. Well known for his role in developing clandestine US operations in Vietnam during the 1950s and 1960s, Lansdale was a devout believer in and proponent of psychological warfare, a military strategy that emphasized close familiarity with one's enemy and keeping civilian populations compliant and away from communist ideologies with orchestrated demonstrations of kindness. He honed these counterinsurgency tactics during his time spent quashing communist activity in the Philippines, largely with the help of his future wife, Patrocinio "Pat" Yapcinco Kelly. The Lansdale-Kelly affair began in 1946, though Lansdale was already married to Helen Lansdale, a white American woman. Lansdale found Kelly, a recent widow, appealing not just for her beauty but also for the intelligence she provided on the whereabouts of Hukbalahap military leaders in the islands.[6] The peasant-led Huk movement, which fought against the Japanese occupation and later the US-backed independent Philippine government, sought land reform and political inclusion via the Communist Party of the Philippines. Kelly was a former classmate of one of the highest-ranking Huk leaders, and as in decades before, dangerous intercourse was key to American incursions in the islands. Pat Kelly was Lansdale's guide in the Huk-friendly Luzon countryside, although recent writings on Kelly suggest that she was sympathetic to the Huk cause and likely misdirected Lansdale on some of their trips.[7] As Lansdale later recounted, however, "Pat showed me a lot of the back country that the Huks went through. . . . She showed me all these things up in the mountains that I would have never known otherwise."[8] A few years after they met, she accompanied him to Vietnam and played her own part in winning the hearts and minds of military and political elites, as she and Lansdale became close associates of Ngo Dinh Diem—the US-backed president of South Vietnam—and his family. In Vietnam, Lansdale often donned Philippine attire and regaled Vietnamese informants in his home with Philippine songs and games.[9] As Lansdale built his persona as a friend to Asian nations and peoples, Pat Kelly was perhaps the most conspicuous marker of the intimate strategy that Lansdale sought to embody.

Kelly's correspondence with Lansdale as she negotiated her move to the United States to be with him in the early 1970s suggests that she was aware of what her presence in his life meant for his personification of intimate counterinsurgency. In one letter, for example, she weighed her life in the Philippines against a potential life with Lansdale in the United States and was not keen on the idea that an exotified domesticity awaited her. Kelly informed Lansdale that she would not risk it all just to "cook adobo in Washington."[10] Though recent biographers point to Pat Kelly as the linchpin of Lansdale's success in the Philippines, and Lansdale himself described her as the love of his life, the unevenness of the US-Philippines relationship was mirrored in their relationship. Though they eventually married in 1973, it was only after the passing of Lansdale's wife in 1972, almost thirty years after the couple had first met in the Philippines.[11] Kelly moved to the United States, and she and Lansdale lived out the rest of their lives in the McLean suburbs of Virginia. Despite Lansdale's deep affection for Kelly, which is amply documented, Kelly is largely immortalized as his diminutive wife/mistress/"Special Filipina friend" in most writings on Lansdale.[12] Only recently have scholars taken a greater interest in her and the role she played in advancing American policy in the Asia-Pacific region. If Pat Kelly's membership in the American family (through her relationship with and eventual marriage to Ed Lansdale) was unstable through the postwar era, as it was for so many Filipinas who were involved with Americans in the colonial decades before, it remains so even in death. While Ed and Helen Lansdale share a large family tombstone in Arlington National Cemetery, Kelly's modest grave marker lies in the ground a few feet away. The Lansdale-Kelly relationship highlights how "going native" remained a cornerstone of US empire building, never a sideshow or an unintended outcome but a foundation. Lansdale was not Kurtz going off the map in the jungle; he was the mapmaker.[13]

The situation for American mestizos has changed since the colonial and commonwealth periods, but the changes have not necessarily improved the prospects of these individuals or addressed the root problems. For one thing, those mixed-race people born in the immediate post–World War II period are now known by many human rights organizations and NGOs as Filipino Amerasians, a label that emerged during the cold war militarization of the Asia-Pacific region and refers to the abandoned children of GIs in Asia more broadly, though many in the Philippines still refer to themselves as mestizos. Filipino Amerasians were excluded from preferential immigration legislation passed by the United States in the 1980s that would have allowed them to more easily enter the United States if they chose to do so. Filipino Amerasians were left out of both the 1982 Amerasian Immigration Act and the 1988 Amerasian Homecoming Act, which listed only Amerasians from Korea, Vietnam, Laos, Kampuchea (now Cambodia), and Thailand. As hundreds of thousands from around the Asia-Pacific region applied to come to the United States under this new legislation, the Philippines was not only overlooked but forced to aid in the repatriation and cultural education of qualifying Amerasians on their way to America. Morong, Philippines, a province just north of Manila and quite close to Subic Bay Naval Base, was home to a Philippine Refugee Processing Center, or PRPC, which was essentially a cultural and language training site for people and families from other Asian nations who were approved for permanent settlement in the United States, Canada, or Europe.[14]

The Morong PRPC opened in the 1980s and could house up to eighteen thousand people at any one time. The camp owed its existence to the historic US-Philippines imperial relationship. As an allied nation in the Pacific with historic ties to the United States, the Philippines hosted this training site, where Filipinos labored to provide refugees from across Southeast Asia with English-language training as well as instruction on American and other Western cultures. Essentially an outsourced humanitarian way station, the Philippines provided the labor, while the United States and other final-destination nations assumed the credit for welcoming those displaced and forced from their homes. Filipinos and Filipino Amerasians who wished to enter the United Stated were limited by the quota system established by the 1965 Immigration Act. With the PRPC operating out of the Philippines, and Filipino Amerasians classified as ineligible for reparative treatment, it was as if the nation had not sustained violence at the hands of the American military but rather was a beneficiary of American tutelage.[15]

Similarly, organizations such as the Philippine American Guardian Association continue to have complicated relations with the United States, and many of the board members (including the current president, chairman, and others) who have leadership roles in the organization are American expats. For example, current beneficiaries of PAGA participate in celebrations of American holidays such as Independence Day and Memorial Day and take trips to the Manila American Cemetery and Memorial, which houses the graves of US personnel killed during World War II. Such field trips and celebrations romanticize American involvement in the islands, closing the door on a more complicated and comprehensive engagement with US imperialism in the Philippines. The beneficiaries of PAGA receive information about the United States that encourages patriotism rather than criticism, romance rather than anger. Though PAGA has done much historically and contemporarily to materially improve the lives of American mestizos and Amerasians, it was and continues to be an organization rooted in US geopolitical dominance, although Filipinos have often challenged from within the asymmetrical relationship reflected in the organization.

Little has been done to assuage or take responsibility for the conditions faced by the newer and older generations of Amerasians or American mestizos who were left behind in the islands. American fathers, on the other hand, have been able to live their lives in the United States, many with veteran pensions, untroubled by the presence of their mixed-race offspring. For the descendants of colonists like H. Otley Beyer and A. V. H. Hartendorp—whose interracial marriages gave their families prominence and prestige in the Philippines—interracial intercourse continues to inform their lives. In addition to material wealth, men like Beyer and Hartendorp were able to access American resources for their families that would have long-lasting impacts, such as jobs for their children through old-timer networks, dual citizenship, and prominent schools. In addition, growing up Asian American in the Philippines opened up opportunities for mixed-race families that were inaccessible to other Filipinos. Also, and perhaps more important, many mixed-race families (largely those with white American ancestors) embrace this colonial ancestry.[16] This embrace, however, does little to shift the narrative of the United States–Philippines colonial romance.

By presenting the history of Filipino mestizos, queridas, sexual and domestic violence, and interracial families, this book has attempted to deconstruct this romance to achieve a more nuanced and complete understanding of how interracial intercourse has and continues to perpetuate an imperial relationship between the United States and the Philippines. Further, this inquiry has not only traced the long history of interracial intercourse but connected these histories to their imperial afterlives in the contemporary problems of sexual tourism and the sexual commodification of Filipina women, contemporary problems that continue to have grave impacts on the lives of Asian and Asian American women more broadly, evidenced by the recent and tragic Atlanta spa shootings. Sociosexual intercourse between Americans and Filipinos cannot be understood outside the framework of imperial control, nor can the exotification and hypersexualization of Filipina women. Indeed, individual choices about sexual intercourse were not necessarily free; Americans and Filipinos made their choices under the destabilizing and unequalizing forces of the imperial regime. US empire in the Philippines was forged by dangerous intercourse. For white and Black men alike, the desire for sexual recreation and experimentation was satisfied under the conditions of imperial rule, which all but guaranteed access to colonial wards. For Filipinas, Indigenous women, and other local women, interracial intercourse was often motivated not by romance and sexual desire but by the very practical considerations of financial and social necessity that had to be negotiated within a shifting imperial terrain. The stakes were and continue to be highest for these women as they continue to navigate the limited choices available to them within the asymmetrical relationship of the United States and the Philippines.

Notes

Introduction

1. James LeRoy, "Manuscript of Travelogue Account of Trip to the Philippine Islands," March 14, 1901, 17, box 1, James A. LeRoy Papers, Bentley Historical Library, University of Michigan, Ann Arbor.

2. LeRoy, "Manuscript of Travelogue," 5–6. Spoken at a dinner with Taft Commission members and the Filipino delegation in Lingayen, Pangasinan.

3. Statistics from Brian M. Linn, *The Philippine War, 1899–1902* (Lawrence: University Press of Kansas, 2000); Daniel B. Schirmer and Stephen R. Shalom, *The Philippines Reader: A History of Colonialism, Neocolonialism, Dictatorship, and Resistance* (Boston: South End Press, 1987).

4. William H. Taft, "Report of the Civil Governor," *Report of the United States Philippine Commission to the Secretary of War, 1900–1903, Bureau of Insular Affairs* (Washington, DC: Government Printing Office, 1904), 495.

5. Herbert D. Fisher, *Philippine Diary* (Burlington: Vantage Press, 2005), 85.

6. Luis Francia, *History of the Philippines: From Indios Bravos to Filipinos* (New York: Overland Press, 2014); Eva Maria Mehl, *Forced Migration in the Spanish Pacific World: From Mexico to the Philippines, 1765–1811* (Cambridge: Cambridge University Press, 2016).

7. "A splendid little war" was how soon-to-be secretary of state John Hay described the Spanish-American War in a letter to Theodore Roosevelt in July 1898. See also Kristin Hoganson, *Fighting for American Manhood: How Gender Politics Provoked the Spanish-American and Philippine-American Wars* (New Haven, CT: Yale University Press, 1998).

8. The commission served as the upper house and had the most power, largely because the governor-general, the highest political office, was also American. The elected Philippine assembly was the lower house.

9. "Report of Major Herbert W. Cardwell," in *Report of the Surgeon-General of the Army to the Secretary of War* (Washington, DC: Government Printing Office, 1899), 136.

10. Richard White, *The Middle Ground: Indians, Empires and Republics in the Great Lakes Region, 1650–1815* (Cambridge: Cambridge University Press, 1991); Raquel Casas, *Married to a Daughter of the Land: Spanish-Mexican Women and Interethnic Marriage in California, 1820–1880* (Reno: University of Nevada Press, 2007).

11. Anne Hyde, *Empires, Nations, and Families: A History of the North American West, 1800–1860* (Lincoln: University of Nebraska Press, 2011); David Wallace Adams and Crista DeLuzio, eds., *On the Borders of Love and Power: Families and Kinship in the Intercultural American Southwest* (Berkeley: University of California Press, 2012).

12. Greg Carter, *United States of United Races: A Utopian History of Racial Mixing* (New York: New York University Press, 2013).

13. Peggy Pascoe, *What Comes Naturally: Miscegenation Law and the Making of Race in America* (New York: Oxford University Press, 2010).

14. Noenoe K. Silva, *Aloha Betrayed: Native Hawaiian Resistance to American Colonialism* (Durham, NC: Duke University Press, 2004); Candace Fujikane and Jonathan Okamura, eds., "Whose Vision? Asian Settler Colonialism in Hawai'i," special issue, *Amerasia Journal* 26, no. 2 (2000).

15. For the history of the term "squaw" as a slur for Indigenous women in the United States, see Stacey Smith, *Freedom's Frontier: California and the Struggle over Unfree Labor, Emancipation and Reconstruction* (Chapel Hill: University of North Carolina Press, 2013), esp. chap. 5; David Smits, "'Squaw Men,' 'Half-Breeds,' and Amalgamators: Late Nineteenth-Century Anglo-American Attitudes toward Indian-White Race-Mixing." *American Indian Culture and Research Journal* 15, no. 3 (1991): 29–61; Rayna Green, "The Pocahontas Perplex: The Image of Indian Women in American Culture. *Massachusetts Review* 16, no. 4 (1975): 698–714.

16. Patrick Wolfe and others emphasize the elimination of Native populations as a method of settler colonialism, while others point to the impossibility of such elimination, highlighting instead the liminal incorporation, or "possession," of Indigenous peoples as a method of settler colonialism. See Maile Arvin, *Possessing Polynesians: The Science of Settler Colonial Whiteness in Hawai'i and Oceania* (Durham, NC: Duke University Press, 2019).

17. Jodi Byrd, *Transit of Empire: Indigenous Critiques of Colonialism* (Minneapolis: University of Minnesota Press, 2011).

18. Julian Go and Anne L. Foster, eds., *The American Colonial State in the Philippines* (Durham, NC: Duke University Press, 2003). The introduction parses out the distinctions between what some scholars have described as "administrative" versus settler colonialism.

19. My thanks to A. B. Wilkinson for suggesting this framing.

20. Katharine Bjork, *Prairie Imperialists: The Indian Country Origins of American Empire* (Philadelphia: University of Pennsylvania Press, 2019).

21. Byrd, *Transit of Empire*, xvii.

22. See, for example, the constant references to the "Indian" of the Philippines in the Schurman Commission interviews in *Report of the Philippine Commission to the President, 1899–1900* (Washington, DC: Government Printing Office, 1900), 2:1–19.

23. Theodore Roosevelt, "Memorial Day Speech, May 30, 1902," in Alfred H. Lewis, ed., *A Compilation of the Messages and Speeches of Theodore Roosevelt, 1901–1905* (New York: Bureau of National Literature and Art, 1906), 1:33. Our historical archives attest to the ways that turn-of-the-century Americans understood the overseas empire as a continuation of the US settler imperial project. It is common for archival material on Native Americans in the United States to also include a smattering of material on the Pacific world. See, for example, the Ayer Collection at the Newberry Library or the collections on the US West at the Huntington Library.

24. "Wilson Reviews Independence Pledge during Staunton Visit," *Filipino People* 1, no. 5 (January 1913): 4.

25. Ned Blackhawk, *Violence over the Land: Indians and Empires in the Early American West* (Cambridge, MA: Harvard University Press, 2009); Albert Hurtado, *Intimate Frontiers: Sex, Gender, and Culture in Old California*, (Albuquerque: University of New Mexico Press, 1999).

26. Margaret Jacobs, *White Mother to a Dark Race: Settler Colonialism, Maternalism, and the Removal of Indigenous Children in the American West and Australia, 1880–1940* (Lincoln: University of Nebraska Press, 2009).

27. There are few examples of US miscegenation laws being applied in the Philippines. At the time of writing, I knew of only one instance: "Moro Widow Will Benefit," *Lincoln Evening Journal*, July 5, 1939, 3. See chapter 4.

28. Pascoe, *What Comes Naturally*.

29. While some scholars assert that racism and imperialism have been incompatible for the reasons laid out here, this project, like others, argues that they were quite compatible and together formed the basis of imperial relations. See Eric Love, *Race over Empire: Racism and U.S. Imperialism, 1865–1900* (Chapel Hill: University of North Carolina Press, 2004).

30. "Letter of Charles Davis to Bess Davis," June 24, 1900, 4–5, box 1, folder 3, Davis Papers, Ayer Collection, Newberry Library, Chicago, Illinois. Davis's letter described his shipboard encounter with three women he presumed were of "ill-fame" on the Hong Kong to Manila leg of his trip. He believed that these women were traveling to Manila to start their own brothel.

31. See note 15.

32. Vernadette Gonzalez uses the framework of intimacy as labor in "Illicit Labor: MacArthur's Mistress and Imperial Intimacies," *Radical History Review* 123 (October 2015): 87–114.

33. *Report of the Surgeon-General of the Army to the Secretary of War, 1899* (Washington, DC: Government Printing Office, 1899), 129–32.

34. Philippa Levine, *Prostitution, Race, and Politics: Policing Venereal Disease in the British Empire* (New York: Routledge, 2003); Ann Laura Stoler, *Carnal Knowledge and Imperial Power: Race and the Intimate in Colonial Rule* (Berkeley: University of California Press, 2002); Durba Ghosh, *Sex and the Family in Colonial India: The Making of Empire* (Cambridge: Cambridge University Press, 2006); Emmanuelle Saada, *Empire's Children: Race, Filiation, and Citizenship in the French Colonies* (Chicago: University of Chicago Press, 2012).

35. See Ngũgĩ wa Thiong'o, *Decolonising the Mind: The Politics of Language in African Literature* (London: J. Currey, 1986); Linda Tuhiwai Smith, *Decolonizing Methodologies: Research and Indigenous Peoples* (London: Zed Books, 1999); Albert Memmi, *The Colonizer and the Colonized*, 3rd ed. (London: Earthscan, 2003).

36. See note 34. For US miscegenation laws, see Pascoe, *What Comes Naturally*.

37. The bulk of the relations examined here were between American men and Filipina/Indigenous women. These made up the majority of sociosexual relations between colonizer and colonized in the colonial Philippines, though other types of relations are discussed here as well. "Unmentionable liberties," for example, was a thinly veiled reference by American officials to same-sex intimacies, also commonly described as "deviant," "unnatural," and so on. See chapter 4.

38. This work is indebted to the feminist scholars who have long asserted that the "personal" is political and international. See Cynthia Enloe, *Bananas, Beaches and Bases: Making Feminist Sense of International Politics*, 2nd ed. (Berkeley: University of California Press, 2014); Joan Scott, "Gender as a Useful Category of Analysis," *American Historical Review* 91, no. 5 (1986): 1053–75.

39. Such gendered depictions were the rule in the United States as political debates about annexation raged. See also the proliferation of romantic songs about liaisons with Filipinas from the turn of the century. Thomas P. Walsh, *Tin Pan Alley and the Philippines: American Songs of War and Love, 1898–1946* (Lanham, MD: Scarecrow Press, 2013).

1. Marshaling Interracial Intercourse during the Philippine-American War, 1898–1902

1. See Cynthia Luz P. Rivera, "Filipino Women's Magazines, 1909–1940: Resistance, Cultural Subversion, and Compromise," *Plaridel* 1, no. 2 (2004): 1–20.

2. See "Local Notes," *Manila Times*, July 7, 1899, 4; "A Timely Order," *Manila Times*, July 7, 1899, 4; "Soldiers and the Liquor Traffic," *Manila Times*, July 11, 1899, 2; "She Loved a Corporal . . . and Her Chinese Husband Found Her Out," *Manila Times*, July 29, 1899, 5; "Colored Soldiers Outrage Women," *Manila Times*, September 2, 1899, 1.

3. Recounted in a letter from Juliana Lopez to Sixto Lopez, January 8, 1902, in Canning Eyot, ed., *The Story of the Lopez Family: A Page from the History of the War in the Philippines* (Boston: James H. West, 1904), 83.

4. Letter from Juliana Lopez to Clemencia Lopez, January 21, 1902, in Eyot, *Story of the Lopez Family*, 96.

5. "Miss Lopez's Speech," *Woman's Journal*, June 7, 1902, 181.

6. Walter Jaeger, "Other Faith Breakers Than Germany," *New York Times*, May 28, 1915, 12.

7. "Battle of Bagsag [*sic*] Forced by Felons," *New York Times*, June 14, 1913, 7.

8. Daniel Roderick Williams, *The Odyssey of the Philippine Commission* (Chicago: A. C. McClurg, 1913), 56.

9. Paul A. Kramer, "Colonial Crossings: Prostitution, Disease, and the Boundaries of Empire during the Philippine-American War," in *Body and Nation: The Global Realm of U.S. Body Politics in the Twentieth Century*, ed. Emily S. Rosenberg and Shanon Fitzpatrick (Durham, NC: Duke University Press, 2014).

10. The US military continued to myopically understand Filipina women mainly as prostitutes during and after World War II. See Susan Zeiger, *Entangling Alliances: Foreign War Brides and American Soldiers in the Twentieth Century* (New York: New York University Press, 2010).

11. Lata Mani, *Contentious Traditions: The Debate on Sati in Colonial India* (Berkeley: University of California Press, 1998); Laura Prieto, "A Delicate Subject: Clemencia López, Civilized Womanhood, and the Politics of Anti-imperialism," *Journal of the Gilded Age and the Progressive Era* 12, no. 2 (2013): 199–233.

12. Lilia Quindoza Santiago, *Sexuality and the Filipina* (Quezon City: University of the Philippines Press, 2007), 30–32.

13. Victoria Lactaw, Felipa Kapuloan, Feliza Kahatol, Victoria Mausig, Patricia Himagsik, Salvadora Dimagiba, Dolores Katindig, Honorata Dimauga, and Deodata Liwanag, "Hibik namin," *El heraldo Filipino*, February 17, 1899. Translation found in Dawn A. Ottevaere, "The Cost Is Sworn to by Women: Gender, Resistance, and Counterinsurgency during the Philippine-American War, 1898–1902" (PhD diss., Michigan State University, 2010), 191–92.

14. Lactaw et al., "Hibik namin."

15. Edward W. Said, *Orientalism* (New York: Vintage Books, 1979); Mary Louise Pratt, *Imperial Eyes: Travel Writing and Transculturation* (London: Routledge, 1992).

16. See note 2.

17. In José Rizal's famous novel *Noli me tángere*, the beautiful and chaste Maria Clara, a Spanish mestiza, was the love interest of the hero. Her father was a Spanish friar and her mother, a native Filipina woman.

18. Vicente L. Rafael, *White Love and Other Events in Filipino History* (Durham, NC: Duke University Press, 2000).

19. Ottevaere, "Cost Is Sworn to by Women."

20. Rivera, "Filipino Women's Magazines"; Georgina Reyes Encanto, *Constructing the Filipina: A History of Women's Magazines, 1891–2002* (Quezon City: University of the Philippines Press, 2004).

21. John Taylor, *The Philippine Insurrection against the United States: A Compilation of Documents with Notes and Introduction* (Pasay City: Eugenio Lopez Foundation, 1971), 3:183.

22. J. Taylor, *Philippine Insurrection*, 3:185.

23. Mina Roces, "Is the Suffragist an American Colonial Construct? Defining 'The Filipino Woman' in Colonial Philippines," in *Women's Suffrage in Asia: Gender, Nationalism and Democracy*, ed. Louise Edwards and Mina Roces (New York: Routledge, 2004); Lilia Quindoza Santiago, *Sa ngalan ng ina: Sandaang taon ng tulang feminista sa Pilipinas, 1889–1989* (Quezon City: University of the Philippines Press, 1997).

24. Specifically, Aguinaldo lists the provinces of "the heroic Cavite, the esteemed Manila, the rich Bataan, the charitable and kindly Bulacan, the famous Pampanga, the fertile Tarlac and Nueva Ecija, the healthful Laguna, the generous Infanta and Morong, the free Tayabas, the great Mindoro and its adjacent isles; and along the coast of the China Sea, from nearby Bataan, Zambales and Pangasinan to distant Union." J. Taylor, *Philippine Insurrection*, 3:186.

25. Homer C. Stuntz, *The Philippines and the Far East* (Cincinnati: Jennings and Pye, 1904), 106–7.

26. J. Taylor, *Philippine Insurrection*, 3:116–24.

27. See "Letter of Severino de las Alas," September 1898, and "Letter of Gregorio Araneta," December 1898, in Taylor, *Philippine Insurrection*, 3:589, 3:619.

28. On the issue of Filipino and Native clergy and the revolutionary government, see Cesar Adib Majul, *The Political and Constitutional Ideas of the Philippine Revolution* (New York: Sentry, 1967), 148–49.

29. General Order No. 68, issued Manila, December 18, 1899, in *Index to General Orders and Circulars Issued from the Office of the U.S. Military Governor in the Philippine Islands* (Washington, DC: Government Printing Office, 1899).

30. J. Taylor, *Philippine Insurrection*, 5:98.

31. J. Taylor, *Philippine Insurrection*, 4:17; see also 2:141. Filipino military leaders distributed similar decrees that promised harsh punishment for rape and other crimes in various provinces. Benito Legarda wrote to Aguinaldo of the Filipino distrust of the revolutionary army due to these reported outrages.

32. J. Taylor, *Philippine Insurrection*, 5:667. One Filipino elite, Magno Abenis, wrote in a December 1900 letter to warn fellow Filipinos about crimes committed by the "insurgent army" and encouraged cooperation with the Americans.

33. J. Taylor, *Philippine Insurrection*, 3:194–95.

34. Depictions like that in figure 1.1 were similar to those common in blackface minstrelsy.

35. *Report of the Surgeon-General of the Army to the Secretary of War* (Washington, DC: Government Printing Office, 1899), 131–32.

36. Ned Blackhawk, *Violence over the Land: Indians and Empires in the Early American West* (Cambridge, MA: Harvard University Press, 2008).

37. Lippincott, like his contemporary Major William H. Corbusier, built his reputation on medical service during the wars of eradication against Native Americans in the late 1800's. Both men were among the first to be recruited by the military to join the expedition to the Philippines. "Correspondence—Philippines," in *United States Congressional Serial Set: Report of the Commission Appointed by the President to Investigate the Conduct of the War Department in the War with Spain*, vol. 2 (Washington, DC: Government Printing Office, 1900), 1213.

38. Statistics from Brian McAllister Linn, *The Philippine War, 1899–1902* (Lawrence: University Press of Kansas, 2000).

39. *Census of the Philippine Islands Taken under the Direction of the Philippine Commission in the Year 1903* (Washington, DC: Bureau of the Census, 1905), 2:42; *Census of the Philippine Islands Taken under the Direction of the Philippine Legislature in the Year 1918* (Manila: Bureau of Printing, 1921), 2:31; *Census of the Philippines: 1939* (Manila: Bureau of Printing, 1941), 2:393. The number of American military personnel were not enumerated for these periods within these census reports.

40. Washington Headquarters Services Directorate for Information Operations and Reports, *Department of Defense, Selected Manpower Statistics: 1986* (Washington, DC: Government Printing Office, 1986), table 2–11, 63.

41. Jennifer L. Morgan, *Laboring Women: Reproduction and Gender in New World Slavery* (Philadelphia: University of Pennsylvania Press, 2004); Anne Hyde, *Empires, Nations, and Families: A History of the North American West, 1800–1860* (Lincoln: University of Nebraska Press, 2011); Shelley Streeby, *American Sensations: Class, Empire and the Production of Popular Culture* (Berkeley: University of California Press, 2002).

42. Anne McClintock, *Imperial Leather: Race, Gender and Sexuality in the Colonial Contest* (New York: Routledge, 1995).

43. See note 2 and Michael C. Hawkins, "Masculinity Reborn: Chivalry, Misogyny, Potency and Violence in the Philippines' Muslim South, 1899–1913," *Journal of Southeast Asian Studies* 44, no. 2 (June 2013): 250–65.

44. Henry Parker Willis, *Our Philippine Problem: A Study of American Colonial Policy* (New York: Henry Holt, 1905), 251.

45. Ian Tyrrell, "New Approaches to American Cultural Expansion," in *Competing Kingdoms: Women, Mission, Nation, and the American Protestant Empire, 1812–1960*, ed. Barbara Reeves-Ellington, Kathryn Kish Sklar, and Connie A. Shemo (Durham, NC: Duke University Press, 2010).

46. "Statement of Rev. W. F. Crafts, Conditions in the Philippines," *Hearings Before the Committee on Military Affairs, U.S. Senate, Dec. 7–14, 1900* (Washington, DC: Government Printing Office, 1900), 20–22.

47. "The Public Forum: Moralist Moralizes," *Manila Times*, June 18, 1907. See also Kristin L. Hoganson and Jay Sexton, eds., *Crossing Empires: Taking U.S. History into Transimperial Terrain* (Durham, NC: Duke University Press, 2020); Paul A. Kramer, "The Darkness That Enters the Home: The Politics of Prostitution during the Philippine-American War," in *Haunted by Empire: Geographies of Intimacy in North American History*, ed. Ann Laura Stoler (Durham, NC: Duke University Press, 2006).

48. An Act Regulating the Sale of Intoxicating Liquors within the City of Manila and Its Attached Barrios," *Acts of the Philippine Commission, nos. 1–1800* (Washington, DC: Government Printing Office, 1901), 1:96–101.

49. "Native" was often a catch-all term that Americans used to describe Filipinos, Chinese, mestizos, and even Spanish. According to these reports, locally made liquor like vino did not harm the nonwhite native inhabitants of the Philippines, but it imperiled the life of the American soldier.

50. For more on the canteen fight between prohibitionists and the military, see Ian Tyrrell, *Reforming the World: The Creation of America's Moral Empire* (Princeton, NJ: Princeton University Press, 2010); Kramer, "Darkness That Enters the Home."

51. Military government over the islands began in August 1898 and ended in July 1901, when William Howard Taft was appointed as the first civil governor of the Philippines. Military rule, however, would continue in parts of the island, notably Mindanao, which was under US military rule until 1913.

52. The American Medical Association, the American Public Health Association, and the Association of Military Naval Surgeons, for example, all passed resolutions condemning the

Anti-Canteen Act. "Miscellaneous Reports," "Sale of Beer and Light Wines in Post Exchanges," *United States Congressional Serial Set* (Washington, DC: Government Printing Office, 1903), 514–16.

53. "Philippine Islands, American Troops," in *Annual Report of the Surgeon General to the Department of War* (Washington, DC: Government Printing Office, 1911), 105.

54. Report of First Lieutenant C. A. Trott, "Sale of Beer and Light Wines in Post Exchanges," *United States Congressional Serial Set* (Washington, DC: Government Printing Office, 1903), 497.

55. Report of Commanding General Potts of the Department of Luzon, P.I., *Congressional Record: Proceedings and Debates of the Sixty-First U.S. Congress* (Washington: U.S. Government Printing Office, 1911), appendix, 203.

56. Report of Jos Garrard, Major, Ninth Cavalry, "Sale of Beer and Light Wines in Post Exchanges," *United States Congressional Serial Set.* (Washington, DC: Government Printing Office, 1903), 438.

57. Kramer, "Darkness That Enters the Home"; Andrew Jimenez Abalahin, "Prostitution Policy and the Project of Modernity: A Comparative Study of Colonial Indonesia and the Philippines, 1850–1940" (PhD diss., Cornell University, 2003).

58. Report of George Byram, Captain and Quartermaster Sixth Cavalry, "Sale of Beer and Light Wines in Post Exchanges," *United States Congressional Serial Set* (Washington, DC: Government Printing Office, 1903), 415.

59. Statement of Capt. Edward L. Munson, Assistant Surgeon, United States Army, in *Miscellaneous Hearings Before the Committee on Military Affairs, U.S. Senate, 1900–1919* (Washington, DC: Government Printing Office, 1900), 75.

60. See chapter 2.

61. Cynthia Marasigan, *Triangulated Amigo Warfare: African American Soldiers, Filipino Revolutionaries, and U.S. Empire* (Durham, NC: Duke University Press, forthcoming); Willard B. Gatewood, *"Smoked Yankees" and the Struggle for Empire: Letters from Negro Soldiers, 1898–1902* (Fayetteville: University of Arkansas Press, 1987).

62. Willard B. Gatewood, *Black Americans and the White Man's Burden, 1898–1903* (Chicago: University of Illinois Press, 1975).

63. Martha Hodes, *White Women, Black Men: Illicit Sex in the 19th Century* (New Haven, CT: Yale University Press, 2014); Amy S. Greenberg, *Manifest Manhood and the Antebellum American Empire* (Cambridge: Cambridge University Press, 2005); Ken De Bevoise, *Agents of Apocalypse: Epidemic Disease in the Colonial Philippines* (Princeton, NJ: Princeton University Press, 1995).

64. Report of Assistant Surgeon General Charles Greenleaf, appended in *Annual Report of Major General Arthur MacArthur, U.S. Army, Commanding, Division of the Philippines, Military Governor in the Philippine Islands*, vol. 1 (Manila, 1901), appendix F, 5.

65. Report of Major Herbert W. Cardwell, "Report of the Surgeon General," *Annual Reports of the War Department; Reports of Chiefs of Bureaus* (Washington, DC: Government Printing Office, 1899), vol. 1, part 2, 488.

66. "Philippine Islands, American Troops," in *Annual Report of the Surgeon General to the Department of War* (Washington, DC: Government Printing Office, 1911), 105.

67. G. E. Seaman, "Some Observations of a Medical Officer in the Philippines," *Milwaukee Medical Journal* 10, no. 7 (1902): 188.

68. *"Pinna chemisa"* (or *piña kamisa*) refers to the pineapple fiber (*piña*) cloth blouse, or *kamisa*, worn by many women in the Philippines.

69. "Sale of Beer and Light Wines in Post Exchanges," *United States Congressional Serial Set* (Washington, DC: Government Printing Office, 1903), 402–10. The gendered assignations of

feminine or masculine modifiers in Spanish given names point to the high number of enterprising women in the liquor business.

70. "Manila without the Canteen," *Manila Times*, cited in "Sale of Beer and Light Wines in Post Exchanges," *United States Congressional Serial Set* (Washington, DC: Government Printing Office, 1903), 498.

71. I tentatively list sexual labor under "informal" economies, as the red-light districts in Manila, for example, were very well regulated by local government authorities.

72. Mrs. Campbell Dauncey, *An Englishwoman in the Philippines* (New York: E. P. Dutton, 1906), 176–77.

73. J. Taylor, *Philippine Insurrection*, 2:50.

74. Maria Luisa T. Camagay, *Working Women of Manila in the 19th Century* (Manila: University of the Philippines Press, 1995).

75. Officials detailed how men would leave their posts, become intoxicated on local drink, and have to sleep off their inebriation in the local towns. See, "Sale of Beer and Light Wines in Post Exchanges," *United States Congressional Serial Set* (Washington, DC: Government Printing Office, 1903), 404, 413, 417, 421.

76. The American colonial government enacted the sedition law in 1901, which forbade public criticism of US colonial rule. Thus, much Filipino critique of American drunkenness comes secondhand from Americans and in American sources. In Filipino plays and dramas banned by the US government for being seditious, however, Americans were often depicted as drunk and disorderly. See Rafael, *White Love and Other Events in Filipino History*, 48; Alfred W. McCoy, *Policing America's Empire: The United States, the Philippines, and the Rise of the Surveillance State* (Madison: University of Wisconsin Press, 2009).

77. "Report of Law Department," in *Annual Report of the Philippine Commission, 1904*, pt. 1 (Washington, DC: Government Printing Office, 1905), 209–10.

78. Philippine Legislature, *Official Gazette* 20, no. 90 (1922): 1622.

79. "History," St. Louise de Marillac College of Bogo (website), accessed February 20, 2022, https://slmcbweb.wordpress.com/history.

80. "News from Planters Association," *Sugar News* 20 (1939): 63.

81. For American expectations of deference, see Steinbock-Pratt, *Educating the Empire: American Teachers and Contested Colonization in the Philippines* (Cambridge: Cambridge University Press, 2019).

82. Camagay, *Working Women of Manila*. See also Kramer, "Darkness That Enters the Home"; De Bevoise, *Agents of Apocalypse*.

83. *Navy Guide to Cavite and Manila: A Practical Guide and Beautiful Souvenir* (Manila: Manila Merchants' Association, 1908), 52; *Beautiful Philippines: A Handbook of General Information* (Manila: Manila Bureau of Printing, 1923), 29. Americans used the diminutive term "little brown brothers" to refer to Filipinos. It conveyed familial or friendly relations between the two nations but also reinforced a patriarchal, hierarchical relationship wherein the United States was the paternal authority.

2. Colonial "Frontiers"

1. According to the notes of Dean Worcester (and those who worked with him) for his photograph collection, Margarita Asuncion de la Cruz was a "Spanish-Tagalog mestizo woman." "German Mestizos," 49-c1, catalogue, Dean C. Worcester Photograph Collection, Museum of Anthropological Archaeology, University of Michigan (hereafter cited as UMMAA).

2. The idea of being the first white person to penetrate a nonwhite community (typically characterized as savage and backward) is a common theme in American settler origin stories, and many white American settlers in the Philippines crafted such reputations for themselves. As Jean O'Brien points out, such works denied the existence of local Indigenous populations or marked the beginning of significant history as the point of contact with white persons. Jean O'Brien, *Firsting and Lasting: Writing Indians out of Existence in New England* (Minneapolis: University of Minnesota Press, 2010).

3. James LeRoy, "Manuscript of Travelogue Account of Trip to the Philippine Islands," June 11–June 20, 1901, box 1, James A. LeRoy Papers, Bentley Historical Library, University of Michigan, Ann Arbor.

4. "German mestiza girl, type 1. Standing with her father," 49-c3, and "German mestiza girl, type 1. Full length front view," 49-c2, Manila (1901), catalogue, Dean C. Worcester Photograph Collection, UMMAA.

5. David P. Barrows, *Circular of Information: Instructions for Volunteer Field Workers; The Museum of Ethnology, Natural History and Commerce* (Manila: Bureau of Non-Christian Tribes for the Philippine Islands, 1901), 3.

6. Report of Captain Arthur Thayer, "Sale of Beer and Light Wines in Post Exchanges," *United States Congressional Serial Set* (Washington, DC: Government Printing Office, 1903), 446–48.

7. While those in the lowlands also expressed opposition, it was easier for the Spanish to protect the settlements they were growing in these areas. Eventually, converted Catholic populations even harbored animosity toward Indigenous highland communities and Muslims for their raids on Spanish-controlled areas.

8. Frank L. Jenista, *The White Apos: American Governors on the Cordillera Central* (Quezon City: New Day, 1987); Stephen Acabado and Grace Barretto-Tesoro, "Places, Landscapes, and Identity: Place Making in the Colonial Period Philippines," in *The Global Spanish Empire: Five Hundred Years of Place Making and Pluralism*, ed. Christine D. Beaule and John G. Douglass (Tucson: University of Arizona Press, 2020).

9. Patricio Abinales and Donna Amoroso, *State and Society in the Philippines* (Lanham, MD: Rowman and Littlefield, 2017), 70.

10. Barrows, *Circular of Information*, 3.

11. Barrows, *Circular of Information*, 3. See also Gerard A. Finin, *The Making of the Igorot* (Quezon City: Ateneo University Press, 2005); Michael Salman, *The Embarrassment of Slavery: Controversies over Bondage and Nationalism in the American Colonial Philippines* (Berkeley: University of California Press, 2003). Many American travel accounts fixate on the first white people to travel within the Cordilleras. Such writings also position American writers as adventurous, as they follow on the heels of the first. See also *Report of the United States Philippine Commission to the Secretary of War 1900–1903, Bureau of Insular Affairs* (Washington, DC: Government Printing Office, 1904), 495.

12. *Census of the Philippine Islands Taken under the Direction of the Philippine Legislature in the Year 1918*, vol. 2 (Manila: Bureau of Printing, 1921).

13. See chapter 3.

14. "Degenerate Americans, He Says," *Manila Times*, March 20, 1908, 6.

15. "Degenerate Americans," 6. The description suggests that these men have "gone native," becoming too much like Filipinos.

16. Homer C. Stuntz, *The Philippines and the Far East* (Cincinnati: Jennings and Pye, 1904), 481.

17. Act No. 1876, An Act Providing for the Establishment of a Province to Be Known as the Mountain Province, *Acts of the First Philippine Legislature*, vol. 9 (Manila: Government Printing Office, 1908), 137–41.

18. Paul A. Kramer, *The Blood of Government: Race, Empire, the United States, and the Philippines* (Chapel Hill: University of North Carolina Press, 2006).

19. For more in US-based "salvage" ethology or anthropology, see Philip Deloria, *Playing Indian* (New Haven, CT: Yale University Press, 1998).

20. Jenista, *White Apos*, 185–206.

21. Jenista, *White Apos*, 185–206.

22. See, for example, H. Otley Beyer, *The Non-Christian People of the Philippines*, Separate from the Census of the Philippine Islands:1918, Vol. 2 (Manila: Bureau of Printing, 1921); Samuel Kane, *Thirty Years with the Philippine Head-hunters* (London: Jarrods ltd. 1934); William Henry Scott, *On the Cordillera: A Look at the Peoples and Cultures of the Mountain Province* (Manila: MCS Enterprises, 1966).

23. Jenista, *White Apos*, 209.

24. A. V. H. Hartendorp, *I Have Lived: Reminiscences of A.V.H. Hartendorp* (Manila: Self-published, 1970), 1:135.

25. Major Wilfrid Turnbull, "Early Days in the Mountain Province," *Bulletin of the American Historical Collection* 3, no. 1 (1975): 49.

26. Nanon Fay Leas Worcester diary, 1909, 37, Joseph Ralston Hayden Papers, Bentley Historical Library, University of Michigan.

27. White women similarly sought to escape the confines of stringent gendered expectations by joining the civil service to work on Native American reservations. See Margaret Jacobs, *White Mother to a Dark Race: Settler Colonialism, Maternalism, and the Removal of Indigenous Children in the American West and Australia, 1880–1940* (Lincoln: University of Nebraska Press, 2009); Cathleen Cahill, *Federal Fathers and Mothers: A Social History of the United States Indian Service, 1869–1933* (Chapel Hill: University of North Carolina Press, 2011).

28. Letter of Dean C. Worcester to Governor-General of the Philippines, William C. Forbes, "Record in the Matter of Charges against Lieutenant Walter F. Hale in Connection with the Guinabal Expedition," October 6, 1911, Correspondence, 1900–1924, box 1, Dean C. Worcester Papers, Bentley Historical Library.

29. Stenographer's report of interview between Lt.-Gov. Hale, Dean C. Worcester, and people of the Guinabal District, October 6, 1911, 3, Correspondence, 1900–1924, box 1, Dean C. Worcester Papers, Bentley Historical Library.

30. For more about the role of women as intermediaries between Indigenous and settler populations, see Juliana Barr, *Peace Came in the Form of a Woman: Indians and Spaniards in the Texas Borderlands* (Chapel Hill: University of North Carolina Press, 2007).

31. Stenographer's report of interview between Lt.-Gov. Hale, Dean C. Worcester, and people of the Guinabal District, 3. Lubo and Mañgali are both located within the Kalinga region of Mountain Province.

32. Nanon Fay Leas Worcester diary, 1909, descriptions on pp. 35 and 45.

33. Stenographer's report of interview between Lt.-Gov. Hale, Dean C. Worcester, and people of the Guinabal District, 5.

34. Herbert D. Fisher, *Philippine Diary* (Burlington: Vantage Press, 2005), 85. Americans often mentioned "squaw men" in their writings, poetry, and accounts. See Stanley Karnow, *In Our Image: America's Empire in the Philippines* (New York: Random House Press, 2010); Bobby Wintermute, *Public Health and the US Military: A History of the Army Medical Department, 1818–1917* (New York: Routledge, 2011). Americans also used the pejorative to refer to white men in Hawaii who married native women.

35. For more on Scheerer's trouble with the US military, see Rebecca Tinio McKenna, *American Imperial Pastoral: The Architecture of US Colonialism in the Philippines* (Chicago: University of Chicago Press, 2017), 87–89.

36. Lewis E. Gleeck, "Fulfillment in the Philippines," *Bulletin of the American Historical Collection* 18, no. 2 (April–June 1990).

37. Dale Riley, "A Little Trip to 'Haight's Place,'" *Mid-Pacific* 17, no. 2 (1919): 159.

38. Riley, "Little Trip," 159. For more on the menu prepared by Susie at Haight's Place, see N. W. Jenkins, "Haight's Place," *Philippine Magazine* 27, no. 12 (1931): 760.

39. Jenkins, "Haight's Place," 759.

40. John Bancroft Devins, *An Observer in the Philippines: Or, Life in Our New Possessions* (Boston: American Tract Society, 1905), 127; "Marry for Keeps Here," *Manila Times*, July 25, 1907, 1. The US commission disapproved of divorce in the Philippines, saying that Americans who married in the islands should "marry for keeps," likely in the hopes that Americans would not marry Filipinas if they could not divorce them. In 1908, Secretary of War William H. Taft described his preference for unmarried men in the US Army, as married men were a "nuisance." "Secretary Taft's Recommendations for the Army in the Philippines," *Manila Times*, February 24, 1908, section 2, 9.

41. Jenista, *White Apos*. The term "Apo" is a Philippine honorific to describe a grandparent, an elder, or an ancestor. Jenista describes how some Ifugao people would refer to higher-ranking American colonial officials in the Cordillera as "Apo."

42. Jenista, *White Apos*.

43. Jenista, *White Apos*, 215.

44. General Orders, No. 68, issued Manila, December 18, 1899, in *Index to General Orders and Circulars Issued from the Office of the U.S. Military Governor in the Philippine Islands* (Washington, DC: Government Printing Office, 1899).

45. Jenista, *White Apos*, 216. I say "given" dubiously because Dosser essentially returned land to its previous stewards.

46. Americans compared people of the Cordillera's to Native Americans in the United States and also saw Filipino mestizos who had Spanish ancestry as more civilized. Many of the lowland Filipinos on the island of Luzon, especially the elites, were mestizo or claimed Spanish ancestry.

47. An Act to Establish Divorce, No. 2710, *Laws of the Fourth Philippine Legislature*, vol. 1 (Washington, DC: Government Printing Office, 1918), 190–91.

48. Finin, *Making of the Igorot*.

49. Jenista, *White Apos*, 220.

50. Reports on American constabulary officials often included their marital status and if they were otherwise known to be bound to local women. See Harry Hill Bandholtz, memorandum, 1904, Correspondence, box 1, folder 4, Harry H. Bandholtz Papers, Bentley Historical Library; Harry Hill Bandholtz, endorsement, April 20, 1905, Correspondence, box 1, folder 5, Harry H. Bandholtz Papers, Bentley Historical Library.

51. Harry Bandholtz to George McVey Hally, June 6, 1905, Correspondence, box 1, folder 5, Harry H. Bandholtz Papers, Bentley Historical Library. In private correspondences to other colonial officials, Bandholtz made his animosity toward Filipinos and his belief in their inferiority clear. See also chapter 3.

52. "Lingayu" is spelled as "Lengñngayu" by her son, William, and as "Lingngayu" by Beyer colleague Arsenio Manuel. Here I use the most commonly used spelling of the Beyer-Gambuk descendants. Arsenio Manuel, "The Wake and Last Rites over H. Otley Beyer," *Philippine Studies* 23 (1975): 123; William Gambuk Beyer, "The Beyer Bone Washing Ritual," *Bulletin of the American Historical Collection* 8, no. 2 (1980): 31.

53. H. Otley Beyer, *The Non-Christian People of the Philippines*, Separate from the Census of the Philippine Islands:1918, Vol. 2 (Manila: Bureau of Printing, 1921), 957.

54. Juan R. Francisco, "H. Otley Beyer's Contribution to Indo-Philippine Scholarship," *Bulletin of the American Historical Collection* 4, no. 2 (April 1976): 25–28.

55. Hartendorp, *I Have Lived*, 2:260. "Datu" is the title for a local ruler in Mindanao, lower in the hierarchy of leadership than a sultan.

56. Henry Ngayawan Beyer (grandson of H. Otley Beyer and Lingayu Beyer), interview by Tessa Winkelmann, June 21, 2012, Baguio, Philippines.

57. Beyer, interview.

58. Beyer, interview.

59. Manuel, "Wake and Last Rites," 121–23.

60. Hartendorp, *I Have Lived*, 1:137.

61. Beyer, interview.

62. Devins, *Observer in the Philippines*, 126–27.

63. "Moro" was the name applied by the Americans (as well as by the Spanish) to both the Muslim inhabitants of the southern Philippines and the geographical region itself. "Moroland" was also used to refer to the island of Mindanao and the Sulu islands.

64. Salman, *Embarrassment of Slavery*.

65. Oliver Charbonneau, *Civilizational Imperatives: Americans, Moros, and the Colonial World* (Ithaca, NY: Cornell University Press, 2020).

66. Paul A. Kramer, "Colonial Crossings: Prostitution, Disease, and the Boundaries of Empire during the Philippine-American War," in *Body and Nation: The Global Realm of U.S. Body Politics in the Twentieth Century*, ed. Emily S. Rosenberg and Shanon Fitzpatrick (Durham, NC: Duke University Press, 2014.

67. A. Lester Hazlett, "A View of the Moral Conditions Existing in the Philippines," in *Affairs in the Philippine Islands: Hearings Before the Committee on the Philippines of the United States Senate* (Washington, DC: Government Printing Office, 1902), 1736–44, quote on 1736.

68. Adrian B. French to C. Guy Robbins, October 30, 1901, in *Affairs in the Philippine Islands*, 1855–56.

69. Owen Sweet to Adjutant General U.S. Army, February 7, 1902, in *Affairs in the Philippine Islands*, 1746–50.

70. Letter of James A. Moore, in *Affairs in the Philippine Islands*, 1884.

71. Letter of W. A. Nichols, in *Affairs in the Philippine Islands*, 1860.

72. Letter of R. R. Stevens, in *Affairs in the Philippine Islands*, 1878.

73. Paul A. Kramer, "The Darkness That Enters the Home: The Politics of Prostitution during the Philippine-American War," in *Haunted by Empire: Geographies of Intimacy in North American History*, ed. Ann Laura Stoler (Durham, NC: Duke University Press, 2006); Paul A. Kramer, "The Military-Sexual Complex: Prostitution, Disease, and the Boundaries of Empire during the Philippine-American War," *Asia-Pacific Journal: Japan Focus* 9, no. 30 (2011).

74. Report of Samuel Seay, in *Affairs in the Philippine Islands*, 1873.

75. Report of R. C. Croxton, in *Affairs in the Philippine Islands*, 1867.

76. "Philippine Islands, American Troops, Prevalence of Special Diseases," in *Annual Report of the Surgeon General to the Department of War* (Washington, DC: Government Printing Office, 1911), 105.

77. Katharine Bjork, *Prairie Imperialists: The Indian Country Origins of American Empire* (Philadelphia: University of Pennsylvania Press, 2019).

78. Bjork follows the domestic and overseas careers of Hugh Lenox Scott, Robert Lee Bullard, and John J. Pershing as they made names for themselves as military leaders in "Indian country," and how those experiences colored their approach to military service in the Philippines, particularly in Mindanao and Sulu.

79. Samuel Tan, *The Filipino Muslim Armed Struggle, 1900–1972* (Manila: Filipinas Foundation, 1977); Moshe Yegar, *Between Integration and Secession: The Muslim Communities of the Southern Philippines, Southern Thailand, and Western Burma/Myanmar* (Lanham, MD: Lexington Books, 2002), 223; Reuben Canoy, *The Quest for Mindanao Independence* (Cagayan de Oro, Mindanao: Mindanao Post, 1987). For deportation of Manila prostitutes to Mindanao, see chapter 3 and Ken De Bevoise, "A History of Sexually Transmitted Diseases and HIV/AIDS in the Philippines," in *Sex, Disease and Society: A Comparative History of Sexually Transmitted Diseases and HIV/AIDS in Asia and the Pacific*, ed. Milton Lewis, Scott Bamber, and Michael Waugh (Westport, CT: Greenwood, 1997). For American plans for the Black colonization of the South, see Guy E. Mount, "The Last Reconstruction: Slavery, Emancipation and Empire in the Black Pacific" (PhD diss., University of Chicago, 2018).

80. James Tyner, *Iraq, Terror, and the Philippines' Will to War* (Lanham, MD: Rowman and Littlefield, 2005), 15.

81. Frank Carpenter, "Report of the Department of Mindanao and Sulu—Agricultural Colonies," in *Annual Report of the Philippine Commission* (Washington: Government Printing Office, 1915), 377. See also Karl Pelzer, *Pioneer Settlement in the Asiatic Tropics: Studies in Land Utilization and Agricultural Colonization in Southeastern Asia* (New York: American Geographical Society, 1945); Peter G. Gowing, *Mandate in Moroland: The American Government of Muslim Filipinos, 1899–1920* (Quezon City: Philippine Center for Advanced Studies, University of the Philippines, 1977).

82. Eva Maria Mehl, *Forced Migration in the Spanish Pacific World: From Mexico to the Philippines, 1765–1811* (Cambridge: Cambridge University Press, 2016).

83. Homestead Act of 1862, Pub. L. No. 37–64, 12 Stat. 392 (1862).

84. Black Americans could acquire homesteads after the passage of the Fourteenth Amendment several years after the passage of the Homestead Act.

85. "Primer Containing Questions and Answers on the Public-Land Laws in Force in the Philippine Islands," in *Annual Report of the Philippine Commission to the War Department* (Washington: Government Printing Office, 1908), 533.

86. Kilmer O. Moe, "Young Man, Go South!," *Philippine Farmer* 7, no. 1 (January 1921): 9.

87. Pelzer, *Pioneer Settlement*; Gowing, *Mandate in Moroland*; Yegar, *Between Integration and Secession*.

88. Report of the Director of Lands, in *Annual Report of the Philippine Commission to the War Department* (Washington: Government Printing Office, 1908), 202.

89. J. J. Heffington, "Homesteads," *Annual Report of the Provincial Governor of Lanao for the Period from January First to November Fourteenth 1935*, box 28, folder 8, Joseph Ralston Hayden Papers, Bentley Historical Library; "Memorandum on Agricultural Colonies," July 3, 1930, box 29, folder 29–7, Joseph Ralston Hayden Papers, Bentley Historical Library, 5–6.

90. Tan, *Filipino Muslim Armed Struggle*, 175.

91. Heffington, "Homesteads," 29.

92. Despite "Filipinization" efforts, most of the top colonial positions remained occupied by Americans. For more on Lang and the MCA, see Nicholas Trajano Molnar, *American Mestizos, The Philippines, and the Malleability of Race, 1898–1961* (Columbia: University of Missouri Press, 2017), 46–49.

93. Charles Burke Elliott, *The Philippines: To the End of the Commission Government; A Study in Tropical Democracy* (Indianapolis: Bobbs-Merrill, 1917), 373.

94. Ludovico Hidrosollo, "Memorandum on Agricultural Colonies," July 3, 1930, box 29, folder 73, Joseph Ralston Hayden Papers, Bentley Historical Library. The Bureau of Non-Christian

Tribes was created by the US colonial government to administer to and "civilize" the Indigenous peoples in the northern Philippines, as well as the Muslim populations in the South.

95. "Mr. C. J. Walker, the Man Who Made Good in Mindanao," *Philippine Farmer*, April 1920, 31.

96. "Mr. C. J. Walker, the Man Who Made Good in Mindanao," 31.

97. "Lanao's Best Agricultural Colony—Was Founded by Americans in the Face of Untold Difficulty," *Graphic*, August 1933, 11.

98. Rafael Bautista, "The Last American Frontier," *Philippines Free Press*, April 6, 1940, 22–23.

99. Salman, *Embarrassment of Slavery*.

100. The name Mose Faggin is likely a reference to one of the most well-known Black Americans in the Philippines during the colonial period, David Fagen. Fagen deserted the US Army and joined the Philippine revolutionary army fighting against the Americans. Fagen's transnational reputation grew as he evaded capture by Americans. Accounts tell of his marriage to a Filipina and his eventual death at the hands of Filipinos eager to collect the bounty on his head, although this last detail is still disputed today for its accuracy.

101. "A Darky's Mournful Wail," *American Oldtimer* 1, no. 9 (July 1934): 37.

102. It was commonly white men who wrote minstrel gags and poems that depicted Black men. Also, most of the readership of and contributors to the *Oldtimer* were white veterans of the Spanish-American and Philippine-American Wars.

103. Salman, *Embarrassment of Slavery*.

104. "Querida" describes the nonmarital or extramarital relationships popularized by the Spanish during their occupation of the Philippines. For a man to have a querida was in essence to have a mistress while married to another. One could likewise be unmarried and have several queridas at one time. "Querida" was used to reference the Filipina or native woman involved in such an arrangement. Relations typically involved the male partner providing remuneration for sexual and other domestic services: payments, the purchase of a home, or the giving of gifts. The querida system continued in both name and practice when Americans took over the Philippines. See chapter 3 for more on the querida system.

105. By looking at the census of the Philippines for the years 1903, 1918, and 1939, one sees the population of mixed-race American Filipino residents increase, whereas the American resident population slowly decreases. Programs dedicated to the care of American Filipino mixed-race children abandoned by their American fathers started up in the early 1920s, including the Manila-based American Guardian Association, which, as the Philippine American Guardian Association, exists to this day.

3. Colonial Sociality and Policing Dangerous Intercourse, 1898–1907

1. "The Taft Tour's Gayer Side," *San Francisco Argonaut*, October 9, 1905.

2. "Taft Tour's Gayer Side."

3. "Taft Tour's Gayer Side."

4. See Mary Racelis Hollnsteiner, *Bearers of Benevolence: The Thomasites and Public Education in the Philippines* (Pasig City: Anvil, 2001); Sarah Steinbock-Pratt, *Educating the Empire: American Teachers and Contested Colonization in the Philippines* (Cambridge: Cambridge University Press, 2019); Vicente L. Rafael, *White Love and Other Events in Filipino History* (Durham, NC: Duke University Press, 2000); Genevieve Clutario, *Beauty Regimes: Disciplining Filipina Labor under U.S. Empire* (Durham, NC: Duke University Press, forthcoming). Concerns over sexual contagion

and discipline emerged in domestic and educational spaces as well but mostly did not engender the same type of panic or modes of policing among American colonists as did the gateway sites I describe here.

5. Clutario, *Beauty Regimes*.

6. Clutario, *Beauty Regimes*; Paul A. Kramer, *The Blood of Government: Race, Empire, the United States, and the Philippines* (Chapel Hill: University of North Carolina Press, 2006); Steinbock-Pratt, *Educating the Empire*.

7. Emilio Aguinaldo, military leader against both the Spanish and American occupations and subsequent first president of the independent Philippine republic under the Malolos constitution, was of mixed Tagalog and Chinese ancestry. For more on Spanish colonial racial classifications, see Richard Chu, *Chinese and Chinese Mestizos of Manila: Family, Identity, and Culture, 1860s–1930s* (Leiden: Brill, 2010); Megan C. Thomas, *Orientalists, Propagandists, and Ilustrados: Filipino Scholarship and the End of Spanish Colonialism* (Minneapolis: University of Minnesota Press, 2012); Luis Francia, *History of the Philippines: From Indios Bravos to Filipinos* (New York: Overland, 2014).

8. Interview with Jose Roderigues Infante, in *Lands Held for Ecclesiastical or Religious Uses in the Philippine Islands, Etc.: Message from the President of the United States* (Washington, DC: Government Printing Office, 1901), 147.

9. Manfred F. Boemeke, Roger Chickering, and Stig Förster, *Anticipating Total War: The German and American Experiences, 1871–1914* (Cambridge: Cambridge University Press, 1999); John M. Gates, "War-Related Deaths in the Philippines," *Pacific Historical Review* 53 (November 1983): 367–78.

10. Eva Johnson to Bertha Schaffer, July 21, 1902, 6, Bertha Schaffer Letters, Bentley Historical Library, University of Michigan.

11. Eva Johnson to Bertha Schaffer, December 6, 1902, 3, Bertha Schaffer Letters, Bentley Historical Library.

12. Steinbock-Pratt, *Educating the Empire*, 230. Steinbock-Pratt describes the experiences of Thomasite teachers who often complained of so many fiesta and party invitations that they often felt as though the local community judged them as segregationist or snobbish if they failed to attend.

13. Fiestas more often than bailes coincided with or were planned around religious observances.

14. For more on the political functions of bailes, see Kramer, *Blood of Government*; Clutario, *Beauty Regimes*.

15. James LeRoy, "Manuscript of Travelogue Account of Trip to the Philippine Islands," April 10, 1901, 81, box 1, James A. LeRoy Papers, Bentley Historical Library.

16. LeRoy, "Manuscript of Travelogue," March 23, 1901, 43.

17. Elsie Clews Parsons, "American Snobbishness in the Philippines," *Independent*, February 8, 1906, 332–33.

18. Mrs. Campbell Dauncey, *An Englishwoman in the Philippines* (New York: E. P. Dutton, 1906).

19. Mary Summers Bowler, interview by Petra Fuld Netzorg, January 24, 1980, box 1, Luce Philippine Project Interviews, Bentley Historical Library. As Bowler, an American mestiza, recalls, her Filipina mother's wealthy and influential family objected to the marriage of her parents. The family did not consider Mary's father (a white American Thomasite teacher of modest means) to be a suitable match.

20. For more on appearance politics, see Mina Roces, "Gender, Nation and the Politics of Dress in Twentieth-Century Philippines," *Gender and History* 17, no. 2 (2005): 354–377; Linda Levy Peck, *Consuming Splendor: Society and Culture in Seventeenth-Century England* (Cambridge: Cambridge University Press, 2005); Ruth Barnes and Joanne B. Eicher, eds., *Dress and Gender:*

Making and Meaning (Oxford: Berg, 1993); Verity McInnis, *Women of Empire: Nineteenth-Century Army Officers' Wives in India and the U.S. West* (Norman: University of Oklahoma Press, 2017).

21. Elite Filipinos complained, for example, about the US display of the Indigenous communities of the northern Philippines in the human zoos of the Chicago and St. Louis world's fairs, and how such displays perpetuated ideas of the islands and peoples as uncivilized. This is one reason why Filipino elites often sought to distance themselves from Indigenous communities. See Nancy J. Parezo and Don D. Fowler, *Anthropology Goes to the Fair: The 1904 Louisiana Purchase Exposition* (Lincoln: University of Nebraska Press, 2007).

22. Doreen Fernandez, "Pompas y Solemnidades: Church Celebrations in Spanish Manila and the Native Theater," *Philippine Studies* 36, no. 4 (1988): 403–26.

23. The forthcoming work of Genevieve A. Clutario describes the significant wealth of Filipina elites as opposed to many of the American women of modest means who came to the islands.

24. Harry Bandholtz to Major General W. H. Carter, May 16, 1910, box 2, Harry H. Bandholtz Papers, Bentley Historical Library.

25. Wider American prohibition discussions reflected colonialists attitudes about the supposedly imitative nature of Filipinos. In reports by the Philippine commission, locally made gin, rum, and wines were considered imitations, adulterated, and not on par with US- or European-made intoxicants. See *Report of the United States Philippine Commission to the Secretary of War* (Washington, DC: Government Printing Office, 1906), 203.

26. Dauncey, *Englishwoman in the Philippines*.

27. Dauncey, *Englishwoman in the Philippines*, 59–61.

28. Dauncey, *Englishwoman in the Philippines*, 123.

29. "In Spanish Society," *Freedom*, May 1, 1899, 10. While the author describes the women as Spanish "senoritas," it is likely that the company was ethnically mixed, as Spanish mestizos, Chinese mestizos, and others made up a large part of the elite population of the islands.

30. Dauncey, *Englishwoman in the Philippines*, 62. Dauncey often uses the racial/ethnic identifiers "mestizo," "Filipino," and even "Spanish" flexibly and interchangeably based on what appears to be simple visual identification of the various racial types that she understands to exist in the islands. She comments on her flexible usage of these terms: "The Spaniards and *Mestizos* dance very well, and by that, of course, I mean Filipinos in general, for it is very difficult to distinguish between them, and to say where one race begins and the other leaves off" (60).

31. For more on fiesta politics, see Kramer, *Blood of Government*.

32. "Memorandum of what occurred at the dinner of the governors of provinces at the Hotel Metropole on Monday noon, Aug. 7, 1905," box 1, James A. LeRoy Papers, Bentley Historical Library.

33. "Memorandum of what occurred at the dinner," 2–3.

34. "Memorandum of what occurred at the dinner," 5.

35. "Memorandum of what occurred at the dinner," 6–7.

36. Parsons, "American Snobbishness in the Philippines," 332–33.

37. Parsons, "American Snobbishness in the Philippines," 332–33.

38. The term "gugu" was a pejorative term Americans used to describe native Filipinos, thought to have been coined by soldiers during the Philippine-American War.

39. Elsie Clews Parsons had a reputation as a liberal feminist, a nonconformist, and an antiracist, which she built largely through her interest in Indigenous life and folklore. She pursued ethnological studies of Native American communities. While she espoused liberal ideas of cultural relativism rather than the more popular ideas of native cultural inferiority, she also believed in ideas of "true" or "universal" native identity. This stance, as scholars have shown, did

not reflect how Indigenous peoples understood modernity, nor did it consider their desires for change on their own terms. See Margaret D. Jacobs, *Engendered Encounters: Feminism and Pueblo Cultures, 1879–1934* (Lincoln: University of Nebraska Press, 1999).

40. See Antoinette Burton, *Burdens of History: British Feminists, Indian Women, and Imperial Culture, 1865–1915* (Chapel Hill: University of North Carolina Press, 1994); Roland Sintos Coloma, "White Gazes, Brown Breasts: Imperial Feminism and Disciplining Desires and Bodies in Colonial Encounters," *Paedagogica Historica: International Journal of Education* 48, no. 2 (2012): 243–61; Rafael, *White Love*; Philippa Levine, *Prostitution, Race, and Politics: Policing Venereal Disease in the British Empire* (New York: Routledge, 2003).

41. Both American and Filipino presses covered the racial animosity at bailes. The secretary of the Taft Commission, James LeRoy, kept records of such articles.

42. Alice Roosevelt Longworth, *Crowded Hours: Reminiscences of Alice Roosevelt Longworth* (New York: C. Scribner's Sons, 1933), 88.

43. "Memorandum of what occurred at the dinner," 1–2, box 1, James A. LeRoy Papers. Mrs. Wright, wife of the ranking American official in the islands, was singled out by Herrera for her unwillingness to mix socially with Filipinos. Supposedly, she was later disciplined by Taft or another American official and made a show of publicly dancing with a Filipino at the baile.

44. Some of these social clubs were de facto segregated while others more explicitly so. See, for example, Virginia Benitez Licuanan, *Filipino and Americans: A Love-Hate Relationship* (Manila: Baguio Country Club, 1982).

45. *Navy Guide to Cavite and Manila: A Practical Guide and Beautiful Souvenir* (Manila: Manila Merchants' Association, 1908), Ayer Collection, Newberry Library; Paul A. Kramer, "The Military-Sexual Complex: Prostitution, Disease and the Boundaries of Empire during the Philippine-American War," *Asia-Pacific Journal: Japan Focus* 9, no. 30 (2011): 1–35.

46. A large body of literature exists on the sexual impunity of American men who transgressed sexual color lines versus the policing of white women's sexuality. See the work of Peggy Pascoe, Martha Hodes, John D'Emilio and Estelle B. Freedman, Walter Johnson, and Linda Dorr.

47. This was already the case in the United States, where white women were held to far different standards than men in cases of interracial intercourse. See Martha Hodes, *White Women, Black Men: Illicit Sex in the 19th-Century South* (New Haven, CT: Yale University Press, 1999).

48. For more about the subject of white women as upholders of the white race, especially in cases of empire in foreign lands, see note 46.

49. "Memorandum of what occurred at the dinner," box 1, James A. LeRoy Papers.

50. A large US military presence remained in the islands in an effort to cow the imperial aspirations of Japan as well as to continue dealing with the ongoing Filipino uprisings. American troops did dwindle while the Philippine Scouts, a US army organization composed mostly of Filipinos, grew. The United States controlled bases in the islands until 1992, when ownership was finally returned to the local government after Philippine leaders refused to renew the base agreement.

51. Emanuel A. Baja, *Philippine Police System and Its Problems* (Manila: Pobre's Press, 1933), 319. "Morals police" is the term Baja used to refer to those who policed immorality.

52. "Let us oppose . . . too familiar friendships, immodest clothing, popular amusements" is a quote from the Minutes of the Second Annual Convention of the Woman's Christian Temperance Union of the Philippines, December 31–January 4, 1926, 17–19. See note 104 in chapter 2 for more on queridas.

53. In Woman's Realm, *Manila Times*, February 21, 1907, 3. Tourist pamphlets, handbooks, and guides also sprang up toward the end of the first decade of US rule, many of them published by the Manila Merchants' Association, which would eventually become the American Chamber

of Commerce in Manila. These published guides include Hamilton M. Wright, *A Handbook of the Philippines* (Chicago: A. C. McClurg, 1907); *Navy Guide to Cavite and Manila*; Daniel O'Connel and the Manila Merchants' Association, *Manila: The Pearl of the Orient* (Manila, 1908).

54. See, for example, Ronald Hyam, *Empire and Sexuality: The British Experience* (Manchester: Manchester University Press, 1990). Ann Stoler and other scholars have critiqued Hyam's work, pointing to his focus on the desires and fantasies of male colonialists rather than on the racial politics of sexuality. A more critical analysis, they argue, underscores the coercive and uneven nature of British men's relations with colonized women.

55. Warwick Anderson, *The Cultivation of Whiteness: Science, Health and Racial Destiny in Australia* (Durham, NC: Duke University Press, 2006), 122. Anderson describes the prevailing attitudes about tropical neurasthenia: "Whites near the equator seemed to become nervy and irresolute, their character dissolved under the strain, and their willpower failed" (117).

56. Evangelina Lewis Postcard Collection, Ayer Collection, Newberry Library, Chicago. Popular postcards of the time often depicted American soldiers. Several postcards in this collection described these young men as "happy go lucky" and as "boys."

57. For more on Brent's efforts against the opium traffic in the Philippines, see Ian Tyrrell, *Reforming the World: The Creation of America's Moral Empire* (Princeton, NJ: Princeton University Press, 2010). For more on his "muscular Christianity" efforts as well as his segregationist attitudes, see Gerald R. Gems, *Sport and the American Occupation of the Philippines: Bats, Balls, and Bayonets* (Lanham, MD: Rowman & Littlefield, 2016).

58. Lewis E. Gleeck Jr., *The Manila Americans (1901–1964)* (Manila: Carmelo & Bauermann, 1977), 68.

59. Gleeck, *Manila Americans*, 77.

60. Charles Henry Brent, "Othello Preaches," in *Liberty and Other Sermons* (London: Longmans, Green, 1906), 169–79.

61. Brent, "Othello Preaches," 173.

62. Brent, "Othello Preaches," 175.

63. Brent, "Othello Preaches."

64. Brent, "Othello Preaches."

65. "Needs of Manila's Young Men," *Manila Times*, February 21, 1907. 3.

66. "Caused Scandal," *Manila Times*, June 14, 1907, 5.

67. *Hearings Before the Secretary of War and the Congressional Party Accompanying Him to the Philippine Islands Held at Manila, August 29–30, 1905* (Manila: Bureau of Printing, 1905), 119. US colonial officials kept close watch on the Lukban family, as they were prominent voices for immediate independence and had close ties with the Philippine revolutionary government.

68. For taxi-dance halls in the United States, see Linda España-Maram, *Creating Masculinity in Los Angeles's Little Manila: Working-Class Filipinos and Popular Culture, 1920s–1950s* (New York: Columbia University Press, 2006).

69. "Lukban against the Dance Halls," *Manila Times*, April 26, 1917, 1; "Bailarinas Are Diseased," *Manila Times*, July 24, 1917, 1.

70. Popular Filipino newspapers like *La Vanguardia* and *El Ideal* frequently printed their support of Lukban and his campaign to close the dance halls during this period.

71. "Bailarinas Are Diseased," *Manila Times*, July 24, 1917, 1.

72. Hazel M. McFerson, *Mixed Blessing: The Impact of the American Colonial Experience on Politics and Society in the Philippines* (Westport: Greenwood, 2002). Pura Villanueva was from a prominent family from the Visayas. She was also one of the first Filipina queens of the Manila Carnival (1908).

73. Robert W. Rydell, *All the World's a Fair: Visions of Empire at American International Expositions, 1876–1916* (Chicago: University of Chicago Press, 1987); Parezo and Fowler, *Anthropology Goes to the Fair.*

74. "Bailarinas Are Diseased," *Manila Times*, July 24, 1917, 1, 3.

75. "Bailarinas Are Diseased," 1, 3.

76. "Dance Halls," *Manila Times*, July 25, 1917, 4.

77. "Campaign Not Wise Measure," *Manila Times*, July 25, 1917, 1.

78. "Says Word for Dance Halls," *Manila Times*, July 27, 1917, 2.

79. "Fair Play for Bailarinas," *Manila Times*, July 27, 1917, 2.

80. "Y Directors Back Women," *Manila Times*, July 28, 1917, 2.

81. "The Iron Mayor" was a nickname other Filipino politicians gave to Lukban. They referred to him in this manner, for example, in census reports from 1918. *Census of the Philippine Islands Taken under the Direction of the Philippine Legislature in the Year 1918* (Manila: Bureau of Printing, 1921), 2:1088.

82. A kalesa, or calesa, is a horse-drawn carriage that was the popular mode of transportation in Manila before automobile travel became affordable.

83. Andrew Jimenez Abalahin, "Prostitution Policy and the Project of Modernity: A Comparative Study of Colonial Indonesia and the Philippines, 1850–1940" (PhD diss., Cornell University, 2003), 346–54.

84. "Public Opinion in the Manila Presses," *Manila Times*, July 28, 1917, 4.

85. "Public Opinion in the Manila Presses," 7.

86. Villavicencio v. Lukban, G.R. No. 14639, March 25, 1919. Found in *Reports of Cases Determined in the Supreme Court of the Philippine Islands*, vol. 39 (Manila: Bureau of Printing, 1920), 802, 804, 812.

87. Lata Mani, *Contentious Traditions: The Debate on Sati in Colonial India* (Berkeley: University of California Press, 1998).

88. "Autocracy in Action," *Manila Times*, October 26, 1918, 4.

89. The top position of power in the islands was still the American governor-general.

90. Santa Ana Cabaret advertisement, *The Philippine Yearbook, Vol. 1 (1933–1934): Anniversary Supplement of the Philippines Herald* (Manila: Philippines, 1933), 100.

91. Carina E. Ray, "Decrying White Peril: Interracial Sex and the Rise of Anticolonial Nationalism in the Gold Coast," *American Historical Review* 119, no. 1 (February 2014): 78–110.

4. The Trials of Intercourse

1. "Manila's Case of Dementia Americana," *Manila Times*, June 13, 1907, 1, 6. The same "diagnosis" was applied in the sensationalized Harry Thaw murder trial that took place in New York in May 1907, just one month prior.

2. "Tomorrow at Eight O'Clock," *Manila Times*, June 17, 1907, 1.

3. "Davis Sentenced to Life," *Manila Times*, June 29, 1907, 1.

4. The United States v. Chester Davis, G.R. No. 4340, August 15, 1908. Cited in *Reports of Cases Determined in the Supreme Court of the Philippine Islands*, vol. 11 (Manila: Bureau of Printing, 1909), 96–99.

5. For more on this case, see Elizabeth Mary Holt, *Colonizing Filipinas: Nineteenth-Century Representations of the Philippines in Western Historiography* (Quezon City: Ateneo de Manila University

Press, 2002); Alex Molnar, *American Mestizos, the Philippines, and the Malleability of Race* (Columbia: University of Missouri Press, 2017).

6. "Girl Says She Loved Pitman Rather Than Davis," *Manila Times*, June 14, 1907, 1.

7. "Girl Says She Loved Pitman," 5.

8. The makeup of the court continued until 1936, when, under the commonwealth president Manuel Quezon, Filipinos were appointed in all seven justice positions.

9. "An American Woman on Marriage between Americans and Filipino Women," *Manila Times*, July 2, 1907, 6.

10. Holt, *Colonizing Filipinas*, 146.

11. "Davis Awaits Unknown Fate," *Manila Times*, June 28, 1907. 6.

12. "Schenck Dropped: Fireman Who Testified at Davis Trial Is Suspended," *Manila Times*, June 29, 1907, 3.

13. "Schenck Discharged," *Manila Times*, July 24, 1907, 3.

14. "Davis Awaits Unknown Fate," 6.

15. Margot Pimental, "Dénouement, Closure and Remembrance: Part One," *The Kelly Family of Manila* (blog), August 19, 2010, http://thekellysfrommanila.blogspot.com.

16. "Kelly Kills Filipino Wife," *Manila Times*, May 23, 1917, 1.

17. "Kelly Tells of His Crimes," *Manila Times*, May 24, 1917, 1.

18. "Kelly Tells of His Crimes," 1. In 1917, P1,000 would have been roughly around $2000 USD.

19. In March 2014, Kelly and Velasco's youngest child passed away at the age of ninety-eight. An article about Irene Velasco Kelly's life describes how she and her sisters were orphaned in 1917 after both of their parents "died tragically." It is more than likely, and indeed believed by many of the Kelly family descendants, that Kelly committed suicide after his sentencing in 1917. The narrative in the 2014 article is one that elides the complete truth of events, but the Kelly children may have been told a similar story to spare them from the burden of the truth. "Military Salute to Former Guerilla Nurse," *Kalatas Australia*, April 28, 2014.

20. Margot Pimental, *The Kelly Family of Manila* (blog).

21. The United States vs. Augustus Hicks, G.R. No. 4971, September 23, 1909, http://www.lawphil.net/judjuris/juri1909/sep1909/gr_4971_1909.html.

22. Willard B. Gatewood Jr., *Black Americans and the White Man's Burden, 1898–1903* (Chicago: University of Illinois Press, 1975); Willard B. Gatewood Jr., *"Smoked Yankees" and the Struggle for Empire: Letters from Negro Soldiers, 1898–1902* (Fayetteville: University of Arkansas Press, 1987).

23. Stuart Creighton Miller, *Benevolent Assimilation: The American Conquest of the Philippines, 1899–1903* (New Haven, CT: Yale University Press, 1982), 193; Cynthia Marasigan, *Triangulated Amigo Warfare: African American Soldiers, Filipino Revolutionaries, and U.S. Empire* (Durham, NC: Duke University Press, forthcoming).

24. See, for example, the work of scholars such as Aimé Cesairé and Frantz Fanon, both of whom lived under the French empire in the Caribbean, and W. E. B. Du Bois, who was deeply influenced by Black postcolonial thinkers.

25. E. San Juan Jr., "African American Internationalism and Solidarity with the Philippine Revolution," *Socialism and Democracy* 24, no. 2 (July 2010): 32–65.

26. Nerissa Balce, *Body Parts of Empire: Visual Abjection, Filipino Images, and the American Archive* (Ann Arbor: University of Michigan Press, 2016), Michael Morey, *Fagen: An African American Renegade in the Philippine-American War* (Madison: University of Wisconsin Press, 2019), Michael C. Robinson and Frank N. Schubert, "David Fagen: An Afro-American Rebel in the Philippines, 1899–1901," *Pacific Historical Review* 44, no. 1 (1975): 68–83.

27. Gatewood, *Black Americans and the White Man's Burden*, 289.

28. Morrey, *Fagen.*

29. Robinson and Schubert, "David Fagen."

30. Gatewood, *"Smoked Yankees."*

31. Marasigan, *Triangulated Amigo Warfare.*

32. Peggy Pascoe, *What Comes Naturally: Miscegenation Law and the Making of Race in America* (New York: Oxford University Press, 2010).

33. Victor Román Mendoza, *Metroimperial Intimacies: Fantasy, Racial-Sexual Governance, and the Philippines in U.S. Imperialism, 1899–1913* (Durham, NC: Duke University Press, 2015), 74.

34. De Court's military service record is detailed in Julian De Court v. United States, G.R. No. E-159, June 18, 1928. Cited in *Cases Decided in the Court of Claims of the United States*, vol. 66 (Washington, DC: Government Printing Office, 1929), 131–34.

35. Military Laws of the United States (Army), 4th ed. (Washington, DC: Government Printing Office, 1911), 1006. Article 61 reads, "Any officer who is convicted of conduct unbecoming an officer and a gentleman shall be dismissed from the service."

36. Mendoza, *Metroimperial Intimacies.*

37. "The Army," *Army and Navy Register*, September 21, 1912, 343.

38. The fact that Reese's death directly followed his dismissal from the military suggests that the death was self-inflicted or otherwise accelerated by Filipinos or Americans who knew the details of his courts-martial trials and were not satisfied with the commuted sentence he received. See also Mendoza, *Metroimperial Intimacies*, 93.

39. Mendoza, *Metroimperial Intimacies*, 66.

40. Letter to General Wood, June 28, 1910, 2, Correspondence, box 2, Harry H. Bandholtz Papers, Bentley Historical Library, University of Michigan.

41. Letter to General Wood, , June 28, 1910, 3.

42. Mendoza, *Metroimperial Intimacies*, 92.

43. Just a small sample of headlines from Manila include "Colored Soldiers Outrage Women," *Manila Times*, September 2, 1899, 1; "Brutal Assault—Committed by Private of the 6th Infantry," *Manila Times*, October 8, 1906, 1; "Violation Alleged," *Manila Times*, December 1, 1909, 9. See also Michael C. Hawkins, "Masculinity Reborn: Chivalry, Misogyny, Potency and Violence in the Philippines' Muslim South, 1899–1913," *Journal of Southeast Asian Studies* 44, no. 2 (2013).

44. Nieves Umali Makalinao, "The Filipina and the Law," *Woman's World*, August 1935, 41.

45. Alva Hill, *An American Lawyer in the Philippines* (Manila: Self-published, 1946–48), 318. While there is no specific publication date, it was completed sometime between 1946 and 1948, as President Manuel Roxas wrote the introduction to the manuscript while in office (his presidency ended abruptly with his death in 1948).

46. Maria Bancosta v. John Doe, G.R. No. L-20996, September 20, 1923. Cited in *Reports of Cases Determined in the Supreme Court of the Philippine Islands*, vol. 46 (Manila: Bureau of Printing, 1925), 843–47.

47. Bancosta v. Doe, 843–47.

48. See discussion of American mestizos in chapter 6.

49. In the matter of the estate of Emil H. Johnson. Ebba Ingeborg Johnson, G.R. No. L-12767, November 16, 1918. *Reports of Cases Determined in the Supreme Court of the Philippine Islands*, vol. 39 (Manila: Bureau of Printing, 1918), 156–75.

50. Intestate of the deceased William Gitt, G.R. No. 45829, July 15, 1939. *Reports of Cases Determined in the Supreme Court of the Philippines*, vol. 68 (Rochester, NY: Lawyers Co-Operative, n.d.), 385–94.

51. "The Gold Mines Are Their Ace in the Hole," *Life*, February 13, 1939, 58. In 1908, the nationalist Filipino newspaper *El Renacimiento* published "Aves de Rapiña," a thinly veiled indictment of US rule. It pointed specifically to education reform and the "benevolent" mission professed by Americans and suggested that these were a smoke screen for the seizure of Philippine gold through mining enterprises.

52. I like Maile Arvin's understanding of "regenerative refusals" as the acts, ideas, and practices of colonized native Hawaiian subjects who reject the imperial logics rooted in notions of white supremacy (and possession through whiteness), opting instead to seek out other ways of being and alternative futures outside these logics. Maile Arvin, *Possessing Polynesians: The Science of Settler Colonial Whiteness in Hawai'i and Oceania* (Durham, NC: Duke University Press, 2019).

53. Intestate of the deceased William Gitt. G.R. no. 45829, 385–94.

54. "Manila Court Holds Moro Woman Widow of a Kentuckian," *Detroit Tribune*, July 15, 1939, 2; "Moro Widow Will Benefit," *Evening State Journal*, July 5, 1939, 3.

55. "Moro Widow Will Benefit," 3.

56. *Annual Report of the Chief of the Bureau of Insular Affairs to the U.S. War Department* (Washington, DC: Government Printing Office, 1936), 7.

57. Statement of Manuel Briones, in *Exclusion of Immigration from the Philippine Islands: Hearings Before the Committee on Immigration and Naturalization* (Washington, DC: Government Printing Office, 1930), 125–29.

58. "Manila Court Holds Moro Woman Widow," 2.

59. Peggy Pascoe, *What Comes Naturally: Miscegenation Law and the Making of Race in America* (New York: Oxford University Press, 2010). The US Supreme Court ruled interracial marriage bans unconstitutional in the *Loving v. Virginia* case of 1967.

60. See, for example, the discussions of childlike Filipino wards in Abe Ignacio et al., *The Forbidden Book: The Philippine-American War in Political Cartoons* (San Francisco: T-Boli, 2004); Robert W. Rydell, *All the World's a Fair: Visions of Empire at American International Expositions, 1876–1916* (Chicago: University of Chicago Press, 1987); Nancy J. Parezo and Don D. Fowler, *Anthropology Goes to the Fair: The 1904 Louisiana Purchase Exposition* (Lincoln: University of Nebraska Press, 2007); Kristin L. Hoganson, *Fighting for American Manhood: How Gender Politics Provoked the Spanish-American and Philippine-American Wars* (New Haven, CT: Yale University Press, 1998).

5. Depicting Dangerous Intercourse

1. John Hohenberg, *Between Two Worlds: Policy, Press, and Public Opinion in Asian-American Relations* (New York: Frederick A. Praeger, 1967), 199.

2. Rosalinda Pineda-Ofreneo, *The Manipulated Press: A History of Philippine Journalism since 1945* (Manila: Cacho Hermanos, 1984), 67–68.

3. A. V. H. Hartendorp, *History of Industry and Trade in the Philippines: The Magsaysay Administration* (Manila: Philippine Education, 1961), 367; An Act to Regulate the Retail Business, Republic Act. No. 1180 (1954). See also Caroline Hau, *The Chinese Question: Ethnicity, Nation and Region in and beyond the Philippines* (Singapore: National University of Singapore Press, 2014).

4. Lewis E. Gleeck Jr., *The Manila Americans (1901–1964)* (Manila: Carmelo & Bauermann, 1977), 379.

5. The phenomenon of seeking out empire to find success when success was more elusive in the metropole continues today. In Hong Kong, for example, the derisive acronym "FILTH" is used by Chinese residents to refer to the high life lived by British expats in the former territory. The acronym stands for "Failed in London, try Hong Kong."

6. I put "wives" in quotation marks because his first marriage was admittedly not legalized by any Filipino or American authority. It was typical for American men to not legally wed their Filipina liaisons, though they often lived together. The informality of common-law marriage made it easier for Americans to leave and abandon their Filipina "wives" and children with impunity.

7. A. V. H. Hartendorp, *An Autobiographical Sketch* (Manila: Self-published, July 1964), 17.

8. Many Americans use this term nostalgically to refer to an earlier period of the occupation, when most of the top governing positions in the Philippines were filled by US citizens.

9. Ignacio et al., *The Forbidden Book: The Philippine-American War in Political Cartoons* (San Francisco: T-Boli, 2004); Robert W. Rydell, *All the World's a Fair: Visions of Empire at American International Expositions, 1876–1916* (Chicago: University of Chicago Press, 1987); Nancy J. Parezo and Don D. Fowler, *Anthropology Goes to the Fair: The 1904 Louisiana Purchase Exposition* (Lincoln: University of Nebraska Press, 2007).

10. See chapter 1.

11. *Maganda* is the Filipino word for "beautiful." In some precolonial origin stories, Maganda was the feminized personification of the Philippines.

12. For more on the construction of popular history and the phenomenon of romanticized settler narratives, see Patricia Nelson Limerick, *The Legacy of Conquest: The Unbroken Past of the American West* (New York: W. W. Norton, 1987); Anne Curthoys, "Constructing National Histories," in *Frontier Conflict: The Australian Experience*, ed. Bain Attwood and Stephen Foster (Acton: National Museum of Australia, 2003), 185–200; Susan Lee Johnson, *Writing Kit Carson: Fallen Heroes in a Changing West* (Chapel Hill: University of North Carolina Press), 2020.

13. Christina Klein, *Cold War Orientalism: Asia in the Middlebrow Imagination, 1945–1961* (Berkeley: University of California Press, 2003), 23; Edward W. Said, *Orientalism* (New York: Vintage Books, 1979); Mary Louise Pratt, *Imperial Eyes: Travel Writing and Transculturation* (London: Routledge, 2008).

14. Frank Cheney, "Brown of the Volunteers," undated, Frank W. Cheney Poems, folder 1, Bentley Historical Library, University of Michigan, Ann Arbor.

15. "Brown of the Volunteers," *American Oldtimer* 4, no. 11 (1937): 21.

16. Cheney, "Brown of the Volunteers"; "Brown of the Volunteers," 21.

17. Lewis E. Gleeck Jr., *Americans on the Philippine Frontiers* (Manila: Carmelo & Bauermann, 1974), 49.

18. Filipinos and Americans alike used the term "Filipinista" to describe someone as having nationalist, pro-independence aspirations.

19. See Peggy Pascoe, *What Comes Naturally: Miscegenation Law and the Making of Race in America* (New York: Oxford University Press, 2010).

20. Hammon Buck, for example, purchased large tracts of land in Tagaytay, a few hours' drive outside of Manila, and encouraged its development as a recreation destination. Hartendorp owned mining stock. Other old-timers owned farms and plantations or had other lucrative business dealings in the islands, and they took these into consideration when deciding whether or not to stay in the Philippines.

21. The "old-timer" designation was common in the American press and in old-timer writings from the 1930s onward. The term generally referred to veterans of the Spanish-American and Philippine-American Wars.

22. Margaret D. Jacobs, *White Mother to a Dark Race: Settler Colonialism, Maternalism, and the Removal of Indigenous Children in the American West and Australia, 1880–1940* (Lincoln: University of Nebraska Press, 2009); Cathleen Cahill, *Federal Fathers and Mothers: A Social History of the United States Indian Service, 1869–1933* (Chapel Hill: University of North Carolina Press, 2011); Maile Arvin, *Possessing Polynesians: The Science of Settler Colonial Whiteness in Hawai'i and Oceania*

(Durham, NC: Duke University Press, 2019); Carol Hess, *Representing the Goods Neighbor: Music, Difference, and the Pan American Dream* (Oxford: Oxford University Press, 2013).

23. For discussions of childlike Filipino "wards," see Ignacio et al., *The Forbidden Book*; Rydell, *All the World's a Fair*; Parezo and Fowler, *Anthropology Goes to the Fair*.

24. Kristin L. Hoganson, *Fighting for American Manhood: How Gender Politics Provoked the Spanish-American and Philippine-American Wars* (New Haven, CT: Yale University Press, 1998). See also the discussion of the US-Philippine relationship as a "romance" in Faye Caronan, *Legitimizing Empire: Filipino American and U.S. Puerto Rican Cultural Critique* (Urbana: University of Illinois Press, 2015). There was a stateside proliferation of "race romance" novels that featured interracial American-Filipino romances, following the pulp fiction trend of sensationalizing interracial relations in the United States. See Nerissa S. Balce, *Body Parts of Empire: Visual Abjection, Filipino Images, and the American Archive* (Ann Arbor: University of Michigan Press, 2016). The *Congressional Record* of the United States is also full of marital metaphor when referencing the US-Philippines relationship. See, for example, *Congressional Record: Proceedings and Debates of the Second Session of the Sixty-Seventh Congress* (Washington, DC: Government Printing Office, 1922), 1483–84.

25. *Congressional Record: Proceedings and Debates of the Second Session of the Seventy-Sixth Congress* (Washington, DC: Government Printing Office, 1939), 4358. Montana congressman Thorkelson argued for the repeal of the 1934 Tydings-McDuffie Act.

26. Sarah Steinbock-Pratt, *Educating the Empire: American Teachers and Contested Colonization in the Philippines* (Cambridge: Cambridge University Press, 2019).

27. Gleeck, *Americans on the Philippine Frontiers*; *Bulletin No. 25: Official Roster of the Bureau of Education, Corrected to March 1, 1906* (Manila: Bureau of Printing, 1906), 7.

28. "Four O'Clock in the Editors Office," *Philippine* 32, no. 6 (June 1935): 314.

29. Hammon H. Buck, *Chronicles of Sam and Maganda* (Manila: Concuera Press, 1935). Though this version is undated (and previously published in *Philippine Magazine* in 1927), Hartendorp's editor's note in *Philippine Magazine* in 1935 describes how Buck recently published the stand alone pamphlet in Manila.

30. Herminia Quimpo Meñez, *Explorations in Philippine Folklore* (Quezon City: Ateneo de Manila Press, 1996); Mabel Cook Cole, *Philippine Folk Tales* (Chicago: A. C. McClurg, 1916).

31. Buck, *Chronicles*, 7.

32. Buck, *Chronicles*, 9.

33. Buck, *Chronicles*, 10.

34. Buck, *Chronicles*, 13.

35. Buck, *Chronicles*, 3; Gleeck, *Americans on the Philippine Frontiers*, 49.

36. Buck, *Chronicles*, 24.

37. Buck, *Chronicles*, 3.

38. Buck, *Chronicles*, 50.

39. See Edward W. Said, *Culture and Imperialism* (New York: Vintage Books, 1994); Pratt, *Imperial Eyes*; Laura Wexler, *Tender Violence: Domestic Visions in an Age of U.S. Imperialism* (Chapel Hill: University of North Carolina Press, 2000); Amy Kaplan and Donald E. Pease, eds., *Cultures of United States Imperialism* (Durham, NC: Duke University Press, 1993).

40. Gleeck, *Americans on the Philippine Frontiers*, 49. Buck was described by Gleeck and others (in *Philippine Magazine*, as Gleeck points to) as a "Filipinista."

41. Buck, *Chronicles*, 15.

42. The Dutch Hans and John Bull that Buck references are allusions to the Dutch and British empires, respectively.

43. Buck, *Chronicles*, 25–26.

44. A. V. H. Hartendorp, *I Have Lived: Reminiscences of A.V.H. Hartendorp* (Manila: Self-published, 1970), 1:125.

45. Hartendorp, *An Autobiographical Sketch*, 1. "Negrito" is a diminutive label previously used by the Spanish and later Americans to refer to the Ati, Aeta, Agta, and Mamanwa people, who are widely considered to be among the first inhabitants of the Philippine islands.

46. Hartendorp, *An Autobiographical Sketch*, 2.

47. See, for example, Gleeck, *Manila Americans*; Thomas Carter, *The Way It Was* (Quezon City: R.P. Garcia, 1985). Gleeck and Carter compiled stories about the American community in the Philippines, following in Hartendorp's footsteps. They cite him as a foundational "pro-Filipino" American. This pro-Filipino position was apparently compatible with imperialism, as Hartendorp was a self-proclaimed imperialist.

48. Anicia Garcia Canseco, "'Let Your Hair Down': A.V.H. Hartendorp—the Man and His Works" (master's thesis, University of the Philippines, 1974), viii.

49. Frank H. Golay, "Hartendorp Remembered," *Bulletin of the American Historical Collection* 5, no. 2 (April 1977): 42.

50. Hartendorp, *An Autobiographical Sketch*, 17–18.

51. Hartendorp lost his American citizenship in 1951, five years after Philippine independence. US law stipulated that a naturalized citizen living in a foreign country for five years or longer would lose their citizenship. Over the course of the next six years, he fought diligently to have his citizenship restored, which it finally was through an act of Congress. An Act for the Relief of Abraham van Heyningen Hartendorp, Private Law No. 85–163, August 14, 1957. Detailed in *United States Statutes at Large*, vol. 71 (Washington, DC: Government Printing Office, 1958), a62.

52. For works that explore the colonial site as laboratory space, see Alfred W. McCoy and Francisco Antonio Scarano, eds., *Colonial Crucible: Empire in the Making of the Modern American State* (Madison: University of Wisconsin Press, 2009); Warwick Anderson, *Colonial Pathologies: American Tropical Medicine, Race, and Hygiene in the Philippines* (Durham, NC: Duke University Press, 2006); Laura Briggs, *Reproducing Empire Reproducing Empire: Race, Sex, Science, and U.S. Imperialism in Puerto Rico* (Berkeley: University of California Press, 2002); Julian Go and Anne L. Foster, eds., *The American Colonial State in the Philippines: Global Perspectives* (Durham, NC: Duke University Press, 2003).

53. Hartendorp, *I Have Lived*, 1:110–12.

54. Hartendorp, *I Have Lived*, 1:137.

55. Matthew Frye Jacobson, *Barbarian Virtues: The United States Encounters Foreign Peoples at Home and Abroad, 1876–1917* (New York: Hill and Wang, 2001).

56. Hartendorp, *I Have Lived*, 1:138–40.

57. See the details of Beyer and Lingayu's relationship in chapter 2.

58. Hartendorp, *I Have Lived*, 1:139.

59. For more on porno tropics, see Anne McClintock, *Imperial Leather: Race, Gender and Sexuality in the Colonial Contest* (New York: Routledge, 1995).

60. Hartendorp, *I Have Lived*, 1:161.

61. Hartendorp, *I Have Lived*, 1:162.

62. Hartendorp, *I Have Lived*, 1:162.

63. Steinbock-Pratt, *Educating the Empire*.

64. Hartendorp, *I Have Lived*, 1:125.

65. Hartendorp, *I Have Lived*, 1:203. The prematurity of baby Esther may also be worth considering. If Hartendorp was, as he states, careful to avoid pregnancy and used birth control, Cornelia might have already been pregnant before entering into her relationship with Hartendorp.

Becoming pregnant out of wedlock may have also provided her with the motivation to pursue a relationship with Hartendorp.

66. Hartendorp, *I Have Lived*, 2:285.

67. Hartendorp, *I Have Lived*, 2:294–95.

68. Hartendorp, *I Have Lived*, 4:673; reprinted from the *American Chamber of Commerce Journal*, January 1954.

69. Hartendorp, *I Have Lived*, 4:753.

70. See Catherine Lutz, ed., *The Bases of Empire: The Global Struggle against U.S. Military Posts* (New York: New York University Press, 2009); Setsu Shigematsu and Keith Camacho, eds., *Militarized Currents: Towards a Decolonized Future in Asia and the Pacific* (Minneapolis: University of Minnesota Press, 2010); David Vine, *Base Nation: How U.S. Military Bases Abroad Harm American and the World* (New York: Metropolitan Books, 2015).

71. In December 2012, a legislative measure passed in the Philippines to ensure more access to sexual health education, birth control, and maternal health care. Its passage was highly divisive, and conservatives as well as the local Catholic church continue to fight the bill.

72. Hartendorp, *I Have Lived*, 4:754–55.

73. Hartendorp, *I Have Lived*, 4:756.

74. Sarah De Mul, *Colonial Memory: Contemporary Women's Travel Writing in Britain and the Netherlands* (Amsterdam: Amsterdam University Press, 2011).

75. See Ann Laura Stoler, *Carnal Knowledge and Imperial Power: Race and the Intimate in Colonial Rule* (Berkeley: University of California Press, 2002), particularly the chapter titled "Memory Work." Domestic intimacies, as Stoler points out, were remembered by Dutch colonists as affective engagements with those who worked for them, while Indonesian workers remembered their time in colonial households as labor.

76. See, for example, Rey Illeto, *Pasyon and Revolution: Popular Movements in the Philippines, 1840–1910* (Quezon City: Ateneo de Manila University, 1979); Vicente L. Rafael, *White Love and Other Events in Filipino History* (Durham, NC: Duke University Press, 2000).

77. An Act Defining the Acts of Treason, Insurrection, Etc., No. 292, *Annual Reports of the War Department, Acts of the Philippine Commission*, vol. 11 (Washington, DC: Government Printing Office, 1902), 51–54.

78. See chapter 1 and Rafael, *White Love*, 45.

79. Behn Cervantes, "The Seditious Theater: Coded Characters Heighten the Dramatic Irony of the Committed Play," in *Filipino Heritage: The Making of a Nation*, vol. 9, *The American Colonial Period (1900–1941)*, ed. Alfredo Roces (Manila: Lahing Pilipino, 1978), 2284–90.

80. Resil B. Mojares, *The War against the Americans: Resistance and Collaboration in Cebu 1899–1906* (Quezon City: Ateneo de Manila Press, 1999); Resil B. Mojares, *Cebuano Literature: A Survey and Bio-Bibliography with Finding List* (Cebu City: San Carlos, 1975). Alonso is credited with translating Jose Rizal's fictional "El Filibusterismo," a scathing rebuke of Spanish rule in the Philippines, into Cebuano, the main language spoken in the central Philippines.

81. Mina Roces, "Is the Suffragist an American Colonial Construct? Defining 'The Filipino Woman' in Colonial Philippines," in *Women's Suffrage in Asia: Gender, Nationalism and Democracy*, ed. Louise Edwards and Mina Roces (New York: Routledge, 2004).

82. Tomas Alonso, "Little Pickanniny Girl," *Woman's Outlook* 1, no. 6 (March 1923): 6.

83. M. Roces, "Is the Suffragist an American Colonial Construct?"

84. See chapter 3.

85. M. Roces, "Is the Suffragist an American Colonial Construct?," 36.

86. Robin Bernstein, *Racial Innocence: Performing American Childhood from Slavery to Civil Rights* (New York: New York University Press, 2007).

87. See, for example, the pejorative use of the word "pickaninny" used to describe Filipino children in the postcard collection of Evangelina Lewis, a white American woman living in the Philippines during the colonial period. Evangelina Lewis Postcard Collection, Ayer Collection, Newberry Library, Chicago.

88. Willard B. Gatewood Jr., *Black Americans and the White Man's Burden, 1898–1903* (Chicago: University of Illinois Press, 1975).

89. Georgina Reyes Encanto, *Constructing the Filipina: A History of Women's Magazines, 1891–2002* (Quezon City: University of the Philippines Press, 2004), 44–47.

90. Mojares, *The War against the Americans.*

91. "Example," *China Monthly Review* 53 (1930): 288.

92. Dawn Mabalon, *Little Manila Is in the Heart: The Making of the Filipina/o American Community in Stockton, California* (Durham, NC: Duke University Press, 2013).

93. Taihei Okada, "Underside of Independence Politics: Filipino Reactions to Anti-Filipino Riots in the United States," *Philippine Studies: Historical and Ethnographic Viewpoints* 60, no. 3 (September 2012): 307–36.

94. Mae Ngai, *Impossible Subjects: Illegal Aliens and the Making of Modern America* (Princeton, NJ: Princeton University Press, 2004).

95. Michael Cullinane, *Illustrado Politics: Filipino Elite Responses to American Rule, 1898–1908* (Quezon City: Ateneo de Manila Press, 2003). Georgina Encanto also points to this shift in her historical study of women's magazines in the Philippines, *Constructing the Filipina.*

96. Lilia Quindoza Santiago, *Sexuality and the Filipina* (Quezon City: University of the Philippines Press, 2007).

97. Edna Zapanta-Manlapaz, *Filipino Women Writers in English, Their Story: 1905–2002* (Quezon City: Ateneo de Manila University Press, 2003).

98. The full short story is reprinted in Santiago, *Sexuality and the Filipina,* 191–96.

99. Alfred McCoy and Alfredo Roces, *Philippine Cartoons: Political Caricature of the American Era, 1900–1941* (Quezon City: Vera Reyes, 1985), 17. For more on Philippine publishing and politics, see Rosalinda Pineda-Ofreneo, *The Manipulated Press: A History of Philippine Journalism since 1945* (Manila: Cacho Hermanos, 1984); Carson Taylor, *History of the Philippine Press* (Manila: n.p., 1927).

100. Princess Orig, "Kayumanggi versus Maputi: 100 Years of America's White Aesthetics in Philippine Literature," in *Mixed Blessing: The Impact of the American Colonial Experience on Politics and Society in the Philippines,* ed. Hazel M. McFerson (Westport: Greenwood Press, 2002), 99–134.

101. Gregorio Coching, "Puso ng Dios," *Liwayway,* December 15, 1933, 105–9.

102. Coching, "Puso ng Dios," 105.

103. Coching, "Puso ng Dios," 108.

104. This phrase probably dates back to World War II and was popularized by a 1946 Philippine movie titled *Hanggang Pier.* By the 1970s and 1980s, "Hanggang pier ka lang" was a fairly common expression in the Philippines, especially around military bases, and was frequently used in literature and media. For example, see Nick Joaquin, *Almanac for Manileños* (Manila: Mr. and Mrs. Publications, 1979); Nick Joaquin, *Language of the Street and Other Essays* (Manila: National Book Store, 1980).

105. Stephanie Fajardo, "Authorizing Illicit Intimacies: Filipina-G.I. Interracial Relations in the Postwar Philippines," *Philippine Studies: Historical and Ethnographic Viewpoints* 65, no. 4 (2017): 485–513.

6. Making Mestizos

1. "Gang of 10 Raid, Loot Hacienda, Murder Planter," *Daily Tribune*, July 24, 1937.

2. "Suspects Admit Part in Murder of Hill; Implicates 7 Others," *Manila Bulletin*, July 26, 1937.

3. I use the term "American mestizo" (or simply "mestizo") to refer to the children born in the Philippines to one American parent (typically the father) and one Filipino parent. While most of these children were not American by law, my use of the term reflects the common terminology of the time, similar to "Spanish mestizo" and "Chinese mestizo."

4. "Suspects Admit Part in Murder of Hill; Implicates 7 Others."

5. Durba Ghosh, *Sex and the Family in Colonial India: The Making of Empire* (Cambridge: Cambridge University Press, 2006), 213.

6. See Anne F. Hyde, *Empires, Nations, and Families: A History of the North American West, 1800–1860* (Lincoln: University of Nebraska Press, 2011); Carter, *United States of United Races*.

7. Nicholas Trajano Molnar, *American Mestizos, the Philippines, and the Malleability of Race, 1898–1961* (Columbia: University of Missouri Press, 2017).

8. The common practice of the time was to refer to American mestizo children as "orphans" or "wards," despite the fact that many were raised by their Filipina mothers or extended families. To challenge the disparagement of Filipino caretakers, my use of the term "orphan" will largely appear in quotation marks.

9. *Report of the Philippine Commission to the President, 1899–1900* (Washington, DC: Government Printing Office, 1900), 1:154.

10. "The American Mestizo," *New York Times*, October 16, 1925, 20.

11. In the Schurman Commission interviews, interviewee and interviewer alike often refer to the various ethnolinguistic groups in the Philippines, such as Tagalogs and Visayans, as "Indians."

12. Mark Rice, *Dean Worcester's Fantasy Islands: Photography, Film, and the Colonial Philippines* (Quezon City: Ateneo de Manila University Press, 2015). See also Dean Worcester, *Index to Philippine Photographs*, (Manila: n.p., 1905), 375–78, Dean C. Worcester Collection of Philippine Photographs, Ayer Collection, Newberry Library. Even Worcester's white traveling companions were not free from the gaze of his camera lens, as his intermarried European and American guides were also featured in his "mestizo" photos. Otto Scheerer and Samuel Kane, as well as their mixed-race families, are included alongside pictures of Spanish and Chinese mestizos. Whether they knew that their photos would be included in his research is unknown, as some of the pictures (particularly of Kane and his family) look more candid than others.

13. "Statement of Edwin H. Warner," in *Report of the Philippine Commission to the President, 1899–1900* (Washington, DC: Government Printing Office, 1900), 2:19.

14. "Testimony of William A. Daland," in *Report of the Philippine Commission to the President, 1899–1900* (Washington, DC: Government Printing Office, 1900), 2:168.

15. "Testimony of William A. Daland," 2:168.

16. "Testimony of Señor Legarda," in *Report of the Philippine Commission to the President, 1899–1900* (Washington, DC: Government Printing Office, 1900), 2:179. See also Richard Chu, *Chinese and Chinese Mestizos of Manila: Family, Identity, and Culture, 1860s–1930s* (Leiden: Brill, 2010).

17. "Testimony of William A. Daland," 2:167.

18. "Testimony of Carlos Palanca," in *Report of the Philippine Commission to the President, 1899–1900* (Washington, DC: Government Printing Office, 1900), 2:224.

19. Often individuals with mixed Spanish and native ancestry were referred to as "Filipino."

20. This sale of lands to Americans and US agribusiness sparked controversy in the Philippines, drawing criticism from Americans and Filipinos, and was investigated by members of the US Congress. See "The Friar-Land Inquiry, Philippine Government," *Administration of Philippine Lands Report*, vol. 2 (Washington, DC: Government Printing Office, 1911); Jennifer Conroy Franco, *Elections and Democratization in the Philippines* (New York: Routledge, 2001), 43.

21. *Lands Held for Ecclesiastical or Religious Uses in the Philippine Islands, Message from the President of the United States, Senate Report* (Washington, DC: Government Printing Office, 1901).

22. "Interview with Señor Don Felipe Calderon, October 17, 1900," in *Lands Held for Ecclesiastical or Religious Uses*, 133–44.

23. *Lands Held for Ecclesiastical or Religious Uses*, document no. 190, 146–47.

24. See chapter 1.

25. See chapter 3.

26. Ian Tyrrell, *Woman's World/Woman's Empire: The Woman's Christian Temperance Union in International Perspective, 1880–1930* (Chapel Hill: University of North Carolina Press, 2010), 214.

27. Smith went on to be an associate justice of the Supreme Court of the Philippines in 1901 and the governor-general of the Philippines in 1906. At the time of the interview, he was temporarily (as brigadier general) in control of the Visayan military district.

28. "Testimony of General Smith," in *Lands Held for Ecclesiastical or Religious Uses*, 247.

29. John Bancroft Devins, *An Observer in the Philippines* (New York: E. P. Dutton, 1906), 127.

30. "Testimony of General Smith," 247.

31. Devins, *Observer in the Philippines*, 127.

32. Ibid.

33. Parker later filled other positions in the Bureau of Education in the Philippines, helping to shape American-style education in the islands for decades.

34. *Census of the Philippine Islands Taken under the Direction of the Philippine Commission in the Year 1903* (Washington, DC: Bureau of the Census, 1905), 2:44.

35. *Census of the Philippine Islands Taken under the Direction of the Philippine Legislature in the Year 1918*, vol. 1 (Manila: Bureau of Printing, 1921). There was no recorded category for American mestizos or "half-breeds" in the 1903 census.

36. Mrs. Samuel Francis Gaches, *Good Cooking and Health in the Tropics* (Manila: American Guardian Association, 1922), 8.

37. Molnar, *American Mestizos*, 111.

38. Matthew Frye Jacobson, *Barbarian Virtues: The United States Encounters Foreign Peoples at Home and Abroad, 1876–1917* (New York: Hill and Wang, 2001); Emily Conroy-Krutz, *Christian Imperialism: Converting the world in the Early American Republic* (Ithaca, NY: Cornell University Press, 2015).

39. Luther Parker, *Verses of the Philippines* (Manila: Squires and Bingham, 1911), 1.

40. Parker, *Verses of the Philippines*, 2.

41. See chapter 5 on colonial fantasy and interracial intercourse.

42. Parker, *Verses of the Philippines*, 4.

43. Reprint of Parkers letter to the *Cablenews-American* found in Parker, *Verses of the Philippines*, 4–7.

44. Molnar, *American Mestizos*, 33–37.

45. "Condition in Philippine Islands," in *Report of the Special Mission to the Philippine Islands to the Secretary of War* (Washington, DC: Government Printing Office, 1922), 7.

46. See, for example, descriptions and pictures of nipa homes in *Navy Guide to Cavite and Manila: A Practical Guide and Beautiful Souvenir* (Manila: Manila Merchants' Association, 1908),

Ayer Collection, Newberry Library; Evangeline E. Lewis Photographic Postcard Collection of the Philippine Islands, Ayer Collection, Newberry Library; David Brody, *Visualizing American Empire: Orientalism and Imperialism in the Philippines* (Chicago: University of Chicago Press, 2010). Though the types of housing in the Philippines varied (from the Spanish hacienda to the nipa palm house), Brody describes how American descriptions of nipa huts as "typical" supported the ideas of Filipinos as backward, uncivilized, diseased, and so on.

47. Molnar, *American Mestizos*, 68–69.

48. Kern was a notable financial campaigner for US hospitals and advertised her services as a fundraiser in medical and hospital journals prior to her work for the AGA.

49. For more on eugenics and the politics of sterilization, see Alexandra Stern, *Eugenic Nation: Faults and Frontiers of Better Breeding in Modern America* (Berkeley: University of California Press, 2016); Laura Briggs, *Reproducing Empire: Race, Sex, Science, and U.S. Imperialism in Puerto Rico* (Berkeley: University of California Press, 2002); Rebecca M. Kluchin, *Fit to Be Tied: Sterilization and Reproductive Rights in America, 1950–1980* (New Brunswick, NJ: Rutgers University Press, 2009).

50. "Our Mestizos Ask Help: Hundreds of Children of American Fathers and Filipino Mothers Are Made Homeless by Economic Changes," *New York Times*, October 18, 1925, 24.

51. "Asks Facts in the Philippines: Admiral Fiske Wants the Children Taught to Be Americans," *New York Times*, March 6, 1926, 5.

52. "The American Mestizo," *New York Times*, October 16, 1925, 20.

53. "Asks Fund to Help Mestizo Children," *New York Times*, September 29, 1925, 27.

54. "The American Mestizo," 20.

55. See Ignacio, et al., *The Forbidden Book: The Philippine-American War in Political Cartoons* (San Francisco: T-Boli, 2004); Servando D. Halili, *Iconography of the New Empire: Race and Gender Images and the American Colonization of the Philippines* (Quezon City: University of the Philippines Press, 2006).

56. "Mestizo Problem in the Philippines," *New York Times*, November 15, 1925, E6.

57. Christina Klein, *Cold War Orientalism: Asia in the Middlebrow Imagination, 1945–1961* (Berkeley: University of California Press, 2003).

58. "Asks Fund to Help Mestizo Children," 27.

59. Frederick Cunliffe—Owen, C.B.E., "Mestizo Problem in the Philippines: Situation Which Demands Attention, According to General Wood, Discussed," *New York Times*, November 15, 1925, E6.

60. Alva Hill, *An American Lawyer in the Philippines* (Manila: Self-published, 1946–48).

61. Parker, *Verses of the Philippines*, 6.

62. Gaches, *Good Cooking and Health in the Tropics*, 8. See also Judith R. Walkowitz, *City of Dreadful Delight: Narratives of Sexual Danger in Late-Victorian London* (Chicago: University of Chicago Press, 1992). On the sexualization of Mestizas, see Gladys Nubla, "The Sexualized Child and Mestizaje: Colonial Tropes of the Filipino/a," in *Gendering the Trans-Pacific World*, ed. Catherine Ceniza Choy and Judy Wu (Leiden: Brill, 2017), 165–95.

63. "Our Mestizos Ask Help," 24; "The American Mestizo," 20. On American campaigns against white slavery, see Brian Donovan, *White Slave Crusades: Race, Gender and Anti-vice Activism, 1887–1917* (Champaign: University of Illinois Press, 2006).

64. Photograph "Wards of Union Church Hall," appears in E. A. Perkins, *Programe Benefit of Union Church Hall*, 1926, 14, American Historical Collection, Ateneo de Manila University; "How the American Guardian Association Works," *American Oldtimer* 6, no. 11 (1939): 12.

65. "Mestizos Call across Pacific: Orphans in Philippines, Children of American Fathers and Native Mothers, Need Our Aid to Escape an Evil Fate," *New York Times*, May 23, 1926, 14; Display ad 6, *New York Times*, June 26, 1926, 6.

66. "Plea for Outcasts in the Philippines," *New York Times*, January 23, 1926, 18.

67. "Our Mestizos Ask Help," 24.

68. "Plea for Outcasts in the Philippines," *New York Times*, January 23, 1926, 18.

69. Paul A. Kramer, *The Blood of Government: Race, Empire, the United States, and the Philippines* (Chapel Hill: University of North Carolina Press, 2006), 275–79.

70. Leti Volpp, "American Mestizo: Filipinos and Antimiscegenation Laws in California," *U.C. Davis Law Review* 33, no. 4 (2000): 795–835.

71. W. E. B. Du Bois, "Philippine Mulattoes," *Crisis* 31 (December 1925): 61.

72. For critiques of the "tragic Mulatto" myth and archetype, see the works of Werner Sollors, Ariella Gross, and Diana Mafe.

73. Andrew Jimenez Abalahin, "Prostitution Policy and the Project of Modernity: A Comparative Study of Colonial Indonesia and the Philippines, 1850–1940" (PhD diss., Cornell University, 2003).

74. Display ad 6, *New York Times*, June 26, 1926, 6.

75. "Asks Facts in Philippines," 5.

76. "Daughters of America Vets Forming Society in Manila," *Manila Bulletin* (special old-timers edition), June 28, 1928, 1–3.

77. See, for example, the interview of American mestiza Mary Bowler, in which Bowler describes the social world of prominent mestizo families. Mary and Bill Bowler, interview by University of Michigan, Center for South and Southeast Asian Studies, LUCE Philippines Interviews, Bentley Historical Library, Ann Arbor.

78. Mary and Bill Bowler, interview.

79. "Daughters of American Vets Forming Society in Manila," *Manila Bulletin* (special old-timers edition), June 28, 1928, 1–3.

80. "Daughters of American Vets Forming Society in Manila," 1–3.

81. "Daughters of American Vets Forming Society in Manila," 1–3.

82. "Report of Philippine Island State Regent," in *Proceedings of the Forty-Seventh Continental Congress of the National Society of the Daughters of the American Revolution* (Washington, DC: n.p., 1938), 589–91.

83. *Asian and Pacific Islander Americans in Congress, 1900–2017* (Washington, DC: Government Printing Office, 2017), 166.

84. "Report of Philippine Island State Regent," in *Proceedings of the Forty-Seventh Continental Congress of the National Society of the Daughters of the American Revolution* (Washington, DC: n.p., 1938), 591.

85. "Some Things You Should Know about the Philippine Islands," *Woman Citizen: A Weekly Chronicle of Progress* 4, no. 22 (December 1919): 602.

86. "Daughters of U.S. Veterans to Inaugurate Tomorrow," *Manila Bulletin* (special old-timers edition), July 21, 1928, 1.

87. *Census of the Philippine Islands*, vol. 1 (Washington: United States Bureau of the Census, 1939), 393.

88. "Nobodies' Sons," *Philippine Magazine* 34, no. 1 (January 1937).

89. "Citizens of the United States," *Census of the Philippine Islands*, vol. 1 (Washington, DC: United States Bureau of the Census, 1939), 400.

90. See chapter 3 and Cornelia Lichauco Fung, *Beneath the Banyan Tree: My Family Chronicles* (Hong Kong: CBL Fung, 2009); Winifred O'Connor Pablo, "The Child of the Mixed Marriage," *The Woman's World*, May 1935, 6–7.

91. See, for example, Saundra Sturdevant and Brenda Stoltzfus *Let the Good Times Roll: Prostitution and the U.S. Military in Asia* (New York: New Press, 1993); Cynthia H. Enloe, *The*

Morning After: Sexual Politics at the End of the Cold War (Berkeley: University of California Press, 1993); Katharine H. S. Moon, *Sex among Allies* (New York: Columbia University Press, 1997); Joseph M. Ahern, "Out of Sight, out of Mind: United States Immigration Law and Policy as Applied to Filipino-Amerasians." *Pacific Rim Law and Policy Journal* 1, no. 1 (1992): 105–26; Elizabeth Kolby, "Moral Responsibility to Filipino Amerasians: Potential Immigration and Child Support Alternatives," *Asian Law Journal* 2 (1995): 61–85; Robin S. Levi, "Legacies of War: The United States' Obligation toward Amerasians." *Stanford Journal of International Law* 29 (1992): 459–502.

92. The term "Amerasian" is a post–World War II term that refers to the children born of one Asian and one American parent during the wartime militarization of the Pacific. Some historians believe that the term was coined during the late 1940s or early 1950s by philanthropist and author Pearl S. Buck. The term specifically implies that the American parent was in the US military (usually the father) and the other parent is Asian. "Amerasian" is also a more politicized term, often used for campaigns that call for US recognition of these children and legislation that supports them.

93. See note 91. See also Cathy Choy, *Global Families: A History of Asian International Adoption* (New York: New York University Press, 2013); Laura Briggs, *Somebody's Children: The Politics of Transracial and Transnational Adoption* (Durham, NC: Duke University Press, 2012).

Conclusion

1. These lyrics seem to be the most common for the 1940s although some versions differ; for example, "All the sailors' hearts were filled with fond regret" also appears as "Many sailors hearts were filled with sad regret."

2. Thomas P. Walsh, *Tin Pan Alley and the Philippines: American Songs of War and Love, 1898–1946* (Lanham, MD: Scarecrow Press, 2013).

3. For more on blackface minstrelsy in the United States, see Eric Lott, *Love and Theft: Blackface Minstrelsy and the American Working Class* (New York: Oxford University Press, 2013).

4. Ideas of postracial multiraciality have been invoked to abolish affirmative action and college admissions practices that consider racial/ethnic background. Former University of California regent Ward Connerly, for example, used ideas of multiraciality to decry affirmative action policies at UC.

5. Peggy Pascoe, *What Comes Naturally: Miscegenation Law and the Making of Race in America* (New York: Oxford University Press, 2010). See also www.lovingday.org.

6. As Max Boot, a Lansdale biographer, notes, Kelly was "full of good information" for the US counterinsurgency. Max Boot, *The Road Not Taken* (New York: Liveright, 2018).

7. Scott Anderson, *The Quiet Americans: Four CIA Spies at the Dawn of the Cold War* (New York: Doubleday, 2020).

8. Boot, *Road Not Taken*, 73.

9. Andrew Friedman, *Covert Capital: Landscapes of Denial and the Making of U.S. Empire in the Suburbs of Northern Virginia* (Berkeley: University of California Press, 2013).

10. Friedman, *Covert Capital*. Adobo is a Filipino dish of stewed chicken in vinegar and soy sauce.

11. According to Boot, Helen did not seek a divorce when she learned of her husband's affair. This was likely due to the social conventions of the time as well as Helen's consideration of her economic future.

12. Cecil B. Currey, *Edward G. Lansdale, The Unquiet American* (Boston: Houghton Mifflin, 1988).

13. Kurtz here refers to the main antagonist of the 1979 film *Apocalypse Now*, which was, not incidentally, filmed mostly in the Philippines.

14. Yen Li Espiritu, *Body Counts: The Vietnam War and Militarized Refugees* (Berkeley: University of California Press, 2014); Jana K. Lipman, *In Camps: Vietnamese Refugees, Asylum Seekers and Repatriates* (Berkeley: University of California Press, 2020). Both Espiritu and Lipman discuss the PRPC and its function from the 1980s to the early 1990s.

15. "Refugee Processing Center Keeps Welcoming Amerasians from Vietnam Camp in Philippines an Asian Ellis Island," *Baltimore Sun*, March 29, 1992, https://www.baltimoresun .com/news/bs-xpm-1992-03-29-1992089019-story.html.

16. As scholars Cynthia Marasigan and Angelica Allen point out, descendants of Black-Filipino families were (and still are) often less open to embracing or even acknowledging their ancestry because of racism from the American and Filipino communities and the persistent stigma associated with being Amerasian. See Cynthia Marasigan, *Triangulated Amigo Warfare: African American Soldiers, Filipino Revolutionaries, and U.S. Empire* (Durham, NC: Duke University Press, forthcoming) and Angelica Allen, "Afro-Amerasians: Blackness in the Philippine Imaginary" (PhD diss., University of Texas, 2020).

Bibliography

Archives

The Philippines

Ateneo de Manila University, Quezon City
    American Historical Collection
    Filipiniana Collection
    Pardo de Tavera Collection
Beyer Family Private Papers, Baguio City
López Museum and Library, Pasig City, Metro Manila
    Filipiniana Collection
Mario Feir Filipiniana Library, Makati
National Library of the Philippines, Ermita
    Otley Beyer Ethnographic Collection
    Rizaliana Collection
Nielson Tower Filipinas Heritage Library, Makati
University of the Philippines, Diliman, Quezon City
    Filipiniana Collection, Beyer Collection

The United States

Library of Congress
National Archives and Records Administration, College Park, Maryland (NARA)
    Philippine Archives Collection (RG 350, RG 395)
National Personnel Records Center, St. Louis, Missouri (NPRC)

The Newberry Library, Chicago, Illinois
    Ayer Collection
        Davis Papers
        Evangeline E. Lewis Photographic Postcard Collection of the Philippine
            Islands
        Pullman Railroad Collection
        Dean C. Worcester Collection of Philippine photographs
University of Illinois, Urbana-Champaign
University of Michigan, Ann Arbor, Bentley Historical Library
    Bertha Schaffer Letters
    Harry H. Bandholtz Papers
    Dean C. Worcester Papers
    James A. LeRoy Papers
    Joseph Ralston Hayden Papers
    Luce Philippine Project Interviews
University of Michigan, Ann Arbor, Harlan Hatcher Graduate Library
    Worcester Collection
University of Michigan, Ann Arbor, Museum of Anthropological Archaeology
    Dean C. Worcester Photograph Collection

Published Primary Sources

Acts of the First Philippine Legislature. Vol. 9. Manila: Government Printing Office,
    1908.
Acts of the Philippine Commission, nos. 1–1800. 7 vols. Washington, DC: Government
    Printing Office, 1901.
*Affairs in the Philippine Islands: Hearings Before the Committee on the Philippines of the United
    States Senate.* Washington, DC: Government Printing Office, 1902.
*Annual Report of Major General Arthur MacArthur, U.S. Army, Commanding, Division of
    the Philippines, Military Governor in the Philippine Islands.* Vol. 1. Manila, 1901.
Annual Report of the Chief of the Bureau of Insular Affairs to the U.S. War Department.
    Washington, DC: Government Printing Office, 1936.
Annual Report of the Philippine Commission. Washington, DC: Government Printing
    Office, 1900–1915.
Annual Report of the Philippine Commission, 1904, pt. 1. Washington, DC: Government
    Printing Office, 1905.
Annual Report of the Surgeon General to the Department of War. Washington, DC: Gov-
    ernment Printing Office, 1911.
Annual Report of the War Department. Washington, DC: Government Printing Office,
    1899.
Annual Reports of the War Department, Acts of the Philippine Commission. Vol. 11. Wash-
    ington, DC: Government Printing Office, 1902.

Asian and Pacific Islander Americans in Congress, 1900–2017. Washington, DC: Government Printing Office, 2017.

Baja, Emanuel. *Philippine Police System and Its Problems.* Manila: Pobre's Press, 1933.

Barrows, David P. *Circular of Information: Instructions for Volunteer Field Workers; The Museum of Ethnology, Natural History and Commerce.* Manila: Bureau of Non-Christian Tribes for the Philippine Islands, 1901.

Beautiful Philippines: A Handbook of General Information. Manila: Manila Bureau of Printing, 1923.

Brent, Charles Henry. "Othello Preaches." In *Liberty and Other Sermons,* 169–79. London: Longmans, Green, 1906.

Buck, Hammon H. *Chronicles of Sam and Maganda.* Manila: Concuera Press, ca. 1935.

Bulletin No. 25: Official Roster of the Bureau of Education, Corrected to March 1, 1906. Manila: Bureau of Printing, 1906.

Bulletin of the American Historical Collection. Quezon City, Philippines: Ateneo de Manila University.

Canseco, Anicia Garcia. "'Let Your Hair Down': A.V.H. Hartendorp—the Man and His Works." Master's thesis, University of the Philippines, 1974.

Carter, Thomas. *The Way It Was.* Quezon City, Philippines: R.P. Garcia, 1985.

Cases Decided in the Court of Claims of the United States. Vol. 66. Washington, DC: Government Printing Office, 1929.

Census of the Philippine Islands. Vol. 1 Washington: United States Bureau of the Census, 1939.

Census of the Philippine Islands Taken under the Direction of the Philippine Commission in the Year 1903. 2 vols. Washington, DC: Bureau of the Census, 1905.

Census of the Philippine Islands Taken under the Direction of the Philippine Legislature in the Year 1918. 2 vols. Manila: Bureau of Printing, 1921.

Census of the Philippines: 1939. 2 vols. Manila: Bureau of Printing, 1941.

Cole, Mabel Cook. *Philippine Folk Tales.* Chicago: A. C. McClurg, 1916.

Congressional Record: Proceedings and Debates of the Second Session of the Sixty-Seventh Congress. Washington, DC: Government Printing Office, 1922.

Congressional Record: Proceedings and Debates of the Second Session of the Seventy-Sixth Congress. Washington, DC: Government Printing Office, 1939.

Congressional Record: Proceedings and Debates of the Sixty-First U.S. Congress. Washington, DC: Government Printing Office, 1911.

Currey, Cecil B. Currey. *Edward G. Lansdale, The Unquiet American.* Boston: Houghton Mifflin, 1988.

Dauncey, Mrs. Campbell. *An Englishwoman in the Philippines.* New York: E. P. Dutton, 1906.

Devins, John Bancroft. *An Observer in the Philippines: Or, Life in Our New Possessions.* Boston: American Tract Society, 1905.

Du Bois, W. E. B. "Philippine Mulattoes." *Crisis* 31 (December 1925).

Elliott, Charles Burke. *The Philippines: To the End of the Commission Government; A Study in Tropical Democracy.* Indianapolis: Bobbs-Merrill, 1917.

Exclusion of Immigration from the Philippine Islands: Hearings Before the Committee on Immigration and Naturalization. Washington, DC: Government Printing Office, 1930.

Eyot, Canning [pseud.], ed. *The Story of the Lopez Family: A Page from the History of the War in the Philippines.* Boston: James H. West, 1904.

The Filipino People, Vol. 1, No. 5, January 1913.

Fisher, Herbert D. *Philippine Diary.* Burlington: Vantage Press, 2005.

"The Friar-Land Inquiry, Philippine Government." *Administration of Philippine Lands Report.* Vol. 2. Washington, DC: Government Printing Office, 1911.

Fung, Cornelia Lichauco. *Beneath the Banyan Tree: My Family Chronicles.* Hong Kong: CBL Fung, 2009.

Gaches, Mrs. Samuel Francis. *Good Cooking and Health in the Tropics.* Manila: American Guardian Association, 1922.

Gleeck, Lewis E., Jr. *Americans on the Philippine Frontiers.* Manila: Carmelo & Bauermann, 1974.

——. "Fulfillment in the Philippines." *Bulletin of the American Historical Collection* 18, no. 2 (April–June 1990).

——. *The Manila Americans (1901–1964).* Manila: Carmelo & Bauermann, 1977.

Hartendorp, A. V. H. "An Autobiographical Sketch." Manila: Self-published, 1964.

——. *History of Industry and Trade in the Philippines: The Magsaysay Administration.* Manila: Philippine Education, 1961.

——. *I Have Lived: Reminiscences of A.V.H. Hartendorp.* 6 books. Manila: Self-published, 1970.

Hearings Before the Committee on Immigration and Naturalization. Washington, DC: United States Government Printing Office, 1930.

Hearings Before the Committee on Military Affairs, U.S. Senate, Dec. 7–14, 1900. Washington: Government Printing Office, 1900.

Hearings Before the Committee on the Philippines of the United States Senate in Relation to Affairs in the Philippine Islands. Washington, DC: Government Printing Office, 1900–1902.

Hearings Before the Secretary of War and the Congressional Party Accompanying Him to the Philippine Islands Held at Manila, August 29–30, 1905. Manila: Bureau of Printing, 1905.

Hohenberg, John. *Between Two Worlds: Policy, Press, and Public Opinion in Asian-American Relations.* New York: Frederick A. Praeger, 1967.

Index to General Orders and Circulars Issued from the Office of the U.S. Military Governor in the Philippine Islands. Washington, DC: Government Printing Office, 1899.

Jenkins, N. W. "Haight's Place." *Philippine Magazine* 27, no. 12 (1931).

Lands Held for Ecclesiastical or Religious Uses in the Philippine Islands, Etc.: Message from the President of the United States. Washington, DC: Government Printing Office, 1901.

Laws of the Fourth Philippine Legislature. Vol. 1. Washington, DC: Government Printing Office, 1918.

Liberty and Other Sermons. Boston: The Merrymount Press, 1906.

Longworth, Alice Roosevelt. *Crowded Hours: Reminiscences of Alice Roosevelt Longworth.* New York: C. Scribner's Sons, 1933.

MacArthur, Arthur. *Annual Report of Major General Arthur MacArthur, U.S. Army, Commanding, Division of the Philippines.* Vol. 1. Manila: n.p., 1901.

Message from the President of the United States, Senate Report, "Lands Held for Ecclesiastical of Religious Use in the Philippine Islands, Etc." Washington, DC: Government Printing Office, 1901.

Military Laws of the United States (Army). 4th ed. Washington, DC: Government Printing Office, 1911.

Miscellaneous Hearings Before the Committee on Military Affairs, U.S. Senate, 1900–1919. Washington, DC: Government Printing Office.

Moe, Kilmer O. "Young Man, Go South!" *Philippine Farmer* 7, no. 1 (January 1921).

Navy Guide to Cavite and Manila: A Practical Guide and Beautiful Souvenir. Manila: Manila Merchants' Association, 1908.

O'Connel, Daniel, and the Manila Merchants' Association. *Manila: The Pearl of the Orient.* Manila: n.p., 1908.

Parker, Luther. *Verses of the Philippines.* Manila: Squires and Bingham, 1911.

"Periscope: Measures Instituted to Diminish the Frequency of Venereal Infections and Results," *Eclectic Medical Journal,* John Scudder, Ed. State Eclectic Medical Association, Ohio, Vol. 72, 1912.

Philippine Studies Journal

The Philippine Yearbook, Vol. 1, (1933–1934): Anniversary Supplement of The Philippines Herald. Manila: Philippines, 1933.

Proceedings of the Forty-Seventh Continental Congress of the National Society of the Daughters of the American Revolution. Washington, DC: n.p., 1938.

Public Laws and Resolutions Passed by the U.S. Philippine Commission. Washington: Government Printing Office, 1901.

Public Laws and Resolutions Passed by the U.S. Philippine Commission, Division of Insular Affairs, War Department. Washington: U.S. Government Printing Office, 1901.

Report of the Philippine Commission to the President, 1899–1900, vols. 1 and 2. Washington, DC: Government Printing Office, 1900.

Report of the Special Mission to the Philippine Islands to the Secretary of War. Washington, DC: Government Printing Office, 1922.

Report of the Surgeon-General of the Army to the Secretary of War (Washington, DC: Government Printing Office, 1899).

Report of the United States Philippine Commission to the Secretary of War. Washington, DC: Government Printing Office, 1906.

Report of the United States Philippine Commission to the Secretary of War, 1900–1903. Washington, DC: Government Printing Office, 1904.

Reports of Cases Determined in the Supreme Court of the Philippines. Vol. 68. Rochester, NY: Lawyers Co-Operative, n.d.

Reports of Cases Determined in the Supreme Court of the Philippine Islands. Vol. 11. Manila: Bureau of Printing, 1909.

Reports of Cases Determined in the Supreme Court of the Philippine Islands. Vol. 39. Manila: Bureau of Printing, 1918.

Reports of Cases Determined in the Supreme Court of the Philippine Islands. Vol. 46. Manila: Bureau of Printing, 1925.

Riley, Dale. "A Little Trip to 'Haight's Place.'" *Mid-Pacific* 17, no. 2 (1919).

Roosevelt, Theodore. *A Compilation of the Messages and Speeches of Theodore Roosevelt, 1901–1905.* Edited by Alfred H. Lewis. 2 vols. New York: Bureau of National Literature and Art, 1906.

"Sale of Beer and Light Wines in Post Exchanges." *United States Congressional Serial Set.* Washington, DC: Government Printing Office, 1903.

Seaman, G. E. "Some Observations of a Medical Officer in the Philippines." *Milwaukee Medical Journal* 10, no. 7 (1902).

Stuntz, Homer C. *The Philippines and the Far East.* Cincinnati: Jennings and Pye, 1904.

Sugar News, Vol. 20. Manila: Sugar News Press, 1939.

Taft, William H. "Report of the Civil Governor." *Report of the United States Philippine Commission to the Secretary of War, 1900–1903, Bureau of Insular Affairs.* Washington, DC: Government Printing Office, 1904.

Taylor, Carson. *History of the Philippine Press.* Manila: n.p., 1927.

Taylor, John. *The Philippine Insurrection against the United States: A Compilation of Documents with Notes and Introduction.* 5 vols. Pasay City: Eugenio López Foundation, 1971.

Turnbull, Wilfrid, Major. "Early Days in the Mountain Province." *Bulletin of the American Historical Collection* 3, no. 1 (1975).

United States Bureau of the Census. *Census of the Philippine Islands: 1903.* Vol. 2. Washington, DC: United States Bureau of the Census, 1905.

United States Bureau of Insular Affairs, Annual Report of the Chief of the Bureau of Insular Affairs to the U.S. War Department (U.S. Government Printing Office, 1936.

United States Congressional Serial Set: Report of the Commission Appointed by the President to Investigate the Conduct of the War Department in the War with Spain. Vol. 2, Appendices. Washington, DC: Government Printing Office, 1900.

United States Statutes at Large. Vol. 71. Washington, DC: Government Printing Office, 1958.

Washington Headquarters Services Directorate for Information Operations and Reports, *Department of Defense, Selected Manpower Statistics: 1986.* Washington DC: Government Printing Office, 1986.

Williams, Daniel Roderick. *The Odyssey of the Philippine Commission.* Chicago: A. C. McClurg, 1913.

Willis, Henry Parker. *Our Philippine Problem: A Study of American Colonial Policy.* New York: Henry Holt, 1905.

Wright, Hamilton M. *A Handbook of the Philippines.* Chicago: A. C. McClurg, 1907.

Secondary Sources

Abalahin, Andrew Jimenez. "Prostitution Policy and the Project of Modernity: A Comparative Study of Colonial Indonesia and the Philippines, 1850–1940." PhD diss., Cornell University, 2003.

Abinales, Patricio. *Making Mindanao: Cotabato and Davao in the Formation of the Philippine Nation-State.* Quezon City: Ateneo de Manila University Press, 2000.

Abinales, Patricio, and Donna Amoroso, eds. *State and Society in the Philippines.* Lanham, MD: Rowman and Littlefield, 2017.

Acabado, Stephen, and Grace Barretto-Tesoro. "Places, Landscapes, and Identity: Place Making in the Colonial Period Philippines." In *The Global Spanish Empire: Five Hundred Years of Place Making and Pluralism,* edited by Christine D. Beaule and John G. Douglass, 200–220. Tucson: University of Arizona Press, 2020.

Adams, David Wallace, and Crista DeLuzio, eds. *On the Borders of Love and Power: Families and Kinship in the Intercultural American Southwest.* Berkeley: University of California Press, 2012.

Ahern, Joseph M. "Out of Sight, out of Mind: United States Immigration Law and Policy as Applied to Filipino-Amerasians." *Pacific Rim Law and Policy Journal* 1, no. 1 (1992): 105–26.

Ahmed, Sara. *Strange Encounters: Embodied Others in Post-Coloniality.* London: Routledge, 2000.

Allen, Angelica. "Afro-Amerasians: Blackness in the Philippine Imaginary." PhD dissertation, University of Texas, Austin, 2020.

Alvah, Donna. *Unofficial Ambassadors: American Military Families Overseas and the Cold War, 1946–1965.* New York: NYU Press, 2007.

Anderson, Benedict R. *Imagined Communities: Reflections on the Origin and Spread of Nationalism.* London: Verso, 2006.

Anderson, James N. *Critical Issues in Philippine Research: A Selected and Annotated Literature Review on the Women's Movement, Conflict in Luzon's Cordillera, Muslim Autonomy, and Recent Political Resistance.* Berkeley, CA: Centers for South and Southeast Asia Studies, University of California Press, 1996.

Anderson, Scott. *The Quiet Americans: Four CIA Spies at the Dawn of the Cold War.* New York: Doubleday Press, 2020.

Anderson, Warwick. *Colonial Pathologies: American Tropical Medicine, Race, and Hygiene in the Philippines.* Durham, NC: Duke University Press, 2006.

——. *The Cultivation of Whiteness: Science, Health and Racial Destiny in Australia.* Durham, NC: Duke University Press, 2006.

Arista, Noelani. *The Kingdom and the Republic: Sovereign Hawai'i and the Early United States.* Philadelphia: University of Pennsylvania Press, 2018.

Arondekar, Anjali R. *For the Record: On Sexuality and the Colonial Archive in India.* Durham, NC: Duke University Press, 2009.

Arvin, Maile. *Possessing Polynesians: The Science of Settler Colonial Whiteness in Hawai'i and Oceania.* Durham, NC: Duke University Press, 2019.

Azuma, Eiichiro. *Between Two Empires: Race, History, and Transnationalism in Japanese America.* Oxford: Oxford University Press, 2005.

——. *In Search of Our Frontier: Japanese America and Settler Colonialism in the Construction of Japan's Borderless Empire.* Berkeley: University of California Press, 2019.

Balce, Nerissa S. *Body Parts of Empire: Visual Abjection, Filipino Images, and the American Archive.* Ann Arbor: University of Michigan Press, 2016.

———. "The Filipina's Breast: Savagery, Docility, and the Erotics of the American Empire." *Social Text* 24, no. 2 (2006): 89–110.

Barr, Juliana. *Peace Came in the Form of a Woman: Indians and Spaniards in the Texas Borderlands.* Chapel Hill: University of North Carolina Press, 2007.

Bederman, Gail. *Manliness & Civilization: A Cultural History of Gender and Race in the United States, 1880–1917.* Chicago: University of Chicago Press, 1996.

Bender, Daniel, and Jana Lippman, eds. *Making the Empire Work: Labor and United States Imperialism.* New York: New York University Press, 2015.

Bennett, Herman L. *Colonial Blackness: A History of Afro-Mexico.* Bloomington: Indiana University Press, 2009.

Bernstein, Robin. *Racial Innocence: Performing American Childhood from Slavery to Civil Rights.* New York: New York University Press, 2007.

Beyer, William Gambuk. "The Beyer Bone Washing Ritual." *Bulletin of the American Historical Collection* 8, no. 2 (1980).

Bhabha, Homi K. *The Location of Culture.* London: Routledge, 1994.

Bjork, Katharine. *Prairie Imperialists: The Indian Country Origins of American Empire.* Philadelphia: University of Pennsylvania Press, 2019.

Blackhawk, Ned. *Violence over the Land: Indians and Empires in the Early American West.* Cambridge, MA: Harvard University Press, 2008.

Blain, Keisha. *Set the world on fire: Black Nationalist Women and the Global Struggle for Freedom.* University of Pennsylvania Press, 2018.

Boemeke, Manfred F., Roger Chickering, and Stig Förster. *Anticipating Total War: The German and American Experiences, 1871–1914.* Cambridge: Cambridge University Press, 1999.

Bonilla-Silva, Eduardo. *Racism Without Racists: Color-Blind Racism and the Persistence of Racial Inequality in the United States.* 2nd ed. Lanham: Rowman & Littlefield, 2006.

Boot, Max. *The Road Not Taken.* New York: Liveright, 2018.

Borras, Saturnino M. *Competing Views and Strategies on Agrarian Reform.* Ateneo de Manila University Press, 2009.

Brewer, Carolyn. *Shamanism, Catholicism, and Gender Relations in Colonial Philippines, 1521–1685.* Aldershot, Hants, England: Ashgate, 2004.

Briggs, Laura. *Reproducing Empire: Race, Sex, Science, and U.S. Imperialism in Puerto Rico.* Berkeley: University of California Press, 2002.

———. *Somebody's Children: The Politics of Transracial and Transnational Adoption.* Durham, NC: Duke University Press, 2012.

Brody, David. *Visualizing American Empire: Orientalism and Imperialism in the Philippines.* University of Chicago Press, 2010.

Brooks, James. *Captives & Cousins: Slavery, Kinship, and Community in the Southwest Borderlands.* Chapel Hill, NC: University of North Carolina Press, 2002.

Brown, Kathleen M. *Good Wives, Nasty Wenches, and Anxious Patriarchs: Gender, Race, and Power in Colonial Virginia.* Chapel Hill: University of North Carolina Press, 1996.

Burns, Kathryn. *Colonial Habits: Convents and the Spiritual Economy of Cuzco, Peru.* Durham, NC: Duke University Press, 1999.

Burns, Lucy Mae San Pablo. *Puro Arte: Filipinos on the Stages of Empire.* New York: New York University Press, 2012.

Burton, Antoinette M. *Burdens of History: British Feminists, Indian Women, and Imperial Culture, 1865–1915.* Chapel Hill: University of North Carolina Press, 1994.

——, ed. *Gender, Sexuality, and Colonial Modernities.* Routledge Research in Gender and History 2. London: Routledge, 1999.

Byrd, Jodi. *Transit of Empire: Indigenous Critiques of Colonialism.* Minneapolis: University of Minnesota Press, 2011.

Cahill, Cathleen. *Federal Fathers and Mothers: A Social History of the United States Indian Service, 1869–1933.* Chapel Hill: University of North Carolina Press, 2011.

Camagay, Maria Luisa T. *Working Women of Manila in the 19th Century.* Manila: University of the Philippines Press, 1995.

Canaday, Margot. *The Straight State: Sexuality and Citizenship in Twentieth-Century America.* Princeton: Princeton University Press, 2009.

Canoy, Reuben. *The Quest for Mindanao Independence.* Cagayan de Oro, Mindanao: Mindanao Post, 1987.

Capino, Jose B. *Dream Factories of Former Colony: American Fantasies, Philippine Cinema.* Minneapolis, University of Minnesota Press, 2010.

Capo, Julio. *Welcome to Fairyland: Queer Miami before 1940.* Chapel Hill: University of North Carolina Press, 2017.

Capozzola, Chris. *Bound By War: How the United States and the Philippines Built America's First Pacific Century.* New York: Basic Books, 2020.

Carby, Hazel V. *Reconstructing Womanhood: The Emergence of the Afro-American Woman Novelist.* New York: Oxford University Press, 1987.

Caronan, Faye. *Legitimizing Empire: Filipino American and U.S. Puerto Rican Cultural Critique.* Urbana: University of Illinois Press, 2015.

Carter, Greg. *United States of United Races: A Utopian History of Racial Mixing.* New York: New York University Press, 2013.

Casas, Raquel Casas. *Married to a Daughter of the Land: Spanish-Mexican Women and Interethnic Marriage in California, 1820–1880.* Reno: University of Nevada Press, 2007.

Chang, David. *The World and All the Things upon It: Native Hawaiian Geographies of Exploration.* Minneapolis: University of Minnesota Press, 2016.

Chang, Kornel S. *Pacific Connections: The Making of the U.S.-Canadian Borderlands.* Berkeley: University of California Press, 2012.

Charbonneau, Oliver. *Civilizational Imperatives: Americans, Moros, and the Colonial World.* Ithaca, NY: Cornell University Press, 2020.

Chauncey, George. *Gay New York: Gender, Urban Culture, and the Makings of the Gay Male World, 1890–1940.* Basic Books, 1995.

Cho, Yu-Fang. *Uncoupling American Empire: Cultural Politics of Deviance and Unequal Difference, 1890–1910.* Albany: State University of New York Press, 2014.

Choy, Catherine Ceniza. *Empire of Care: Nursing and Migration in Filipino American History.* Durham, NC: Duke University Press, 2003.

——. *Global Families: A History of Asian International Adoption.* New York: New York University Press, 2013.

Choy, Catherine Ceniza, and Judy Wu, eds. *Gendering the Trans-Pacific World*. Leiden: Brill, 2017.

Chu, Richard. *Chinese and Chinese Mestizos of Manila: Family, Identity, and Culture, 1860s–1930s*. Leiden: Brill, 2010.

Clancy-Smith, Julia, and Frances Gouda. *Domesticating the Empire: Race, Gender, and Family Life in French and Dutch Colonialism*. Charlottesville: University Press of Virginia, 1998.

Clutario, Genevieve. *Beauty Regimes: Disciplining Filipina Labor under U.S. Empire*. Durham, NC: Duke University Press, forthcoming.

Cocks, Catherine. *Tropical Whites: The Rise of the Tourist South in the Americas*. Philadelphia: University of Pennsylvania Press, 2013.

Cohen, Lizabeth. *Consumers Republic: The Politics of Mass Consumption in Postwar America*. New York: Knopf Doubleday, 2003.

Colby, Jason M. *Business of Empire: United Fruit, Race, and U.S. Expansion in Central America*. Ithaca, NY: Cornell University Press, 2013.

Collins, Patricia Hill. *Black Feminist Thought: Knowledge, Consciousness, and the Politics of Empowerment*. New York: Routledge, 2000.

Coloma, Roland Sintos. "White Gazes, Brown Breasts: Imperial Feminism and Disciplining Desires and Bodies in Colonial Encounters." *Paedagogica Historica: International Journal of Education* 48, no. 2 (2012): 243–61.

Conroy-Krutz, Emily. *Christian Imperialism: Converting the World in the Early American Republic*. Ithaca, NY: Cornell University Press, 2015.

Cott, Nancy F. *The Bonds of Womanhood: "Woman's Sphere" in New England, 1780–1835*. New Haven, CT: Yale University Press, 1997.

Crenshaw, Kimberle, ed. *Critical Race Theory: The Key Writings That Formed the Movement*. New York: New Press, 1995.

Cruz, Denise. *Transpacific Femininities: The Making of the Modern Filipina*. Durham, NC: Duke University Press, 2012.

Cullinane, Michael. *Illustrado Politics: Filipino Elite Responses to American Rule, 1898–1908*. Quezon City: Ateneo de Manila Press, 2003.

Cummings, Bruce. *Dominion from Sea to Sea: Pacific Ascendancy and American Power*. New Haven, CT: Yale University Press, 2009.

Curthoys, Anne. "Constructing National Histories." In *Frontier Conflict: The Australian Experience*, edited by Bain Attwood and Stephen Foster, 185–200. Acton: National Museum of Australia, 2003.

Daniel, G. Reginald. *Race and Multiraciality in Brazil and the United States: Converging Paths?* University Park: Pennsylvania State University Press, 2006.

Dávila, Jerry. *Diploma of Whiteness: Race and Social Policy in Brazil, 1917–1945*. Durham, NC: Duke University Press, 2003.

Dawley, Alan. *Changing the World: American Progressives in War and Revolution*. Princeton, NJ: Princeton University Press, 2005.

De Bevoise, Ken. *Agents of Apocalypse: Epidemic Disease in the Colonial Philippines*. Princeton, NJ: Princeton University Press, 1995.

——. "A History of Sexually Transmitted Diseases and HIV/AIDS in the Philippines." In *Sex, Disease and Society: A Comparative History of Sexually Transmitted Diseases and HIV/AIDS in Asia and the Pacific,* edited by Milton Lewis, Scott Bamber, and Michael Waugh, 113–38. Westport, CT: Greenwood, 1997.

De Guzmán, María. *Spain's Long Shadow: The Black Legend, Off-Whiteness, and Anglo-American Empire.* Minneapolis: University of Minnesota Press, 2005.

Deloria, Philip Joseph. *Playing Indian.* New Haven, CT: Yale University Press, 1998.

DeLuzio, Crista, and David Adams, eds. *On the Borders of Love and Power: Families and Kinship in the Intercultural American Southwest.* Berkeley: University of California Press, 2012.

D'Emilio, John, and Estelle B. Freedman. *Intimate Matters: A History of Sexuality in America.* Chicago: University of Chicago Press, 1998.

De Mul, Sarah. *Colonial Memory: Contemporary Women's Travel Writing in Britain and the Netherlands.* Amsterdam: Amsterdam University Press, 2011.

Donovan, Brian. *White Slave Crusades: Race, Gender and Anti-vice Activism, 1887–1917.* Champaign: University of Illinois Press, 2006.

Dorr, Linda. *White Women, Rape, and the Power of Race in Virginia, 1900–1960.* Chapel Hill: University of North Carolina Press, 2004.

Dower, John. *War without Mercy: Race and Power in the Pacific War.* New York: Pantheon, 1986.

DuVal, Kathleen. *The Native Ground: Indians and Colonists in the Heart of the Continent.* Philadelphia: University of Pennsylvania Press, 2006.

Encanto, Georgina Reyes. *Constructing the Filipina: A History of Women's Magazines, 1891–2002.* Quezon City: University of the Philippines Press, 2004.

Enloe, Cynthia H. *Bananas, Beaches and Bases: Making Feminist Sense of International Politics.* 2nd ed. Berkeley: University of California Press, 2014.

——. *Maneuvers: The International Politics of Militarizing Women's Lives.* Berkeley: University of California Press, 2000.

——. *The Morning After: Sexual Politics at the End of the Cold War.* Berkeley: University of California Press, 1993.

Erman, Sam. *Almost Citizens: Puerto Rico: The U.S. Constitution, and Empire.* Cambridge: Cambridge University Press, 2019.

España-Maram, Linda. *Creating Masculinity in Los Angeles's Little Manila: Working-Class Filipinos and Popular Culture, 1920s–1950s.* New York: Columbia University Press, 2006.

Espiritu, Augusto Fauni. *Five Faces of Exile: The Nation and Filipino American Intellectuals.* Stanford, CA: Stanford University Press, 2005.

Espiritu, Yen Li. *Asian American Panethnicity: Bridging Institutions and Identities.* Philadelphia: Temple University Press, 1992.

——. *Body Counts: The Vietnam War and Militarized Refugees.* Berkeley: University of California Press, 2014.

Fajardo, Stephanie. "Authorizing Illicit Intimacies: Filipina-G.I. Interracial Relations in the Postwar Philippines." *Philippine Studies: Historical and Ethnographic Viewpoints* 65, no. 4 (2017): 485–513.

Fanon, Franz. *Black Skin, White Masks.* New York: Grove Press, 1952.

Fernandez, Doreen. "Pompas y Solemnidades: Church Celebrations in Spanish Manila and the Native Theater." *Philippine Studies* 36, no. 4 (1988): 403–26.

Findlay, Eileen. *Imposing Decency: The Politics of Sexuality and Race in Puerto Rico, 1870–1920.* Durham, NC: Duke University Press, 1999.

Finin, Gerard A. *The Making of the Igorot: The Contours of Cordillera Consciousness.* Quezon City: Ateneo de Manila University Press, 2005.

Fojas, Camilla. *Islands of Empire: Pop Culture and U.S. Power.* Austin: University of Texas Press, 2014.

Foley, Neil. *The White Scourge: Mexicans, Blacks, and Poor Whites in Texas Cotton Culture.* Berkeley: University of California Press, 1997.

Francia, Luis. *History of the Philippines: From Indios Bravos to Filipinos.* New York: Overland, 2014.

Francisco, Juan R. "H. Otley Beyer's Contribution to Indo-Philippine Scholarship." *Bulletin of the American Historical Collection* 4, no. 2 (April 1976).

Franco, Jennifer Conroy. *Elections and Democratization in the Philippines.* New York: Routledge, 2001.

Freeman, Estelle. *Redefining Rape: Sexual Violence in the Era of Suffrage and Segregation.* Cambridge, MA: Harvard University Press, 2013.

Friedman, Andrew. *Covert Capital: Landscapes of Denial and the Making of U.S. Empire in the Suburbs of Northern Virginia.* Berkeley: University of California Press, 2013.

Fujikane, Candace, and Jonathan Okamura, eds. "Whose Vision? Asian Settler Colonialism in Hawai'i." Special issue, *Amerasia Journal* 26, no. 2 (2000).

Gaines, Kevin. *American Africans in Ghana: Black Expatriates and the Civil Rights Era.* Chapel Hill: University of North Carolina Press, 2012.

Garraway, Doris Lorraine. *The Libertine Colony: Creolization in the Early French Caribbean.* Durham, NC: Duke University Press, 2005.

Gates, John M. "War-Related Deaths in the Philippines, 1898–1902." *Pacific Historical Review* 53, no. 3 (1984): 367–78.

Gatewood, Willard B., Jr. *Black Americans and the White Man's Burden, 1898–1903.* Chicago: University of Illinois Press, 1975.

——. *"Smoked Yankees" and the Struggle for Empire: Letters from Negro Soldiers, 1898–1902.* Fayetteville: University of Arkansas Press, 1987.

Gerald R. Gems. *Sport and the American Occupation of the Philippines: Bats, Balls, and Bayonets.* Lanham, MD: Rowman & Littlefield, 2016.

Gershman, John. "Is Southeast Asia the Second Front." *Foreign Affairs* 81, no. 4 (2002): 60–74.

Ghosh, Durba. *Sex and the Family in Colonial India: The Making of Empire.* Cambridge: Cambridge University Press, 2006.

Gillem, Mark. *America Town: Building the Outposts of Empire.* Minneapolis: University of Minnesota Press, 2007.

Gilroy, Paul. *The Black Atlantic: Modernity and Double Consciousness.* New York: Verso Press, 1993.

Go, Julian, and Anne L. Foster, eds. *The American Colonial State in the Philippines: Global Perspectives.* Durham, NC: Duke University Press, 2003.

Gobat, Michael. *Empire by Invitation: William Walker and Manifest Destiny in Central America.* Cambridge, MA: Harvard University Press, 2018.

Golay, Frank H. "Hartendorp Remembered." *Bulletin of the American Historical Collection* 5, no. 2 (April 1977): 42.

González, Deena J. *Refusing the Favor: The Spanish-Mexican Women of Santa Fe, 1820–1880.* New York: Oxford University Press, 1999.

Gonzalez, Vernadette Vicuna. *Empires Mistress, Starring Isabel Rosario Cooper.* Durham, NC: Duke University Press, 2021.

——. "Illicit Labor: MacArthur's Mistress and Imperial Intimacies." *Radical History Review* 123 (October 2015): 87–114.

——. *Securing Paradise: Tourism and Militarism in Hawai'i and the Philippines.* Durham, NC: Duke University Press Books, 2013.

Gordon, Linda. *The Great Arizona Orphan Abduction.* Cambridge, MA: Harvard University Press, 1999.

Gowing, Peter G. *Mandate in Moroland: The American Government of Muslim Filipinos, 1899–1920.* Quezon City: Philippine Center for Advanced Studies, University of the Philippines, 1977.

Grandin, Greg. *Fordlandia: The Rise and Fall of Henry Ford's Forgotten Jungle City.* New York: Metropolitan Books, 2010.

Green, Rayna. "The Pocahontas Perplex: The Image of Indian Women in American Culture." *Massachusetts Review* 16, no. 4 (1975): 698–714.

Greenberg, Amy S. *A Wicked War: Polk, Clay, Lincoln, and the 1846 U.S. Invasion of Mexico.* New York: Vintage Press, 2013.

——. *Manifest Manhood and the Antebellum American Empire.* Cambridge: Cambridge University Press, 2005.

Greene, Julie. *The Canal Builders: Making America's Empire at the Panama Canal.* New York: Penguin, 2009.

Grewal, Inderpal. *Home and Harem: Nation, Gender, Empire, and the Cultures of Travel.* Durham, NC: Duke University Press, 1996.

Gross, Ariela J. *What Blood Won't Tell: A History of Race on Trial in America.* Cambridge, MA: Harvard University Press, 2008.

Guglielmo, Thomas A. *White on Arrival: Italians, Race, Color, and Power in Chicago, 1890–1945.* Oxford: Oxford University Press, 2003.

Gutiérrez, Ramón A. *When Jesus Came, the Corn Mothers Went Away: Marriage, Sexuality, and Power in New Mexico, 1500–1846.* Stanford: Stanford University Press, 1991.

Halili, Servando D. *Iconography of the New Empire: Race and Gender Images and the American Colonization of the Philippines.* Quezon City: University of the Philippines Press, 2006.

Hall, Stuart, ed. *Culture, Media, Language: Working Papers in Cultural Studies, 1972–79.* London: Hutchinson, 1980.

——, ed. *Representation: Cultural Representations and Signifying Practices.* Culture, Media and Identities. London: Sage, 1997.

Hamalainen, Pekka. *Comanche Empire*. New Haven, CT: Yale University Press, 2008.

Hattori, Anne Perez. *Colonial Dis-Ease: US Navy Health Policies and the Chamorros of Guam, 1898–1941*. Honolulu: University of Hawai'i Press, 2004.

Hau, Caroline. *The Chinese Question: Ethnicity, Nation and Region in and beyond the Philippines*. Singapore: National University of Singapore Press, 2014.

Hawkins, Michael C. "Masculinity Reborn: Chivalry, Misogyny, Potency and Violence in the Philippines' Muslim South, 1899–1913." *Journal of Southeast Asian Studies* 44, no. 2 (2013): 250–65.

Hess, Carol. *Representing the Good Neighbor: Music, Difference, and the Pan American Dream*. Oxford: Oxford University Press, 2013.

Hill, Alva. *An American Lawyer in the Philippines*. Manila: Self-published, ca. 1946–48.

Hobson, Emily. *Lavender and Red: Liberation and Solidarity in the Gay and Lesbian Left*. Berkeley: University of California Press, 2016.

Hodes, Martha. *White Women, Black Men: Illicit Sex in the 19th Century*. New Haven, CT: Yale University Press, 2014.

Hoen, Maria, and Suengsook Moon, eds. *Over There: Living with the U.S. Military Empire from World War Two to the Present*. Durham, NC: Duke University Press, 2010.

Hoganson, Kristin L. *Consumers' Imperium: The Global Production of American Domesticity, 1865–1920*. Chapel Hill: University of North Carolina Press, 2007.

——. *Fighting for American Manhood: How Gender Politics Provoked the Spanish-American and Philippine-American Wars*. New Haven, CT: Yale University Press, 1998.

Hoganson, Kristin L., and Jay Sexton, eds. *Crossing Empires: Taking U.S. History into Transimperial Terrain*. Durham, NC: Duke University Press, 2020.

Hollnsteiner, Mary Racelis. *Bearers of Benevolence: The Thomasites and Public Education in the Philippines*. Pasig City: Anvil, 2001.

Holt, Elizabeth. M. *Colonizing Filipinas: Nineteenth-Century Representations of the Philippines in Western Historiography*. Quezon City: Ateneo de Manila University Press, 2002.

Hong, Jane. *Opening the Gates to Asia: A Transpacific History of How American Repealed Asian Exclusion*. Chapel Hill: University of North Carolina Press, 2019.

Horne, Gerald. *The Deepest South: The United States, Brazil, and the African Slave Trade*. New York: New York University Press, 2007.

Hurtado, Albert L. *Intimate Frontiers: Sex, Gender, and Culture in Old California*. Albuquerque: University of New Mexico Press, 1999.

Hyam, Ronald. *Empire and Sexuality: The British Experience*. Manchester: Manchester University Press, 1990.

Hyde, Anne F. *Empires, Nations, and Families: A History of the North American West, 1800–1860*. Lincoln: University of Nebraska Press, 2011.

Iger, David. *The Great Ocean: Pacific Worlds from Captain Cook to the Gold Rush*. Oxford: Oxford University Press, 2017.

Ignacio, Abe, Enrique de la Cruz, Jorge Emmanuel, and Helen Toribio. *The Forbidden Book: The Philippine-American War in Political Cartoons*. San Francisco: T-Boli, 2004.

Illeto, Rey. *Pasyon and Revolution: Popular Movements in the Philippines, 1840–1910*. Quezon City: Ateneo de Manila University, 1979.

Imada, Adria. *Aloha America: Hula Circuits Through the U.S. Empire*. Durham, NC: Duke University Press, 2012.

Jacobs, Margaret D. *Engendered Encounters: Feminism and Pueblo Cultures, 1879–1934*. Lincoln: University of Nebraska Press, 1999.

———. *White Mother to a Dark Race: Settler Colonialism, Maternalism, and the Removal of Indigenous Children in the American West and Australia, 1880–1940*. Lincoln: University of Nebraska Press, 2009.

Jacobson, Matthew Frye. *Barbarian Virtues: The United States Encounters Foreign Peoples at Home and Abroad, 1876–1917*. New York: Hill and Wang, 2001.

Jagodinsky, Katrina. *Legal Codes and Talking Trees: Indigenous Women's Sovereignty in the Sonoran and Puget Sound Borderlands, 1854–1946*. New Haven, CT: Yale University Press, 2016.

Jenista, Frank Lawrence. *The White Apos: American Governors on the Cordillera Central*. Quezon City: New Day, 1987.

Joaquin, Nick. *Almanac for Manileños*. Manila: Mr. and Mrs. Publications, 1979.

———. *Language of the Street and Other Essays*. Manila: National Book Store, 1980.

Johnson, Susan Lee. *Writing Kit Carson: Fallen Heroes in a Changing West*. Chapel Hill: University of North Carolina Press, 2020.

Johnson, Walter. *Soul By Soul: Life Inside the Antebellum Slave Market*. Cambridge, MA: Harvard University Press, 1999.

Jung, Moon-Ho. *Coolies and Cane: Race, Labor, and Sugar in the Age of Emancipation*. Baltimore: Johns Hopkins University Press, 2006.

Jung, Moon-Kie. *Reworking Race: The Making of Hawaii's Interracial Labor Movement*. New York: Columbia University Press, 2006.

Kahn, Jeffery. *Islands of Sovereignty: Haitian Migration and the Borders of Empire*. Chicago: University of Chicago Press, 2019.

Kaplan, Amy, and Donald E. Pease, eds. *Cultures of United States Imperialism*. Durham, NC: Duke University Press, 1993.

Karnow, Stanley. *In Our Image: America's Empire in the Philippines*. New York: Random House Press, 2010.

Karuka, Manu. *Empire's Tracks: Indigenous Nations, Chinese Workers, and the Transcontinental Railroad*. Berkeley: University of California Press, 2019.

Kauanui, J. Kehaulani. *Paradoxes of Hawaiian Sovereignty: Land, Sex, and the Colonial Politics of State Nationalism*. Durham, NC: Duke University Press, 2018.

Keys, Barbara. "Spreading Peace, Democracy, and Coca-Cola®: Sport and American Cultural Expansion in the 1930s." *Diplomatic History* 28, no. 2 (2004): 165–96.

Khalidi, Rashid. *Resurrecting Empire: Western Footprints and America's Perilous Path in the Middle East*. Boston: Beacon Press, 2005.

———. *Sowing Crisis: The Cold War and American Dominance in the Middle East*. Boston: Beacon Press, 2009.

Kim, Claire Jean. *Bitter Fruit: The Politics of Black-Korean Conflict in New York City*. New Haven, CT: Yale University Press, 2000.

Klein, Christina. *Cold War Orientalism: Asia in the Middlebrow Imagination, 1945–1961*. Berkeley: University of California Press, 2003.

Kluchin, Rebecca M. *Fit to be Tied: Sterilization and Reproductive Rights in America, 1950–1980*. New Brunswick, NJ: Rutgers University Press, 2009.

Kolby, Elizabeth. "Moral Responsibility to Filipino Amerasians: Potential Immigration and Child Support Alternatives." *Asian Law Journal* 2, no. 1 (1995): 61–85.

Kramer, Paul A. *The Blood of Government: Race, Empire, the United States, and the Philippines*. Chapel Hill: University of North Carolina Press, 2006.

——. "Colonial Crossings: Prostitution, Disease, and the Boundaries of Empire during the Philippine-American War." In *Body and Nation: The Global Realm of U.S. Body Politics in the Twentieth Century*, edited by Emily S. Rosenberg and Shanon Fitzpatrick, 17–41. Durham, NC: Duke University Press, 2014.

——. "The Darkness That Enters the Home: The Politics of Prostitution during the Philippine-American War." In *Haunted by Empire: Geographies of Intimacy in North American History: Geographies of Intimacy in North American History*, edited by Ann Laura Stoler, 366–404. Durham, NC: Duke University Press, 2006.

——. "The Military-Sexual Complex: Prostitution, Disease and the Boundaries of Empire during the Philippine-American War." *Asia-Pacific Journal: Japan Focus* 9, no. 30 (2011): 1–35.

Kramm, Robert. *Sanitized Sex: Regulating Prostitution, Venereal Disease, and Intimacy in Occupied Japan, 1945–1952*. Berkeley: University of California Press, 2017.

Kurashige, Scott. *The Shifting Grounds of Race: Black and Japanese Americans in the Making of Multiethnic Los Angeles*. Princeton, NJ: Princeton University Press, 2008.

Laderman, Scott. "Tourists in Uniform: American Empire-Building and the Defense Department's Cold War Pocket Guide Series." *Radical History Review* 129 (October 2017): 74–102.

Lair, Meredith. *Armed with Abundance: Consumerism and Soldiering in the Vietnam War*. Chapel Hill: University of North Carolina Press, 2011.

Lasker, Bruno. *Filipino Immigration to the Continental United States and to Hawaii*. New York: Arno, 1969.

Lavrin, Asunción. *Sexuality and Marriage in Colonial Latin America*. Lincoln: University of Nebraska Press, 1992.

Lee, Erika. *The Making of Asian America: A History*. New York: Simon and Schuster, 2016.

Levi, Robin S. "Legacies of War: The United States' Obligation toward Amerasians." *Stanford Journal of International Law* 29 (1993): 459–502.

Levine, Philippa. *Prostitution, Race, and Politics: Policing Venereal Disease in the British Empire*. New York: Routledge, 2003.

Licuanan, Virginia Benitez. *Filipino and Americans: A Love-Hate Relationship*. Manila: Baguio Country Club, 1982.

Limerick, Patricia Nelson. *The Legacy of Conquest: The Unbroken Past of the American West*. New York: W. W. Norton, 1987.

Linn, Brian McAllister. *The Philippine War, 1899–1902*. Lawrence: University Press of Kansas, 2000.

Lipman, Jana K. *Guantánamo: A Working-Class History between Empire and Revolution*. Berkeley: University of California Press, 2009.

——. *In Camps: Vietnamese Refugees, Asylum Seekers and Repatriates.* Berkeley: University of California Press, 2020.

Lipsitz, George. *The Possessive Investment in Whiteness: How White People Profit from Identity Politics.* Philadelphia: Temple University Press, 1998.

Loewen, James W. *Lies across America: What Our Historic Sites Get Wrong.* New York: New Press, 2013.

Lott, Eric. *Love and Theft: Blackface Minstrelsy and the American Working Class.* New York: Oxford University Press, 2013.

Love, Eric. *Race over Empire: Racism and U.S. Imperialism, 1865–1900.* Chapel Hill: University of North Carolina Press, 2004.

Lutz, Catherine, ed. *The Bases of Empire: The Global Struggle against U.S. Military Posts.* New York: New York University Press, 2009.

——. *Homefront: A Military City and the American 20th Century.* Boston: Beacon Press, 2001.

Mabalon, Dawn Bohulano. *Little Manila Is in the Heart: The Making of the Filipina/o American Community in Stockton, California.* Durham, NC: Duke University Press, 2013.

Mafe, Diana Adesola. *Mixed Race Stereotypes in South African and American Literature: Coloring Outside the (Black and White) Lines.* New York: Palgrave Press, 2013.

Majul, Cesar Adib. *Muslims in the Philippines.* Quezon City: University of the Philippines Press, 1999.

——. *The Political and Constitutional Ideas of the Philippine Revolution.* New York: Sentry, 1967.

Malloy, Sean. *Out of Oakland: Black Panther Party Internationalism during the Cold War.* Ithaca, NY: Cornell University Press, 2017.

Man, Simeon. *Soldiering Through Empire: Race and the Making of the Decolonizing Pacific.* Berkeley: University of California Press, 2018.

Mani, Lata. *Contentious Traditions: The Debate on Sati in Colonial India.* Berkeley: University of California Press, 1998.

Manuel, Arsenio. "The Wake and Last Rites over H. Otley Beyer." *Philippine Studies* 23 (1975).

Marasigan, Cynthia. *Triangulated Amigo Warfare: African American Soldiers, Filipino Revolutionaries, and U.S. Empire.* Durham, NC: Duke University Press, forthcoming.

Marino, Katherine. *Feminism for the Americas: The Making of an International Human Rights Movement.* Chapel Hill: University of North Carolina Press, 2019.

Matsuda, Matt K. *Empire of Love: Histories of France and the Pacific.* Oxford: Oxford University Press, 2005.

McAlister, Melani. *Epic Encounters: Culture, Media, and U.S. Interests in the Middle East since 1945.* Berkeley: University of California Press, 2005.

McClintock, Anne. *Imperial Leather: Race, Gender and Sexuality in the Colonial Contest.* New York: Routledge, 1995.

McCoy, Alfred W. *An Anarchy of Families: State and Family in the Philippines.* Madison: University of Wisconsin Press, 2009.

——. *Policing America's Empire: The United States, the Philippines, and the Rise of the Surveillance State.* Madison: University of Wisconsin Press, 2009.

McCoy, Alfred, and Alfredo Roces. *Philippine Cartoons: Political Caricature of the American Era, 1900–1941*. Quezon City: Vera Reyes, 1985.

McCoy, Alfred W., and Francisco Antonio Scarano. *Colonial Crucible: Empire in the Making of the Modern American State*. Madison: University of Wisconsin Press, 2009.

McFerson, Hazel M., ed. *Mixed Blessing: The Impact of the American Colonial Experience on Politics and Society in the Philippines*. Westport: Greenwood, 2002.

McInnis, Verity. *Women of Empire: Nineteenth-Century Army Officers' Wives in India and the U.S. West*. Norman: University of Oklahoma Press, 2017.

McKenna, Rebecca Tinio. *American Imperial Pastoral: The Architecture of US Colonialism in the Philippines*. Chicago: University of Chicago Press, 2017.

Mehl, Eva Maria. *Forced Migration in the Spanish Pacific World: From Mexico to the Philippines, 1765–1811*. Cambridge: Cambridge University Press, 2016.

Meixsel, Richard B. "United States Army Policy in the Philippine Islands, 1902–1922." MA Thesis, University of Georgia, 1988.

Memmi, Albert. *The Colonizer and the Colonized*. London: Earthscan, 2003.

Mendoza, Victor Román. *Metroimperial Intimacies: Fantasy, Racial-Sexual Governance, and the Philippines in U.S. Imperialism, 1899–1913*. Durham, NC: Duke University Press, 2015.

Meñez, Herminia Quimpo. *Explorations in Philippine Folklore*. Quezon City: Ateneo de Manila Press, 1996.

Meyer, Leisa D. *Creating GI Jane: Sexuality and Power in the Women's Army Corps during World War II*. New York: Columbia University Press, 1998.

Meyerowitz, Joanne Jay. *Not June Cleaver: Women and Gender in Postwar America, 1945–1960*. Philadelphia: Temple University Press, 1994.

Miles, Tiya. *Ties That Bind: The Story of an Afro-Cherokee Family in Slavery and Freedom*. Berkeley: University of California Press, 2005.

Miller, Stuart Creighton. *Benevolent Assimilation: The American Conquest of the Philippines, 1899–1903*. New Haven, CT: Yale University Press, 1982.

Mills, Sara. *Gender and Colonial Space*. Manchester: Manchester University Press, 2005.

Mojares, Resil B. *Cebuano Literature: A Survey and Bio-Bibliography with Finding List*. Cebu City: San Carlos, 1975.

——. *The War against the Americans: Resistance and Collaboration in Cebu, 1899–1906*. Quezon City: Ateneo de Manila University Press, 1999.

Molnar, Nicholas Trajano. *American Mestizos, the Philippines, and the Malleability of Race, 1898–1961*. Columbia: University of Missouri Press, 2017.

Moon, Katharine H. S. *Sex among Allies*. New York: Columbia University Press, 1997.

Morey, Michael. *Fagen: An African American Renegade in the Philippine-American War*. Madison: University of Wisconsin Press, 2019.

Morgan, Edmund Sears. *American Slavery, American Freedom: The Ordeal of Colonial Virginia*. New York: Norton, 1975.

Morgan, Jennifer L. *Laboring Women: Reproduction and Gender in New World Slavery*. Early American Studies. Philadelphia: University of Pennsylvania Press, 2004.

Mount, Guy E. "The Last Reconstruction: Slavery, Emancipation and Empire in the Black Pacific." PhD diss., University of Chicago, 2018.

Mufti, Aamir, Ella Shohat, and Anne McClintock, eds. *Dangerous Liaisons: Gender, Nation, and Postcolonial Perspectives*. Minneapolis: University of Minnesota Press, 1997.

Mullen, Bill. *Afro-Orientalism*. Minneapolis: University of Minnesota Press, 2004.

Neptune, Harvey R. *Caliban and the Yankees: Trinidad and the United States Occupation*. Chapel Hill: University of North Carolina Press, 2007.

Ngai, Mae M. *Impossible Subjects: Illegal Aliens and the Making of Modern America*. Princeton, NJ: Princeton University Press, 2004.

Ngũgĩ wa Thiong'o. *Decolonising the Mind: The Politics of Language in African Literature*. London: J. Currey, 1986.

Nubla, Gladys. "The Sexualized Child and Mestizaje: Colonial Tropes of the Filipino/a." In *Gendering the Trans-Pacific World*, edited by Catherine Ceniza Choy and Judy Wu, 165–95. Leiden: Brill, 2017.

O'Brien, Jean. *Firsting and Lasting: Writing Indians out of Existence in New England*. Minneapolis: University of Minnesota Press, 2010.

Okada, Taihei. "Underside of Independence Politics: Filipino Reactions to Anti-Filipino Riots in the United States." *Philippine Studies: Historical and Ethnographic Viewpoints* 60, no. 3 (2012): 307–36.

Okihiro, Gary. *Pineapple Culture: A History of the Tropical and Temperate Zones*. Berkeley: University of California Press, 2009.

Omi, Michael, and Howard Winant. *Racial Formation in the United States: From the 1960s to the 1990s*. New York: Routledge, 1994.

Ong, Aihwa. *Flexible Citizenship: The Cultural Logics of Transnationality*. Durham, NC: Duke University Press, 1999.

Orig, Princess. "Kayumanggi versus Maputi: 100 Years of America's White Aesthetics in Philippine Literature." In *Mixed Blessing: The Impact of the American Colonial Experience on Politics and Society in the Philippines*, edited by Hazel M. McFerson, 99–134. Westport: Greenwood Press, 2002.

Ottevaere, Dawn A. "The Cost Is Sworn to by Women: Gender, Resistance, and Counterinsurgency during the Philippine-American War, 1898–1902." PhD diss., Michigan State University, 2010.

Padoongpatt, Mark. *Flavors of Empire: Food and the Making of Thai America*. Berkeley: University of California Press, 2017.

Parezo, Nancy J., and Don D. Fowler. *Anthropology Goes to the Fair: The 1904 Louisiana Purchase Exposition*. Lincoln: University of Nebraska Press, 2007.

Pascoe, Peggy. *Relations of Rescue: The Search for Female Moral Authority in the American West, 1874–1939*. New York: Oxford University Press, 1990.

——. *What Comes Naturally: Miscegenation Law and the Making of Race in America*. New York: Oxford University Press, 2010.

Peck, Linda Levy. *Consuming Splendor: Society and Culture in Seventeenth-Century England*. Cambridge: Cambridge University Press, 2005.

Pelzer, Karl J. *Pioneer Settlement in the Asiatic Tropics: Studies in Land Utilization and Agricultural Colonization in Southeastern Asia*. New York: American Geographical Society, 1945.

Perez, Erika. *Colonial Intimacies: Interethnic Kinship, Sexuality, and Marriage in Southern California, 1769–1885*. Norman: University of Oklahoma Press, 2018.

Pérez, Louis A. *Cuba in the American Imagination: Metaphor and the Imperial Ethos.* Chapel Hill: University of North Carolina Press, 2008.

Pineda-Ofreneo, Rosalinda. *The Manipulated Press: A History of Philippine Journalism since 1945.* Manila: Cacho Hermanos, 1984.

Pleck, Elizabeth H. *Not Just Roommates: Cohabitation after the Sexual Revolution.* Chicago: University of Chicago Press, 2012.

Poblete, Joanna. *Balancing the Tides: Marine Practices in American Samoa.* Manoa: University of Hawai'i Press, 2019.

———. *Islanders in the Empire: Filipino and Puerto Rican Laborers in Hawai'i.* Champaign: University of Illinois Press, 2014.

Pratt, Mary Louise. *Imperial Eyes: Travel Writing and Transculturation.* London: Routledge, 1992.

Prieto, Laura. "A Delicate Subject: Clemencia López, Civilized Womanhood, and the Politics of Anti-imperialism." *Journal of the Gilded Age and the Progressive Era* 12, no. 2 (2013): 199–233.

Rafael, Vicente L. "Colonial Domesticity: White Women and United States Rule in the Philippines." *American Literature* 67, no. 4 (December 1995): 639–66.

———. *White Love and Other Events in Filipino History.* Durham, NC: Duke University Press, 2000.

Ray, Carina E. *Crossing the Color Line: Race, Sex, and the Contested Politics of Colonialism in Ghana.* Athens: Ohio University Press, 2015.

———. "Decrying White Peril: Interracial Sex and the Rise of Anticolonial Nationalism in the Gold Coast." *American Historical Review* 119, no. 1 (2014): 78–110.

Reagan, Leslie J. *When Abortion Was a Crime: Women, Medicine, and Law in the United States, 1867–1973.* Berkeley: University of California Press, 1997.

Reeves-Ellington, Barbara, Kathryn Kish Sklar, and Connie A. Shemo, eds. *Competing Kingdoms: Women, Mission, Nation, and the American Protestant Empire, 1812–1960.* Durham, NC: Duke University Press, 2010.

Renda, Mary. *Taking Haiti: Military Occupation and the Culture of U.S. Imperialism, 1915–1940.* Chapel Hill: University of North Carolina Press, 2001.

Rice, Mark. *Dean Worcester's Fantasy Islands: Photography, Film, and the Colonial Philippines.* Quezon City: Ateneo de Manila University Press, 2015.

Rivera, Cynthia Luz P. "Filipino Women's Magazines, 1909–1940: Resistance, Cultural Subversion, and Compromise." *Plaridel* 1, no. 2 (2004): 1–20.

Robinson, Michael C., and Frank N. Schubert. "David Fagen: An Afro-American Rebel in the Philippines, 1899–1901." *Pacific Historical Review* 44, no. 1 (1975): 68–83.

Roces, Alfredo, ed. *Filipino Heritage: The Making of a Nation.* Vol. 9, *The American Colonial Period (1900–1941).* Manila: Lahing Pilipino, 1978.

Roces, Mina. "Is the Suffragist an American Colonial Construct? Defining 'The Filipino Woman' in Colonial Philippines." In *Women's Suffrage in Asia: Gender, Nationalism and Democracy,* edited by Louise Edwards and Mina Roces, 24–58. New York: Routledge, 2004.

——. *Women, Power, and Kinship Politics: Female Power in Post-War Philippines.* Westport, CT: Praeger, 1998.

Rodriguez, Dylan. *Suspended Apocalypse: White Supremacy, Genocide, and the Filipino Condition.* Minneapolis: University of Minnesota Press, 2010.

Roediger, David. *How Race Survived US History: From Settlement and Slavery to the Obama Phenomenon.* New York: Verso, 2008.

——. *The Wages of Whiteness: Race and the Making of the American Working Class.* London: Verso, 1999.

Rosen, Ruth. *The Lost Sisterhood: Prostitution in America, 1900–1918.* Baltimore: Johns Hopkins University Press, 1982.

Rosenberg, Emily. *Spreading the American Dream: American Economic and Cultural Expansion, 1890–1945.* New York: Hill and Wang, 1982.

Rosenberg, Emily S., and Shanon Fitzpatrick, eds. *Body and Nation: The Global Realm of U.S. Body Politics in the Twentieth Century.* Durham, NC: Duke University Press Books, 2014.

Rydell, Robert W. *All the World's a Fair: Visions of Empire at American International Expositions, 1876–1916.* Chicago: University of Chicago Press, 1987.

Saada, Emmanuelle. *Empire's Children: Race, Filiation, and Citizenship in the French Colonies.* Chicago: University of Chicago Press, 2012.

Said, Edward W. *Culture and Imperialism.* New York: Vintage Books, 1994.

——. *Orientalism.* New York: Vintage Books, 1979.

Salman, Michael. *The Embarrassment of Slavery: Controversies over Bondage and Nationalism in the American Colonial Philippines.* Berkeley: University of California Press, 2001.

San Juan, E., Jr. "African American Internationalism and Solidarity with the Philippine Revolution." *Socialism and Democracy* 24, no. 2 (July 2010): 32–65.

Santiago, Lilia Quindoza. *Sa ngalan ng ina: Sandaang taon ng tulang feminista sa Pilipinas, 1889–1989.* Quezon City: University of the Philippines Press, 1997.

——. *Sexuality and the Filipina.* Quezon City: University of the Philippines Press, 2007.

Saxton, Alexander. *The Rise and Fall of the White Republic: Class Politics and Mass Culture in Nineteenth-Century America.* London: Verso, 2003.

Schaeffer, Felicity A. *Love and Empire: Cybermarriage and Citizenship across the Americas.* New York: New York University Press, 2013.

Schirmer, Daniel B., and Stephen R. Shalom. *The Philippines Reader: A History of Colonialism, Neocolonialism, Dictatorship, and Resistance.* Boston: South End Press, 1987.

Schulz, Joy. *Hawaiian by Birth: Missionary Children, Bicultural Identity, and U.S. Colonialism in the Pacific.* Lincoln: University of Nebraska Press, 2020.

Scott, Joan. "Gender as a Useful Category of Analysis." *American Historical Review* 91, no. 5 (1986): 1053–75.

Sexton, Jared. *Amalgamation Schemes: Antiblackness and the Critique of Multiracialism.* Minneapolis: University of Minnesota Press, 2008.

Shah, Nayan. *Contagious Divides: Epidemics and Race in San Francisco's Chinatown.* Berkeley: University of California Press, 2001.

——. *Stranger Intimacy: Contesting Race, Sexuality and the Law in the North American West.* Berkeley: University of California Press, 2012.

Sharpe, Jenny. *Allegories of Empire: The Figure of Woman in the Colonial Text.* Minneapolis: University of Minnesota Press, 1993.

Shigematsu, Setsu, and Keith Camacho, eds. *Militarized Currents: Towards a Decolonized Future in Asia and the Pacific.* Minneapolis: University of Minnesota Press, 2010.

Shimizu, Celine Parreñas. *The Hypersexuality of Race: Performing Asian/American Women on Screen and Scene.* Durham, NC: Duke University Press, 2007.

Shoemaker, Nancy. *Native American Whalemen in the World: Indigenous Encounters and the Contingency of Race.* Chapel Hill: University of North Carolina Press, 2015.

——. *A Strange Likeness: Becoming Red and White in Eighteenth-Century North America.* New York: Oxford University Press, 2004.

Silva, Noenoe K. *Aloha Betrayed: Native Hawaiian Resistance to American Colonialism.* Durham: Duke University Press, 2004.

Smith, Linda Tuhiwai. *Decolonizing Methodologies: Research and Indigenous Peoples.* London: Zed Books, 1999.

Smith, Stacey. *Freedom's Frontier: California and the Struggle over Unfree Labor, Emancipation and Reconstruction.* Chapel Hill: University of North Carolina Press, 2013.

Smits, David. "The 'Squaw Drudge': Prime Index of Savagism." *Ethnohistory* 29, no. 4 (1982): 281–306.

——. "'Squaw Men,' 'Half-Breeds,' and Amalgamators: Late Nineteenth-Century Anglo-American Attitudes toward Indian-White Race-Mixing." *American Indian Culture and Research Journal* 15, no. 3 (1991): 29–61.

Sollors, Werner. *Neither Black nor White yet Both: Thematic Explorations of Interracial Literature.* Cambridge, MA: Harvard University Press, 1999.

Spivak, Gayatri Chakravorty. *In Other Worlds: Essays in Cultural Politics.* New York: Methuen, 1987.

Steinbock-Pratt, Sarah. *Educating the Empire: American Teachers and Contested Colonization in the Philippines.* Cambridge: Cambridge University Press, 2019.

Stern, Alexandra. *Eugenic Nation: Faults and Frontiers of Better Breeding in Modern America.* Berkeley: University of California Press, 2016.

Stoler, Ann Laura. *Carnal Knowledge and Imperial Power: Race and the Intimate in Colonial Rule.* Berkeley: University of California Press, 2002.

——. *Haunted by Empire: Geographies of Intimacy in North American History.* Durham, NC: Duke University Press, 2006.

——. *Race and the Education of Desire: Foucault's History of Sexuality and the Colonial Order of Things.* Durham, NC: Duke University Press, 1995.

——. "Tense and Tender Ties: The Politics of Comparison in North American History and (Post) Colonial Studies." *Journal of American History* 88, no. 3 (December 2001): 829–65.

Streeby, Shelley. *American Sensations: Class, Empire and the Production of Popular Culture.* Berkeley: University of California Press, 2002.

Strobel, Margaret, and Nupur Chaudhuri, eds. *Western Women and Imperialism: Complicity and Resistance.* Bloomington: Indiana University Press, 1992.

Sturdevant, Saundra, and Brenda Stoltzfus. *Let the Good Times Roll: Prostitution and the U.S. Military in Asia*. New York: New Press, 1993.

Takagi, Dana Y. *The Retreat from Race: Asian-American Admissions and Racial Politics*. New Brunswick, NJ: Rutgers University Press, 1992.

Takaki, Ronald T. *Strangers from a Different Shore: A History of Asian Americans*. Boston: Little, Brown, 1998.

Tan, Samuel. *The Filipino Muslim Armed Struggle, 1900–1972*. Makati: Filipinas Foundation, 1977.

Terami-Wada, Motoe. "Karayuki-San of Manila: 1890–1920." *Philippine Studies* 34, no. 3 (1986): 287–316.

Thomas, Lynn M. *Politics of the Womb: Women, Reproduction, and the State in Kenya*. Berkeley: University of California Press, 2003.

Thomas, Megan C. *Orientalists, Propagandists, and Ilustrados: Filipino Scholarship and the End of Spanish Colonialism*. Minneapolis: University of Minnesota Press, 2012.

Torget, Andrew. *Seeds of Empire: Cotton, Slavery, and the Transformation of the Texas Borderlands, 1800–1850*. Chapel Hill: University of North Carolina Press, 2015.

Torres, Cristina Evangelista. *The Americanization of Manila, 1898–1921*. Quezon City: University of the Philippines Press, 2010.

Trask, Haunani-Kay. *From a Native Daughter: Colonialism and Sovereignty in Hawaii*. Honolulu: University of Hawaii Press, 1999.

Tyner, James. *Iraq, Terror, and the Philippines' Will to War*. Lanham, MD: Rowman and Littlefield, 2005.

Tyrrell, Ian. "New Approaches to American Cultural Expansion." In *Competing Kingdoms: Women, Mission, Nation, and the American Protestant Empire, 1812–1960*, edited by Barbara Reeves-Ellington, Kathryn Kish Sklar, and Connie A. Shemo, 43–66. Durham, NC: Duke University Press, 2010.

——. *Reforming the World: The Creation of America's Moral Empire*. Princeton, NJ: Princeton University Press, 2010.

——. *Woman's World/Woman's Empire: The Woman's Christian Temperance Union in International Perspective, 1880–1930*. Chapel Hill: University of North Carolina Press, 2010.

Vine, David. *Base Nation: How U.S. Military Bases Abroad Harm America and the World*. New York: Metropolitan Books, 2015.

Volpp, Leti. "American Mestizo: Filipinos and Anti-miscegenation Laws in California." *U.C. Davis Law Review* 33, no. 4 (2000): 795–835.

Von Eschen, Penny M. *Race against Empire: Black Americans and Anticolonialism, 1937–1957*. Ithaca, NY: Cornell University Press, 1997.

——. *Satchmo Blows Up the World: Jazz Ambassadors Play the Cold War*. Cambridge, MA: Harvard University Press, 2009.

Walkowitz, Judith R. *City of Dreadful Delight: Narratives of Sexual Danger in Late-Victorian London*. Chicago: University of Chicago Press, 1992.

Walsh, Thomas P. *Tin Pan Alley and the Philippines: American Songs of War and Love, 1898–1946*. Lanham, MD: Scarecrow Press, 2013.

Wexler, Laura. *Tender Violence: Domestic Visions in an Age of U.S. Imperialism*. Chapel Hill: University of North Carolina Press, 2000.

White, Richard. *The Middle Ground: Indians, Empires and Republics in the Great Lakes Region, 1650–1815*. Cambridge: Cambridge University Press, 1991.

Wintermute, Bobby. *Public Health and the US Military: A History of the Army Medical Department, 1818–1917*. New York: Routledge, 2011.

Wolfe, Patrick. *Settler Colonialism and the Transformation of Anthropology: The Politics and Poetics of an Ethnographic Event*. New York: Cassell, 1999.

Wu, Judy. *Radicals on the Road: Internationalism, Orientalism, and Feminism during the Vietnam Era*. Ithaca, NY: Cornell University Press, 2013.

Yegar, Moshe. *Between Integration and Secession: The Muslim Communities of the Southern Philippines, Southern Thailand, and Western Burma/Myanmar*. Lanham, MD: Lexington Books, 2002.

Yokota, Kariann A. *Unbecoming British: How Revolutionary America Became a Postcolonial Nation*. Oxford: Oxford University Press, 2014.

Zapanta-Manlapaz, Edna. *Filipino Women Writers in English, Their Story: 1905–2002*. Quezon City: Ateneo de Manila University Press, 2003.

Zeiger, Susan. *Entangling Alliances: Foreign War Brides and American Soldiers in the Twentieth Century*. New York: New York University Press, 2010.

Zimmerman, Andrew. *Alabama in Africa: Booker T. Washington, the German Empire, and the Globalization of the New South*. Princeton, NJ: Princeton University Press, 2012.

Index

Page numbers in italics refer to figures and maps.